DATE DUE

OC 30 96

John Dewey's Theory of
Art, Experience, and Nature

SUNY Series in Philosophy
Robert Cummings Neville, Editor

John Dewey's Theory of Art, Experience, and Nature

The Horizons of Feeling

Thomas M. Alexander

State University of New York Press

Published by
State University of New York Press, Albany

© 1987 State University of New York

For information, address State University of New York
Press, State University Plaza, Albany, N.Y., 12246

Library of Congress Cataloging in Publication Data

Alexander, Thomas M., 1952-
    John Dewey's theory of art, experience, and nature.

    (SUNY series in philosophy)
    Bibliography: p.
    Includes index.
    1. Dewey, John, 1859-1952.   2. Empiricism—History—
20th century.   3. Aesthetics, Modern—20th century.
I. Dewey, John, 1859-1952.   II. Title.   III. Series.
B945.D44A67   1987   191   86-14545
ISBN 0-88706-425-6
ISBN 0-88706-426-4 (pbk.)

10 9 8 7 6 5 4 3 2 1

For Jill

Love is the bright foreigner, the foreign self.
                                           Emerson

A true friend of man; almost the only friend of human progress. . . . I do not see how he can ever die; Nature cannot spare him.

Thoreau, Walden

Contents

Acknowledgments

I would like to express the deepest gratitude to all those who have helped me complete this project, most of all to my wife, Jill E. Adams, my parents, Hubert and Mildred Alexander, Dr. James Gouinlock of Emory University, John, Beverly, and Rebecca Troth, E. Maynard and Phyllis Adams, Gary Cesarz, and Robert Reeves. I would also like to acknowledge the patience and help of William Eastman of SUNY Press, the labor of several editors, the expert typing of Ruth Cook, and The Society for the Advancement of American Philosophy for the rejuvenating role it is playing in American Philosophy.

I would also like to thank the SIU Press for permission to quote extensively from *The Works of John Dewey*. Jo Ann Boydston, the editor of this series, deserves a special thanks for all her help and kindness.

As this manuscript was completed, I received a copy of R.W. Sleeper's fine book, *The Necessity of Pragmatism*. Aside from a couple of references, I have not been able to incorporate its valuable insights into the text.

Introduction

The last decade has witnessed the gradual but steady revival of interest in the philosophy of John Dewey, whose thought had suffered virtual total eclipse since his death at the age of ninety-three in 1952. The man who was the most actively involved and widely read professional philosopher in the first part of this century in America survives only as a dim memory in the popular mind. He is hazily recalled as an educator (or, worse, as the culprit responsible for the progressive education disaster), while Christian fundamentalists and right-wing demagogues still link his name with those of Darwin and Marx. Until recently, his fate was hardly better in academic circles. I have seen tenured philosophy professors struggle to associate his name with a library cataloguing system or with the opponent defeated by Truman. Aside from the handful of scholars who continued to be engaged by his thought and The Society for the Advancement of American Philosophy's tenacious and revitalizing presence, the revival of interest in Dewey is largely attributable to the sudden appearance of his name in a provocative work by a widely respected thinker within the analytic tradition. Ever since the publication of Richard Rorty's *Philosophy and the Mirror of Nature* in 1979, followed three years later by a collection of his essays, *Consequences of Pragmatism*, Dewey's name, along with those of Wittgenstein and Heidegger, has been invoked in the crusade against "foundationalism." These thinkers constitute the anti-essentialist, anti-systematic, anti-Cartesian, anti-speculative triumvirate who have "deconstructed" the absolutist pretensions of "the Tradition." "In our time," Rorty asserts, "Dewey, Wittgenstein, and Heidegger are the great edifying, peripheral thinkers"—"peripheral" because they work from the "margins" of the Tradition in their efforts to dissolve or undercut the authority of the central text of Philosophy, which has been its claim to Truth. "All three make it as difficult as possible to take their thought as expressing views on traditional philosophical problems, or making constructive proposals for philosophy as a cooperative and progressive discipline."[1] They are not thinkers in the traditional sense, but rather types of high-grade intellectual acids to be used for dissolving, not solving, philosophical problems.

All of a sudden, then, we are given a new picture of Dewey as a protodeconstructionist, a quiet, subversive thinker silently eroding the foundations of the ancien régime. This is the sort of popular image destined to be attractive to academics, projected as it is upon the blank screen of wide-spread, fundamental ignorance of his work. In contrast with this rather unconvincing "new look," there have been several recent serious scholarly and philosophical studies of Dewey's thought. These include James Gouinlock's *John Dewey's Philosophy of Value*, Victor Kestenbaum's *The Phenomenological Sense of John Dewey*, Ralph W. Sleeper's *The Necessity of Pragmatism* and Raymond Boisvert's *Dewey's Metaphysics*.[2] In addition, mention should be made of course of the monumental project now nearing completion, the publication of the works of John Dewey by Southern Illinois University Press under the editorship of Jo Ann Boydston. The physical presence of these volumes and their high quality of scholarship and editorial skill alone will revolutionize Dewey research. They have already inaugurated a new era in assessing Dewey's stature as a philosopher. Maverick interpretations as well as glib dismissals of Dewey are becoming less and less possible. Like Homeric warriors battling for the fallen, the struggle over Dewey's corpus has begun in earnest.

This work is meant to enter the fray. Dewey's work is a sprawling vista both in terms of sheer quantity and in the intricacy and subtlety of his thought. Aside from the demand to ingest so much written material, one of the major problems to overcome in treating Dewey as a philosopher is his own style. To read Dewey, someone once said, is like swimming through oatmeal. A better comparison might be that of Heidegger's "woodpaths." There are tremendous views to be had by following Dewey through the circuitous, tangled underbrush of his prose, but they can only be reached by following those paths carefully. Added to the problem of the order of Dewey's presentation is that of his deceptive effort to speak plain English. Here his manner of approach is quite the opposite of someone like Heidegger, who forces the difficulty of his thought upon the reader by a bewildering technical style. Dewey's thought is equally difficult and elusive, I believe, but this fact is often hidden by Dewey's conscious adoption of terms with an established meaning, both in popular as well as philosophical senses. Dewey, in other words, sought to reconstruct an existing language rather than fabricate a new one. There were serious reasons for this choice, I think, namely, Dewey wanted his thought to reach and affect a widespread audience rather than merely an academic few who were the "elect." Dewey wanted his philosophy to transform the culture itself, and so he attempted to co-opt its language. This is a dangerous game, as he found out. The predictable result was that Dewey's genuinely novel ideas were translated back into the pre-established habits of understanding, where they then either seemed to be patently false or trivial. A prime instance was the term "experience," the very heart and center of Dewey's thought. Ever since Locke, the term had come to mean a subjective event, a constellection of "ideas" lodged inside a "mind" brought about by the operation of certain physical powers upon us. From the start, Dewey's philosophy was opposed to such a theory. "Experience" for him meant a process situated in a natural environment, mediated by a socially shared symbolic system, actively exploring and responding to the ambiguities of the world by seeking to render the most problematic of them determinate. The persistent failure of his critics to adapt themselves to these new meanings had Dewey so frustrated by his eighties, that he toyed with dropping the term "experience" altogether, along with several others. *Experience and Nature,* his major work, was to be retitled *Nature and Culture.*

The primary task of this work, then, is to undertake a systematic thinking-through of Dewey's philosophy. Instead of providing a survey of the numerous topics of his thought, such as his ethics, his theory of inquiry, his views on education, and so on, I propose to investigate what I consider to be the central, guiding thought in his philosophy: the aesthetic dimension of experience. It is the thesis of this book that the best approach to what Dewey means by "experience" is not to be gained by focusing primarily on the theme by which Dewey is generally known, his "instrumentalism," but instead by looking at experience in its most complete, most significant, and most fulfilling mode: experience as art. In short, I claim that when we explore experience which has been shaped into an aesthetically funded process, into *"an* experience," we will discover Dewey's paradigmatic understanding of experience. And this, in turn, may lead to a more coherent understanding of the rest of Dewey's philosophy. Experience as artistically shaped and aesthetically funded gives us also Dewey's paradigmatic understanding of meaning. Instead of taking scientific discourse or formal logic as constituting the paradigms of meaning and communication, Dewey explicitly selects art and the aesthetic. This is a radical and relatively ignored theme in treatments of Dewey's philosophy. By focusing on "instrumentalism." Dewey was read as a proto-positivist who sought to reduce meaning to scientific procedure. Seen in this light, not only did Dewey seem to be saying much the same thing as his fellow philosophers in Vienna or Cambridge, but he didn't seem to be saying it half so well. Instead of arguing that philosophy ought to concentrate on the cognitive value of experience, however, Dewey in fact maintained exactly the converse. The primary fallacy of Western philosophy, he states, is "the intellectualist's fallacy" which reads all types of experience as ultimately a form of cognition (EN, 24; *LW* 1:28-29). To be sure, Dewey does give emphasis to the idea of experimental inquiry when he comes to treat the problem of knowledge. Not only did Dewey locate the project of human knowledge within the wider and richer context of the project of human life, but his treatment of knowledge as a process of learning rather than a body of "facts" points to his understanding of science as an artistic and creative enterprise. In contrast with most philosophies of experience, which begin by focusing on highly constrained, determinate moments of conceptual certainty (whether these be "impressions," "sense data," or intuited "essences"), Dewey's empiricism rejects such thin, watery instances as paradigmatic and looks instead for thick kinds.

Instrumentalism was a tool, an organon, built to serve a far more general theory of experience. If instrumentalism argued for a conception of experience in which experience was intrinsically capable of intelligent transformation, one is still left with the question, transformation to what? To expose the teleological possibilities of experience is not enough; a treatment of ends is also required. The telos of experience is the aesthetic. The aesthetic marks the fulfillment of the possibilities of experience for funded expressiveness and intrinsic value. The aesthetic becomes, then, the ultimate concern for any philosophical understanding. Dewey explicitly states this in *Art as Experience:* "To the aesthetic experience, then, the philosopher must go to understand what experience is. For this reason, . . . the theory of esthetics put forward by a philosopher. . . is a test of the capacity of the system he puts forth to grasp the nature of experience itself. There is no test that so surely reveals the one-sidedness of a philosophy as its treatment of art and esthetic perception" (AE, 274; *LW* 10:278). Given this, is it an excessive proposal to urge that the test of Dewey's philosophy to grasp the nature of experience lies in his treatment of art and aesthetic perception?

Unfortunately, Dewey's aesthetics has been subjected to a harsh battery of criticisms which render its connection to the rest of his philosophy suspect. It has been argued that the doctrines of *Art as Experience* rely upon premises more in keeping with idealism than with Dewey's professed naturalistic empiricism.[3] These commitments have made the work internally inconsistent as well as contrary to the spirit of his thought as a whole. Stephen Pepper was the first to raise this objection and he was immediately followed by Benedetto Croce. For this reason I have labelled the criticism "the Pepper-Croce thesis," though it has been taken up and expanded by a number of other critics as well. Dewey, of course, responded to both Pepper and Croce with dismissals which did nothing toward dissuading either critic from his convictions. Thus, before one can securely point to the theory of aesthetic experience as the central idea in Dewey's philosophy, the charges of the Pepper-Croce thesis must be laid to rest.

The problems exposed by the debate take on a twofold character, one with respect to the development of Dewey's ideas and the other with the systematic nature of his mature philosophy. The first is a fairly limited issue. The claim that Dewey's aesthetics relies subversively upon certain idealist assumptions is not altogether implausible when one recalls that Dewey began philosophizing in the Hegelian mode and continued to do so well into his mid-thirties. One can suspect that after Dewey abandoned absolute idealism, he focused on developing his instrumentalism without any further thought about the higher stages of Spirit. As he got around toward systematizing his philosophy in old age, he decided to round it out with an aesthetics (not to mention a philosophy of religion). To do this he had to dredge up from the murky, undisturbed depths of his memory various ideas on art and the aesthetic. The problem was that "instrumentalism" was a philosophy of experimental inquiry and really had little to do with the topic of art. And so we are presented with the case of a philosopher of Dewey's acumen badly bungling when it came time for him to produce an aesthetics.

This is a possibility, of course, though not a very desirable one for anyone wishing to preserve Dewey's stature as a philosopher. It becomes incumbent, at least, to explore Dewey's early idealism for any telltale similarities it may reveal with his mature philosophy, especially in the area of aesthetics. By examining the articles of the 1880s and his first systematic work, the *Psychology* of 1887, a number of striking comparisons do come to light, in fact. These comparisons coincide, furthermore, with the problematic topics discovered in *Art as Experience*. Initially, it would seem that the Pepper-Croce thesis is vindicated. A more important finding also comes to light. From the start, Dewey was intensely concerned to develop a philosophy which would treat experience in all its richness, complexity, and ambiguity without forcing it into some sort of reductionistic schema. This is what attracted Dewey to idealism in the first place and never allowed him to be tempted with the dreary, mercantile scientism of British empiricism or the constricting, dogmatic moralism of Scottish realism. Dewey commenced his philosophical life as a radical Hegelian, and as his Hegelianism became more radical it began to butt up against the fundamental commitments of idealism. It was in the name of his original concern for articulating a theory of experience that Dewey left the Hegelian fold and struck out on his own. From this perspective, it should not surprise us to find certain similarities between the early idealist writings and the key ideas of *Art as Experience*. Indeed, the fact that these similarities exist argues *for* the importance of this book in interpreting Dewey's mature thought, for it would be there that Dewey would, as he said, have presented his answer to his original demand for a theory that could treat experience as fully as possible. This, at any rate, is my proposal. The search for an adequate aesthetics of experience is what drives the development of Dewey's philosophy.

This does not resolve the problem of consistency, of course. The Pepper-Croce thesis exposes a more wide-ranging problem: is Dewey's mature philosophy as a whole troubled with the problems of a double allegiance to idealism and naturalism? Did Dewey, in other words, fail to work out the truly conflicting nature of his philosophical commitments? It is one thing to argue that *Art as Experience* is inconsistent with the masterpiece of his later thought, *Experience and Nature*, but what if the same riddling inconsistencies are found in the latter work as well? This prospect offers to view a fault-line of gigantic proportions running through Dewey's most significant philosophical achievements. There is a wide-ranging critical literature suggesting just this, extending from 1905 to, once again, Richard Rorty.[4] The critics, coming from a number of philosophical positions, wish to save whatever part of Dewey's thought they regard as valuable, but to remove the part which seems an undesirable dead weight, or even a malignant growth. This part is what is regarded as responsible for Dewey's desire to do metaphysics. Generally he lived an upright philosophical life, but then the old Adam (or old Hegel) would grab hold of him and he would go off on a speculative tear. It is necessary, therefore, to come to grips with what is probably unhappily called Dewey's "metaphysics of experience."[5] This area of his thought involves a number of issues, such as the relation of experience to nature, the status of knowledge, and the proposed aims and methods of metaphysics.

Here, once again, I believe that the importance of Dewey's theory of aesthetic experience comes to the fore. For those who believe that "experience" must refer to some sort of immediate perceptual event causally arising from nature or for those who hold that the primary relation of experience to nature is determined in terms of knowledge, Dewey's attempt to construct a metaphysics must appear to be incomprehensible and unnecessary. But when experience is understood from the Deweyan standpoint, as an involved, meaningful, and shared response to the world and to each other, the possibility of such a project not only is recognized but is seen to be necessary. To keep experience from being taken in a subjective or reductionistic manner, one requires a theory which will maintain its situational and transactional features in full view. To keep experience from being treated always as a form of cognition (or even primarily as a form of cognition), one needs to articulate a position where the larger issues of human meaning and value contextualize the pursuit of knowledge. Knowledge is only possible because we can respond to the world as a dramatically enacted project in which meanings and values can be won, lost, and shared. The fundamental "impulsion" (as Dewey calls it) of human beings is to engage the world with a heightened sense of meaning and the realization of value. This is precisely what is illuminated in aesthetic experience.

Dewey's metaphysics articulates a philosophical theory which attempts to give a comprehensive, critical view of the human project of making sense. One problem with the traditional view of reality is that it has sought to suppress the elements of chance, indeterminacy, and potentiality. While I argue that in many ways Dewey relies on an Aristotelian form of naturalism, it is one which does not share Aristotle's bias against the potential or his prejudice in favor of fixed forms. With the restoration of the status of the potential, Dewey presents us with a view of reality as a developing continuity rather than as some sort of self-same identity. The "principle of continuity," in other words, is the key to Dewey's metaphysics. It is also the underlying idea in Dewey's conception of "an experience" in his aesthetics. By connecting potentiality with naturalism, Dewey successfully allowed for the realization of human meanings, values, and ideals as genuine

possibilities of nature. In this manner he avoids a reductionistic naturalism by espousing an emergentism. In Dewey's metaphysics, as in
Whitehead's or Heidegger's, the concept of time as a teleologically
determined structure is essential. Once again, *an* experience reveals
the temporality as well as the continuity of experience.

Dewey's metaphysics establishes the context for his understanding of meaning as a transactional event mediated by symbolic communication. Although experience arises from the interaction of the organism with its environment, for human beings it is primarily an
event within a social or cultural context, a "lifeworld." The world of
human activity constitutes the matrix within which any symbol system must function. The body provides the primary structures for
meaning in its capacity for organized action. Dewey severely criticizes
the sort of behaviorism which sees the live body as a passive or
reactive stimulus-response mechanism. The body is better regarded
as a center of life activity, as a developer of experience, an explorer of
its world. It is the central instrument in organizing the world into an
integrated order through its own activity. As William James said,
"The body is the storm centre, the origin of co-ordinates, the constant
place of stress in all that experience-train."[6] The primary demand is
for experience to grow in a dynamic but coherent way. There is a
general impulsion for wholeness in all activity, according to Dewey,
and art and aesthetic experience are but refined developments of this
essential desire to make sense of the world. In this manner, the live
body connects the creature with its environment actively and thereby
provides for the very possibility of meaning.

Because human beings are social, they require a shared world
which allows for common ends to be articulated and for cooperative
activity to be regulated so that they may be attained. Symbolic interaction arises from this need. Meaning, in other words, originates in the
act of communication. Communication is a process involving members as participants; the members, moreover, understand themselves
as conjoint participants and use that understanding as part of the
regulative meaning of the situation. Individuals become aware of
their individuality only through a social context and the ability to
regard themselves from the social perspective. The theory of meaning
which emerges from such a view is far removed from that which
attempts to see meaning in purely formal terms, as a timeless, impersonal structure. Meaning is rather the very struggle to make the world
coherent; it is the on-going process of trying to make sense. This is a
communally shared task or project. In such a theory, meaning includes the ambiguous as well as the clear, the indeterminate as well as

the determinate. The activity of communication is a constant process of interaction, adjustment, determination, and development. Instead of seeking a paradigm of meaning in fixed categorial structures or in logical or syntactic laws, Dewey looks toward the narrative, dramatic, and expressive modes of communication. Meaning inhabits the dramatic universes of human action and interpretation which are called "culture." The body is born into a social or cultural environment as much as an organic environment. From the moment of birth, the body is trained to become a medium for expressive activity; the body becomes cultured or civilized by the education of its talents. As the body becomes "encultured," to coin a term, so culture becomes embodied.

Because the body becomes the event of meaning, consciousness must be understood functionally within this transactional process. It is a field-event in which the transformations of meaning are possessed and directed. Consciousness appropriates meaning in a variety of ways. As a field-event, it is characterized by an immediate focus of intensive concern, a proximate sense of context, and a tacitly felt horizon which provides the ultimate determining ground of meaning. This horizonal aspect is largely ignored in ordinary experience, but it is made manifest in those moments which are peculiarly aesthetic. In this manner, then, art and the aesthetic provide a unique and central instance of meaning for Dewey's philosophy. The aesthetic marks the realization of the impulsion for wholeness rendered conscious through the expressiveness of a medium transformed through activity.

Thus, when one comes to treat aesthetic experience for Dewey, it is hardly an issue of peripheral concern, illuminating as it does the central themes of his philosophy of experience. The tendency of philosophy to displace aesthetics for epistemology reflects the dualistic habits of a culture which displaces art from life. Dewey is forced to search for the aesthetic initially by conscientiously ignoring works of fine art. The origin of art is not to be found in the desire to become housed in a museum. Instead, art originates when life becomes fulfilled in moments of intelligently heightened vitality. When the potentialities of experience are intentionally utilized toward such a complete end, the sense of its own meaning becomes intrinsically present as a consummation of the event. This is what Dewey calls "an experience." In an experience, we genuinely come to inhabit the world; we dwell within the world and appropriate it in its meaning. The human impulsion for meaning and value is manifestly fulfilled.

Several dimensions of an experience can be noted: expression, form, and quality. The artistic-aesthetic event, an experience, is a primary instance of expression for Dewey. To the extent, however, that expression theory of art has come under a good deal of criticism, it is necessary to distinguish its claims and problems from the theory Dewey holds. Dewey likewise has a radical theory of form. Instead of regarding form as the abstractable Platonic skeleton of a work of art, Dewey construes it functionally, as the "working" of the work of art. Form becomes the temporal process through which the "substance" of the work, what the work is ultimately about, shows itself. Not only is form the enactment of the work in individual experience, it is also the *historical* enactment of the work by the culture. The work of art is a social event, and it lives a life within a culture. The immanent, guiding presence of the quality of the experience as a whole turns out to be the most crucial feature of *an* experience, however. Aesthetic quality is the integrating and sense-giving horizon of the work which brings forth the consummatory value of the work. As the realization of the ideal possibilities of experience to embody meaning and value, it reveals at the same time the possibility for experience to be rendered luminous by ideals. Aside from the intrinsic value of aesthetic experience, in other words, art teaches the moral that experience can be transformed toward fulfilling human ends. This has political implications.

Art is by its very nature bound up with the human ability to create ideals which can become controlling forces in culture. Art is social not because it occurs within culture, but because in a very real sense art is culture. It becomes one with the community's ability to realize itself in a significant manner. Culture is the artistic appropriation of the ideal possibilities for human life, the creative endeavor to live with meaning and value. Dewey calls this project "democracy." The democratic community is consciously founded on the recognition of the possibility for the perpetual liberation of life. It is the community which understands itself in terms of the art of conduct. The arts of inquiry, intelligence, and communication are directed toward this end. In doing so, they point to the paramount importance of the ideal of education, which is the means whereby the community brings itself forth into existence. Democracy is not founded on a fixed idealogy for Dewey, but on a collective recognition of our Socratic ignorance. The democratic community recognizes the human situation as inherently problematic, something ever to be inquired into, ever sought out, and ever submitted to criticism for reconstruction. In short, it is the community dedicated to life as art. This is the utmost creative task human existence can set for itself, offering as it does the possibility of a genuinely shared, consummatory life. Democratic life realizes itself as the expression of utmost care for the significant possibilities of human existence. As a form of life, democracy is the progressive liberation of man. This includes the articulation of those horizons of human care which provide the meaning-determining contexts of culture. Democracy is therefore an inherently philosophical mode of life so understood.

At a time when the humanities have faltered and given themselves over to projects of deconstruction or the negation of their own histories, Dewey's philosophy offers an alternative. Between naive optimism and cynical despair there are courage and commitment. These must be based on intelligence and faith as well as on a sense of human limitation, a tragic self-consciousness. I contend that if Dewey has truly succeeded in providing a coherent theory of aesthetic experience he has accomplished a good deal more than to allow room for an academic "conversation," as Rorty would have it. Instead of deconstruction, Dewey's is a philosophy of reconstruction. He exhibits the possibility of a meaningful response to the world which refuses to gloss over ambiguities, conflicts, or problematic depths; nor does it hold itself hubistically above self-interrogation. In *The American Scholar*, Emerson said, "The office of the scholar is to cheer, to raise, and to guide men by showing them the facts amid appearances." The central fact by which Dewey sought to offer cheer was that of art as experience.

List of Abbreviations

Since 1967, Southern Illinois University Press has been in the process of publishing the complete works of John Dewey under the editorship of Jo Ann Boydston. The first two series, the Early and Middle Works, are now complete and the third, the Later Works, is nearing completion. As this will constitute the standard edition of Dewey, I have, wherever possible, cross-cited references to these volumes. I have also referred to commonly used editions in citing Dewey's texts (not always first editions, either) for the sake of convenience to the reader.

Abbreviations for the SIU Edition:

EW   The Early Works (1882-1898)
MW   The Middle Works (1899-1924)
LW   The Later Works (1925-1953)

Abbreviations for Dewey's Texts:

AE   Art as Experience (New York: Capricorn Books, 1958)
CF   A Common Faith (New Haven: Yale University Press, 1960)
DE   Democracy and Education (New York: The Free Press, 1966)
EEL   Essays in Experimental Logic (New York: Dover Publications, n.d.)
EN   Experience and Nature (New York: Dover Pulibications, Inc., 1958)
ENF   On Experience, Nature, and Freedom, Richard Bernstein ed. (Indianapolis: Bobbs Merrill Company, Inc., 1960)
FC   Freedom and Culture (New York: Capricorn Books, 1962)

HNC Human Nature and Conduct (New York: The Modern Library, 1930)

IDP   The Influence of Darwin on Philosophy (New York: Peter Smith, 1951)

KK   Knowing and the Known, with Arthur Bentley (Boston: Beacon Press, 1949)

LTI   Logic: The Theory of Inquiry (New York: Henry Holt and Company, 1938)

PC   Philosophy and Civilization (New York: Peter Smith, 1968)

PP   The Public and Its Problems (Chicago: The Swallow Press Inc., n.d.)

QC   The Quest for Certainty (New York: Capricorn Books, 1960)

RP   Reconstruction in Philosophy (Boston: Beacon Press, 1957)

Abbreviations for Journals Cited:

JAAC The Journal of Aesthetics and Art Criticism

JHP   The Journal for the History of Philosophy

JP   The Journal of Philosophy

PPR   Phenomenology and Philosophical Research

PR   The Philosophical Review

RM   The Review of Metaphysics

TPS   The Transactions of the Charles S. Peirce Society

Chapter 1

The Pepper-Croce Thesis

Of *Art as Experience* Monroe Beardsley has said, "It is, by widespread agreement, the most valuable work on aesthetics written in English (and perhaps in any language) so far in our century."[1] A similar estimate of the book was made by Stephen Pepper shortly after its publication. "I am personally convinced that *Art as Experience* is one of the four or five great books on esthetics," he said, "and is a classic though but five years old."[2] Yet Pepper himself raised what was to be the greatest critical challenge to the book, claiming that it presented a confused welter of pragmatist and idealist notions. The charge was taken up and developed by Benedetto Croce. Subsequently a number of others have upheld and expanded this view.[3]

The importance of this controversy exceeds a mere critics' war concerning a secondary issue in Dewey's aesthetics. One does not have to read far in Dewey to discover the central emphasis he places on art and aesthetic experience. Art epitomizes the resolution of "hard and fast dualisms"; it is the "culmination of nature"; as intelligent action integrating means and ends, art is the "greatest intellectual achievement in the history of mankind"; art is not only the ultimate judgment on a civilization, it *is* civilization. Finally, as noted, Dewey himself acknowledges that the crucial test for any philosophy's claim to understand experience is its aesthetics.[4] Certainly Dewey's whole philosophy is just that effort to "grasp the nature of experience itself" which should find itself best articulated in an aesthetics. Therefore, any criticism questioning the coherency of Dewey's aesthetic theory must stand also as a judgment of his philosophy as a whole.

In this chapter I will examine the reasons why Pepper, Croce, and George H. Douglas believed that some or all of the tenets of *Art as*

1

Experience are inconsistent with Dewey's naturalistic instrumentalism. The central issue of the Pepper-Croce thesis rests, I contend, on a misunderstanding of Dewey's theory of aesthetic meaning, particularly that aspect of it described as "the pervasive qualitative whole." This idea is not only important in Dewey's aesthetic theory but reflects major concepts and underlying themes of his mature philosophy. One cannot, in fact, claim to understand Dewey as an instrumentalist or as a naturalist without understanding basic issues in his philosophy of experience which become highlighted under the topic of aesthetic meaning. While it is the task of this book to examine in detail the relationship of experience and the aesthetic, this chapter will be concerned simply with showing how the Pepper-Croce thesis is inconsistent and ambiguous. Nevertheless, it provides a valuable means of access to what is the central problem of Dewey's philosophy, his theory of experience.

I. The Pepper-Croce Thesis and Dewey's Response

Pepper records that he was at work on a pragmatist aesthetics when *Art as Experience* appeared in 1934. Since he had been relying on scattered remarks about art in Dewey's works, Pepper was pleased to find a number of his predictions correct. Yet, he recalls, "I was also amazed to find Dewey saying many things which I had deliberately excluded from my tentative account, believing them contrary to the spirit of pragmatism—things which an organic idealist would have said and which I should have thought Dewey would have rather bitten his tongue than to have said . . ."[5] Pepper concluded that this idealist side stood out more than the pragmatist, and he wrote *Aesthetic Quality* (1937) to present a purified pragmatic aesthetic.

Pepper's assessment that Dewey was "reverting to Hegelianism in his later years"[6] seemed to confirm Croce's own reading of *Art as Experience*. Croce did not see two incompatible doctrines interwoven in the book, however. He found himself presented with a coherent idealist aesthetic which was inconsistent, of course, with the rest of Dewey's writings. Welcoming Dewey back to the fold, Croce wondered whether Dewey had "availed himself of some Italian authors" in writing the book.[7] Croce remarked that "an Italian reader is pleasantly surprised to meet on every page observations and theories long since formulated in Italy and familiar to him."[8] Later, Croce made this insinuation blatant, claiming that Dewey "arrived on almost every point at the same conclusions regarding art which had been reached in Italian aesthetics during the past thirty years."[9] The "Italian authors" were of course Croce and his disciples, and the "observations and theories" were the ideas presented in Croce's *Estetica* of 1902, developed in subsequent works. While Croce praised Dewey at least for the "freshness and spontaneity" in his treatment, he confessed ultimately to "discovering his own ideas in a new form."[10] Thus, Croce encouraged Dewey to drop his "Anglo-Saxon empiricism," to forget the "fanaticism and emptiness" of his old Hegelian masters, and to ally himself with the left-wing Hegelians.

Before examining Dewey's testy and unhelpful responses, here are the chief points of Pepper's and Croce's evaluations. Pepper's approach was first to describe in outline the tenets of "the" organicist (i.e. idealist) and "the" pragmatist aesthetics, and then to compare Dewey's theory against each. According to Pepper, organicist aesthetics emphasizes the implicit coherence in experience on the basis of its inherrent rational and internally related structure. Pragmatism, on the other hand, emphasizes that experience is dependent on the environmental context, and so may or may not be coherent. The organicist finds aesthetic value in the greater degrees of coherency while the pragmatist finds value in the intensity of the quality. Pepper erroneously believes that idealist aesthetics is committed ultimately to a harmony theory of beauty, grounded in a subjective state, while pragmatist aesthetics finds its criteria in vividness, contrast, and tension in experience brought about by objective features. Finally, Pepper states that the idealist position holds that in a given instance there is only one work of art, while the pragmatist believes that there are an indefinite number of equally valid though different responses to a work of art, depending on the context.

This procrustean approach might be faulted for many reasons. Pepper seems to believe that any coherent philosophical theory can be categorized under one of a limited number of possible positions (four or five, actually) and measured for the degree to which it lives up to the consistency of that position. In spite of the value of the insight that philosophical theories may be governed by paradigmatic "root metaphors," this approach certainly fails to do justice to the variety and complexity of positions which can be held on philosophical grounds. This becomes evident in Pepper's inability to distinguish "organic" from "idealist." While Dewey's philosophy does rely on the concept of organism, this concept does not have to be construed in the sense of Schelling or Hegel. It will be seen that Dewey was fascinated by a similar reliance on the concept of organism in the evolutionary biology of his day as well as in the dominant schools of idealism. Because Dewey tried to make naturalism an intermediary theory between materialism and idealism, he has often been faulted for being (or failing to be) one or the other.

Pepper believed that Dewey could have circumvented his organic terminology by focusing instead on the concept of fusion, the "funding" of experience in an intensely vivid "seizure."[11] Both Pepper and Croce had remarked on this feature of Dewey's theory, comparing it to the clear but confused cognition described by such eighteenth-century philosophers as Baumgarten.[12] The ambiguity of equating such a notion with pragmatism is evident from the similarities Croce himself noted between it and his concept of "expression = intuition."

Pepper was primarily distressed with Dewey's remarks about the aesthetic experience being "integrated through its inner relations into a single qualitative whole."[13] Pepper asks whether this is not the organization of implicitly coherent feelings into a whole through their internal relations as commented on by the idealists. "From the vague appearance to the clear reality," concludes Pepper, "from the abstract and conflicting to the concrete and coherent: thesis, antithesis, synthesis. . . . Is this not the very chorus voiced by Schelling, Hegel, Bradley and Bosanquet?"[14] Pepper's final assessment of Dewey's aesthetics is that the "vital kernel of a new esthetic struggles to grow . . . But is finally mulched under a rich layer of organicism."[15]

Pepper found the paradigmatic instance of Dewey's commitment to organicism in the following passage:

> The undefined pervasive quality of an experience is that which binds together all the defined elements, the objects of which we are focally aware, making them a whole. The best evidence that such is the case is our constant sense of things as belonging or not belonging, a sense which is immediate (*AE*, 194; *LW* 10:198).

Certainly, this passage describes what might be called the ineffable unity of contexts of experience, an apprehension which locates specific objects of consciousness within a whole situation, itself immediately grasped or felt to be balanced or discordant. This passage contains a lucid summary of what Dewey means by "aesthetic meaning," but Pepper sees it as implicitly containing the most idealist (and so contradictory) part of Dewey's aesthetics.

The question, of course, is whether Dewey's "pervasive qualitative whole", which unifies and controls experience so that it does have immediate sense or meaning, is necessarily committed to idealist metaphysics. Bertrand Russell, like Pepper, felt uneasy with Dewey's use of words like "coherence," "whole," and "integration." Dewey objected that his use of these terms was quite dependent on the primary concept of "situation" in his philosophy. To Russell, Dewey said, "From one angle, almost everything I have written is a commentary on the fact that situations are immediate in their direct occurrence, and mediated and mediating in the temporal continuum constituting life experience."[16] Dewey unfortunately did not elaborate on how situations provided an alternative basis for claiming that an experience could be internally mediated but immediately had or that immediately had experiences led to a complete or total experience which was whole.

Dewey's response to Pepper's criticisms was equally unilluminating. Instead of explaining how his ideas fitted into a naturalistic framework, Dewey tried to turn the tables on Pepper by accusing him of not being a good pragmatist for his deducing the content of aesthetic theories a priori. Though this is, I believe, a justified criticism of Pepper's attitude, Dewey had a tendency in defending his ideas to resort to the posture that his observations were simply innocent discoveries arrived at by a method of empirical inquiry, as if there were no underlying theory to be accounted for. Thus Dewey claimed that "coherence" and "organic unity" were simply features present in experience, to greater or lesser degree, which could be observed to be there. In other words, Dewey maintains that there are *some* experiences which have the character attributed by the idealists to *all* experience. The trouble came when this aspect or part of experience was reified into a metaphysical absolute. Another aspect of Dewey's response was to claim that each part of his philosophy was subject to the method appropriate to the subject matter at hand, so that the results arrived at in his aesthetics should naturally be expected to be different from those arrived at in his theory of knowledge and inquiry. However legitimate this emphasis on pluralism in methodology is—especially when its significance in Aristotle's thought is remembered—one is naturally left wondering whether Dewey did have an organized unified philosophical perspective, if not a system in the grand manner.

Croce noted how weak Dewey's response to Pepper was and so took encouragement that Dewey, in spite of himself, was providing evidence for the truth of idealism, especially that of "some Italian authors." To substantiate this, Croce pointed out over a dozen similarities between his own and Dewey's aesthetics. Most of these are, as Dewey himself remarked, rather secondary. Both, for example, distinguish expression from emoting, subject matter from substance in the artwork, or technique from art; both affirm the continuity of ordinary and aesthetic experience and the rhythmic and temporal nature of all art; both say that the work is a process not a thing and that aesthetic meaning cannot be construed solely in terms of form.[17] The significant difference was that these ideas were located in vastly different overall theories. Croce proceeded to defend idealism as the *only* coherent basis for upholding these valuable insights. In *Art as Experience*, Dewey had specifically criticized Croce (as he later did Pepper) for having superimposed philosophic preconceptions upon an "arrested esthetic experience" (*AE*, 294; *LW* 10:299). By this Dewey meant that Croce's theory of "expression = intuition" could only be understood in terms of Croce's contention that Spirit alone is real; the concrete intuitions of experience are expressive only because they are created by the mind—they are *its* states, instead of the passive impressions of an external world. The insights of Croce's aesthetics were dyed with the color of a metaphysics which Dewey firmly rejected. Croce did not object to this characterization of his position, affirming that "I hold nothing can exist separate from knowing."[18] Dewey had not refuted this doctrine, Croce rejoined, and so his criticisms may be dismissed. Croce dogmatically stated that Dewey in fact was theoretically incapable of refuting idealism because he had repudiated "philosophical reflection" for "reconstructive intelligence" which led him into "vicious circles and positivistic tautologies."[19] To opt for reflection, of course, would automatically have led him to accept the fundamental commitments of idealism.

Dewey's short response to Croce's article was uncharacteristically testy. Once again, Dewey seemed either to substantiate the charges or at least to indicate that his own philosophy was casually inconsistent. Dewey rashly denied that his aesthetics had any relation to his instrumentalism. He couldn't really do more than comment on Croce's criticisms, he said, because a reply implied there was some common ground, and there was none in this case. Croce, unlike Dewey, regarded aesthetic experience as cognitive, a form of knowledge superior to science. Asserting the independence of his aesthetic theory, Dewey was led into making the even wilder claim that he "did *not* write *Art as Experience* as an appendix to or application of my pragmatism . . . or in subjection to *any* system of philosophy."[20] Dewey concluded by complaining that Croce had read traditional empiricist meanings into his position and that the similarities noted by Croce in their theories were "of the order of commonplaces" at least as far as people familiar with the subject were concerned.[21] The point which Dewey struggled to make, however, is significant: idealism, like other philosophies, treated *all* types of experience ultimately as forms of cognitive events (here as forms of "self knowledge"). Dewey contended that the range of non-cognitive but meaningful experiences exceeded that of experiences primarily concerned with the question of truth. "Instrumentalism" was Dewey's theory to account for those latter situations; it was concerned with a *type* of experience. But aesthetic experience is not a *type* for Dewey—it is an inherent possibility of most experience; it is concerned with the fulfillment of *meaning*, not truth.

Neither Pepper nor Croce was convinced. Pepper reminisced years later that Dewey's book, in spite of its "greatness," was "adulterated and confused" so that "my criticism still holds."[22] Croce was more bitter, saying Dewey "was not very courteous in his reply to me, but that has no importance because it is true that he who does not lose control of himself ends by being right and having it recognized."[23] Croce himself launched a vitriolic attack on Dewey in 1952, saying he was not amused to have philosophized "commonplaces" with Dewey, especially since it was these points alone which constituted the value of Dewey's aesthetics. If they were commonplaces, it was only because of Croce's influence. Dewey's commitment to pragmatism prevented him from "demonstrating the luminous affirmations which an inborn sense of the truth has brought him to achieve"; and so Croce concluded with the malicious irony that "empirically and pragmatically Dewey cannot overcome the dualism of mind and nature."[24] Only by regarding nature as a product of mind or Spirit, reaffirmed Croce, could one overcome dualism. This retort was lost on Dewey, who died three months before the article appeared. Croce himself had only a few months to live. The controversy itself has quietly persisted.

II. Douglas' Evaluation and Further Problems

The controversy received attention after Dewey's death in articles by Patrick Romanell, Charles E. Gause, and, most recently, by George H. Douglas, who tried to find the common ground that did exist—pace Dewey—between his and Croce's positions. Douglas also explored why there had been misunderstandings on both sides. Douglas exonerated Dewey from Croce's insinuation of plagiarism, but he found that Dewey erred in categorizing Croce as Hegelian, probably due to an influential misinterpretation of Santayana's.[25] Douglas confessed to a degree of "residual idealism" in Croce's writings, but there also was some in Dewey's, so that the main tenets of the Pepper-Croce thesis were in substance correct. Douglas surprisingly expanded the theory to include *Experience and Nature*, considered by many to be Dewey's major book, among Dewey's deviations from naturalistic pragmatism into idealist historicism. Like Croce, Douglas was left wondering why Dewey could not bring himself to abandon pragmatism, unless "he never wanted to cut himself loose from the philosophy which had made him a great public figure and for which he is still best known. . . . Of course in the process of maintaining a cleavage between a philosophy of knowing and a philosophy of perceptual experience Dewey was sponsoring a dualism of the sort that he was always inveighing against."[26] In short, then, Douglas supported the charge and carried it to the heart of Dewey's mature philosophy.

The similarities that Douglas pointed out between Dewey's and Croce's accounts are intriguing: both treat aesthetic experience as a form of precognitive experience; both base their aesthetic theories on the concept of expression (nor is their common stress on the continuity of aesthetic experience with ordinary experience as secondary as Dewey believed); and both emphasize the importance of activity in organizing experience into objects. Douglas was correct in selecting these features as important concepts, central to the theories of either thinker. The issue is whether they share more than superficial similarities because of the different theoretical contexts which provide their meaning.

Placed against the general philosophies of both men, rather startling differences emerge. Croce, as noted, is strident about the idealist commitments of his philosophy. Croce denies "above all that art is a physical fact. . . . If it is asked why art cannot be a physical fact, it is necessary to state first of all that physical facts *lack reality.* On the other hand, art . . . is *supremely real.* Consequently it cannot be a physical fact which is something unreal."[27] Now, while Dewey also insists that the work of art must go beyond the physical art product and be realized in experience, this is only to be understood as incorporating as well as transforming a biophysical as well as cultural environment. There is no artistic activity without interaction with a definite medium, according to Dewey.[28]

Perhaps there is no greater disparity between Dewey's and Croce's positions than their respective views of activity. According to Douglas, this should be the central area of their common ground, for both assert that expression, the key concept in aesthetics, is expressive activity. For Croce, expression is the spiritual activity whereby automatic sensations are constituted into objects of conscious perception. Douglas is willing to attribute the same doctrine to Dewey, saying:

> Man's human activity, his spiritual activity, which Croce calls 'expression,' forms and structures these impressions, fuses them into a

single whole. Expressive activity focuses the scattered rays of reality, gives meaning to the chaos of animal life. That human spirit is developed out of the flux of animal life by means of individuating expressive qualities is obviously a commonly shared belief of Dewey and Croce.[29]

Douglas failed to note that experience for Dewey, unlike Croce, emerges from the complex interplay between the biological organism and a physical environment mediated by participating in a culture of symbols. Activity for Dewey is a dynamic phase of adjustment, adaptation and assimilation long before any objects of conscious perception are constituted. It is a feature of an interactive or transactional, natural situation. Activity for Croce is a magical internal product of Spirit, unrelated to anything like an external environment. In short, activity for Dewey is in the world before it is either subjective or objective; for Croce activity is the objectification of a subjective consciousness.

This difference stands out in the stringent distinction Croce draws between theory and practice. Since art is a form of knowledge for Croce, and knowledge is characterized best by theory rather than practice, art and aesthetic intuitions are purely theoretical unless one wills to externalize the intuition into a public object through some practical activity. In other words, though the aesthetic intuition, like any intuition, is an objectification or expression of Spirit, objectification does not necessarily imply externalization. The latter is incidental to the expression, because, for Croce (and unlike Hegel), practice is incidental to theory. Though occasionally Croce speaks as if expression were only realized through some external activity, or as if the work of art and the intuition were the same, this is not so. For example, Croce seemingly appropriates Hegel's criticism of the "beautiful souls," those who claim to have great aesthetic inspirations but either lack the technique to realize them or refuse to do so because that would degrade the work. Instead of a Deweyan—or Hegelian—respect for practical technique, however, this is really a defense by Croce of the superior intuition of the artist which precedes embodiment in a medium. "It is usual to distinguish the internal from the external work of art," remarks Croce, "the terminology seems to us infelicitous, for the work of art (the aesthetic work) is always *internal.*'[30] Croce's theory, even to one barely acquainted with Dewey's philosophy, must seem a paradigmatic instance of the classic split between theory and practice which Dewey vigorously rejected, not to mention a fairly conservative form of Hegelianism itself. The difference is evident in the following passage from *Experience and Nature:*

To call action thought in constituting objects direct is the same as to say that it is miraculous. For it is not thought as idealism defines thought which exercises the reconstructive function. Only action, interaction, can change or remake objects. The analogy of the skilled artist still holds. His intelligence is a factor in forming new objects which mark a fulfillment. But this is because intelligence is incarnate in overt action . . . (*EN*, 158; *LW* 1:126).

As for the observation that both Croce and Dewey treat art and aesthetic perception as a type of precognitive experience, this too does not bear scrutiny. Croce himself had tried to link Dewey's observation that "tangled scenes of life are made more intelligible in esthetic experience; not, however, as reflection and science render things more intelligible by reduction to conceptual form, but by presenting their meanings as the matter of a clarified, coherent, and intensified or 'impassioned' experience" (*AE*, 290; *LW* 10:295) with the traditional notion of experience which is *"cognitio inferior, clara sed non distincta.'*[31] Croce's theory owes much to this idea; for him, aesthetic intuition is a primary, precognitive type of knowledge. Intuitions can be worked up into self-articulate concepts, and can sink back from the level of cognition to aesthetic intuition.[32] Art, like philosophy, for Croce, is part of "science," not natural science, obviously, for that is tainted by practical activity and consequently is "impure."[33] Rather, science refers to the science of Spirit, *Geisteswissenschaft*; and so art becomes an inferior way in which Spirit comes to know itself. "Intuition gives us the world," he says, "the phenomenon; the concept gives us the noumenon, the Spirit."[34] In the concept, Spirit becomes self-conscious, so that intuition is "expression in and for itself."[35] However "precognitive" art is for Croce, it is a moment of Spirit's self-knowledge.

One of the major points stressed throughout *Art as Experience* is Dewey's complaint that previous philosophers have done injustice to aesthetic experience by trying to turn it into a form of knowledge. It is ironic that the very passage Croce quoted above was taken from an extended criticism of this theory which mentioned Croce by name.[36] As will be seen, not only is there a place for what may be called "prereflexive" experience in Dewey's thought, but art and aesthetic experience arise from it, since the fulfillment of aesthetic experience as consummatory is really a "postcognitive" rather than a "precognitive" state. Experience is mediated by intelligence so that its meanings fuse and become funded in *"an* experience" which carries its critical, intellectual phase within the pervasively felt qualitative unity. In other words, aesthetic meaning for Dewey is "supracognitive" rather than precognitive. This is a crucial point in understanding how Dewey can claim that aesthetic experience is expressive of meaning and produces "the sense of disclosure and heightened intelligibility" (*AE*, 289; *LW* 10:294), without advocating a cognitive theory of art.

Again it seems clear that Dewey's idea of the pervasive qualitative whole marks a central aspect of his theory which has led critics to connect it with idealism. This can be further brought out, though Douglas fails to note it, by Croce's and Dewey's uses of the term "intuition". "Intuition," states Croce "is the undifferentiated unity of the perception of the real and simple image of the possible."[37] It is simply a whole, *unanalyzed* perception unrelated to questions of its reality, relationships or implications, much like Santayana's use of "essence." It is the immediate object of Spirit's activity. For Dewey, aesthetic or consummatory experience is also ultimately intuited, which is to say that the pervasive qualitative whole is realized throughout the whole developing experience as the binding or grounding of all the phases so that they belong together—they are all parts of *an* experience. This quality is not directly the object of consciousness, but it is what focuses and contextualizes consciousness. In other words, for Dewey "Intuition . . . signifies the realization of a pervasive quality such that it regulates the determination of relevant distinctions or of whatever . . . becomes the accepted object of thought" ("Qualitative Thought"; *PC*, 101; *LW* 5:249).

Whereas intuitions for Croce are preanalyzed and unrelated essences, for Dewey they are the immediate or significant sense of the situation within which all analysis and relating are contained. Though superficially one might say that aesthetic meaning is intuited for Croce and Dewey, this is at best misleading and ambiguous. The full understanding of Dewey's theory of situations, context, and sense is necessary before what he means by "intuition" will be clear. But from these simple comparisons it should be evident that there are profound differences underlying the apparent similarities between his thought and Croce's. It is also plain that Douglas was only able to maintain the Pepper-Croce thesis by ignoring these fundamental dissimilarities.

III. Conclusion: The Significance and Scope of the Problem

Much of the force behind the Pepper-Croce thesis comes from a failure to understand Dewey's aesthetics in the context of his general philosophy. To show that the thesis is founded on misunderstandings and confusions is not to disprove it, however. Many philosophers have had difficulties with Dewey's ideas, and after a certain point, no matter what special topic is being examined, a certain similarity or pattern in the criticisms emerges. In Dewey's metaphysics, for example, there is a problem about his "phenomenological" versus his "naturalistic" approach or between his theory of quality and his theory of relation. The controversy began almost at the beginning of his instrumentalist period and persisted until his death and beyond.

The nature of the problem can be brought out by contrasting statements. "In every work of art," he says, ". . . meanings are actually embodied . . ." (*AE*,273; *LW* 10:277). Elsewhere, however, he says, "Genuinely to think of a thing is to think of implications that are no sooner thought of than we are hurried on to *their* implications" (*EN*, 118; *LW* 1:98). Again, we hear, "Quality is quality, direct, immediate and undefinable," whereas, "Order is a matter of relation, of definition, of placing and describing" (*EN*, 110; *LW* 1:92). "It cannot be asserted too strongly," claims Dewey, "that what is not immediate is not aesthetic (*AE*, 119; *LW* 10:123); elsewhere he says that "Immediacy of existence is ineffable" (*EN*, 85; *LW* 1:74). How can the aesthetic have meaning if it must be both mediated and ineffable? Dewey repeatedly insists that aesthetic experience is one of enjoyed meanings, yet he seems to have severed meaning from immediacy completely. Thus, while the Pepper-Croce thesis may have rested on ambiguities, there is good evidence that Dewey's theory itself contained ambiguities or contradictions or both. Perhaps, in short, Dewey *was* grafting a pragmatist branch onto an idealist trunk and roots so that this strange fruit was the result.

My thesis, however, is that Dewey did present a coherent, viable philosophy of experience and aesthetic meaning, though, surely, not a tidy one. This is not to deny that Dewey was frequently ambiguous or vague or that he contradicted himself. These features, however, have been so over-emphasized that I believe it is worthwhile to attempt a systematic and sympathetic reading of his thought. The difficulty of Heidegger's writing or the fragmentary presentation of Wittgenstein's later thought tend to postpone the reader from making hasty, premature criticisms. For better or worse, Dewey's rambling, matter-of-fact tone, which tries to present rather extraordinary ideas in ordinary American street-English, often gives the reader the impression that he has grasped the thought when he has grasped the ordinary sense. The fact that Dewey availed himself of terms deeply embedded in the very tradition which he was overthrowing, like "experience," "nature," "metaphysics," "organism," and so on, represents, I think, his genuine desire to co-opt the habits of speech. If his new meanings, in other words, could succeed in attaching themselves to the old terms, he would have gone far in changing the very "form of life" of the culture, diverting it from its dualistic habits to more constructive ones. Dewey, it must be recalled, wrote for a much broader audience than philosophers do today. That such an enterprise backfired is no great surprise, but the result has been a systematic misreading of Dewey's thought. How often, for example, is Dewey presented as a "naturalist," i.e., someone who believed that all man's higher functions could be reduced to and explained by organic laws of biology, chemistry, and physics, or that it was the genuine thrust of his theory of experimental intelligence that all questions, including those of value, should be handed over to research scientists for resolution? Such a misreading is reflected in the attempts to treat Dewey as a half-hearted or unsystematic positivist-utilitarian—positions to which he was deeply opposed. Before, however, we undertake an examination of his mature philosophy, it will be illuminating to explore the outlines of his first idealistic system, focusing on those problematic ideas raised by the Pepper-Croce thesis. It will then be easier to determine whether there are skeletons—or ghosts—lurking in the cellars and attics of his later thought.

Chapter 2

The Logic of Life

Dewey's short intellectual biography, "From Absolutism to Experimentalism" (written when he was seventy-one), is, like most autobiographies, deceptive as well as revealing. It is particularly maddening for stopping where it does, at the very commencement of Dewey's instrumentalist period, as well as for what it leaves out. But we do get a map of what Dewey regarded as the motivating tensions and crucial turning points of his early philosophical career. Dewey does remark perceptively enough "that my development has been controlled largely by a struggle between a native inclination toward the schematic and formally logical" and those things which were "contrary to his natural tendencies," namely issues of a "concrete, empirical, and 'practical' " sort—the very characteristics for which he became best known (LW 5:150-51). Dewey says that he recognized his attraction to the formal to be a weakness, indeed, a form of cowardice. In any case, we do well to remember that he says "when anyone is unduly concerned with controversy, the remarks that seem to be directed against others are really concerned with a struggle going on inside himself." When the "schematic side" was dominant, Dewey says, "writing was comparatively easy" (and his early essays, placed next to the later, substantiate this remarkably), "since then thinking and writing have been hard work" (LW 5:151). Perhaps this accounts too for the otherwise incomprehensible stories of Aristotle ranked as a stylist with Plato. After an influential brush with Transcendentalism by way of Marsh's edition of Coleridge's *Aids to Reflection*, Dewey found his first intellectual synthesis in the dynamic Hegelianism of his teacher in graduate school, George Sylvester Morris. Recognizing his "heritage of New England culture", with its dualisms of self and world, soul and body, nature and God, and the consequent "painful oppression", Dewey found that "Hegel's synthesis of subject and object, matter and spirit, the divine and the human, was, however, no mere intellectual formula; it operated as an immense release. Hegel's treatment of human culture, of institutions and the arts, involved the same dissolution of hard-and-fast dividing walls, and had a special attraction for me" (*LW* 5:153). Dewey continues:

> I drifted away from Hegelianism in the next fifteen years; the word "drifting" expresses the slow and, for a long time, imperceptible character of the movement, though it does not convey the impression that there was an adequate cause for the change. Nevertheless I should never think of ignoring, much less denying, what an astute critic occasionally refers to as a novel discovery—that acquaintance with Hegel has left a permanent deposit in my thinking. The form, the schematism, of his system now seems to me artificial to the last degree. But in the content of his ideas there is often an extraordinary depth; in many of his analyses, taken out of their mechanical dialectical setting, an extraordinary acuteness. Were it possible for me to be a devotee of any system, I still should believe that there is greater and variety of insight in Hegel than in any other single systematic philosopher—though when I say this I exclude Plato, who still provides my favorite philosophical reading (*LW* 5:154).[1]

Dewey points out very briefly four other factors in the development of his mature thought: the philosophical importance of his involvement with experimental education, the frustrating methodological dualism between science and ethics, the biological functionalism of William James' *Principles of Psychology,* and the increasingly important implications of the social sciences for philosophy in general (especially those concerned with communication) and the arts. These points in themselves are worth remembering, the last one in particular, but for now we may wonder at Dewey's rather congenial recollection of the importance of Hegel for his thinking just after noting the firm rejections we encountered in his debates with Pepper and Croce. Clearly, whatever insights he considered to be of value for his own philosophy found in Hegel's writings, especially Hegel's treatment of human culture, Dewey believed had been successfully translated into his own philosophy. Had Dewey, in his responses to Pepper and Croce, tried to indicate precisely where his theory was indebted to idealism in general or to Hegel's system in particular, it would have been easier to see whether his own aesthetic theory presented a consistent position.

The question therefore to be asked is: to what extent does Dewey's early theory of aesthetic meaning resemble his mature theory, and how firmly are both theories committed to idealism? This chapter will deal with this issue in the following manner. First, Dewey's attempt to treat experience in its wholeness will be shown to be the central underlying dynamism of his philosophy, from first to last. It accounts for his earliest blending of idealist metaphysics with scientific psychology to create his first "system", represented by the *Psychology* of 1887. The centrality of psychology as the "science of the self" and therefore the "science of reality" will be contrasted with Dewey's mature position which, although concerned with experience, interprets it in terms of a biosocial theory of meaning, which almost distributes the area of psychology to the fields of biology and sociology. Both the early and the mature theories are concerned with the subject of meaning, especially meaning as immediately embodied in concrete experience. The importance of imagination and art is also parallelled in the early and later work, art providing the fusion of ideal and habitual meanings in creative activity. While the idealist theory characteristically attributes this activity to a metaphysical "Self", the naturalistic theory refers to concrete, practical modes of activity grounded in the transactional situation. In a sense, both theories view meaning as a particular phase of experience within some larger whole, bound by a pervasive feeling, which establishes art as a mode of intimate communication. Yet there is a vast gulf between the idealist treatment of this topic, which ultimately interprets meaning as the Self coming to understand its internal content, and the naturalistic treatment, which sees the self, or the nexus of meanings and values, as a developing process realized through interaction or creative participation in the natural and cultural environment. Dewey's theory of aesthetic meaning in *Art as Experience* does bear a number of similarities with the idealist position in his writings prior to 1903, but this does not mean that his later theory is either idealist in intent or inconsistent with his overall philosophy. It demonstrates that there was a continuity of concern with certain key ideas which Dewey came to believe were dealt with better in his later philosophy than in his earlier. And this is quite significant in understanding the purpose of Dewey's philosophy. It will be the tasks of subsequent chapters to define the context of Dewey's mature theory of aesthetic meaning and to describe that theory itself.

I. The "New Psychology"

Another important clue to understanding Dewey's intellectual history is given in the essay already cited. As an undergraduate,

Dewey encountered Huxley's *Lessons in Elementary Physiology*, from which, he claimed, "subconsciously, at least, I was led to desire a world and a life that would have the same properties as had the human organism in the picture of it derived from the study of Huxley's treatment" (*LW* 5:147-48).[2] This alone might have predestined young Dewey to a career in biology. But there was another force being felt in New England: The Transcendentalist movement had opened the doors to German idealism and romanticism. In addition to Huxley, Dewey read Coleridge's *Aids to Reflection*. Years later, Herbert Schneider recalled Dewey's saying that Marsh's American edition of the work "was our spiritual emancipation in Vermont" and that "Coleridge represents pretty much my religious views still, but I quit talking about them because nobody else is interested in them."[3]

This tension between a biologically functional, if materialistic, world-view and one which asserted the inherent spirituality and creativity of the cosmos was to be repeated in Dewey's graduate education. Dewey's two most influential teachers at Johns Hopkins were the idealist George Sylvester Morris and the psychologist G. Stanley Hall. Dewey's first semester consisted of a heavy dose of Morris' strange synthesis of Christianity, Hegel, and Trendelenburg's Aristotelianism; his second semester was almost entirely devoted to courses in laboratory behavioral psychology given by Hall, himself a student of Wundt.[4] What idealism, Trendelenburg's teleological philosophy, Darwinian biology, and Wundtian psychology all had in common was, of course, the concept of *organism*. To a remarkable degree, Dewey's philosophical development arose from the attempt to mediate and harmonize these highly divergent viewpoints into one coherent theory.

Accompanying Dewey's youthful enthusiasm, which promisingly found so much in common between such seemingly opposed doctrines, was a marked distaste for those aspects of each position which seemed reductionistic, abstract, or atomizing. This was dramatically presented in a series of early articles from 1884 to the publication of his *Psychology* in 1887. His first attempt to bridge psychology with idealism was, therefore, to insist on the original integrity and wholeness of experience. He regarded both Wundtian psychology and Hegelian logic as reductionistic attempts to replace primary experience with abstractions. Mill's empiricism, it should be noted, was not even a contestant. In an early article, "The New Psychology" (1884), Dewey directly implies that art, rather than philosophy or science, has done more justice to experience in preserving this original texture, individuality and depth:

> That rich and colored experience, never the same in two nations, in two individuals, in two moments of the same life—whose thoughts, desires, fears and hopes have furnished the material for the ever-developing literature of the ages, for a Homer and a Chaucer, a Sophocles and a Shakespeare, for the unwritten comedies and trage-dies of daily life—was neatly and carefully dissected, its parts la-beled and stowed away in their pigeon-holes, the inventory taken, and the whole stamped with the stamp of *un fait accompli (EW* 1:48).

While the remark above is directed against the atomizing tradition of British empiricism, Dewey also had stern criticisms of Hegelian logic, which attempts to arrive at the concrete individual via the abstract universal. Because even dialectical logic by itself is a purely abstract discipline, it never can make the final leap to its required living embodiment in nature:

> There is no way of getting from logic to the philosophy of nature *logically.* . . . For logic, being thus confessedly determined as ab-stract, is still retained to determine the nature of the concrete. Logic, while it is thus declared to be only one moment of spirit, is still used to determine the nature of the whole. . . . Spirit is reached by a *logical* process, and the *logical* result is that as fact it is not reached at all. As concrete it is beyond the reach of any abstract process ("Psy-chology as Philosophical Method," *EW* 1:164-65).[5]

The question then is typically Deweyan: what is the appropriate method for coming to understand experience in its wholeness which neither anatomizes it nor treats it from a purely formal dilectical standpoint? Dewey did not choose to reject reason for mysticism or aestheticism. Instead he attempted to create a new science or, rather, radically to transform and reground the science of psychology. Dewey's "new psychology" would start with lived experience and attempt to understand it in terms of its organic movement and whole-ness. Abstractions, in other words, were to be understood in terms of *it* rather than vice versa. Though immediately beginning with human experience, this method would necessarily lead not only to the sci-ences of nature, but dialectically proceed to the study of reality as Absolute Self, for "we know that man is indeed the microcosm who has gathered into himself the riches of the world. . . ." ("The New Psychology"; *EW* 1:49). Dewey would reveal the ontological dimen-sion of psychology by making idealism more empirical.

At the time of Dewey's early essays in the 1880s psychology was divided between the old-fashioned introspectionists and the new physiology coming from Germany. Typically, Dewey attempted to bridge this dualism as well. The way through this dilemma lay, he thought, by first of all acknowledging the invaluable contribution of physiological psychology: method. This brand of psychology, states Dewey:

> Has given a new instrument, introduced a new *method*—that of experiment, which has supplemented and corrected the old method of introspection. Psychical facts still remain psychical, and are to be explained through psychical conditions; but our means of ascertaining what these facts are and how they are conditioned have been indefinitely widened (*EW* 1:53).

Dewey in fact denies that the "old method of introspection" was really a method at all, since no experimental controls were used. The purpose of method is to explain and "To explain is to mediate; to connect the given fact with an unseen principle; to refer the phenomenon to an antecedent condition—while introspection can only deal with the immediate present, with the given now" (*EW* 1:53-54). Though, as Dewey puts it later in the *Psychology*, introspection "must ultimately be the sole source of the *material* of psychology" (*EW* 2:12), correct perception must involve the mediation of reflection. In other words, perception deals with constructed objects, meanings, not brute sensations.

By this route Dewey sought to ground the "hard" method of experimental, physiological psychology upon the equally "hard" fact that human experience is primarily encountered neither as atomic bits of sense data, nor as a series of mechanical jerks, but as a world of developing *meanings*. Insofar as any experiment relies on a method and any method relies upon certain theoretical assumptions, "To observe truly a mental fact demands a true hypothesis in the mind and proper material with which to correlate it" (*EW* 2:13). The "true hypothesis" of psychology is that it is ultimately concerned with the "facts of self" or self-consciousness, which constitute its proper subject matter.

Because meanings, the content of the self, are universal while the self itself is individual, "Psychology is the science of the reproduction of some universal content or existence, whether of knowledge or action, in the form of individual, unsharable consciousness" (*EW* 2:11). While Dewey does describe the experimental method in psychology as an indirect means of investigating "the connection of the soul with the body" (*EW* 2:13), instead of regarding this relationship as one of psycho-physical parallelism, he points to the structure and function of organic processes as indications of the way psychical processes work. In other words, the functional concept of the organism, common to biology and idealism, will provide the connecting link. In "The New Psychology" he states:

> The present theory that memory is not a chamber hall for storing up ideas and their traces or relics, but is lines of activity along which the mind habitually works, was certainly suggested from the growing physiological belief that the brain cells which form the physical basis of memory do not in any way store upon past impressions or their traces, but have, by these impressions, their structure so modified as to give rise to a certain functional mode of activity. . . . The influence of biological science in general upon psychology has been very great. . . . To biology is due the concept of organism. . . . In psychology this conception has led to the recognition of mental life as an organic unitary process developing according to the laws of all life, and not a theatre for the exhibition of independent autonomous faculties or a *rendezvous* in which isolated atomic sensations and ideas may gather, hold external converse, and then forever part (*EW* 1:55-56).

This comparison led Dewey to make a crucial decision which would affect the entire course of his philosophy. For, if psychical life is akin to physical, especially with regard to its organic, functional nature, then one can no more look upon consciousness as an independent, unrelated entity, hovering spectrally above the waters of life. Just as organisms develop in response to environmental circumstances and are united through functional integration, so too must consciousness be in touch with its environment, realized through interaction with it:

> Along with this recognition of the solidarity of mental life has come that of the relation in which it stands to other lives organized in society. The idea of environment is a necessity to the idea of organism, and with the conception of environment comes the impossibility of considering psychical life as an individual, isolated thing developing in a vacuum (*EW* 1:56).

The environment of consciousness is the entire social world which defines the individual's functions. The "new psychology" will then incorporate "those vast and as yet undefined topics of inquiry which may be vaguely designated as the social and historical sciences—the sciences of the origin and development of the various spheres of man's activity" (*EW* 1:57). Thus, instead of introspection or the study of merely physical reflexes, psychology will be a study encompassing linguistics, anthropology, sociology, ethnology, and child psychology (to list Dewey's examples); in short, it will be the foundation of the human studies as well as of all the sciences pertaining to man.

While the natural sciences may have provided the ideal as far as the concept of experimental method and the functional nature of the organism goes, the growth of the new psychology will be due to "sciences of humanity in general, giving us the method of objective observation" (*EW* 1:58). In other words, the program laid out will study the objective manifestations of meaning in the human world by an experimental and functional approach:

> The broadest and most fundamental method of correcting and extending the results of introspection, and of interpreting these results, so as to refer them to their laws, is the study of the objective manifestations of mind. Mind has not remained a passive spectator of the universe, but has produced and is producing certain results. These results are objective, can be studied as all objective historical facts may be, and are permanent. They are the most fixed, certain, and universal signs to us of the way in which mind works. Such objective manifestations of mind are, in the realm of intelligence, phenomena like language and science; in that of will, social and political institutions; in that of feeling, art; in that of the whole self, religion (*EW* 2:15).

It should be remembered here that, even though Dewey abandoned the "true hypothesis" of his new program, the Absolute Self, and with it the "fixed, certain and universal" character of its results, he did not abandon the ultimate task. In the last analysis, as will be seen, philosophy for Dewey stands for a method of cultural interpretation, evaluation and criticism, a study and creation of cultural meanings.[6]

One might question exactly how, at this phase in Dewey's career, he differed from Hegel, who also had argued for a rigorous study of the objective manifestations of Spirit in human culture. Dewey's rejection of the abstract a priori nature of Hegelian dialectic clearly dictated an alternative methodology. But Dewey was not impressed either with the inductive or deductive methodologies of the current science and logic. These seemed too committed to the empiricist treatment of every separate idea involving a separate existence, to subjectivism, and to other nominalist presuppositions. In "The New Psychology," Dewey announces that "the logic of concrete experience, of growth and development, repudiates such abstractions. The logic of life transcends the logic of nominalistic thought" (*EW* 1:59). Such "formalistic intuitionalism" must be rejected for a new, dynamic methodology which will reveal that truth and reality are present in living, developing experience. This is because:

Experience is realistic, not abstract. Psychical life is the fullest, deepest, and richest manifestation of this experience. The New Psychology is content to get its logic from this experience, and not to do violence to the sanctity and integrity of the latter by forcing it to conform to certain preconceived abstract ideas. It wants a logic of fact, of process, of life (*EW* 1:59-60).

What Dewey meant by "the logic of life" in this enthusiastic essay is not clear—he was making an impassioned call for a new program and not announcing a new discovery. Though eventually this underlying sense of fidelity to the richness, wholeness, and primacy of experience led Dewey to develop his instrumentalism as "the logic of life", since it alone seemed to have regard for the functional relationships in experience without setting up a priori intellectual categories, Dewey at this period saw the unity and process of experience as due to the will, which was "a living bond connecting and conditioning *all* mental activity" (*EW* 1:60). The teleology of the will introduced, furthermore, an ethical dimension into all "psychological research." The new psychology was to be a science of creating man as well as understanding him. The result of this was the abiding sensitivity in Dewey's philosophy to the frequent tendency in thinkers to abstract a phase, idea or element from its total "lived context" where it operated as a functional part, and posit these constituents as prior in some epistemological or metaphysical sense. In another essay, "The Psychological Standpoint," Dewey states, "What is denied is the correctness of the procedure which, discovering a certain element *in* knowledge to be necessary for knowledge, therefore concludes that this element has an existence prior to or apart from knowledge" (*EW* 1:123).[7] Once this path has been taken, the whole can easily be reduced to its parts—in fact, all parts can be reduced to or explained by one part.

By starting with experience as it is lived, the method of psychology can come to understand how the various phases or elements arise within it and so be understood in terms of their functional origins. Ultimately, Dewey claims, all these distinctions exist for consciousness. For example, "From the psychological standpoint the relation of subject and object is one which exists within consciousness" (*EW* 1:131). This leads Dewey to postulate the "true hypothesis" of absolute idealism, because ultimately one cannot posit, without contradiction, the existence of another consciousness totally unrelated to one's own. Instead of arguing for a solipsistic position, Dewey emphasizes the universal, objective content of consciousness, reconciling the becoming of individual consciousness with its objects "by the postulate of a universal consciousness" (*EW* 1:138). Consciousness in fact is "the unity of the individual and the universal" or "the unity of subject and object" (*EW* 1:140, 138).

Because psychology is the science of consciousness, it is not just another science alongside other sciences; rather, it is "the ultimate science of reality, because it declares what experience in its totality is; it fixes the worth and meaning of its various elements by showing their development and place within this whole. It is, in short, *philosophic method*" (*EW* 1:144). Dewey believes that idealism disregarded psychology as a method because psychology had been identified with British empiricism. This, however, left a dualism between man as the subject of an empirical science and man as a self-conscious and "infinite" being. All other forms of knowledge rely on consciousness, so that "the psychological standpoint is necessarily a universal standpoint . . ." (*EW* 1:141). It is the science of the self-realization of the universe through the individual. Man is an "individualized universe" (*EW* 1:149). Psychology, therefore, both represents man as a conscious being and grounds all other empirical investigations: "Or, in a word, if the reality of spirit be the presupposition, the *prius* and goal, the condition and end of all reality, the science of spirit must occupy a corresponding position with relation to all science" (*EW* 1:167).

Consciousness is the mediation of a transient fact into a universal meaning for Dewey at this state. Psychology is primarily concerned with both meaning and value and how these are realized as parts of a whole. Self-realization on the level of consciousness is "the absolute meaning of experience" (*EW* 1:151). The primacy of experience over cognition or sensation is indicated in Dewey's assertion that "the real *esse* of things is neither their *percipi,* nor their *intelligi* alone; it is their *experiri*" (*EW* 1:151). "Experience", therefore, comes to signify for Dewey the fullest, richest and most dynamic unity of universal meaning embodied in concrete individuality, that is, as absolute self-realization.

It is evident that central themes which appear in Dewey's mature work, especially his aesthetics, are urgently present in the early phase of his career. Dewey is already fighting against artificial dualisms which force experience from its primacy, immediacy, and dynamic vitality into arid, fixed abstractions. Especially important for this struggle is the model of the organism, conceived of both biologically and along the lines of the idealists' organic unity of Spirit. Dewey calls for the wedding of empirical methodology with the human studies to provide a disciplined appropriation of the domain of meanings as concretely embodied. Philosophy itself must be the study of experience in its functional modes of existence, and experience is broader than the mere categories of cognitive understanding.

The outstanding difference between the early and late Dewey is, of course, the contrast between the commitment to absolute idealism and to pluralistic naturalism. Originally Dewey saw idealism as providing the proper framework for working out the program described. The very truth of these studies, in fact, rested upon the underlying assumption that everything was an aspect or phase contained within an Absolute Individual coming to full self-consciousness. It was this belief and the ambitious program announced in Dewey's articles of the 1880s which led to his first complete philosophical system, represented by the *Psychology* of 1887 and its two subsequent revisions (1889; 1891).

II. Dewey's System: The Psychology

Perhaps the reason why Dewey insisted so strongly in his later years, when replying to Pepper, Croce and others, that he had no system was that he had, in fact, had one—which he came to see as representing all the errors that his later philosophy set out to avoid. Although written as a textbook in psychology, Dewey's first book was nothing less than an attempt to use the latest scientific research in psychology to prove the truth of objective idealism. While demonstrating the a priori necessity of the Absolute Self, Dewey cites the works of Helmholtz, Stumpf, Wundt, Bain, and others. References to idealist philosophers are kept to a minimum, limited mainly to the works of Lotze, Bradley, and Thomas Hill Green.[8] Though Dewey's later books tend to be rambling and unsophisticated, the *Psychology* is a detailed, intricate tapestry in which each phase and moment dialectically dovetails into the others, and Hegelian terms are dextrously manipulated. It was meant to be a stunning and subversive book.

Though Dewey's former teacher, Granville Stanley Hall, and another psychologist, William James, had deep reservations, no one denied it was an impressive first book.[9] Its influence would have been more widely felt had James' own *Principles of Psychology* not eclipsed it three years later. Dewey attempts to demonstrate the internal integrity of experience by showing how its three major modes, knowing, feeling, and willing, all mutually imply each other. It is significant that once again he appeals to the analogy of the living organism.

> Any state of consciousness is really knowledge since it makes us aware of something; feeling, since it has a certain peculiar reference to ourselves; and will, since it is dependent upon some activity of

ourselves. ̃. . . . Just as in the organic body the progress of digestion cannot go on without that of circulation, and both require respiration and nerve action, which in turn are dependent upon other processes, so in the organic mind. Knowledge is not possible without feeling and will and neither of these without the other two (EW 2:20).

To rephrase, cognition is concerned with the objective and universal aspect of experience; feeling deals with the subjective and qualitative side, while willing is the active mediation of the two into a concrete individual. Since knowing and feeling are activities of Spirit, they are forms of willing; since feeling and willing are concerned with the content of Spirit, they are knowledge, and since knowing and willing refer to some subject, they involve feeling.

Later, Dewey will insist that all experience involves both phases of doing and undergoing, and, when these are done in relation to each other, experience is mediated by intelligence. To this extent, at least, one may catch an echo of the early philosophy in the later. In both periods Dewey insists that there is no such thing as brute, hard, unmediated experience or sense data, though there is a qualitative "had" or "undergone" aspect which can also be described as immediate. All experience, however, involves interaction, which is to say, interpretation. Truth, for example, is described as a "system of interpretation".[10] Likewise, in both philosophies there is no experience without interest. In the *Psychology*, Dewey says:

Our consciousness . . . is not indifferent or colorless, but it is regarded as having importance, having value, having *interest*. It is this peculiar fact of *interest* which constitutes the emotional side of consciousness, and it signifies that the idea which has this interest has some unique connection with the self (EW 2:19).

In *Art as Experience*, Dewey will make the same general point arguing against Kant's view of the aesthetic as "disinterested interest" and the formalist doctrines of critics like Roger Fry.[11] There would be no experience for us to see, Dewey insists, unless we are oriented to it through some sort of interest. But here, in the early position, Dewey's problem is the relation of the particular individual to the absolute. To summarize, then, for the early and late Dewey, experience must have both meaning and value inherently.

The outstanding divergence between the two positions is that in this early phase Dewey's theory of activity is virtually identical with that noted in Croce: activity is due to the associating or dissociating spiritual power of the will.[12] Every passing moment of experience is an instance of self-realization leading inevitably to a higher stage of Absolute Spirit. For Dewey and Hegel alike, however much Dewey may insist on the non-cognitive aspects of experience like feeling and willing, experience is ultimately mediated "through and through", but mediation is not *simply* knowledge or reason. In other words, self-realization cannot be summed up for Dewey as "self-knowledge". Though one can say of Dewey's later account of experience that there is no pure, unmediated form, there is a world of difference between ascribing mediation to a universal, creative spiritual power or to the attitudes or dispositions of habits acquired by interacting with an environment. In the former, there is an eventual total mediation of the system while in the latter there is never any absolute mediation achieved, no final, "objective" universal standpoint which determines everything else. The later Dewey denied that there was any one, fixed perspective from which the world received its ultimate meaning. Instead, the world was intrinsically pluralistic and unfinished.

An important feature of Dewey's idealism is the interpretation of knowledge as fundamentally concerned with *meaning*. This doctrine will also have its parallels with his later theory. According to absolute idealism, knowledge is really the meaning of self-realization—Spirit comes to a full and absolute understanding of itself as self-consciousness objectified in a system of relations or meanings. In "Knowledge as Idealization", Dewey's own views are apparent in the claim that "When Psychology recognizes that the relating activity of mind is one not exercised *upon* sensations, but one which supplies relations and thereby makes meaning . . . Psychology will be in a position to become Philosophy" (*EW* 1:190). "There is but one world," he says elsewhere, "the world of knowledge, not two, an inner and an outer, a world of observation and a world of ordinary conception; and this one world is everywhere logical" (*EW* 3:81-82).

Dewey's emphasis upon taking experience in its primacy dictated that, however convinced one might be of the internal, a priori necessity of the world, one must begin with examining experience itself and not by positing a metaphysical doctrine. One starts, then, by looking at the *meaning* of terms like "truth" and "reality." For example:

> If reality is itself an element in conscious experience, it must come under the scope of significance, the meaning of experience, and hence cannot be used as an external standard to measure this meaning. The reality of experience is, in short, an element of its . . . ideal quality or relation to intelligence. . . . Reality, like everything else that has meaning, is a function of our ideas (*EW* 1:192-93).

Thus, even here, method and inquiry are prior, and only function within a context of meaning. To begin with experiences is to begin with encountered meanings and values, not with sense data or pure theory.

Though in Dewey's later views much the same can be said, it is important to be clear what Dewey means here by meaning and value. Value, as we saw, deals with the subjective or particular and qualitative emotional interest of consciousness. This is quite different from value as the situational functioning of intelligence relating ends and means toward consummatory, continuous experience.[13] In this idealist version, meaning is described as follows:

> Meaning constitutes the worth of every psychical experience; meaning is not bare existence, but is an inferential mediate factor; it is relation and is ideal; as ideal it is supplied by intelligence out of its own content; this constitutes, indeed, the reality of intelligence (*EW* 1:192).

While later Dewey will also describe meaning as a mediating and relating function, it certainly will not be taken out of intelligence's "own content." It will involve various active modes of participation, inquiry, deliberation, evaluation, and resolution through which the world is appropriated and the self, the system of meanings, *grows*. The difference between these two types of relating can best be summarized as the difference between an internal act of remembering and having a conversation with a new acquaintance. However active relations may be in Dewey's idealism, the spectator model still predominates, while in his instrumentalism the dramatic model comes to the fore. In either case, however, the concepts of meaning and value are based upon the original, functional, organic metaphor noted. That is, to be aware of the meaning or value of something is to see it in terms of being *a functioning part within a larger whole*. For example, "heart" refers to the role of a specific organ within the whole living system, and its value is determined by this function. Likewise, the whole will be understood as the integration of various component functions into one continuous activity.[14]

Dewey strenuously rejects the British empiricist theory of meaning, essentially the nominalist interpretation, that meanings are associations held in the mind between ideas on bits of sense data. This theory explains nothing, Dewey cogently argues, since previous sensations are vanished, and, if they were in need of interpretation before, they are doubly so if one merely adds more sensations onto them: "Multiplication of sensations is not the interpretation of sensations previously existent" (*EW* 1:187). Sensations do not duplicate the world—they are "virtual creations" of Spirit in response to the world—and they provide instead the *material* rather than the *subject matter* of knowledge. Nor do sensations come to us in discrete bundles. Experience is encountered as a continuum of feeling bound by fusion:

> We have . . . a continuous whole of sensation constantly undergoing modification and constantly expanding, but never parting with its unity. This process may be termed *fusion* or *integration* to indicate the fact that the various elements are continually entering into a whole in which they lose their independent existence (*EW* 2:86).

This critical concept of fusion will reappear in Dewey's aesthetics. Pepper himself, to recall, saw it as Dewey's major contribution to pragmatic aesthetic theory, though ironically it first appears in the context of Dewey's most idealist work. Dewey's discussion of feeling is also important in terms of its future treatment in his mature theory of experience. "Feeling, in all cases," notes Dewey, "seems to serve as a matrix in which ideas are embedded, and by which they are held together. There is no more permanent tie between ideas than this identity of emotion" (*EW* 2:95). Dewey will later stress that all thought must be bounded by a "pervasive qualitative whole" and be governed by a sense or feeling of the context to take on meaning.[15] At this point, however, the fusing of sensations as well as the role of feeling are ascribed to the "interpreting activity of intelligence" (*EW* 1:189). It is important to note that what we perceive in experience is not "clusters of sensations" but associated *meanings* integrated into a continuum of feeling as well as knowing. "What is perceived is, in short, significance, meaning," claims Dewey (*EW* 1:178). Though a baby, a bricklayer and a chemist may receive similar optical stimuli, they will have quite different perceptions of the same event. As Dewey insists, "Perceiving . . . is interpreting. The content of perception is what is signified. . . . Meaning constitutes for us the whole value of experience" (*EW* 1:178). Were this aspect removed from experience, Dewey denies there would be consciousness at all: "Take away the meaning, and consciousness vanishes" (*EW* 1:179). That Dewey retained this insight is well testified by his remark in *Studies in Logical Theory*: "*Meaning* is the characteristic object of thought. . . . We need only to recognize that association is of matters or meanings, not of ideas as existences or events. . . ." The main difference is that instead of understanding this association as due to an abstract "intelligence," Dewey speaks of thought controlled "in reference to an end" and as a "reconstructive movement of actual contents of experience in relation to each other" (EEL, 158, 116, 176; MW 10:352, 324, 363).[16]

Since knowledge is of meanings, and meanings are relations, it follows that "There is no such thing as purely *immediate* knowledge" (EW 2:192). Dewey rephrases this by saying that "what is *immediately* present is never known" (EW 1:179). We see here the beginning of the problem that was to haunt Dewey and his critics: If knowledge or meanings are purely relational, then nothing can ever be known or understood *now*. Whatever one may say of aesthetic experience, insofar as it deals with immediate perception, one cannot speak of it having "aesthetic meaning." Yet, as we have seen, there really is no such thing as "immediate perception," or if there were, Dewey denies we would really "experience" it. What Dewey is trying to say, of course, is that pure sensations alone are meaningless. Sensation is always involved in a complex, organized activity and comes to have meaning because of this organization. But Dewey often lapses into the terminology of British empiricism while attempting to refute it. This comes out in his speaking of knowledge as purely relational and meaning as treating immediate sensation as "signs":

> The sensuous material is of worth only as it is a sign; it is a sign only as it signifies or points out meaning. This meaning is present as mediated. . . . Psychical result or significance is all intelligence cares for. . . . Processes, whether of perception or reasoning, are of no account to intelligence except as they lead to meaning. Perception is well defined as unconscious reasoning (EW 1:180).

Relations must always be relations *of*; if one over-emphasizes them and their transitoriness, one faces the problems which arose from Hegel's philosophy, with which later idealists like Bradley had to deal.[17] On the one hand, the internally related nature of the whole must be defended; on the other, the immediate, present moment seems to evaporate into an impossible skein of relations. Dewey himself struggled with this paradox, and came to the conclusion that idealism was incapable of resolving it. As will be seen, James' observation that relations had a qualitative, felt aspect was one of the most influential ideas for Dewey in the *Principles of Psychology*.[18] Dewey saw this as fundamental to his mature theory of experience; and his aesthetics, especially his theory of aesthetic meaning, relies on his attempted resolution of the problem.

At this stage of Dewey's development, however, the role of "unconscious reasoning" must be invoked to explain why everything is ultimately related.[19] In an important sense, though, conscious experience is never stationary, and part of the significance it has lies in its intrinsic orientation toward the future in terms of a developing process. Dewey will always insist that experience has meaning because it is developing and because it is *of* something. "We simply take one *meaning* at a time, and then go on to the next meaning. Reasoning is the way in which we separate and unite meanings into one complex meaning" (*EW* 1:180-81). This organization comes about through focusing attention and "Attention has always an end in view, with express consideration of what it selects. The mind at-tends; it is stretched out toward something" (*EW* 2:119). There is meaning because experience is temporal and concerned about projects, as Heidegger subsequently has shown.

Another important aspect of Dewey's early theory of meaning is the importance he places on habit. This idea, so central in Dewey's subsequent philosophy and so novel in any idealist theory of meaning, is nevertheless placed in the context of Dewey's presuppositions about the "unconscious reasoning" of Spirit. Habit is important in Dewey's idealism because it represents his attempt to connect the mediating function of reason to the immediate world of sensation through fusion. With habit, "the sign has become fused with the act signified" (*EW* 2:101). Dewey notes here, as he will later, that habit frees consciousness from the stable aspects of experience to cope with the novel. Habit represents the "instinctive" union of the individual with the world, including the social world. Though Dewey makes growth itself depend on habit, growth under the rubric of idealism refers to increasing self-conscious awareness of the organic unity of Spirit. Habit illustrates the relation between unconscious and conscious Spirit and owes its active synthesizing, as well as analyzing, powers to a nonphysical, autonomous agency. Long before relations are translated into action, Dewey claims "that relations are thoroughly *ideal*" (*EW* 1:185).

By "ideal," Dewey means that the a priori necessity of active Spirit is presupposed. In other words, something cannot come from nothing, a higher reality cannot come from a lesser.[20] "Significance, meaning, must already be there," states Dewey. "Intelligence, in short, is the one indispensable condition of intelligent experience" (*EW* 1:189). Since bare, passive impressions of sense cannot transcend or synthesize themselves, Spirit must, explicating what was implicit, making conscious what was unconscious:

> This process is properly called one of *idealization* because it goes beyond the present sensuous *existence*, which is actually *present*, and

gives the present datum meaning by connecting it with the self, and thus putting into it significance, which as bare existence it does not have. Meaning, in short, is connection, is relation, is going beyond the mere presentation to something beyond. This element must be supplied by the self or mind, and hence is ideal (*EW* 2:122).

Meaning is produced because of "the development—the manifestation—of internal content of intelligence" (*EW* 1:188). The self, according to this model, must be the source and content of all experience of knowledge. The more the external is integrated into internal categories of Spirit, the more it has value, meaning and reality: "Experience begins when intelligence projects something of itself into sensations. We have now to recognize that experience grows, or gets more meaning, just in the degree in which intelligence reads more ideal content into it" (*EW* 1:191).

While the later Dewey will insist that growth is growth of meaning due to the role of intelligence, how different these phrases are without the metaphysics of idealism behind them! A crude comparison between the two versions might be said to be that according to the idealist model the external testifies to some ontologically prior, completed reality, whereas according to the naturalist model growth is the genuine realization of possibilities between the organism and its environment, a truly creative development of nature. Dewey does not reverse the relationship in his later philosophy, making the mind a passive *tabula rasa* to a world of external powers (even Locke could not maintain that theory). But experience is the product of interactions between the organic, habitual, and social structures the individual inherits from the past, his openness to the world, and the world itself. Novelty and method are crucial for experience in Dewey's later work, whereas self-consciousness recognizing its own "internal content" is the goal of experience in the early work. Therefore Dewey can say in 1887, "Self consciousness is the idealizing process of all knowledge continued until it becomes conscious of itself," and "Knowledge might be indifferently described, therefore, as a process of idealization of experience, or of realization of intelligence" (*EW* 1:186, 192). In short, for idealism the Self is never truly at risk and its growth finally is a type of recapitulation or remembrance, for it realizes as it develops that it *was* those things all along.

Part of the impressive nature of Dewey's *Psychology* is how the various phases and elements of experience are analyzed to fit into the model described. Of central importance is imagination, because with it experience becomes consciously aware of its idealizing capacities and of the freedom of the mind itself.

> Creative imagination . . . is the only free action of that idealizing activity which is involved in all knowledge whatever. Perception is idealization of sensations so that they become symbolic of some present reality; memory is such an extension of this idealization that past experiences are represented. Imagination takes this idealized element by itself, and treats it with reference to its own value, without regard to the actual existence of the things symbolized. . . . Perception and memory both have their worth because of the *meaning* of the perceived or remembered thing, but this meaning is subordinate to the existence of the thing. Imagination reverses this process; existence is subordinate to meaning (*EW* 2:171-72).

Dewey will later discuss aesthetic meaning in similar terms: the appreciation of meanings as intrinsic and ideal. But again, the change of context determines a fundamental change in the expression. The worth and value of imagination here comes from the place it occupies on the road to full self-consciousness. Later, Dewey will point to the aesthetic experience as a paradigmatic example of all experience because it is a complete integration of means and ends, self and world, in a dynamic mode of participation which realizes communication and expression.

Imagination occupies a midway position between pure sensation at one extreme and pure reason at the other. In this respect it comes to stand as a symbol of the concrete individual. Knowledge *uses* images as symbols or tools, but does not abide within the sensuous image since it is concerned with the universal, mediating principle behind it.[21] It must be recalled though that knowledge for Dewey is not of the universal itself, but of the concrete universal, the Absolute Individual or Self: "All knowledge is . . . of an individual" (*EW* 2:200). As the next section will discuss, imagination can be said to deal with "immediate meaning" insofar as it recognizes both sensuous and universal features in experience.

This idea finds its parallel in Dewey's mature views, where the imagination is described as "the only gateway through which these meanings can find their way into a present interaction; or, rather, . . . the conscious adjustment of the new and old *is* imagination" (*AE*, 272; *LW* 10:276). The previous meanings of adjusted, habitual behavior are creatively applied to interpret and control novel elements of experience. Imagination grasps the *possibilities* of the present, but *as* possibilities and not as forms of a higher, truer reality. Instead of the subsumption of a particular sensuous image under a universal concept, even if that concept is also a "general mode of action" which leads to a concrete individual, Dewey's mature treatment of imagination repudiates the notion of a "special and self-contained faculty . . .

in possession of mysterious potencies" (*EW*, 267; *LW* 10:271). The "free idealizing creative activity of spirit" disappears for the tension between "inner and outer vision" which strives to create new forms *in the world* so that "varied materials of sense quality, emotion, and meaning come together in a union that marks a new birth in the world" (*AE* 267; *LW* 10:272). In both accounts one may say that imagination is the interface between the ideal and the real; but in the idealist version, ultimately, the ideal *is* the real while in the instrumentalist version the ideal is the *possibility* of the real. In naturalistic terms, creation is a genuine emergence, a *phusis*, the birth of the new.

A final comparison must be made regarding the role of intuition. Since knowledge deals with mediation, the question arises with the idealist position, can the whole be known unless it is related to something else, and so on *ad infinitum*? However infinite the whole may be, it must also be actually realized to be an individual. Since every higher stage is presupposed in a lower, the total system of knowledge must be presupposed in any particular mediating activity, making that activity itself possible. Ultimate knowledge therefore must be a grasping of the whole individual, and this grasping is "intuition." "It follows, in a word," asserts Dewey, "that every concrete, actually-performed psychological result is an *intuition*, or knowledge of an individual" (*EW* 2:205). The absolute individual cannot refer to anything beyond itself. Intuition marks the final synthesis of reason and sense, universal and particular. Intuition is not an unmediated mode of perception but a fully mediated one, concerned with grasping "ultimate wholes," like World, Self, and God (the Absolute).

As will be noted later, and as has already been mentioned in discussing Douglas' position, Dewey does retain "intuition" as this power of sensing the parts within the whole.[22] The difference lies in the fact that in Dewey's later use there are no ultimate wholes, though in the religious quality of experience we may have a feeling of an overall satisfying integration with the universe.[23] Intuition here is a condition of knowledge in the sense that all knowledge relies on a sense of context, but it is by no means the highest form of knowledge. As Dewey came to a more sober understanding of experience, he continued to value those moments when experience achieved an integrated, intelligent, and qualitatively felt sense of unity. But he no longer saw them as indications of what a hidden reality was really like; instead they symbolized what reality *could* achieve and *might* become again with the agency of intelligence working with the powers of nature. One of the fundamental shifts from idealism to naturalism is the shift from necessity to possibility.

III. Dewey's Idealist Aesthetics

Dewey found a special role for aesthetic imagination and feeling in this early idealist system. Ever since Kant, the imagination had indicated the synthesizing, and to that extent, creative, power of the mind to unite percepts with concepts, to create the sensed and known world. Dewey is clearly in this tradition when he ascribes the elements in experience which transcend sensation to the imagination:

> In the perception of an object . . . there are actually present only a few sensations. All the rest of the perception is supplied by the mind. The mind supplies sensations coming from other senses besides those in use; it extends and supplements them; it adds the emphasis of its attention, and the comment of its emotions; it interprets them. Now all this supplied material may fairly be said to be the work of the imagination (EW 2:168-69).

The imagination is further able to distinguish the ideal from the real through its capacity to exercise freedom upon the senses. Most importantly, however, it recognizes a meaning fused with an image.

Dewey gives a detailed analysis of the various levels of imagination, ascending from mere association to fancy to creative imagination itself. Only the creative imagination achieves a full synthesis between ideal meaning and sensuous image; this process, moreover, is described as the "direct perception of meaning":

> The highest form of imagination, however, is precisely an organ of penetration into the hidden meaning of things—meaning not visible to perception of memory, nor reflectively attained by the processes of thinking. It may be defined as the *direct perception of meaning*—of ideal worth in sensuous forms; or as the spontaneous discovery of the sensuous forms which are most significant, most ideal, and which, therefore, reveal most to the intellect and appeal most to the emotions (EW 2:171, emphasis added).

This anticipates, of course, Dewey's claim in *Art as Experience* that the aesthetic experience is essentially an appreciative awareness of "immediate meanings." Here, in contrast to Dewey's later book, the *Psychology* attributes this perception of meaning, as well as its creation, to a totally "spiritual" power. The imagination creates by:

> A direct and spontaneous sense of the relative values of detail in reference to the whole. All is left out that does not aid in developing the image of this whole; all is put in that will round out the meaning of the details and elevate them into universal and permanent significance (EW 2:171).

The paradox between meanings, interpreted as wholly mediating and relational, and aesthetic meaning as immediate, noted in the first chapter, is present as far back as 1887 in Dewey's philosophy. In the context of Dewey's Hegelian psychology, a "mediated immediacy" is not the sort of contradiction which should bother one committed to the dialectical synthesis of polarities. By "immediate" Dewey does not mean "unmediated." There is nothing, on this account, which is unmediated; this is the same as claiming there is something real which is abstract, unrelated, and indefinite. Such an object cannot exist or be known, for to be either it must be related and in some way definite. Nevertheless, insofar as Spirit has bound itself into a whole integrated system which is actualized, that actuality exists now, "immediately." Thus we may distinguish two senses of "immediate," both, unfortunately, used by Dewey. The first refers to the impossible objects of British empiricism: unmediated, brute sense data, or to the equally impossible objects of classical rationalism: unmediated, self-evident, intuited concepts. The second sense refers to the Hegelian insistence on the presence of the whole in the part. Relations are *of* this whole, understood in terms of it as its distinctions. Insofar as this whole is grasped as being more than the sum of its parts, it is intuited as *one* whole. Instead of the bare, isolated intuition of the rationalists, this intuition, to be known, involves a thorough process of mediation.[24]

Imagination provides the *symbol* of the whole *to be known*. It is the first realization of the role of meaning in sensuous existence, since it distinguishes ideal meanings from sensuously present reality. It is also the realization that mind itself is creative and active. Art, says Dewey, is merely a symbol or developed form of the immanent creativity of Spirit.[25] In his later philosophy, Dewey also appeals to art as a realization of the aesthetic possibilities of common, everyday experience. But at this stage the point is just the reverse: Every perception testifies to the reality of a transcendent Spirit. Science Dewey notes, relies more and more on imagination as it goes beyond mere sensation to "the realm of hidden, ideal significance and meaning" (*EW* 2:175). Clearly, on this model, the creative self-realization of the artist is the paradigm of knowledge simply because it can mediate between sense and knowledge, the bare moment and universal meaning. While Dewey retained this ideal in many respects, he gradually downplays the romanticist and voluntarist interpretation of creativity and the emphasis on "creative imagination," supplementing it with his discussion of intelligence, shared meaning, and sensitivity to the relation between means and ends. Imagination still remains the way in which the immediate situation is transcended in terms of its possibility, especially its possibilities for consummatory meaning. But these possibilities of the situation do not testify to any underlying spiritual reality or power hiddenly at work.

Imagination, according to the theory of the *Psychology,* creates meanings. It does this through feeling and emotion as well as cognition. Dewey places a high value on the role of feeling:

> The intensity of feeling shuts out from the discourse all inharmonious images and irrelevant ideas far more effectually than any direct purpose of attention could bring about. The contingent and accidental detail that usually accompanies the course of our ideas vanishes, and they follow each other in an original and vital unity, a unity which reflective thought may imitate, but only overmastering emotion produce.
>
> The poet not only detects subtler analogies than other men, and perceives the subtle link of identity where others see confusion and difference, but the form of his expression, his language, images, etc., are controlled also by deeper unities . . . of feeling. The objects, the ideas, connected are perhaps remote from each other to the intellect, but feeling fuses them. Unity of feeling gives artistic unity, wholeness of effect, to the composition (*EW* 2:96).

Art does not refer to an idle faculty of day-dreaming or fancy on this account; it provides a sense of those wholes which discover the interrelated unity of Spirit and can be clarified by reason. Again a comparison may be made to Dewey's later theory, where all thinking is claimed to be akin to that of the artist, proceeding by feeling first and reason afterward.[26] Feeling itself remains the significant sense or tacit awareness of the context which gives discursive meaning its import and reference. The passage cited above, taken out of context, could easily be fitted into *Art as Experience* or *Experience and Nature.* The central difference is that here art and aesthetic perception are cited as evidence of the higher reality of Spirit; even though the imagination is described as creative, in truth it merely discovers the predetermined system of Spirit, more fully revealed by reason and absolute self-understanding. In Dewey's later philosophy creativity becomes a challenge rather than a guarantee and an intrinsically consummatory process rather than a mere stepping stone to Spirit's self-knowledge.

Another analogy between the early and later Dewey is the importance in both versions of the role of rhythm in experience, which Dewey says "can hardly be overestimated." "It is a native form under which the soul tends to apperceive all with which it comes in contact. . . . "It is the language of the manifestation of emotion. . . .

Poetry is everywhere an earlier and more natural mode of expression than prose" (*EW* 2:161-62). Later, Dewey will insist on the origin of art from basic biological rhythms of interacting, loss and recovery, growth and fulfillment, and will repeat the dubious claim regarding the priority of poetry over prose.[27] Rhythm is perhaps the best symbol of identity and difference, of unity and variety, or of the temporal dynamic growth of experience; Dewey clearly uses the idea to antici-pate his later remarks on the funded quality of consummatory expe-rience, where each part or phase sums up and carries forward the developing meaning. Here he says that each element "carries the mind backwards and forwards at once; and this, amid the succession, preserves the idea that the successive parts are members of one whole. It is only because of this that time relations are perceived" (*EW* 2:163).[28]

Because imagination involves the creative synthesizing power which ultimately realizes Spirit concretely, it is the power of self-realization; it is a "universalizing activity," as Dewey puts it (*EW* 2:172). In *Art as Experience*, Dewey says that with art, "We are carried out beyond ourselves to find ourselves," and that art is concerned with what is "ideal" and "universal." This would seem to be in line with his idealist doctrines.[29] Once again, however, the meaning of these expressions has changed. Self-realization means the capacity for experience to grow, take on deeper and more extensive meanings, and be integrated through evaluation and intelligence. The ideal refers not to a transcendental mode of being, but to a paradigmatic integration with the world which has significance and enjoyment, while univer-sality for Dewey comes to mean the general way something functions in experience so that a common bond is realized. This is quite differ-ent from the interpretation given in the *Psychology*, where imagination reveals the capacity of the self to construct transcendental meanings "out of its own internal content" and so comes to represent "the subjective side of self acting in its freedom" (*EW* 2:173). This idea leads Dewey to adopt Kant's and Schiller's theory of art as the play of the imagination.[30] This is why, for Dewey, imagination is the "sym-bol" of the concrete universal; it presents freedom as an *ideal* to be realized through perfect integration and mediation which will be ultimately intuited as Self.

Though Dewey later repeatedly praises art as "the most effective mode of communication that exists" (*AE*, 286; *LW* 10:20), this also must be interpreted in a quite different context from his discussion in the *Psychology* of how art, through arousing "universal feelings and interests" unites men with each other and nature. As before, there is a continuity between these positions, arising from Dewey's ideal of an experience which is perfectly, organically integrated:

> It must be observed that the sole basis of such action of imagination as is controlled by the universal feelings is a fundamental unity between man and man and between man and nature. . . . There must be an organic connection between man and nature. Man must find himself in some way in nature. . . . All products of the creative imagination are testimonies of spirit which binds man to man and man to nature in one organic whole (EW 2:174).

Dewey's understanding here is that art *discovers* the unity of Spirit, which is tacitly lurking beneath appearance. Speaking of Wordsworth, who exemplifies this attitude for Dewey, he says, "we do not find ourselves in a strange, unfamiliar land; we find Wordsworth penetrating into those revelations of spirit, of meaning in nature, of which we ourselves already had some dumb feeling, and this the poetry makes articulate" (EW 2:174). Though Dewey continued with his appreciation of romantic art, and even some of its ideals, he rejects his commitment to its metaphysics. Instead of discovering the spiritual unity of all things via the power of "creative imagination," art, in Dewey's later account, *creates* feelings and bonds of unity between men and between man and nature by working with meanings embodied in definite media.

One final but important parallel between Dewey's early and late theory lies in his affirmation that feelings are not purely internal or subjective states but are objective modes of the way experience reveals the world. Some feelings, it is true, refer to the internal state of the organism or its psychic attitudes. Nevertheless, all feelings are felt to be *of* objects which they *qualify*: "The object and the feeling cannot be separated; they are factors of the same consciousness. . . . The connection is not an external one of the feeling *with* the object, but an internal and intimate one; it is feeling *of* the object. The feeling loses itself in the object" (EW 2:239). Dewey then proceeds to use an example which occurs repeatedly throughout his work: "Thus we say that food *is* agreeable . . . that the landscape *is* beautiful or that the act *is* right" (EW 2:239).[31]

The central difference between how this is understood on Dewey's idealist model and his naturalistic one must remain to be discussed in later chapters. Briefly, however, the former sees the world ultimately as a projection of Spirit, delving mysteriously into its internal but inarticulate content, manifesting itself, and becoming united with the object through an awareness of identity. The later works, as I will argue, offer a more Aristotelian account, whereby a process of interaction realizes *potentialities of the world*. Although the self is also realized in this process, this does not point to any underlying identity existing a priori between the whole cosmos and a transcendental Self. Experience, especially in the form of art, achieves *continuity* with the world, rather than bare identity, and continuity must be understood in the sense of establishing a creative, growing, and dynamic relation, where novelty and emergent qualities have a necessary role.

The greatest divergence between the briefly developed theory of the *Psychology* and the complex doctrine of *Art as Experience* can be seen in the following points. Aesthetic feeling, according to the early theory, seeks an ideal which is "universal, permanent, and out of reach of individual desires and impulses," and which, when experienced, makes us "transcend our immediate self and realize our being in the widest way" (*EW* 2:245). Aesthetic sentiment means establishing a "harmonious ideal" which, through its sense of harmony, creates a sense of truth or coherency. Art must follow the "laws of the self" which are freely imposed on sense. There can be no sense of ownership in the aesthetic experience, nor any awareness of a practical purpose: "The universality of aesthetic feeling requires that the beautiful object be not subordinated to *any* external end" (*EW* 2:271). Utility detracts from Beauty, states Dewey, reaffirming Schiller's connection between art and play, though art does have a purpose insofar as it creates "a perfectly harmonized self." Finally, Dewey gives a thoroughly Hegelian classification and ranking of the arts according to their degree of spirituality and universality, with "practical" arts like architecture on the bottom, ascending to "material" arts like sculpture and painting, followed by "dynamic" arts like music, and ending with literature as the highest, since in it meaning dominates sense entirely.[32]

IV. Conclusion: Dewey's Shift Away from Idealism

The *Psychology* represents Dewey's most systematic attempt to present a philosophy of idealism. It is possible to divide Dewey's idealist period (1882–1903) into three phases.[33] The first stage (1882–1890), which culminates in the *Psychology*, is dominated by the thought of Hegel and Thomas Hill Green, as well as by the personal influence of Morris. Dewey's desire was to fuse the biological and idealist understanding of organism, thereby preserving experience in all its wholeness and dynamic unity. Dewey strongly agreed with

Green's view that "unless the validity of the deeper ideas of poetry and religion can be shown, the conception of man as a moral being must also vanish. If the underlying ideas of poetry are incompatible with natural science, ethics must also be eliminated."[34] Green was not only an idealist but a theist as well, and as a result, unlike Hegel, he had a dualistic metaphysics. For Green, there was an eternal, infinite Self already realized; it merely reproduced itself in piecemeal fashion in human experience. As Dewey described it, in an essay on Green, "Experience thus means the continual reproduction in man of an eternal consciousness" (EW 3:24). The question of *why* such a consciousness had to reproduce itself was, of course, left inexplicable.

Dewey's second period (1890–1893) is marked by his attempt to assimilate James' seminal *Principles of Psychology*. The teleological functionalism of James appealed to Dewey and seemed to provide a far sounder interpretation of the structures and relations in experience than the passive mirroring of the eternal order of an Absolute Spirit. Dewey wrote in this period two articles highly critical of Green and moved much closer to Hegel, who, he said, represented "the quintessence of the scientific spirit" (EW 3:138). Dewey's central problem was clearly becoming the integration of scientific methodology, "logic," with human values, ethics.

This double influence of James and Hegel led Dewey in his third period (1894-1903) to advocate an even more radical form of idealism which he called "experimental idealism."[36] In retrospect, it is hard to see it as other than proto-instrumentalism. Dewey's former concern with demonstrating the implicit ideality of experience is eclipsed by his concern to adapt the method of experimental inquiry to ethics. During this period he became involved in the experimental Dewey School in Chicago and began his lifelong association with George Herbert Mead. The fundamentals of his mature theory of action begin to become evident: his genetic understanding of experience, its phases broken down on the basis of adjustment and adaptation, intelligence as the mediator of experience in a practical rather than a transcendental manner, and so on. Dewey's two most important articles during this period are "The Theory of Emotion" (1894–1895) and "The Reflex Arc Concept in Psychology" (1896).[37] The latter essay especially presents in miniature the basis of Dewey's understanding of how experience begins from a whole situation, is mediated by intelligent inquiry during a problematic phase, and is reconstructed toward integration and growth of meaning. This essay marks the breakthrough toward which Dewey had been struggling from the start and is the foundation upon which his later philosophy is erected.

In 1903, Dewey officially broke with idealism and joined the new pragmatic movement with his *Studies in Logical Theory*. Even so, to perceptive critics like Charles S. Peirce, Dewey's opposition to "the German School" would not have been so obvious "had he not put so much emphasis on it."[38]

Aside from an occasional article or review, Dewey's concern with logic, experimental inquiry and ethics did not demonstrate much concern for aesthetics. In his *Outlines of a Critical Theory of Ethics* (1891), Dewey rejects the distinction between fine and useful art on the basis that "utility" refers to a limited, narrow end, while "beauty" refers to a "complete use or service, and hence . . . self-expression" (*EW* 3:310-11).[39] this will be Dewey's position in *Art as Experience* as well.[40] In reviewing Bosanquet's *History of Aesthetic*, Dewey makes a number of interesting and revealing comments, such as redefining idealism so that showing the "natural" origin of ideals in no way discredits their "reality." Dewey also criticizes Bosanquet by saying that, "The entire conception . . . of a fixed distinction between the realm of art and that of commonplace reality seems to me to need a good deal of explanation" (*EW* 4:196). This is a problem "lying at the very heart of aesthetic." Dewey proceeds to say that the concept of fine art as something opposed to ordinary experience occurs whenever new ideas ("principles of action") have not yet found forms of embodiment and so seem incapable of aesthetic expression. "Commonplace reality, in other words," says Dewey, "is simply the material which art has not yet conquered, which has not yet become a plastic medium of expression" (*EW* 4:197). The alternative to Bosanquet's view of art as "a form of symbolism" is to see art "as the expression of life in its entire range" (*EW* 4:197). Most important for our purposes, however, is Dewey's statement that metaphysics and aesthetics share a problem: "how to reconcile feeling with reason; how sense material may be pregnant with meaning—this problem being first a practical one and only afterwards a theoretical one" (*EW* 4:195).

Clearly, Dewey's initial commitment to the dynamic organic unity of lived experience persists from "The New Psychology" clear through to the end of his life. This does not mean that Dewey ended espousing the same ideas he began with. It might be illuminating to summarize some of the basic objections Dewey raised against idealism in later years to understand why he thought that it was inadequate to provide a theory of experience. The story of Dewey's increasing marital problems with the Absolute, their divorce (itself a quiet matter), and their continuing custody battles is too long a tale to be told here. Looking at Dewey's case we must remember we are hearing the side of the husband who charges his wife with infidelity as well as barrenness. If the Absolute were to make her case (as Brand Blanshard has represented it), I'm sure she would accuse Dewey of asking her to do things which only a base-born Yankee could dream up.[41] In any case, their relationship had become very estranged in the late 1890's and with Dewey's attack on Lötze in the *Studies in Logical Theory* the marriage was publically ended. But there are certain fundamental themes which can be detected and are of central importance for understanding Dewey's mature theory of experience, especially as it gets developed in *Art as Experience*. Unfortunately, there is no one place where Dewey undertakes a prolonged analysis of absolute idealism, especially Hegelian idealism. By looking at his 1906 article, "Experience and Objective Idealism," the major outlines of his criticisms can be determined. After exploring these, I will briefly turn to some of the scattered and rather dialectical criticisms which are to be found in *Experience and Nature* and *The Quest for Certainty*.

Dewey's criticisms resolve themselves basically into two. The first is that idealism simply has conflated two distinct orders, the real and the ideal or the actual and the possible. The underlying point of Dewey's later thought is to keep these orders distinct without creating a dualism. Indeed, he defines the central task of philosophy as the perpetual appropriation of the clearing defined by these two orders.[42] The second criticism of idealism is that the confusion represented in the first mistake has disastrous consequences for the meaning and value of human life and conduct. Instead of providing a basis for intelligent moral action which genuinely strives to create meaning and value in human existence, the Absolute in fact undermines such a project, rendering human action unnecessary and doomed to incompletion, forever straining toward and never capable of attaining the self-certainty of the Absolute as it is in and for itself. This is Dewey's version of Nietzsche's insight that "the highest values devaluate themselves." That is, in their very claim for being the ultimate, final, imperative criteria determining the meaning and value of human existence, they render human existence valueless and meaningless; thus they are not questioned so much as they call themselves into question.[43] The outcome of this reflection on the metaphysics of idealism and its ethical implications, will lead Dewey toward a new ontology as well as a new methodology. The names of his mature philosophy are various—"immediate empiricism," "instrumentalism," "naturalistic empiricism," "naturalistic humanism," and, his final choice, "cultural naturalism"—but they reflect the exploration and articulation of one path set upon the moment Dewey renounced idealism. A progression can, in fact be revealed in these names, going from a focus on the richness of immediate experience to the theory of method which it indicates, from recognition of the significance of the dimension of nature in experience to the emphasis on the human dimension which reveals man less as the individual shaper of the world than as a participant in the shared task of the community to cultivate and enculture nature with meaning and value which fund life and expand it rather than negate and diminish it.

Idealism, says Dewey in "Experience and Objective Idealism," stands in "such a delicate relation to experience" that it demands a careful analysis and evaluation rather than wholehearted acceptance and dismissal (*IDP*, 198; *MW* 3:129). Not only does idealism take on many forms, it seeks to accomplish several tasks. It stands "half opposed to empiricism and half committed to it," but the opposition to empiricism ultimately creates such an instability that idealism "can find release only by euthanasia in a thorough-going empiricism" (*IDP*, 198-99; *MW* 3:128). In other words, Dewey ironically indicates that the inner dialectical oppositions of idealism will negate it, uplifting it at the same time into a more robust, genuine empiricism. Idealism is committed to experience insofar as experience is organized and prophetic of the source and goal of all organization, value, and meaning, the Absolute. It is opposed to experience to the extent that experience is fragmentary, indeterminate, or "tainted" with sense unmediated by reason. There are, Dewey asserts, three historic episodes in the idealist interpretation of the relation of reason and experience. The first, represented by classic Platonism, contrasts experience as the source of practical crafts which aim at artfully dealing with a world full of changing particular objects with reason which "is direct apprehension, self-revealing and self-validating, of an eternal and harmonious content" (*IDP*, 199; *MW* 3:129). Experience deals with a natural world of genesis and decay and at best achieves true opinion; reason finds its object in Being and terminates in necessary knowledge from which demonstration is possible. The antithesis revealed here is interpreted by Dewey as that between "the historically achieved *embodiments* of meaning, partial, multiple, insecure" and "reason as the source, author, and container of *meaning*, permanent, assured, unified" (*IDP*, 200; *MW* 3:129). Dewey also points to the various Neo-Kantian idealisms which have seen themselves as upholding the case for intrinsic human dignity and the authority of moral ideals against the "crudeness and insensitivity" of naturalism and empiricism. We have as a result "Experience considered as the summary of past episodic adventures and happenings in relation to fulfilled and adequately expressed meaning" (*IDP*, 201; *MW* 3: 130).

The second historic episode, represented by modern rationalism, focuses on the respective claims of experience and reason as the origin and validation of true, absolute, scientific knowledge. Experience, as described by Locke, Peirce, and James, stands for "the foreign element which forces the hand of thought and controls its efficacy" (*IDP*, 202; *MW* 3: 130-31). Empiricism urges the critical test and evaluation of the established, traditional claims of knowledge—it represents the right to question authority in light of one's own encounters with the world.[45] Idealism as the rationalist response argues that science or knowledge, taken in its classical sense as being of what is self-evident, necessary, and unchanging, cannot possibly be grounded on such an individualistic, relative, unstable, or *foreign* thing as experience. Experience, in short, cannot transform itself into true knowledge. This can only be done by inner concepts. The question that emerges is the relation of percepts to concepts.

The third episode, represented by critical and transcendental idealism, reveals the tension between the subjectivity of experience and objectivity of reason. Experience here is now less the external, foreign intrusion of the world acting on us than our own subjective or internal impression or perception. Thought or conception thus indicates the basis in terms of which any experience has cognitive objectivity. Thus idealism argues that reason is (1) the cause of all meaning and value in experience, the good, the beautiful and the true, (2) the power to transform percepts into science by means of the active intervention of pure concepts, and (3) the objective order of experience itself, without which it would be private, subjective flux.

In typical fashion, after spelling out these three issues, Dewey chooses to deal with them in reverse order (thereby ending as well as beginning with the issue which he regards as the main concern, the relation of value to the world). Starting with the last episode, the transcendental argument, Dewey points out an inherent confusion between two senses of the a priori: on the one hand the a priori conditions for the possibility of objective judgments are treated as the immanent and constitutional order of *all* experience and on the other as an active, regulative agency which constructively determines or controls experience. In the first sense, the "*a priori* conceptions of Kant as immanent fall, like the rain, upon the just and the unjust; upon error, opinion, and hallucination," but in the second sense the concept is treated "as that which makes an experience actually different, controlling its evolution towards consistency, coherency, and objective reliability" (*IDP*, 207; *MW* 3:133). The first sense gave rise to objective idealism, seeing reason as a metaphysical condition for any and every experience. Dewey sees no reason for retaining such a doctrine provided that one simply accepts that experience *comes* ordered as well as disordered. Applying the lesson of James' radical empiricism, Dewey states, "Experience always carries with it and within it certain systematized arrangements, certain classifications" (*IDP*, 208; *MW* 3:134). As examples Dewey offers either the organization of the biological structures of the live creature or the social and political customs of a culture. It is one thing to say that thought played a role in the establishment of these institutions at one time, says Dewey, but quite another to say it continues to do so. "As *organizations*, as established, effectively controlling arrangements of objects in experience, their mark is that they are not thoughts but habits, customs of action" (*IDP*, 209-10; *MW* 3:135). The significance of this comment cannot be overestimated, for Dewey here is placing the organizations of experience within the larger domain of life-activity. Reason, in short, is a function of the lifeworld, not vice versa, and this changes everything. Our capacity to do geometry no longer betrays an underlying constitutive intuition of the mind (much less is it an indication of a higher, suprasensible realm), but it is "a practical locomotor function of arranging stimuli in reference to maintenance of life activities *brought into consciousness*" (*IDP*, 210; *MW* 3:135).[46] We may be grateful to Kant, Dewey says, for defending the order of experience against the rhapsodic accounts given by Locke and Hume, but we do not need his appeal to transcendental conditions as the cause or source for it. Dewey seeks to rehabilitate Kant toward "an improved and revised empiricism" (*IDP*, 208; *MW* 3:134). This saves the directive, reconstructive role of thought as well, "thought as an act, an art of skilled mediation" (*IDP*, 209; *MW* 3:135). In *r*eorganizing experience, "The concept is a practical activity doing consciously and artfully what it had aforetime done blindly and aimlessly, and thereby not only doing it better but opening up a freer world of significant activities" (*IDP*, 210; *MW* 3:135). Thought is an expression of "vital activity" rather than of a transcendental ego.

In dealing with the claim that the justification of scientific knowledge must be grounded on reason rather than experience, Dewey rather bluntly calls into question the two thousand year old theory of knowledge. If the order of experience is simply the institutionalization of past efforts at reorganization, then there is no particular appeal to be found in making the present or the future conform to the traditions of the past outside of their *present* teleological and experimental value. " 'Law and order' are good things," Dewey tersely notes, "but not when they become rigidity, and create mechanical uniformity or routine. Prejudice is the acme of the *a priori*. Of the *a priori* in this sense we may say what is always to be said of habits and institutions: They are good servants, but harsh and futile masters" (*IDP*, 211; *MW* 3:136). Here idealism is charged with sacrificing "novelty, flexibility, freedom, creation" to the dead hand of the past; only "genuine thought, empirical reflective thought" has the sensitivity, openness, and creativity to constitute an art of knowledge. With this, not only does Dewey charge idealism with being bound to a reactionary conception of knowledge (the movement itself being a conserving reaction to modern science in the cause of defending the moral and human dimension of our self-understanding), but he claims that this faintheartedness led to what it sought to avoid, that is, the undermining of the sense of meaning and value of life. Only a philosophy committed to the open-ended present, which embraced the problematic, could do this.

This prepares the way for Dewey's analysis of the relation of perception and concepts. Perception, he notes, has two different senses. It may refer to a concrete, vital activity "predominantly practical in character though carrying at its heart important cognitive and esthetic qualities," or to a peculiar type of experience which occurs in the process of cognitive inquiry, to the "object" of observation (*IDP*, 214; *MW* 3:137). The first regards perception as an act of adjustment in which discrimination is called forth by the demands of action in need of direction. This is the "cognitive phase," but it includes "collateral objects and qualities that give additional range and depth of meaning to the activity of adjustment, perceiving is esthetic as well as intellectual" (*IDP*, 215; *MW* 3:215). In this sense, perception is not opposed to thought, to conception, for it is saturated throughout with "ideal factors" supplied by imagination and reflectively sustained in order to organize experience and guide action. The more mature and intelligent, the more experienced and educated the individual is, the less will there be an opposition of perception and conception, Dewey maintains. Experience, in short, will be encultured. It is only when we take perception in the second sense, which involves the "deliberate, artful exclusion of affectional and purposive factors" for the sake of impartiality and neutrality in scientific observation, that the trouble occurs. Here, in the context of inquiry, we may contrast the need for detailed observation with the theoretical elaboration of hypotheses. One may recall the story of Louis Agassiz who demanded his students to study, draw, redraw, and redraw over and again a small fish and only then allowed them to commence speculating on the functions of the various parts.[47] Dewey is, of course, not denying the need for detailed empirical description in inquiry. "But in so far as thought is identified with the conceptual phase as such of the entire logical function," he argues, "observation is, of course, set over against thought: deliberately, purposely, and artfully so" (*IDP*, 217; *MW* 3:139). Such experience is not "neutral" in a ubiquitous sense, but only in a highly restrictive sense; overall it is guided by the purposes and needs of the inquiry. Here Dewey points the accusing finger at Locke, whose theory of experience arrived at just such an impasse by taking one moment as a paradigmatic instance of the meaning of experience or perception, thereby laying the foundations for the idealist interpretation of experience as something constituted through the activity of mind or spirit. This is simply a "perversion of experience; a perversion for which, indeed, professed empiricists set the example, but which idealism must perpetuate if it is not to find its end in an improved, functional empiricism" (*IDP*, 219; *MW* 3:141).

This brings us to Dewey's major criticism, the problem of the "ideality of experience." It is one thing to say that experience is fragmentary or incomplete and that we may desire moments when it becomes coherent and whole, but it is another to explain on what basis such a claim can be made at all. Here the absolute idealists had an unanswerable criticism directed toward the classical empiricists: it's all well and good to say experience consists of a swarming hive of ideas or impressions, but there must be some *ground* for making that judgment, a ground which reveals an underlying, active, constitutive power which transcends the particular and fragmentary and organizes them into a whole. In short, how is it *possible* to judge experience as incomplete and have an ideal of a complete, organized system of fulfilled meaning? Up through the 1890s Dewey had seen the idealist's answer as the only possible one: there is some transcendental reality in which we participate through our capacity to organize experience in terms of an underlying unity, the self. From the start of his philosophical life, Dewey had stood opposed to any view which condemned man to a partial, piece-meal acceptance of the world as it was; philosophy, in other words, had to provide a basis for criticism and evaluation, it had to account for having ideals.

Dewey approaches the problem by looking at the function of memory, for this is what reveals experience as multifarious as well as suggestive of some sort of continuity. Memory thus helps organize the present by indicating similarities, differences, and general modes of possible action. If, however, memory weren't selective and provided us with total recall, not only would new action be stymied, but we would simply relive the past. So, as Dewey puts it, "Dis-membering is a positively necessary part of re-membering" (*IDP*, 220-21; *MW* 3:141). Memory must fragment experience for the sake of the conduct of present experience toward its integration, toward "the most excellent meaning or value conceived." Dewey continues: "If the remembering is efficacious and pertinent, it reveals the possibilities of the present; that is to say, it clarifies the transitive, transforming character that belongs inherently to the present. The dismembering of the vital present into the disconnected past is correlative to an anticipation, an idealization of the future" (*IDP*, 221; *MW* 3:142). The very tentativeness of the rules arising from this process is thereby inherently capable of further refinement and perfecting. One's attitude toward them becomes experimental, flexible, and open-ended rather than cleaving to them with dogmatic certainty. "The fixed or necessary law," says Dewey, "would mean a future like the past—a dead, an unidealized future" (*IDP*, 221; *MW* 3: 142). Dewey finds it "exasperating" to think of how different Aristotle's attitude toward the contingent features of experience would have been had he opted for the view of intelligence as a progressive development of evaluation rather than the fixation upon an unchanging object. The implication is that he would have broken free from his Platonism, reflected in the artificial hierarchies of perfection, and developed a more dynamic, pluralistic, and emergentistic type of naturalism. Aside from the question whether Aristotle could have taken this step, the comment is very revealing for what it says about Dewey's own aspirations for naturalism and how closely it abides with Aristotle's understanding of nature, of *phusis*, in terms of potentiality and actuality.

"The one constant trait of experience from its crudest to its most mature forms," states Dewey, "is that its contents undergo change of meaning, and of meaning in the sense of excellence, value. Every experience is in-course of becoming worse or better as to its contents, or in course of conscious endeavor to sustain some satisfactory level of value against encroachment or lapse" (*IDP*, 222; *MW* 3:143). Because of this, both doubt and idealization emerge; the present may be evaluated against the past and the past may suggest ways of conducting the present to more desirable issue. Memory and idealization are functions of the present need in the concourse of experience. Direction and control of the present situation call for the *art* of intelligence (and Dewey's insistence on this term should be noted). The meaning of the present must be explored and the meaning of the present reveals itself as an inherently temporal event. "The irrelevancy of an objective idealism," contends Dewey, "lies in the fact that it totally ignores the position and function of ideality in sustained and serious endeavor. Were values automatically injected and kept in the world of experience by any force not reflected in human memories and projects, it would make no difference whether this force were a Spencerian environment or an Absolute Reason. Did purpose ride in a cosmic automobile, it would not cease to be physical and mechanical in quality because labeled Divine Idea, or Perfect Reason" (*IDP*, 223; *MW* 3:143). The moral of determinism, says Dewey, is carpe diem, to abdicate responsibility and take a moral holiday. Whether this is what idealists from Fichte to Royce have *intended* is beside the point, for surely most have desired just the opposite. Their theories relying on the determinist force of the dialectic results in the attitude of, to quote D.H. Lawrence, "Not I, not I, but the wind that blows through me!" Idealism, the philosophical doctrine, has undercut the basis of idealism, the moral struggle to make experience better. No more damning charge could be made, especially by one who had passionately fought under the banner for so many years.

The root of the problem is found in the metaphysics which grounds the world of change or appearance upon a world of absolute, changeless reality. "To suppose values are ideal because they are eternally so given is the contradiction in which objective idealism has entrenched itself," says Dewey, ". . . experimental teleology alone spells ideality. Objective, rationalistic idealism breaks upon the fact that it can have no intermediary between a brutally achieved embodiment of meaning . . . and a total opposition of the given and ideal, connoting their mutual indifference and incapacity" (*IDP*, 224; *MW* 3:143-44). Only a kind of empiricism which "acknowledges the transitive character of experience," Dewey concludes, "and that acknowledges the possible control of the character of the transition by means of intelligent effort, has abundant opportunity to celebrate in productive art, genial morals, and impartial inquiry the grace and the severity of the ideal" (*IDP*, 224-25; *MW* 3:144).[48]

The central insight that emerges from this critique is that for Dewey at least if there were to be a genuine possibility for moral idealism, one *had* to separate the ideal from the real rather than conflate them. In The *Quest for Certainty*, Dewey asserts that "The motivating desire of idealistic systems of philosophy is justified. But the constructive office of thought is empirical—that is, experimental. 'Thought' is not a property of something termed intelligence or reason apart from nature. It is a mode of directed action. . . . The active power of ideas is a reality, but ideas and idealisms have an operative force in concrete experienced situations; their worth has to be tested by the specified consequences of the operation. Idealism is something experimental not abstractly rational" (*QC*, 166-67; *LW* 4:133). We hear in this passage the ghost of Dewey's "experimental idealism" of the 1890s, but here couched entirely within a naturalistic framework—and in one of his most "instrumentalist" writings. To see the ideal *as* ideal means to see it as a possibility of the present, not as a pre-existent, self-established reality. In *Experience and Nature*, Dewey points out that idealists, after magnifying the role of thought and the ideals of human aspiration, "have then sought to prove that after all these things are not ideal but are real—real not *as* meanings and ideals, but as existential being. Thus the assertion of faith in the ideal belies itself in the making; these 'idealists' cannot trust their ideal till they have converted it into existence . . ." (*EN*, 415; *LW* 1:310). Idealism, in short, lacks faith, and the result is that its ideals have no efficacy in concrete action. "It is a light which is darkness, for shining in the void it illumines nothing and cannot reveal even itself. . . . It thus abnegates itself in abjuring footing in natural events, and ceases to be ideal" (*EN*, 416; *LW* 1:311). Ideals are generated in nature as "possibilities of existences" revealed through interaction, intelligence, and imagination.

> The relation between objects as known and objects with respect to value is that between the actual and the possible. "The actual" consists of given conditions; "the possible" denotes ends or consequences not now existing but which the actual may through its use bring into existence. The possible in respect to any given actual situation is thus an ideal for that situation. . . . If we agree to leave out the eulogistic savor of "ideal" and define it in contrast with the actual, the possibility denoted by an idea is the ideal phase of the existent. The problem of the connection or lack of connection of the actual and the ideal has always been the central problem of philosophy in its metaphysical aspect, just as the relation between existence and idea has been the central theme of philosophy on the side of the theory of knowledge. Both issues come together in the problem of the relation of the actual and the possible. Both problems are derived from the necessities of action if that is to be intelligently regulated (*QC*, 299-300; *LW* 4:239).

Idealism as a philosophy undercuts the sort of distinctions which give significance to action, to life. In arguing for the inherent, original unity of reality, it renders evil, error, and fragmentary experience unintelligible—these must be subsummed as "appearances" of what is complete in itself, good, true, and one. "If the universe is in itself ideal," Dewey asks, "why is there so much in our experience of it which is so thoroughly unideal?" (*QC*, 301; *LW* 4:240). Idealism, in its effort to affirm integration, creates dualism, whether theoretically or practically. By absolutizing values as ultimate ideals, they cease to conduct activity. As Dewey wryly notes, "Men hoist the banner of the ideal, and then march in the direction that concrete conditions suggest and reward" (*QC*, 281; *LW* 4:224). On the theoretical level one is faced with the dualisms of being and becoming, phenomena and noumena, appearance and reality. In this way, Dewey states, "the philosophies which go by the name of Idealism are attempts to prove by one method or another . . . that the Real and the Ideal are one, while at the same time they introduce qualifying additions to explain why after all they are not one" (*QC*, 301; *LW* 4:240). The tension in Hegelianism between the unfolding, dynamic view of *The Phenomenology of Spirit* and the abstract atemporal view of *The Science of Logic* would be another illustration. Spirit is historical, but is this to say it is genuinely *temporal*? The *Phenomenology* tells the story of Spirit as a biography while the *Logic* anatomizes the very structure of its psyche, exposing the architecture of its being and why it has to do what it does; it reveals the world of its shadowy motives where, paradoxically, it appears totally transparent to itself. The Absolute Idea schematically reveals the possibility of Spirit's full self-knowing, and knowing this sets it free actually to objectify itself as nature and then to rediscover itself through the history of self-consciousness. But, as Dewey noted, the step from abstract, if dialectical, logic to embodied existence is highly problematic.[49] There is an order to Spirit which is "progressive," but the progress of Spirit is the progress of a circular movement—every going forward is a coming back. Dewey's point is that we are confronted here with a genuine paradox because the process is little more than a monadic unfolding of an internal preestablished (but dialectically produced) harmony. Spirit is all tenses at once—it will be what it already has been and that is what it is. This is not the sort of temporality revealed in human action which confronts the present problematically, where indeterminacy and the possible carry no self-guarantees with them. If Schelling's Identity-philosophy was the night in which all cows are black, Dewey would accuse Hegel's Absolute of being the day in which all geese are glass. Every attempt to draw a shadow in Hegel's system only reveals a further testimony to the rationality of the whole and the cunning of Spirit which can overcome even itself when it sets out to deceive itself. This can only happen because Spirit, instead of being genuinely dramatic and having a story to tell, is a concatenation of histories, a telling of all stories. To preserve the narrative, dramatic structure of existence, for Dewey, is to preserve the dimensions of the possible and the actual; these are not divorced orders but, to repeat, dimensions of nature. In the clearing they establish, events interweave, form histories, enact time.

Most of the problems of modern philosophy, Dewey argues, can be traced to "the dogma which denies temporal quality to reality as such" (*EN*, 149; *LW* 1:120). "Temporal quality," he says elsewhere, "is however not to be confused with temporal order. Quality is quality, direct, immediate, and undefinable. Order is a matter of relation, of definition, dating, placing and describing. It is discovered in reflection, not directly had and denoted as is temporal quality. Temporal order is a matter of science; temporal quality is an immediate trait of every occurrence whether in or out of consciousness" (*EN*, 110-11; *LW* 1:92). Temporality as an event, as passage from past to future in which something is at issue and at stake, in which the actual is set in the possible and the possible opens avenues and closes them to the actual, is "an integral part of the *character* or *nature* of present existence." It is no accident that when Dewey comes to treat of experience in its paradigmatic fulfillment, as *an* experience, its fundamental feature is that it is genuinely and dramatically undergone or had as a temporal event. It begins, opens up or reveals something at issue, brings it to completion or realizes it, and this realization closes it off and demarcates it. Art has the peculiar talent of revealing this aspect of experience, its genuine temporality, which also reveals the proper relation of the dimensions of the actual and the ideal.

There are three ways of idealizing the world, notes Dewey: through pure reason which strives to prove the world has those characters which it seems to lack, through pure dumb luck which accidentally manages to realize a possible fulfilling harmony between self and world, and finally, through art. This is accomplished by "actions directed by thought, such as are manifested in the works of fine art and in all human relations perfected by loving care." It "represents the way of deliberate quest for security of the values that are enjoyed by grace in our happy moments" (*QC*, 302; *LW* 4:241). The moral that Dewey draws from this in his mature thought is "Nature thus supplies potential material for embodiment of ideals. Nature, if I may use the locution, is idealizable. It lends itself to operations by which it is perfected."

A crucial conclusion follows: for Dewey, the human situation in nature (embraced by the term "experience") is radically temporal. This temporality is reflected in the interface and interplay between the dimensions of the possible and the actual: the world which stands forth has features of contingency and conditionality or necessity, of disorder and order, of indeterminacy and determinancy at once. These features cohabit in the fundamental temporal event, the situation. "Nature" is truly a *phusis*, a bringing-forth, where certain potentialities are realized at the expense of others (as Anaximander saw)—the revealing of some is also the concealment of others. The temporality of nature is reflected in the tenses and moods of our verbs. Dewey would agree with Heidegger that our commitment to a metaphysics which has sought to eternalize a timeless present has permeated our understanding so that we think in nouns rather than verbs or approach the verb from the present tense and the "infinitive" (that is, indefinite and atemporal) mode.[50] All the moods and tenses of language are philosophically important. In remembering them we are brought to the recognition that human existence is inherently temporal. Instead of leading Dewey toward a transcendental critique of human existence, as it did Heidegger, however, this question drew Dewey to a radical form of Aristotelian naturalism in which the role of the potential was purged of its degraded associations and raised to equiprimordial status with the actual. Out of the problematic tensions of idealism, then, Dewey deliberately evolved his mature naturalism. It involved, as he clearly saw, ultimately regrounding the basis of his whole thinking. While the next chapter will explore this new basis, it should be evident now that Dewey did not simply happen to drop idealism for naturalism, and it is therefore equally probable that in his later years he did not happen to lapse back into his idealist habits of speech when he strayed beyond the parameters of instrumentalism and into his former haunts in "the realm of Absolute Spirit." At least, before arriving at this judgment, one must try as hard as possible to think the thinker's thought through. While the criticisms of internal inconsistency have not been resolved, the importance of the new relation of the potential and actual is too important to be ignored.

From the beginning of Dewey's philosophical enterprise, as we have seen, the fundamental issue with which he was concerned was to develop as rich and concrete a theory of experience as possible which would thereby do justice to those aspects which had been so summarily ignored in philosophy, particularly the moral and aesthetic dimensions. Dewey first turned to absolute idealism and then attempted to cross-breed it with empirical psychology, the bizarre offspring being his philosophical psychology. In the face of the incipient radical empiricism of James' *Principles of Psychology*, Dewey set upon the road to create a radical idealism, an "experimental idealism," only to discover that it merged with the via moderna of pragmatism. Having entered the path of empiricism through the gates of idealism, however, Dewey was never tempted to read experience as anything like what Locke, Hume, or the Mills had described. For those operating in the pragmatist or realist camps, this would always make Dewey's use of words like "experience" or "nature" sound somewhat suspicious. But Dewey had not divorced a great and noble lady in order to take up with the consumptive school-marm of British empiricism; he had taken a robust American bride and together they set out to meet the possibilities of the land.

In the early years of this century Dewey produced a prodigious quantity of writing, but virtually none of it treated the topic of art and the aesthetic, though his personal interest in poetry abided. In 1917, however, the irascible millionaire-industrialist Albert C. Barnes, owner of the best collection of French impressionists in the Western hemisphere, developed a passion for Dewey's philosophy.[51] After reading *Democracy and Education,* he hung Monets in his factory and commuted to New York to attend Dewey's classes. Thus began one of the strangest and least predictable friendships in Dewey's life. Barnes, playing teacher in his turn, took Dewey to Europe and its museums and artworld. The fruition of the relationship came with Dewey occupying a place on the board of the Barnes Foundation and, by 1925 with *Experience and Nature,* once again directly discussing art—as "the culminating event of nature."

Chapter 3

The Metaphysics of Experience

$\mathbf{B}$y understanding the term "experience" one obtains the Northwest Passage to Dewey's philosophy; failure to understand it inevitably leads to shipwreck. As this chapter will illustrate, the treacherous shoals of Dewey's thought are strewn with the hulks of decades of rash critical sailing. The previous chapters have shown that if we are to understand what Dewey means by "experience" we must focus on the topic of immediate or qualitative meaning and this, in turn, is directly handled in Dewey's aesthetic theory. It was also argued that from the commencement of Dewey's philosophical life he was concerned with developing a theory which would do justice to the fullness, richness, and organic complexity of experience. This is the underlying motive of Dewey's thought from first to last. His original commitment to idealism arose from its promising way of doing just this task, thereby providing the only viable alternative to the mechanistic and reductionistic approaches of materialism or British empiricism. Idealism also promised that it could understand experience in a genuinely dynamic and progressive manner, as a process of growth. After years of trying to reconstruct idealism from within, however, Dewey confronted the fact that its deepest commitments were those of traditional rationalism. It thereby not only converted all forms of experience into forms of cognitive experience (even if the idealists had treated knowledge as ultimately self-knowledge, this meant that to be was to be a knowing self), but also that its professed dynamism and concern with struggle and indeterminacy were, in the last analysis, mere appearances. One could not reconstruct this feature without dismantling the very engine of idealism, the transcendental ego or the Absolute. No doubt Dewey's direct involvement with his experimental school and his study of children in the actual process of learning must have made the whole conceptual ballet of the Hegelian dialectic seem artificial and useless in the extreme. In the end, Dewey realized that his project of experience had been betrayed. But in the meanwhile, James' development of pragmatic radical empiricism had opened another alternative. It was this alternative, loosely formulated by James, which Dewey set out in 1903 to explore systematically.

Dewey's philosophy after 1903 easily falls into two periods, that before the publication of *Experience and Nature* in 1925 and that beginning with the book and incorporating most of Dewey's major philosophical accomplishments, such as *The Quest for Certainty* (1929), *Art as Experience* (1934), and *Logic: The Theory of Inquiry* (1938). It might be useful to characterize the earlier period as one in which Dewey is primarily concerned with developing his instrumentalist methodology and the later period as the systematic effort to ground and articulate the metaphysics of experience. This has led Boisvert to label the periods respectively Dewey's "experimentalist" phase and his "naturalist" phase.[1] While this is perhaps a valuable initial distinction, it is not a hard and fast one. As we shall see, almost from the start of this new beginning Dewey's effort to formulate a radical empirical methodology led to the problems of developing a metaphysics of nature and experience. Nor should we forget that Dewey's continued involvement with the theory of democratic life, ranging from education and conduct to political theory, contributed toward his theory of culture and art which is part and parcel of this theory of naturalism.

There is, however, a puzzling feature about the middle period: whereas in both the early and the later period art and aesthetic experience play a predominant role in Dewey's analysis of experience, there is virtually no significant discussion of these subjects from 1903 to their sudden re-emergence in Experience and Nature, where art is described as "the culminating event of nature" and "the climax of experience" (*EN*, xvi; *LW* 1:8). Art does play an important role in Dewey's theory of education, it is true, and there are exuberant passages in *Reconstruction in Philosophy* and *Human Nature and Conduct* where art is praised for its capacity to make us aware of ideals.[2] This paradox is more apparent than real, for what Dewey is doing during this middle period is working out the implications of his vision of life as art. His theory of artistic, intelligent conduct is nothing other than instrumentalism. And, like any method or tool, it reveals as much about the material it works upon as about its user.

Yet *Experience and Nature* clearly represents a dramatic convergence of themes hitherto only loosely associated in Dewey's mature philosophy. What marks the high tenor of this work is that Dewey now plays off his enriched naturalistic vision of experience against the whole Western philosophical tradition, not merely showing where ancient and modern philosophy have gone wrong, but showing *why* they have gone wrong and where they have gone right. The aesthetic metaphysics of the Greeks and the scientific metaphysics of the moderns are not to be repudiated utterly, for they are rich, valuable interpretations of experience and each preserves its moment of truth (here, perhaps, is the old Hegelian still at work in the new philosophy). And, while Boisvert may be right that Dewey tends rather hazily to typify "the" ancient and "the" modern views, there is an underlying sophisticated, subtle, and profound reading of the history of Western civilization.[3] As Dewey was writing the re-introduction for the book in his nineties, Joseph Ratner tells us that he projected undertaking a Promethean critique, "a philosophical interpretation of the history of Western man" (*LW* 1:329). The powerful and suggestive fragments of Dewey's re-introduction show that this would have been a comprehensive view of the relation of philosophy to its environing culture: economic, social, moral, artistic, and scientific—obviously something far removed from a dry rehearsal of thinkers' opinions or a witty recounting of the history of silly beliefs, such as Russell provided. For my purposes, however, it will be enough to ask whether Dewey's metaphysics of experience is a natural outgrowth of his mature position or whether it is, as many have held, a case of an old man trying to resow the wild oats of a misspent Hegelian youth.

It is the purpose of this chapter, therefore, to examine Dewey's metaphysics of experience and to understand its bearing on the issue of meaning and immediacy. This requires first of all an examination of Dewey's first and not entirely successful effort to reformulate the theory of experience which underlay his instrumentalist methodology. In the course of working this out, Dewey must confront whether "experience" is something merely private, a subjective screen preventing any glimpse of things as they are in themselves, or whether in fact it reveals something about the nature of nature and the nature of man. What is the relationship of experience to nature? If thought is something which transforms experience (which Dewey argues it certainly does), how does this not lead toward the bitter Kantian conclusion that before we can apprehend the genuine article of reality it has been mauled and tampered with by the meddlesome activity of the mind? Finally, if experience does arise from nature, in what legitimate sense can qualitative immediacy and meaning be understood as having natural reference, as being *of* nature and not projections of our subjectivity? In his claim that art is truly revelatory of the relation of experience and nature, has Dewey succumbed to romanticism from a hard-headed pragmatism?

I hope it is now obvious why any study of Dewey's aesthetics cannot rest content with confining itself to what lies between the covers of *Art as Experience*.[4] First of all, such a limitation would not succeed in responding cogently to the Pepper-Croce thesis. Secondly, it would fail to locate the proper role of art and aesthetic experience within the general context of Dewey's thought. This, I believe, is to leave much of Dewey's philosophy wandering in darkness. Finally, one cannot understand the issues or motives of Dewey's aesthetics without understanding them as deeply connected with those of his philosophy as a whole. *Art as Experience*, Dewey tells us from the start, is a book about *life*, not primarily about "fine art." Much spilt ink would have been saved if the first pages of the book had been taken to heart. Art is not some by-product of experience, a refreshing wayside on the arduous highway of our instrumentalist affairs. It is the revelation of what experience is all about. For Dewey, the aesthetic haunts each moment as a near or remote possibility. Its *absence* from experience, not its presence, is what needs to be accounted for. Intelligence—civilization—is born in the shared quest for its recovery. The aesthetic comes to generate the enterprise of the democratic community itself. It represents the possibility of the fulfilling, shared life where human beings realize meaning and value in the creative process of intelligent growth. In short, the aesthetic is the Acropolis *and* the Agora of Dewey's polis.

Our discussion in this chapter will be organized in the following way: By examining the major criticisms of Dewey's theory of experience, beginning in 1905 and continuing today, it becomes evident that the critical issue of the Pepper-Croce thesis is but one disturbance of a faultline running through the center of Dewey's philosophy. The nature of this problem is described differently by different critics at various times, but I believe that the essence of its lies in the claimed opposition of Dewey's statements about the immediate qualitative nature of experience and the naturalistic and instrumental interpretation of empiricism. Instead of being an ultimate contradiction which would reduce Dewey's philosophical edifice to rubble, I contend that this is a coherent and defensible reinterpretation of experience and nature, one which is so radical and divergent from traditional philosophy that thinkers whose intellectual habits have been formed by the tradition are compelled, often against their inclinations, to give a systematic misreading of Dewey. If, on the other hand, Dewey has embraced a contradictory theory, I cannot but see how this would cause a complete revaluation of Dewey as a philosopher and throw doubt upon the safety of accepting any part of his thought.

The first step, after tracing a path through eighty years of criticism, will be to return to Dewey's earliest attempts to formulate his "new" philosophy, the "postulate of immediate empiricism," and to see whether he had made a fatal or a fateful decision there. Dewey immediately becomes embroiled in charges of subjectivism in his attempt to provide a grounding for his instrumentalism. Later we see the project of *Experience and Nature* to be essentially the same as that which was lispingly put forth twenty years previously. But now, in addition to a fuller interpretation of experience in all its noncognitive and culturally social modes, we are presented with Dewey's metaphysical enterprise, the effort to describe the "generic traits of existence as existence." This certainly represents one of the vaguest, most troublesome and most crucial parts of Dewey's philosophy. Is Dewey trying to describe the way nature or existence is apart from human experience and still claim to being an empiricist? How can an empirical methodology claim to arrive at universal or generic categories at all? What, if anything, is the value of this enterprise? Perhaps we should, as Rorty suggests, respectfully but firmly exorcise this last ghost that has haunted the Western tradition and now interrupts our academic conversations. Yet, before we remove the possibility of understanding what Dewey truly has to offer, his reinterpretation of experience and nature, perhaps we should at least make an effort toward understanding what exactly this quest for the generic traits of existence means. It will be shown, I hope, that it is not so foolish or misguided as many have contended. This part of Dewey's philosophy provides the very tools whereby his project of a rich, pluralistic, and dynamic interpretation of experience becomes possible and perpetuates itself. They reveal the very situationality of experience and the regulative means whereby this is kept in view in reflective enterprises.

The generic traits open up the problematic claim that experience and nature are "continuous." Throughout his writings Dewey repeatedly appeals to his "principle of continuity," usually when he happens to be in a particularly troublesome moment. Before one sides with those critics who either see this appeal as a concession to idealism or as Dewey's magic lamp, it is worth trying to understand what this meant for Dewey and how he meant "continuity" to be taken. As will be seen, continuity for Dewey means growth, which involves a creative theory of temporality. The underpinning for Dewey's philosophy of experience is a tenacious insistence on its radical temporality as well as its situationality. This leads to the last topic for this chapter,

Dewey's theory of situations. Situations exemplify continuity, they have the possibility of growth toward consummatory, qualitative meaningful experience. Quality is present from the start as the defining and regulating aspect of situations, constituting the horizon and focus of experience and the teleology of action. That situations are dynamic means that they have the potentiality of becoming realized in their continuity, and this is exactly what happens when experience becomes aesthetic, *an* experience. The human situation in nature creates the possibility for meaning, action, and participation through communication. The *world* can take on shared meaningful structures which are intelligent, structures which reveal as much about the world in which we live as about those beings who dwell upon the earth.

Thus I conclude this chapter by arguing that Dewey's metaphysics of experience does offer a valuable and coherent philosophy, though, perhaps, a far from complete one. It is nevertheless highly important to strive to understand Dewey's project before acceding to those criticisms which may have been profoundly misguided. Dewey's philosophy, like every great philosophy, is full of tensions and not without its contradictions. But it is easy to avoid the vision of the whole and become satisfied with a reading of the part. At the very least, since the promise is so great, it is worth thinking through.

I. The Critical Problem: Contradictions in Dewey's Philosophy

Dewey's ideas generated a vast quantity of criticism, now occupying almost a century of discussion. As Dewey's philosophy changed focus so did the criticisms. Nevertheless, again and again certain issues were raised which have their origin in a basic tension in Dewey's philosophy. This problem comes out in a variety of topics: the nature of immediate experience; whether Dewey is a realist; a naturalist, a materialist, or an idealist; the issue of how experience is related to nature; the dualism of quality and relation, and the consistency of Dewey's aesthetics with his instrumentalism itself.

It is important to note that the critical problem emerges almost simultaneously with the genesis of Dewey's instrumentalist period. Though Dewey had been "drifting," as he put it, away from idealism for many years, he first consciously allied himself with the pragmatism in his articles which appeared in 1903 in *Studies in Logical Theory*.[5] In 1905, Dewey published an article, "The Postulate of Immediate Empiricism," which sought to extend his instrumentalist theory of knowledge through an analysis of qualitative immediacy. Significantly, the article contains in germ the essence of what would later become his theory of aesthetic meaning. Numerous objections were raised to the ideas it presented, the major one being that by focusing almost entirely on experience in its immediacy Dewey could never arrive at a rational, mediated, or even instrumental view of knowledge, not to mention at a metaphysics of nature. Dewey seemed to have retreated into the worst sort of subjectivism and sensationalism.[6] Dewey surprised his critics by emphatically stating that the contrary was true— the method he had outlined in the article was the only way to account for rational inquiry and knowledge and to arrive at a metaphysics which escaped the dilemmas and dead ends of the past. Immediate empiricism, argued Dewey, affirmed rather than denied a mediated, related aspect of experience which placed man in direct relationship to nature and knowledge through the process of inquiry.

When *Experience and Nature* appeared twenty years later, a similar controversy arose over the issue whether Dewey's professed empiricism allowed him the luxury of creating a naturalistic metaphysics. A number of perceptive critics such as Santayana, Morris Cohen, and William E. Hocking did not see the problem as the immediate vs. the mediate aspect of experience. Instead, it was the bewildering relationship Dewey tried to establish between nature and experience. To many, Dewey came dangerously close to idealism by encompassing nature within human experience. Santayana claimed that Dewey's "nearsighted sincerity" to human problems had exaggerated the "dominance of the foreground" in experience. "In nature," Santayana said, "there is no foreground or background. . . . The immediate experience of things, far from being fundamental in nature, is only a dream which accompanies our action, as other dreams accompany our sleep." Dewey had therefore grafted something spiritual upon nature, rendering his philosophy "the specious kind of naturalism possible also to such idealists as Emerson, Schelling, or any of the Hegelian left." For Dewey, claimed Santayana, "Immediacy, which was an epistemological category, has become a physical one; natural events are conceived to be compounded of such qualities as appear to human observers. . . ." Dewey lacked "natural piety," that is, he failed to regard nature on its own account and ascribed human qualities to it.[7]

Morris Cohen spoke of Dewey's philosophy as "anthropocentric naturalism," a charge which was repeated by H.S. Thayer, who evaluated Dewey's position as "animism at best."[8] Cohen repeated Santayana's charge that Dewey was "emphasizing the things nearest to him" and was "denying the existence of things that are not in his field of interest." Because Dewey had described nature in terms of the categories of human experience, he "cannot accept whole-heartedly physical determinism," and so breaks the continuity of man and nature. Cohen, speaking as a naturalist, was echoed by Hocking, speaking as an idealist, much as Pepper's criticisms received support from Croce, an opponent of pragmatism. Because, said Hocking, Dewey had admitted that human experience constitutes the world in some way, he had conceded the central thesis of idealism. Dewey had but to realize that "the more theory, the nearer reality," i.e. to give up his instrumentalism for rationalism. Since the "nonidentity of the immediate and the mediated must be compatible with their objective history," and the mediation of theory is truer than immediate primary experience, only idealism is capable of giving us "eternal truth."[9] One can instantly see how this criticism in particular would destroy the primacy that Dewey, even as an idealist, had wished to place upon immediate, lived experience and the role of action and practice.

The dilemma facing Dewey was succinctly posed by Sholom Kahn:

> For Dewey . . . experience occurs within a framework of "nature," which is a realm of "existence" composed of "events," . . . but the universe he pictures is one in which "experience" bulks large . . . By Dewey's own familiar statement, however, "metaphysics is cognizance of the generic traits of *existence.*" Thus the distinctively metaphysical problem persists: What is the relationship between experience and existence in Dewey's naturalistic universe?[10]

On the one hand Dewey seemed committed to view human nature as well as nature itself objectively, especially in terms of the empirical sciences. Such a view would dispense with immediate appearances except as signs of underlying natural conditions. The *real* world, however, would be expressed in terms of relations, and these relations constituted the object of knowledge. On the other hand, Dewey seemed to insist that ultimately everything had to be understood in terms of "experience." Barring Humean sensationalism, this indicated that nature or matter were constructs of the mind, and that this mediating power of the mind only knew immediate experience in terms of a self-conscious rational system of spiritual self-understanding. In short, Dewey is accused of waffling between materialistic naturalism and objective idealism. On this basis, Dewey's early longing for an organic philosophy which would harmonize Huxley with Hegel would seem to have led inevitably to a magnificently confused failure.

After Dewey's death the controversy rose again, this time in a debate over the status of relations and qualities in Dewey's metaphysics. Paul Welsh, for example, noted that "The first of [Dewey's] assumptions . . . is the view that events and the qualities that make them up are unique. . . ." Yet, since relations are described as recurrent, "For Dewey, every experienced object has a double status."[11] Qualities refer to the immediate aspect of experience, relations to the mediate: how are both combined in *one* event? Richard Bernstein has most forcibly criticized Dewey on this point. "Dewey's analysis of quality," he notes, "is one of the most interesting and original features of his philosophy . . . It is the key for understanding his theory of experience, inquiry, and value . . . Difficulties discovered here are at the core of his thought." Bernstein claims that, in fact, there are two irreconcilable strains in Dewey's theory, a "metaphysical strain" and a "phenomenological strain." He concludes that "Dewey was ever seeing continuity where others claimed there were sharp cleavages; but there is a deep crack, a basic discontinuity that cuts through his naturalism."[12]

Bernstein locates the trouble in the contrary claims Dewey makes about the immediate, yet mediated, nature of experience and about the relation of experience itself to nature. These paradoxes come to a head in Dewey's theory of quality. Here, Dewey's idealist leanings are apparent:

> The pivotal point of Dewey's rejection of idealism is in his insistence that experience is far more extensive than knowing. . . . But in his polemical defense of the integrity of experience, Dewey claimed so much for experience that it became difficult to see what was *not* experience, what if anything controlled and limited experience. It looked as if Dewey, who had so many harsh words about idealism, was serving it up in another form.[13]

The only resolution of this problem, according to Bernstein, was for Dewey to assert that "experience is continuous with and a part of other natural transactions." But, "Dewey glibly passes from experience to nature. . . . He explicitly claims that possession of quality is not only a trait of experience, but a characteristic of all natural existences."[14] If qualities are *had* and not *known*, how does Dewey *know* they are traits of all existences?

A number of issues are packed into these remarks. It is to be noted, however, that Bernstein dismisses Dewey's solution, i.e., his appeal to the "continuity of experience and nature." Instead of trying to ascertain what Dewey meant by this cryptic remark, Bernstein says:

> The difficulties can be seen in what is undoubtedly the most fundamental principle in Dewey—the principle of continuity. It is the heart of his naturalism. . . . What precisely is the meaning and status of

this principle of continuity? Sometimes Dewey speaks as if it were a regulative principle for all inquiry, and sometimes he talks as if it were a generalized conclusion for all science. We are never given a detailed systematic analysis of "continuity." Too frequently, Dewey appears to be guilty of the sin that he detected so clearly in others— confusing metaphysics with morals. The principle of continuity has more of an emotive meaning than a descriptive, informative meaning.[15]

If justified, this criticism demolishes the basis of Dewey's whole philosophy, which, as will be shown, constantly appeals to this "principle of continuity." Bernstein says, furthermore, that "Dewey emphasizes that these qualities can be active; that they can be transformed and mediated. . . . But when Dewey goes on to discuss those qualities which are intrinsically possessed by natural existences . . . he tells us that quality is brute, unconditioned, and unmediated."[16] Dewey speaks two languages about quality, one phenomenological, dealing with it as experience, and one metaphysical, treating it as a category of all existences. The former, states Bernstein, tends toward idealism, the latter to realism. Bernstein concludes that "Dewey thought he had undercut the dispute between idealists and realists, but now it looks as if the old opposition has not been avoided, but rather held together in an unholy alliance."[17]

The breach opened by Bernstein has been widened by other critics who, like Bernstein himself, are far from hostile toward Dewey's general position. Roland Garrett makes a systematic list of Dewey's contradictory account of quality. One account holds that qualities (1) are not involved in causal relationships, (2) are unrelated and exclusive, (3) are absolutely unique in occurrence—no two qualities are ever identical, and (4) cannot be known because they are "ineffable." The other account states that qualities (1) arise from and are caused by certain conditions, (2) are involved in objects, events or situations, and hence are related, (3) can function in causal sequences as signs or universals, which, since they must repeatable to be signs, are not unique, and (4) as universals must be objects of knowledge and reflection. Garrett sees Dewey's mistake in making qualities ineffable, unique, unrelated, and outside of causal relationships, that is, the version offered in the first account. This was a foredoomed project, since one can never give an account of what is ineffable and unknowable. "Dewey is led into confusion by his very attempt to do what cannot be done in metaphysics," states Garrett, "to define and describe what is unrelated and ineffable."[18] Garrett concludes that one must "jettison one half of Dewey's theory of quality."[19] In striving to free qualities from the "ubiquitous knowledge relation" of idealism,

Dewey's metaphysics "became riddled with false starts, ambiguities, and contradictions."[20]

The criticisms of Richard Rorty parallel those of Garrett in a way, except that Rorty believes Dewey's attempt to construct a metaphysics of any kind to be misguided from the start. For Rorty, Dewey's contribution, along with that of Heidegger and Wittgenstein, lies in his negative critique of "the tradition" of Western metaphysics.[21] Rorty poses the dilemma that "either Dewey's metaphysics differs from 'traditional metaphysics' in not having a directing bias concerning social values because Dewey found an 'empirical' way of doing metaphysics . . . or else when Dewey falls into his vein of talking of the 'generic traits manifested by existences of all kinds,' he is in slightly bad faith."[22] Rorty is correct in regarding the issue of the "generic traits" as a vague and troublesome spot in Dewey's philosophy, but he has presented a very distorted view of Dewey's philosophy and pragmatism.[23] Dewey by no means intended philosophy to become a purely formal, even if playful, academic discipline; metaphysics was crucial to the goal of a critically responsible and intelligently evaluative enterprise focused on the real problems of human life, which Dewey saw as philosophy's true subject matter. It is interesting, however, that Rorty raises once again the charge of latent idealism in Dewey's system:

> Dewey wanted not merely skeptical diagnosis but also constructive metaphysical system-building. The system that was built in *Experience and Nature* sounded idealistic, and its solution to the mind-body problem seemed one more invocation of the transcendental ego, because the level of generality to which Dewey ascends is the same level at which Kant worked, and the model of knowledge is the same—the constitution of the knowable by the cooperation of two unknowables.[24]

Like Croce, Rorty believes that Dewey's solution to the mind-body problem was merely to introduce a hyphen and posit an entity called the "body-mind."[25] In summary, for Rorty we should disregard the Dewey who presents us with "answers" to the experience-nature problem, the mind-body problem, or who speaks of philosophy as committed to a serious inquiry into the general meanings governing human existence. This renders, I believe, the critical side of Dewey's philosophy without any basis whatsoever and therefore meaningless. Rorty's comments have nevertheless drawn into focus the central importance of understanding Dewey's metaphysics and metaphysical enterprise in attempting to understand other aspects of his philosophy.

Robert Dewey's recent study, *The Philosophy of John Dewey*, not only repeats the well-worn charge of inconsistency, but seems to make it the guiding principle in interpreting his distant cousin's thought.[26] According to this critic, "The dilemma is this: Either retain empiricism and accept the absurd conclusion that events are organism-dependent for their existence, or accept the independent existence of events and abandon the fundamental commitment to empiricism."[27] Once again, "Dewey's idealist background" is held accountable for this muddle. But Robert Dewey sees a more fundamental factor at work: "If Dewey had not continued the traditional philosophic quest for essence, most of these difficulties would not have arisen."[28] Thus, in abandoning this useless quest, a truer and broader Deweyan empiricism will be forth-coming.

Against, indeed diametrically opposed to, this work is that of Raymond Boisvert, who argues patiently that the quest for essence has a significant place in Dewey's naturalistic project.[29] Writing in the spirit of the American naturalism of Woodbridge and Randall, Boisvert attempts to show how, once the all-important qualifications against the static, atemporal interpretation of the classical conception of form have been made, Dewey does seem to have the doctrine that natural events have a structured and therefore knowable side to them. Though Boisvert's approach may strike many as a subversive attempt to make Dewey serve the cause against which he fought all his life, in fact it is not. Indeed, given the long, gloomy medical reports on the ill health of Dewey's metaphysics, Boisvert's analysis is refreshingly clear-headed and, I believe, substantially correct. If this chapter seems to differ from the approach taken by Boisvert, it will be more in the matter of emphasis than disagreement. Whereas Boisvert has sought to rehabilitate the idea of form in Dewey's metaphysics, I have attempted to indicate the crucial role of potentiality.

To reorient ourselves after traversing this thicket of criticism, three related issues can be detected. The first is the epistemological problem which deals with Dewey's account of experience as both immediate and unknowable and as mediate and providing knowledge. The second is the metaphysical problem, concerning the ultimate commitments of Dewey's position to idealism or naturalism. Finally there is the problem of the generic traits of existence and how the enterprise of Dewey's metaphysics bears on his philosophy in general. This last issue focuses especially on the relationship between two traits, quality and relation, and the contradictory account of quality Dewey seems to give. It is clear that these questions are bound up with each other: quality is immediate in experience and is *of* nature. If the aesthetic develops from our experience in nature and utilizes the inherent capacity of experience to take on meanings and yet be immediately apprehended, it is evident that these questions must be at least partially answered if a coherent account of aesthetic meaning is to be given. At best we see Dewey weakly appealing to a "principle of continuity" or to such terms as "body-mind." What is meant by these expressions, and do they save Dewey's position? It is the contention of this chapter that such terms do make sense and provide a coherent context for Dewey's theory of aesthetic meaning.

II. The Postulate of Immediate Empiricism

This chapter cannot answer nearly a century of criticism; yet the problems raised must be dealt with. There have been numerous accounts and short studies of Dewey's theories of experience and nature, yet there is not really any attempt to understand Dewey's system in terms of the idea of continuity or emergence. The job is more difficult when one looks at Dewey's own works and responses, for he surely was neither a systematic writer nor his own best defender. The blessing and curse of Dewey's writing was to gain a new perspective on a problem by walking all around it, a feature which makes following him both exciting and confusing. Like Heidegger, Dewey chose to wander "wood paths" rather than follow the established streets of thinking. Moreover, Dewey had acquired an aversion to the systematic exposition of his youthful days. The *Psychology* represents his greatest achievement in this genre; it was no doubt Dewey's growing rejection of the ideas in this work which made him realize that one could be very coherent and also very wrong. Had Dewey stuck to a precise terminology, had he tried to relate his thought more closely and accurately to certain ideas in the philosophical tradition, had he tried less to write for the intelligent general reader than for professional philosophers, his philosophy might have suffered fewer distortions and dismissals than it has.

Also, as we have seen with Croce and Pepper, Dewey had a tendency to respond to critics by doggedly repeating the point at question. Towards the end of his life, in response to the dilemma posed by Sholom Kahn, Dewey decided to abjure the term "metaphysics" altogether because he could not erase its traditional connotations.

> I now realize it was exceedingly naive of me to suppose it was possible to rescue the word from its engrained traditional use. I derive what consolation may be possible from promising myself never to use the word again in any connection with any aspect of my

own position. . . . And while I think the *words* used were most unfortunate, I still believe that that which they were used to name is genuine and important.[30]

Unfortunately, relinquishing this term merely left Dewey's ideas open to being interpreted as a type of positivism. However, as Gouinlock has correctly observed, "In all Dewey's work the metaphysical basis is present and operative."[31] It is to be noted that Dewey also came to reject the term "experience" late in his career, and for much the same reasons. It has recently come to attention that in preparing the reintroduction to *Experience and Nature* in 1951 Dewey revised the title itself. He wrote:

> Were I to write (or rewrite) *Experience and Nature* today I would entitle the book *Culture and Nature* and the treatment of specific subject-matters would be correspondingly modified. I would abandon the term "experience" because of my growing realization that the historical obstacles which prevented understanding of my use of experience are, for all practical purposes, insurmountable. I would substitute the term "culture" because with its meanings as now firmly established it can firmly and freely carry my philosophy of experience (*LW* 1:361).

Dewey adds that "I am not convinced that the task I undertook was totally misguided. . . . There was a period in modern philosophy when the appeal to 'experience' was a thoroughly wholesome appeal to liberate philosophy from desiccated abstractions. But I failed to appreciate the fact that subsequent developments inside and outside of philosophy had destroyed and corrupted the wholesomeness of the appeal . . ." (*LW* 1:361-62). "Experience" had come to mean only the process of "experiencing" and to exclude *what* was experienced. Though Dewey's hopes for the security of "culture" as a bias-free term may make us, the inheritors of the post-structuralists, smile, it is remarkably helpful in avoiding the traditional misinterpretations of Dewey's thought. The historical critique that Dewey projected the year before his death was nothing less than an attempt to see how the terms "culture" and "experience" had come to mean such radically different things. In this division, Dewey saw the plight and danger of contemporary civilization and it may be safely said that most of Dewey's philosophical endeavor was an effort to overcome that separation and thereby incorporate nature and experience. For Dewey, then, the traditional mind-body problem is far more intelligible when posed as the "culture-nature" problem.

By "culture," Dewey refers to the complex and various ways in which human beings live together in the world. It refers to how we understand and appropriate the resources of nature and how we understand and appropriate each other. "The name 'culture' in its anthropoligical (not its Matthew Arnold) sense," says Dewey, "designates the vast range of things experienced in an indefinite variety of ways" (LW 1:362). It includes artifacts, activities, customs, beliefs, dispositions, morals, arts, knowledge, and world-views. In addition, "culture" refers to all the uses to which these are put "and which accordingly deserve, philosophically speaking, the name 'ideal' (even the name 'spiritual,' if intelligibly used)" (LW 1:362).[32] Culture refers then to "the material and the ideal in their reciprocal interrelationships" (LW 1:363). It is to be recalled here that the tensive nexus between the ideal and the real is for Dewey *the* human concern. "Culture" is the shared life of human beings upon the earth as it is appropriated in terms of meaning and value. "Experience" designates this relationship and "metaphysics" will attempt to describe it in its most general features. "Nature" will provide the material of "culture," and "culture" ("experience") will be an exploration of the possibilities of nature. Nature will not be something that is "hidden" by culture any more than the nature of clay will be "hidden" by the art of pottery.

That this is what Dewey had in mind when he wrote *Experience and Nature* is well attested by the short but important syllabus for a course Dewey offered in 1922-23 called "Types of Philosophic Thought," and which is obviously an ur-text for his projected magnum opus. Not only does it give in lucid formulations crucial ideas tortuously expressed in *Experience and Nature*, but it provides a clear account of the reading material Dewey had in mind and outlines his views on the nature of Western philosophy. It begins as follows:

> The word "experience" is here taken non-technically. Its nearest equivalents are such words as "life," "history," "culture," (in its anthropological use). It does not mean processes and modes of experiencing apart from *what* is experienced and lived. The philosophical value of the term is to provide a way of referring to the unity or totality between what is experienced and the way it is experienced, a totality which is broken up and referred to only in ready-made distinctions or by such words as "world," "things," "objects" on the one hand and "mind," "subject," "person," "consciousness" on the other. Similarly "history" denotes both events and our record or interpretation of them; while "events" include not only the acts and sufferings of human beings but all the cosmic and institutional conditions and forces which in any way whatsoever enter into and affect these human beings—in short, the wide universe as manifesting itself in the careers and fortunes of human beings (MW 13:351).

The route by which Dewey arrived at this situational view of experience is complex. While certainly one can point to Dewey's idealist background as the likely source for a view which sees nature and culture so cooperatively conspiring, what must be asked is whether Dewey sucessfully naturalized this theory. The key figure in this process is none other than William James. One of the major influences on Dewey even while he was an idealist was James' *Principles of Psychology*. The elements there of what was to become James' doctrine of radical empiricism quickly made an impression upon Dewey because they were so intimately connected with his own attempt to give a full-blooded account of experience. In particular, one can point to James' doctrine that relations are felt (or "had" in Dewey's terminology) as well as known. One need not posit a transcendental ego busily synthesizing the discrete atomata of experience if experience doesn't arrive in discrete bits. Instead it arrives as a temporally moving, dynamic whole, a process of transformation.[33] We have seen that even in Dewey's *Psychology* a significant role was assigned to feeling. James' account of the stream of consciousness, with its emphasis on the teleology, temporality, and functionality of experience as a natural articulation of life showed Dewey that he had no need of "the bare miraculous self," to use James' words. Later on, Dewey even came to criticize James for having too substantial a theory of the self.[34] Experience as it was lived was originally whole; it did not come fallen and in need of salvation by a synthesizing ego. What experience needed as it came to us was not to be "constructed" out of the rubble of sense data, but to be organized and controlled, directed, if possible, toward desirable ends. In short, it needed reconstruction and it needed to have the possibility for its reconstruction safely contained within it.

Dewey was also particularly impressed by what James called "the psychologist's fallacy."[35] In trying to account for how empiricists and idealists had cooked up such a thin and impotent account of experience, James argued that they had merely read the discrete, manipulable *results* of their analytical accounts into the primary, original state from which they had been abstracted as having been there in their pure, pristine shape all along. In short, they had converted the fruits of analysis into the roots of experience. Locke's simple ideas are a paradigmatic instance. We do not receive the "idea" of red, which is jumbled up along with other ideas of "sweet" or "round" and all added together to equal "apple." We learn to point out "red" only as we learn to point out all our colors, which is part of that long, painful effort to organize our world known as education. To be able to see something as an instance of the color red involves already a sophisticated coordination of responses. It was unwarranted for Locke and others to argue that "experience" which was the *result* of a long active process of organization was exactly the *same* experience which originally came to us. Not only did this lead James to see experience as a living, growing process in which transformation played a vital function, but it threw into doubt the privileged status of analytical, cognitive or knowing experiences to report about their origins without changing the subject-matter. Dewey would later expand this observation beyond the limits of psychology and call it the "fallacy of selective emphasis" of which the "intellectualist fallacy" was the worst instance. For Dewey, not only do we tend to select our particular interest as giving primary instances of the way things "really" are, but especially in philosophy where the problem of knowledge has been paramount we tend to treat *all* kinds of experience as varieties of one basic type, cognitive experience.[36] While many have seen in pragmatism an effort to reduce all forms of experience to the grossest utilitarian and self-centered instances, both James and Dewey (and, though to a lesser extent, Peirce and Mead) are emphatic in preserving the richness and autonomy of our non-cognitive experiences in the face of centuries of treating them as modes (usually lower modes) of knowing. Dewey was also extremely impressed with James' interpretation of consciousness as inhabiting a "field" which faded toward a defining penumbra "fringe" or "horizon." Dewey, too, would come to see experience as a horizonal field-event.

James' *Principles* resolved far more successfully than Dewey's *Psychology* the very organic and lived aspects of experience which Dewey himself wished to combine. Yet James' account easily fell prey to the dualistic language and habits of thought which were part of psychology's inheritance. The path out of that wilderness had been opened up in those places where James began developing his radical empiricism. Gradually, as the term "experimental idealism" quietly disappeared from his writings, Dewey began to see in the very idea of organic action the key to resolving the lingering problems of dualism. It is with the publication of "The Reflex Arc Concept in Psychology" (1896) that Dewey presents in miniature what will become his model for interaction. Although the discussion of this article is left for the next chapter, it should be noted here that instead of treating physical movement and sensation as distinct and separate phases of activity, Dewey sees them as mutually coordinating features falling within one whole action. An article in psychology was not the place to work out the mind-body problem and it was enough for Dewey to discredit the mechanical cause-effect model of the reflex arc.

After Dewey's publication of the *Studies in Logical Theory* he rapidly began working out an instrumentalist theory of experience. 1905 shows a dramatic shift in the focus of Dewey's writing, which for the previous ten years had been devoted to problems in the philosophy of education. There begin appearing articles dealing with strictly philosophical issues, in particular those which define the instrumentalist approach to realism, truth, and logic, gathered together in *The Influence of Darwin on Philosophy* (1910) and *Essays in Experimental Logic* (1916). Dewey's attempt to formulate a theory of experience which would better conform to instrumentalism begins with his main article of 1905, "The Postulate of Immediate Empiricism." It was exploratory, ambiguous, and, as it turned out, highly controversial. In trying to make James' dualistic theory more objective, Dewey was accused of advocating the most extreme and unreconstructed form of solipsism. What the article attempted—and this was the major source of confusion—was to distinguish questions of reality from questions of knowledge or truth. This distinction remains fundamental throughout the rest of Dewey's philosophy.

Dewey attempted in the article to define the essential aspect of pragmatism, which was not a body of doctrine so much as "a presupposition as to what experience is and means" (*IDP*, 226; *MW* 3:158). This presupposition, or rather "attitude," was "the postulate and criterion of *immediate empiricism.*" Dewey cautioned at the beginning that "Empiricism, as herein used, is as antipodal to sensationalistic empiricism, as it is to transcendentalism, and for the same reason. Both of these systems fall back upon something which is defined in nondirectly experienced terms in order to justify that which is directly experienced" (*IDP*, 226-27; *MW* 3:158, fn. 2). Here we can see the influence of James clearly. Dewey is trying to take experience as a functioning whole, as it is encountered, rather than trying to posit the refined, analyzed concepts of sensa or categories as prior and underlying realities.

The postulate was couched in the following ambiguous and challenging formulation: "Immediate empiricism postulates that things—anything, everything in the ordinary or non-technical use of the term 'thing'—are what they are experienced as" (*IDP*, 227; *MW* 3: 158). On the face of it, Dewey seemed to be advocating the most naive of naive realism. Did he mean that because I experienced the stick in water as bent, it *really* was bent? Dewey chose as an example the various accounts of a horse that a jockey, a zoologist, a horse trader, and others might give. Each one would differ in significant respects, and yet all would be valid, in their contexts, and *of* the same horse. Nor would these accounts be mere "subjective impressions": where the jockey might see a "winner," the zoologist might see a fine example of a species of *equus* and the trader a "good deal." Nor would one account necessarily be truer than another, since each referred to different ways of interacting with the horse. Least of all should these various accounts be regarded as piecemeal "appearances" of some real, underlying "horse in-itself." These are real responses to a real animal.

Let us concentrate on the term "immediate." Normally it refers to something in direct contact, that which is not separated by a medium. In the seventeenth and eighteenth centuries this came to be applied to the problem of knowledge. With Descartes and then Locke, what is directly or immediately before the mind are its "ideas." No longer is the *idea, eidos,* or *forma* that which connects the mind with an object because of its identity, but it is simply the "effect" of some mysterious "cause" which brings it before the mind's eye. It is the internal content of the mind which at best will stand for or represent the external world. Thus we have the classic statement in Locke's *Essay:* "Since the mind, in all its thoughts and reasonings hath no other immediate object but its own ideas, which it alone does or can contemplate, it is evident that our knowledge is only conversant about them" (IV. i, 1). With this, as Thomas Reid saw, the fatal path to Humean skepticism is inevitable.

The alternative reached in the German tradition of Kant and Hegel was to deny that the mind could passively behold any immediate object without imposing some sort of mediating activity. Clearly, there was a content before the mind, or else it would be empty and unknowing. Hence, there was something "immediate" as an object, but it was a "mediated immediacy." It might not be able to tell us much about things in themselves, but, at least according to Fichte, Schelling, and Hegel, it could tell us a great deal about ourselves. It revealed nothing less than that the mind was a self-constituting and self-transcending process, and that it could grasp itself through and in this process. In other words, knowledge as self-knowledge was possible. But this knowledge was not to be conceived along the immediate act of self-intuition as expressed in Descartes' *cogito.* It was to be understood as the thoroughly mediated result of a process whereby the Absolute ultimately grasped itself wholly, comprehensively, infinitely, and eternally in and for itself. The Absolute's knowledge of itself was utterly rational because it was completely and infinitely internally related. But since these ultimately were *internal* relations, the Absolute grasped itself as a *whole,* as a self-contained and self-constitutive project. (Thus, for Hegel at least, to the extent which Spirit comprehended itself positively as a whole, it was immediate in the good sense of being also mediated and not in the pejorative sense of being a bare and unmediated object set over against consciousness.) In other words, because the Absolute could grasp itself as a whole throughout the various stages of history, that history became *its* history. Immediacy contained the truth about Spirit to the extent it successfully grasped itself in the process of its own becoming. Immediacy could refer then to the immanent organic wholeness of the temporal process instead of to a static relation of a mind to an idea.[37]

Given Dewey's Hegelian background, I think we can understand that he would have had no problems with the idea that experience could be "immediate" and yet also organic, temporal, and internally mediated. Unfortunately, most of Dewey's contemporaries operated within the tradition of Locke rather than Hegel. Dewey, of course, had tried to naturalize this view. Dewey's "postulate" can be rendered, then, not that "subjective appearances are reality" but that the *present* moment of experience is a dynamic orientation to a whole process; it is the attempt to organize that process into a unity. It is not taking a static, subjective, and passive Lockean perspective, but an active, involved and dynamic attitude. It is, in short, a moment of coordination. It is particularly important to emphasize the temporal teleological structure of such a "take" on the world. To the extent any moment is a genuine part of a temporal process, the attitude taken will reflect a certain perspective on the past *as* past and the future *as* future. It is a phase *of* action which is also a phase of interpretation. The solution to discovering how experience becomes intelligently articulated through inquiry does not lie in surmounting the immediate by appeal to a transcendental agency, however. It lies in investigating the possibilities inherent in the present to reconstruct itself, as James said. Knowledge arises from the way we are *in* the world, not from the way we are *out* of it.

The implication of all this is that I may have other attitudes toward the world than those of trying to "know" it. If I am worried that the stick in the water is bent, I may draw it out to see if the shape "really" is as crooked as the water made it appear. If I am concerned with painting the illusory quality of light on water, the problem of whether the stick is bent or not will probably not even arise. The stick can function in a variety of encounters which have nothing to do with knowing its true shape, and these modes of interaction are just as real as those occurring in the instance of knowing. Dewey, in other words, has made the all-important distinction between reality as it is known and reality as it is encountered in other types of experience which are not cases of knowing at all. Unfortunately, a short journal article was not the place for Dewey to try to shift an emphasis in the two thousand year history of Western philosophy, which had been deeply committed to the correlation of reality with the object of knowledge.

Dewey's critics may be excused for misinterpreting him, or, as in the case of F. J. E. Woodbridge's response to the article, challenging Dewey directly on the issue.[38] Knowledge, for Dewey, is only a privileged standpoint in terms of seeking the truth of experience. But there is more to experience than its truth. Thus, he states:

> By our postulate, things are what they are experienced to be, . . . it is fallacious to say that Reality is just and exclusively what it is or would be to an all-competent all-knower; or even that it *is*, relatively and piece-meal, what it is to a finite and partial knower. . . . Knowing is one mode of experiencing, and the primary philosophical demand . . . is to find out what *sort* of an experience knowing is—or, concretely, how things are experienced when they are experienced *as* known things (*IDP*, 228-29; *MW* 3:159-60).

Committing this fallacy, says Dewey, is the root of "all philosophic evil." It is important, from "the immediatist's standpoint," as Dewey calls it, to describe *how* things are experienced *as* when they are known, and "what the knowledge standpoint is itself *experienced as*" (*IDP*, 230; *MW* 3:160). Dewey advocates that by using "the direct descriptive method" (*IDP*, 240; *MW* 3:259) in philosophy just as it is used in "all the natural sciences," with appropriate modifications, numerous traditional philosophical problems will disappear.

As an example, Dewey refers to the experience of hearing a startling noise which, upon investigation, turns out to be the wind making a shade tap. The first experience of the frightful noise is just as real as the discovery of the cause and the return of the feeling of normalcy. The noise "really" is fearful. The experience of knowing the cause effects a change in the attitude to the situation just as the experience of the noise *as* fearful initiated the inquiry. Dewey insists that the first experience was not a knowing experience at all, not even one of knowing "I am frightened." *Being* frightened is not the same as *knowing* fear (as when a psychologist might undertake an inquiry into the phenomenon of fear). There may be experiences where one is worried over whether one is indeed frightened or not, as in war or a test of character. In the situation described, however, that is not the issue, which is simply "fright-at-the-noise." The experience need not end in an instance of knowledge. One might take an artistic interest in the feeling and use it to produce a work like Poe's "The Raven," with its sinister "tapping at my chamber door," or, perhaps, one could treat the noise superstitiously as bad luck or as a sign of the malevolent presence of spirits. These are all possible meanings of the experience but they are not all equally true.

Dewey does admit that the experience of knowing the cause is the truer one, taking "truer" in the pragmatic sense, however. In the example, it would mean that the inquiry and its results would govern future behavior as a guiding interpretation—further similar tapping noises would be initially regarded as blowing window shades. As this behavior came to be reliable it would become habitual, not even disturbing consciousness. Dewey asserts that "the question of truth is not as to whether Being or Non-Being, Reality or mere Appearance, is experienced, but as to the *worth* of a certain correctly experienced thing" (*IDP*, 235; *MW* 3:163). The interpretation is true in the archaic sense of "trustworthy, reliable"—the tapping is not *worth* being frightened at. It is nonsensical, though, to claim on that basis that the original experience was not really frightening, or even that the noise, later encountered as merely a harmless noise, was not itself originally frightful.

Dewey is therefore not making the trivial claim that dreams or illusions are "real" or "really exist" as dreams and illusions. Unless perhaps they are originally *experienced as* illusions, they are open to a number of possible interpretations, including being taken as true situations. As psychologists and parents have discovered, children must be taught how to distinguish dreaming from waking states and which are the proper responses to dreams. Likewise, a scientific response to an illness may be truer, more trustworthy and sophisticated, than a shaman's or a child's; but the latter interpretations are just as real in experiencing the disease *as* the work of witches or *as* punishment from God, and this fact is different from their *worth* in responding to the disease. Immediate experience, as stated, reflects a phase in a situation, which develops along with the situation.

Dewey's insistence, once again, is upon the primary wholeness of experience. Experience must be the ground for both truth and error; in other words, the attitudes we take toward experience must reflect the ways we interact with the world. Dewey makes the important claim that experience is always experienced "as that," i.e., that "things" or "objects" reflect dynamic modes of involvement which are perspectives and that each perspective has its own unique quality integrating it as a whole.

> There are two little words through the explication of which the empiricist's position may be brought out—"as" and "that." We may express his presupposition by saying that things are what they are experienced *as* being; or that to give a just account of anything is to tell what *that* thing is experienced to be. By these words I want to indicate the absolute, final, irreducible and inexpungible concrete *quale* which everything experienced not so much *has* as *is*. To grasp

this aspect of empiricism is to see what the empiricist means by objectivity, by the element of control (*IDP*, 234; *MW* 3:162-63).

To clarify what Dewey means by this, one must keep in mind that experience is an on-going process. The ambiguous, problematical, and even contradictory aspects of a present experience may be useful later in controlling how the experience develops. Dewey uses the illustration of an optical illusion, Zöllner's lines.

Here, lines which are parallel appear to be converging or diverging because of the cross-hatching. The immediate impiricist takes as the starting point the way they are experienced *as being that way* and "sticks in the most uncompromising fashion to *that* experience as real," (*IDP* 235; *MW* 3:163). If we assume the lines are convergent, we ought to be able to chart a point of intersection. But, on measuring the angles or drawing the lines out we see they do not converge; they are judged on *that* experience as "truly" being parallel. The original impression develops into the second, and so can be re-evaluated and corrected; we now see it *as* an optical illusion and can deal with it in an appropriate manner. We have determined the *worth* of the original reading through its own inner tensive nature. "It is because this thing . . . is a concrete *that*, that it develops into a corrected experience . . . whose full content is not a whit more real, but which is true or truer," (*IDP*, 235; *MW* 3:163). We have not used a mysterious intuition of reason to "see through," x-ray like, a false appearance. We have "seen through" the experience by staying with it, by "seeing it through," and by interacting with it, start to finish.

As with the window shade, the reality of the experience leads to or is a condition of its truth. As Dewey says, "If the illusoriness can be detected, it is because the thing experienced is real, having within its experienced reality elements whose *own mutual* tension effect its reconstruction," (*IDP*, 237; *MW* 3:164). We can judge the previous experience in terms of the latter because the latter "has, in its *own* determinate *quale*, elements of real continuity with the former; it is *ex hypothesi*, transformable through a series of experienced reals without break of continuity into the absolute thought experience," (*IDP*, 237-38; *MW* 3:165). The former experience is now *seen as*, or "interpreted as," the initial phase of an inquiry which goes a certain way rather than as an isolated, dream-like, and meaningless experience. The meaning of the noise has changed, or, rather, grown. In other words, the developmental continuity of the experience has been realized. Nothing in Dewey's thought, especially his theory of aesthetic meaning, makes sense unless the basic doctrine that *experience grows*, and in growing takes on *meaning*, is remembered.

What Dewey means by "immediate empiricism" should be clearer now. "Immediate" refers to the quality of the situation as a whole, inclusive of its determinate and indeterminate, cognitive and noncognitive aspects. In his late work, *Logic: The Theory of Inquiry*, Dewey says that it:

> Is of the very nature of the indeterminate situation which evokes inquiry to be *questionable*; or, in terms of actuality instead of potentiality, to be uncertain, unsettled, disturbed. The peculiar quality of what pervades the given materials, constituting them a situation, is not just uncertainty at large; it is a unique doubtfulness which makes that situation to be just and only the situation it is. It is this unique quality that not only evokes the particular inquiry engaged in but that exercises control over its special procedures. . . . It is the *situation* which has these traits. *We* are doubtful because the situation is inherently doubtful (*LTI*, 105-06; *LW* 12:109).

The immediate is the pre-analyzed (or what Merleau-Ponty would call the "prereflective") context in which thought operates—it is in fact what makes thought possible. If one conceives "experience" as a subjective phenomenon, a priori dividing "mind" from "reality," then it is impossible to make sense of Dewey's contextual and situational theory. Dewey criticizes theories of knowledge which start with these abstract dualisms and then must invent transcendental synthesizing agents to join artificially what never should have been sundered. In *Experience and Nature*, Dewey says that experience:

Includes *what* men do and suffer, *what* they strive for, love, believe and endure, and also *how* men act and are acted upon, the ways in which they do and suffer, desire and enjoy, see, believe, imagine—in short, processes of *experiencing*. "Experience" denotes the planted field, the sowed seeds, the reaped harvests, the changes of night and day, spring and autumn . . .; it also denotes the one who plants and reaps, who works and rejoices, hopes, fears, plans. . . . It is "double-barreled" in that it recognizes in its primary integrity no division between act and material, subject and object, but contains them both in an unanalyzed totality. "Thing" and "thought," as James says in the same connection, are single-barreled; they refer to products discriminated by reflection out of primary experience (*EN*, 8, *LW* 1:18-19).[39]

This is what is "immediate" for Dewey, the "gross, macroscopic, crude subject-matters in primary experience" (*EN*, 3; *LW* 1:15), which provide the beginning and the end of all reflection. This immediate world is not the immediate world of traditional empiricism, the world of sense data or "ideas," for these have already come under the cast of philosophical reflection trying to solve "the problem of knowledge." Rather, it is the immediate world of life and action where "things" function *in* experience. Dewey's radical formulation of empiricism, then, would have it begin with the lifeworld as the primary fact; immediacy is "worldy" or, in Dewey's terms, "situational," long before it exists for knowledge in inquiry. Before the world is "experienced-as" phenomenon or "encountered as" providing the material for inquiry, it is *there* and we are *in* it; it is the *way* we are in a situation—that is to say, the situation itself—which is ultimate. A profitable analogy can be drawn to Heidegger's use of *Dasein* for human existence. *Da* means not simply "there" (*dort*), but "here" and "now" as well. Human existence does not fill up space but situates itself, has place, not just in a present instant but in terms of past and future which are filled with plans, concerns, and attitudes. This becomes clearer in Dewey's later philosophy as he develops his theory of situations. In *Logic: The Theory of Inquiry*, Dewey asserts that:

The immediately given is an extensive qualitative *situation*, and . . . that emergence of separate qualities is the result of operations of observation. . . . In other words, they are functional distinctions made by inquiry within a total field for the sake of control of conclusions. . . . Existences *are* immediately given in experience; that is what experience primarily *is*. They are not given *to* experience but their giveness *is* experience. But such immediate qualitative experience is not itself cognitive; it fulfills none of the logical conditions of knowledge and of objects *qua* known (*LTI*, 517, 522; *LW* 12:509-10, 514).

Dewey concluded his essay, "The Postulate of Immediate Empiricism," with the claim:

> From the postulate of empiricism . . . nothing can be deduced, not a single philosophic proposition. . . . But the real significance of the principle is that of a method of philosophical analysis—a method identical in kind (but differing in problem and hence in operation) with that of the scientist. . . . Such a method is not spectacular; it permits of no offhand demonstrations of God, freedom, immortality, nor of the exclusive reality of matter, or ideas or consciousness, etc. But it supplies a way of telling what all these terms mean (*IDP*, 238-39; *MW* 3:165-66).

From this it is clear that Dewey's position at this time is anti-metaphysical; like other thinkers in this century, Dewey wished philosophy to stand for a method which would circumvent traditional metaphysical dilemmas and bring thought into contact with "the things themselves." Dewey's conclusion is put too extremely, however, for a number of "philosophic propositions" are immediately inferable from the article. Nor does Dewey clarify how the philosophical method is like the scientific in anything more than a general way of trying to describe and solve problems in terms of contexts and consequences. It is important to note that Dewey regards his method of experience as both a method of immediacy and one which leads to *meaning*.

As many critics asked, how was Dewey to resolve his emphasis on immediacy with the need for mediated, rational knowledge? He seemed to have left no place for mediation at all.[40] In a footnote later appended to the essay, Dewey said that the article:

> Is not a denial of the necessity of "mediation," or reflection in knowledge, but is an assertion that the inferential factor must *exist*, or must occur, and that all existence is direct and vital, so that philosophy can pass upon its nature . . . only by first ascertaining what it exists or occurs *as*. . . . There is nothing in the text to imply that things exist in experience atomically or in isolation . . . [or] that denies the existence of things temporally prior to human experiencing of them. Indeed, I should think it fairly obvious that we experience most things *as* temporally prior to our experiencing of them (*IDP*, 240; *MW* 3:166-67).

In other words, Dewey seems paradoxically to assert that things are what they are experienced as, and that *some* things are experienced as existing prior to being experienced.

In one sense, Dewey can be seen as trying to revise his "psychological standpoint" articulated twenty years earlier. Both the standpoint and the postulate are dedicated to giving an account of experience in its integrity and are opposed to abstracted substitutions for it. Both try to advance themselves as methods rather than doctrines, appealing to science as an example. Both take what can be called a functional stance toward experience. The difference is that Dewey has abandoned any hypothesis about a final absolute or transcendental perspective which determines experience. Instead he has taken a relativistic standpoint: there are any number of different perspectives, and some views may work better than others, but no one has a privileged view.

While the earlier theory viewed the subject, the Absolute Self, as the ground of all experience, Dewey would eventually locate perspectives within interactions as functions of situations. In other words, the situation as a transactional involvement replaced the Self of idealism.

Gradually Dewey realized that his hope of regrounding a theory of experience by a purely methodological postulate was inadequate. The postulate of immediate empiricism had asked, in effect, philosophers to forget the history of philosophy and all the theoretical interpretations which had separated experience from reality or assumed that experience could be legitimately taken to be essentially an instance of knowledge. One could not simply wipe the slate clean and begin by taking experience in its full, lived, prereflective, worldly complexity. What was needed was a theoretical reinterpretation of experience which could overcome and radically call into question the previous interpretations: the only way to overcome one theory had to be through theory itself. In short, Dewey recognized that a metaphysics of experience had to be undertaken. The culmination of this was *Experience and Nature*, which sustains a prolonged dialectic with the major interpretations of experience and reality throughout its pages. Unfortunately, here too Dewey's reliance on terms long familiar to the very positions his theory called into question, such as "experience," "nature," "ends," "means," and not least, "metaphysics," frequently betrayed him. It is crucial in understanding Dewey to recognize from the outset that these terms stand for things which are questions to be investigated rather than concepts which we have ready to hand. The theoretical inquiry into such problems was what Dewey meant by "metaphysics"; the inquiries undertaken by this discipline would in principle restore the continuity Dewey sought. The signposts for reflective inquirers revealed by such investigations were the "generic traits" which belonged to existence as such, which grounded all inquiry, action, knowing, and having. These traits would methodologically replace the postulate of immediate empiricism; they would reveal the precognitive origins of knowing and the aesthetic fulfillment of experience as inherent and significant issues for philosophical reflection.

III. The Generic Traits of Existence

In 1905 Dewey left the University of Chicago for Columbia, where he came under the influence of the Aristotelian scholar and naturalist F. J. E. Woodbridge. This was also the period in American philosophy when realism was being strongly advocated by Montague, Bush, Perry, Sellars, Lovejoy, and others, and in as many different versions. As Dewey's daughter Jane wrote:

> Dewey found himself at Columbia in a new philosophical atmosphere. By 1905 the realistic movement was in the forefront of philosophy. It was represented at Columbia by Woodbridge. . . . Woodbridge accepted and taught the naturalistic metaphysics of the Aristotelian type. Contact with him made Dewey aware of the possibility and value of a type of metaphysical philosophy which did not profess to rest upon principles not empirically verifiable.[42]

There are many similarities between Woodbridge's naturalism and Dewey's. Both, for example, are pluralists, that is to say, antireductionistic naturalists. Both see subjects and objects in a functionally related rather than constitutive manner. Both regard metaphysics as an empirical and hypothetical enterprise and both importantly find a place for a category of potentiality in nature. But there is one significant and problematic difference. Woodbridge was much closer to the classical Aristotelian view of knowledge. Not only does he treat knowing as a paradigmatic form of experience (which, as we have seen, Dewey rejects), but knowledge is the realization of the objective structure of nature. Knowing for Dewey marks an active transformation of the situation. Dewey kept his idealist heritage in this one respect, although he naturalized it as far as possible. Instead of regarding knowledge as the product of an a priori spiritual power, knowing was the actual transformation of an indeterminate situation into a determinate one. A potter, for example, is someone who has come to know clay through a long process of exploring the potentialites of the material and developing his own habits of sensitive, creative response. We say he "knows" clay because he can transform a lump of fine dust into a beautiful glazed jar or a sculpture which is expressive because of the powerful way the material has been organized. Instead of a state of "knowledge," for Dewey we should, as Georges Dicker suggests, speak of a process of coming-to-know. [43] For an Aristotelian like Woodbridge, knowledge has to consist in the identity of form in the mind with the object. For Dewey, knowing is realizing the potentialities of the situation through active inquiry and toward an end. In other words, the object of knowledge will be in a significant sense *different* from the original material with which the process began. But it will not be *discontinuous*. If the result of inquiry is entirely disconnected with the subject-matter, it will not even be identified as a "result." The full implications of Dewey's view will only be clear once his conception of continuity is discussed, but it is clear that this idea is far broader than that of a mere isomorphic relation.

It would also be illuminating to grasp Woodbridge's understanding of metaphysics before examining Dewey's. Woodbridge agreed with Aristotle's characterization of metaphysics as "first philosophy," i.e., "a science which investigates existence as existence and whatever belongs to existence as such. It is identical with none of the sciences which are defined less generally."[44] Specifically, said Woodbridge,

> With Aristotle, we may define metaphysics as the science of existence and distinguish it from other departments of knowledge by its generality and its lack of attention to those specific features of existence which make many sciences an intellectual necessity. Existence, considered generally, presents itself as an affair of connected varieties, and consequently, as an onward movement. . . . Metaphysics proposes thus both an analysis and a theory of existence; it is descriptive, and it is systematic.[45]

In other words, metaphysics is the description of omnipresent traits in any and all kinds of beings, beings which are inter-related and in process. Thus Woodbridge suggests that metaphysics be both empirical and hypothetical, differing from the sciences only in terms of generality. Unfortunately, Woodbridge does not specify either a methodology or what testability would signify in such an enterprise, though ultimately what he seems to have in mind is a reflective historical discipline which gives a comprehensive and functional order to all other departments of knowledge grounded upon the idea of evolution and natural teleology.

It is clear that Dewey's idea of metaphysics as a quest for the "generic traits" of nature founded on "the principle of continuity" owes much to Woodbridge. In "The Subject-Matter of Metaphysical Inquiry," Dewey distinguished between the sort of metaphysics which sought transcendental causes and that concerned with "certain irreducible traits found in any and every subject of scientific inquiry"

(*ENF*, 213; *MW* 8:4). Here, in 1915, Dewey is still dominated by the ideal of scientific method and obviously conceives of metaphysics as a science of sciences, still concerned with truth. Metaphysics, in other words, is a *cognitive* discipline and its object, Reality, is paradigmatically appropriated in a *cognitive* manner. Dewey distinguishes metaphysics from science by noting that whereas the latter would deal with the conditions and causes of evolution, for example, "metaphysics would raise the question of the sort of world which *has* such an evolution, not the question of the sort of world which causes it" (*ENF*, 213; *MW* 8:4). The *implications* of Dewey's view are thus not simply to arrive at cognitive claims but to reground such claims within the primary context of the full lived situation; The *world* is that which makes metaphysics *possible*. Like Woodbridge, Dewey appealed to Aristotle as a paradigm of this manner of approach, though, unlike Aristotle, he stresses that metaphysicians should seek only to analyze and describe without the ulterior motive to "eulogize" the stable, intelligible, or formed aspects of being over the precarious, changing, or material aspects. With regard to the term "metaphysics" itself, he says:

> The name at least has the sanction of the historical designation given to Aristotle's consideration of existence as existence. But it should be noted that we also find in Aristotle the seeds . . . of the conception of metaphysics rejected above. For he expressly gives the more general traits of existence the eulogistic title "divine" and identifies his first philosophy with theology. . . . But unless one approaches the study with theological presuppositions, there is . . . no ground for thinking that they are any better or any worse . . . than other traits . . . (*ENF*, fn., 215-16; *MW* 8:6-7).

While Dewey's primary concern here is obviously the positive relation of metaphysics to the sciences, as Gouinlock notes, it was later correctly broadened to include existence as revealed in *all* types of experience:

> Dewey might seem to suggest that metaphysics is concerned with the subject-matter of any *scientific* inquiry. In his subsequent works as he developed his notion of metaphysics, he persisted in the endeavor of "detection and description of the generic traits of existence," while rejecting any suggestion that this mode of inquiry was confined only to the examination of man's cognitive transactions with nature or only to those subject matters with which scientists are concerned.[47]

In one sense, Dewey's metaphysics is the broadest application of the postulate of immediate empiricism; it is an attempt to take account of the way things are as revealed through experience. This, in turn, was to provide a basis for intelligent, experimental conduct. Unfortunately, Dewey never specified how the methodology was to be systematically applied or provided a simple list of the generic traits of nature. In "The Subject-Matter of Metaphysical Inquiry," he lists traits of nature which tend to be revealed through the inquiries of the natural sciences, e.g., diversity, interation, and change. Dewey's ambiguity on what these traits are and why they are significant led Rorty to argue that either they were covert, transcendental "causes" and so typical of traditional metaphysics, or they were trivial because, being ubiquitous, they were uninformative.

Rorty ignores the fact that Dewey speaks of the awareness of these traits as "the beginning of wisdom" (EN, 413; LW 1:309).[48] Philosophy for Dewey is ultimately concerned with both criticism and evaluation, and without an attempt to note the generic traits of existence as existence, it is futile. The generic traits are not only the result of the "denotative method" carried to its limit, but they are the determining horizons of those contexts establishing the "universes of discourse" which make meaning and criticism possible. But Dewey's use of the phrase "existence as existence" easily lends suspicion to the relation of Dewey's enterprise to classical metaphysics. Unlike Aristotle's science of Being qua Being, Dewey's approach does not begin with an attempt to *evaluate* the candidates for being or *ousia* (form, matter, the universal, etc.), but with the attempt to *describe* reality as it is encountered through experience in all its forms. Metaphysics for Dewey provides the grounds for our evaluations, but when it takes itself as an evaluative enterprise, it commits the fallacy of "selective emphasis." Metaphysics may be better understood as the broadest, most comprehensive *search* or *inquiry* into an adequate understanding of experience and nature as a transactional whole. Its concepts would provide the regulative contextualizations for all other, special inquiries. In other words metaphysics would act by keeping open the general problematic dimension of the nature of all inquiries, thereby checking their tendency to claim that their special, unique determining concepts in fact provide universal grounding paradigms of interpretation.

Experience and Nature is Dewey's attempt to form a comprehensive exposition of his naturalism, especially his naturalist metaphysics. Three ideas are basic to this endeavor: the denotative method, the generic traits of nature, and the idea of philosophy as criticism. The denotative method is essentially Dewey's old postulate of immediate empiricism, "things are as they are experienced as," applied to the phases of experience. All inquiry, regarded functionally, begins and ends with our involvements in the contexts of ordinary experience, no matter how abstract the actual inquiry may be. This means that any inquiry begins and ends with certain determining conditions which are just those aspects of the situation which are necessarily taken for granted in order for a specific inquiry to be possible and have significance. Experience cannot be understood or made to mean if one initiates inquiry by a "universal doubt"; one only achieves the paradoxical condition of being dogmatic and hypocritical at once, as Peirce observed against Descartes.[49]

We are better off taking the "fallibilistic" attitude of being able to acknowledge that at any point inquiry may demand we question what was otherwise assumed. In other words, experience should control inquiry or, rather, the *situation* should. This means, as Dewey's postulate stated, taking the determining context as regulative:

> Experience includes dreams, insanity, illness, death, labor, war, confusion, ambiguity, lies and error. . . . The value of experience as method in philosophy is that it compels us to note that *denotation* comes first and last, so that to settle any . . . doubt, . . . we must go to some thing pointed to, denoted, and find our answer in that thing. . . . It asserts the finality and comprehensiveness of the method of pointing, finding, showing, and the necessity of seeing what is pointed to and accepting what is found in good faith and without discontent (*EN* 1st ed., 10; *LW* 1:371-72).

Dewey's use of the terms "denotation" and "pointing" are ambiguous. Long before Wittgenstein, Dewey recognized that any act of pointing required a defining context of shared life activity. In *Logic: The Theory of Inquiry*, Dewey recounts the anthropologist Malinowski's story of asking the boys of a tribe for the word for table:

> There were five or six boys standing around, and tapping the table with my forefinger I asked 'What is this?' One boy said it was *dodela*, another that it was *etanda*, a third stated that it was *bokali*, a fourth that it was *elamba*, and the fifth said it was *meza*." After congratulating himself on the richness of the vocabulary of the language the visitor found later "that one boy had thought he wanted the word for tapping; another understood we were seeking the word for the material of which the table was made; another had the idea that we required the word for hardness; another thought we wished the name for that which covered the table; and the last . . . gave us the word, *meza*, table" (*LTI*, 53; *LW* 12:59).

Given, then, that Dewey does not believe that we can begin with a neutral, interpretation-free method of denotation, how can we use the denotative method to settle doubt? The solution to this paradox lies in remembering that the lifeworld is primarily noncognitive, contextual, and social. We do not begin our inquiries, especially metaphysical ones, except under certain defining situations. Unless one has lived and interacted with others, learned a language and participated in a culture with its stories and traditions, one cannot even begin asking questions. Questions which concern the general nature of things only arise after a culture has provided a rich, symbolic, cultural matrix and has come to the point where, as with the Greeks, the idea of inquiry itself had been discovered. To paraphrase Aristotle, although the questions dealt with in "First Philosophy" are primary, in the order of inquiry they come last, not first. The quest, then, for the generic traits of existence only makes sense in the context of a culture which has *already* developed habits of inquiry, reflection and speculation and encountered the problematic questions such pursuits raise. The reason Dewey appeals to denotation as coming "first and last" is that we need to locate *inquiry* itself, and it is located within the more general context of the world as encountered, lived, enjoyed, and suffered by human beings. In short, the denotative approach is the necessary acknowledgment of our humanity as well as our remembrance of the world which is there prior to our speculations and which remains after our theorizing is ended. Even the most abstract reflective enterprises cannot transcend the world or those beings who are reflecting. And the whole thrust of Dewey's approach is based on the point that the world is more than what it is during our moments of inquiry and reflection.

On what ground, then, does Dewey justify introducing such a notion as "the generic traits of nature"? Dewey is quite direct in stating that the purpose of *Experience and Nature* is to "discover some of these general features" and "to interpret their significance for a philosophic theory of the universe in which we live . . ." (EN, 2; LW 1:14). Clearly, Dewey believes that he can show, point to, or denote certain general features of "existence as existence" which are found in "existence of all kinds" and which occur in every "universe of discourse." An analogy might be drawn here to Aristotle's list of categories, which indicates the various ways in which beings are and how we speak of them. The matter is not so simple, however. Dewey never gave a complete list of these traits (for example, at various places he mentions: transaction, the precarious, the stable, qualities or ends, means or relations, histories and processes, individuality, community, selectivity, continuity, emergence, potentiality, actuality, time, process, and history).[50] Nor does Dewey ever indicate how he arrives at them, except to say that they are encountered through empirical inquiry.

But he is involved in a deeper problem. Obviously some of these traits do not occur in existences of all types, but are found uniquely in human situations, e.g., the social, which Dewey described as the most inclusive category of all.[51] On the one hand Dewey seems to be trying to describe nature as it exists both in and outside of human experience, and on the other he seems to be describing the conditions of human experience alone. This confusion has led such critics as Bernstein to the conclusion that Dewey's philosophy hung between naturalism and idealism without healing the breech. Here come Thayer's and Santayana's charges of "animism."

I think it would be helpful to recall that Dewey's appeal to these generic traits occurs in a work which is largely involved with an analysis of a two-thousand five-hundred year old philosophical tradition and what role it has in a contemporary culture in which scientific methodology is directed solely toward obtaining knowledge while the realm of human moral and political life is left to the winds of chance, ideology, or religious dogma. The quest for the generic traits arises out of the inherent possibility of reflective experience to isolate itself, to claim to be autonomous, imperious, and uninvolved with the living problems of human existence. The generic traits will attempt to reveal *to inquiry* its contextual origin and its moral obligations. In one sense, Dewey seeks here what might be called a transcendental or hermeneutic exploration of reflective experience. What is revealed in the objects of *all* reflective experience ("theories") is nothing less than that they have at each and every moment presupposed the larger world which acts as their ground, their origin, their material, and their true end. Without this very special enterprise, the possibility will always remain that inquiry will forget its origin and its end. It will then become a sterile and parasitic occupation, or, at the least, a mere Rortian "conversation." Such projects are, from the Deweyan standpoint, obviously possible, but ultimately self-deceptive and self-ignorant.

Thus Dewey insists that inquiry into the generic traits is vital for philosophy's role as a higher form of criticism. They are permanent warnings against taking a reductionistic attitude by way of framing a vision or *theoria* of nature. This is only possible if they are regarded as *ways* of being, as tools which can make experience meaningful. If one keeps in mind Dewey's early desire to see experience wholly and functionally, it is easy to realize that Dewey saw his quest for the generic traits as a means of attaining this ideal of keeping faith with nature and experience.[52]

Second, Dewey is attempting to point to the fact that nature grows or evolves. Whatever we say of the universe, it is such that life, consciousness, meaning, science, and art arises within it. This is to say that nature has potentialities which are actualized upon certain conditions. It is absurd, according to Dewey, to argue that, because matter is a condition of consciousness, either consciousness is an unreal by-product of a fundamentally material universe or matter is an unreal or degraded form of an underlying conscious reality. "The only way to avoid a sharp separation between the mind which is the center of the processes of experiencing and the natural world," states Dewey, "is to acknowledge that all modes of experiencing are ways in which some genuine traits of nature come to manifest realization" (EN, 24; LW 1:30-31). In this sense, Dewey can be classified as an emergent naturalist. As will be seen, in this view potentiality must play a crucial role.

In what sense are the generic traits generic? If one ceases to try to regard them as fixed constitutive essences instead of broad general ways in which situations behave, the problem becomes easier.[53] As Gouinlock notes:

> It seems to be entirely within the spirit of Dewey's enterprise to say that metaphysical inquiry can be concerned with developing from particular subject matters concepts of the widest possible applicability, even though such applicability may not turn out to be generic.[54]

In other words, the generic traits are interpretive and critical tools which provide a denotative context for keeping situations, experience and nature continuous. They are also of existence as existence; i.e., they indicate how, in a general way, various aspects of nature are integrated functionally within situations. This is why they *work* as critical instruments: A tool which in no way corresponds to the nature of what it works upon will not work.

A final word should be said then about Dewey's idea of philosophy as criticism. Both metaphysics and the denotative method are united by this goal.

> The interests of empirical and denotative method and of naturalistic metaphysics wholly coincide. The world must be such as to generate ignorance and inquiry; doubt and hypothesis, trial and temporal conclusions . . . The ultimate evidence of genuine hazard, contingency, irregularity and indeterminateness in nature is thus found in the occurrence of thinking. The traits natural existence which generate the fears and adorations of superstitious barbarians generate the scientific procedures of disciplined civilization (EN, 69-70; LW 1: 62-63).

Philosophy, as "love of wisdom," meant a concern with value, a reconstruction of the meanings which inhibit experience from consummatory realization. Dewey therefore sees philosophy as "inherently criticism, having its distinctive position among the various modes of criticism in its generality; a criticism of criticisms as it were" (*EN*, 398; *LW* 1:298). The denotative method keeps an eye on the concrete situations and the many ways they manifest themselves in experience. Description is not value-neutral, however. It exists as an evaluative attitude which takes an active, participatory role in the world. Metaphysics provides a generic intelligibility within which criticism operates. The metaphysical enterprise itself makes sense only within the broader context of philosophy as the pursuit of wisdom, i.e., as human conduct made luminous and consummatory through intelligence. Philosophy must not only see situations as unique but as continuous; the study of generic traits achieves this while at the same time acting as a prophylactic against the blinders of dualistic thinking and "the fallacy of selective emphasis." The task of philosophy, for Dewey, is to liberate and clarify meanings: " 'Social reform' is conceived in a Philistine spirit, if it is taken to mean anything less than precisely the liberation and expansion of the meanings of which experience is capable" (*EN*, 411; *LW* 1:307). This is the very alpha and omega of Dewey's thought.

Together, these three aspects of Dewey's philosophy, the denotative method, the description of the generic traits, and the role of philosophy as criticism, converge to an important conclusion. Philosophy is not concerned with truth per se but with *meaning*. Of course this includes the meaning of "truth," but it is also equally concerned with meanings lying outside the scientific domain—moral and aesthetic meanings for instance. Philosophy is neither dictator nor handmaid to the sciences; it is the human drive for understanding and living with meaning in its broadest expression:

> As to truth . . . philosophy has no pre-eminent status; it is a recipient not a donor. But the realm of meanings is wider than that of true-and-false meanings; it is more urgent and more fertile. When the claim of meanings to truth enters in, then truth is indeed pre-eminent. But this fact is often confused with the idea that truth has a claim to enter everywhere . . .; a large part of our life is carried on in a realm of meanings to which truth and falsity as such are irrelevant. And the claim of philosophy to rival or displace science as a purveyor of truth seems to be mostly a compensatory gesture for failure to perform its proper task of liberating and clarifying meanings (*EN*, 410-11; *LW* 1; 307).

In his important essay, "Philosophy and Civilization," Dewey states:

> Meaning is wider in scope as well as more precious in value than is truth. . . . Truths are but one class of meanings. . . . Beyond this

land of meanings which in their own nature are true or false lies the ocean of meanings to which truth and falsity are irrelevant. We do not inquire whether Greek civilization was true or false, but we are immensely concerned to penetrate its meaning. We may indeed ask for the truth of Shakespeare's *Hamlet* or Shelley's *Skylark*, but by truth we now signify something quite different from that of scientific statement and historical record. In philosophy we are dealing with something comparable to the meaning of Athenian civilization or of a drama or a lyric. Significant history is lived in the imagination of man, and philosophy is a further extension of the imagination into its own prior achievements. . . . Knowledge . . . marks in the end but an enrichment of consciousness, of the area of meanings. Thus scientific thought itself is finally but a function of the imagination in enriching life with the significance of things (*PC*, 4-5; *LW* 3:4-5).

Dewey's attitude toward philosophy is that it should strive to encompass the whole of human experience and see that experience as firmly grounded in nature, conceiving nature in the broadest way possible. Metaphysics discerns this connection by seeking the generic traits within every "universe of discourse." A universe of discourse is the immediate informing context for the significance of a situation. The system of meanings which renders an experiment in biology significant is a different type of system from that which constitutes the background for a brilliant interpretation of *Hamlet*. But instead of allowing these universes to go their separate ways, philosophy should attempt to see them both in terms of human experience and nature. As Dewey puts it, "A universe of experience is the precondition of a universe of discourse. Without its controlling presence, there is no way to determine the relevancy, weight, or coherence of any designated distinction or relation. The universe of experience surrounds and regulates the universe of discourse but never appears as such within the latter," (*LTI*, 68; *LW* 12:74). There is always a tacit dimension, to use Polanyi's expression, providing the regulating sense of the context in any inquiry or experience. Words or categories have no meaning or use except as they function in situations; as they function in a situation they render it meaningful. Because philosophy is committed, in Dewey's eyes, to the wholeness and integrity of experience, it seeks for those generic traits which make the universe of discourse disclose the universe of experience in its functional wholeness. These traits therefore provide the "ground-map of criticism":

If philosophy be criticism, what is to be said of the relation of philosophy to metaphysics? For metaphysics, as a statement of the generic traits manifested by existences... seems to have nothing to do with criticism and choice. . . . It begins and ends with analysis and definition. When it has revealed the traits and characters that are sure to turn up in every universe of discourse, its work is done. So at least the argument may run. But the very nature of the traits discovered in every theme of discourse, since they are ineluctible traits of all existence, forbids such a conclusion. Qualitative individuality and constant relations, contingency and need, movement and arrest, are common traits of all existence. This fact is the source both of values and of their precariousness. . . . Any theory that detects and defines these traits is therefore but a groundmap of the province of criticism, establishing base lines to be employed in more intricate triangulations (*EN*, 412-13; *LW* 1; 308-09).

Dewey never suggests that this task is simple or finite; everything in his thought indicates the opposite. This does not mean that it is futile. Aristotle, long before, said that ever and again man must raise the question, "What is being?" For Dewey, this meant nothing short of establishing a completely honest integrity toward experience, of seeing nature as precarious, transient, and emergent as well as stable, structured, and universal. It meant seeing experience as extending beyond cognitive experience. This attitude also meant that instead of its previous role of privileged spectator, philosophy should take a participatory role in the onward flow and sense of events. The world or man may not admit of a final complete interpretation because they may not be something final or complete. We discover ourselves in nature as participants, interpretants, and creators rather than as onlookers. An honest metaphysics acknowledges this human and natural condition and does not try to escape it. For the most part philosophers have seen themselves as trying to chart the features of a stable territory or as framing the changless laws of a moral universe (notice how often even the critical Kant relies on geographical or legal metaphors). For Dewey, the task is rather one of maintaining an acutely sensitive and informed awareness of the whole creative and problematic project of human life. Metaphysics can then recognize itself as arising from the same human need as all our other projects, the need to inhabit the universe with the enjoyed, shared articulate sense of meaning and value.

IV. The Principle of Continuity in Experience and Nature

The ambiguity of Dewey's metaphysics of experience is not resolved by stressing philosophy's critical or interpretive function. The relation of experience to nature must be clarified even if one admits that nature is the sort of thing in which experience occurs. How is one to account, for example, for the rather human traits which Dewey seems to ascribe to nature in general? If nature is known only through experience, how can we distinguish between what is in nature itself and what is contributed by experience? Dewey regards this as a false dilemma. Nevertheless, critics have constantly tried to force Dewey's theory to provide a simple answer to this question when Dewey was in fact taking a profoundly novel approach to the problem. Upon the failure of Dewey's philosophy to "solve" this issue, the tags of "materialist" or "idealist" were attached, depending on the prejudices of the critic.

Dewey repeatedly describes the relationship between experience and nature as continuous. Not only is Dewey's "principle of continuity" the basis of his metaphysics of experience, but it is crucial for an understanding of his aesthetics as well. Most critics, however, have ignored this facet of Dewey's philosophy, and therefore they fail to understand some of the most fundamental features of what Dewey says.

The most common error is the confusion of continuity with identity. To assert continuity is not the same as asserting identity. Because Dewey asserted the continuity of experience and nature, Santayana understood him to be saying that experience and nature were identical, and so called Dewey an idealist. Cohen and Hocking made similar errors, while Bernstein, though recognizing Dewey's principle of continuity, failed to analyze it and consequently dismissed Dewey's discussion of the experience-nature relation. Continuity, as will be seen, is not just the link between Dewey's method of "immediate empiricism" and his theory of situations, it is the basis of his emergentism in *Art as Experience*.[55]

Dewey's attitude is not that experience is a barrier to the world; how would it be of use if it were? Before all else, experience is exactly the way we *do* become acquainted with the world and participate in it. Experience is an explorer, transformer, and liberator of nature. Through experience the ways and potentialities of things and ourselves become apparent. This was the new doctrine expressed in Dewey's postulate of immediate empiricism. In language much like Heidegger's, Dewey states that "experience and nature are not enemies or alien. Experience is not a veil that shuts man off from nature; it is a means of penetrating continually further into the heart of nature. There is in the character of human experience . . . a growing progressive self-disclosure of nature itself" (*EN*, x; *LW* 1:5). But by "self-disclosure," Dewey does not mean either an Hegelian process of self-recognition or a mystical manifestation of a transcendental realm. Scientific inquiry is a pre-eminent way in which nature discloses itself. New powers and aspects of nature are revealed by our activities which explore, discover, and determine possibilities of the world and the human situation. This is what "experience" means for Dewey; it is a structured process, not a "stuff" or substance. Contour plowing, the fission of the atom, penicillin, Beethoven's symphonies, the cathedral of Chartres, and the *Principia Mathematica* are types of experience— they are instances of articulate human exploration into the possibilities of nature taken in the most inclusive sense. Intelligence takes a material, whether it be agriculture, energy, bacteria, sound, a religious ideal, or a set of symbols, and shapes it so that new ways of its working or functioning are revealed. The form is not artificially imposed from without (if it were, chances are the product would *not* work) but comes from an inquiry and understanding of the nature of the material.

Experience is organically or functionally incorporated in nature, according to Dewey. As the next chapter will show, consciousness itself is but the tensive nexus of a situation, arising originally as a means of helping the organism interact and organize its interactions with the environment. From the start consciousness has a role to play in life; it is a way of participating in the world rather than being a superimposed spectator of events. Dewey's point that philosophy should begin with experience is therefore to be understood as urging our reflective inquiries to commence with an understanding of human *activity* and the sort of world disclosed *through* activity.

> These commonplaces take on significance when the relation of experience to the formation of a philosophic theory of nature is in question. They indicate that experience, if scientific inquiry is justified, is no infinitesimally thin layer or foreground of nature, but that it penetrates into it, reaching down into its depths, and in such a way that its grasp is capable of expansion; it tunnels in all directions and in so doing brings to the surface of the earth things at first hidden. . . . These commonplaces prove that experience is *of* as well as *in* nature. It is not experience which is experienced but nature— stones, plants, animals, diseases, health, temperature, electricity, and so on. . . . Experience thus reaches down into nature; it has depth. It also has breadth and to an indefinitely elastic extent. It stretches. That stretch constitutes inference (*EN*, 3a-1; *LW* 1:11-13).

Even though chronologically experience only appeared in the universe with the development of living organisms, occurring only under specific conditions, "when experience does occur . . . it enters into possession of some portion of nature and in such a manner as to render other of its precincts accessible," (*EN*, 1; *LW* 1: 12). A geologist today has access to information of the fossil record which, in his experience, reveals nature as it was long before man appeared. This information is in nature, but it is not easily obtained. A long process of scientific inquiry, conceptual refinement, testing, correlation, and observation lies in the background of the geologist's experience. It cannot be seriously denied, however, that his experience opens up nature as it was, say, 400 million years ago. To a person of no scientific education, the stone may merely be revealed *as* a stone. In this case experience is simply in the foreground of nature delimited by a narrow ambit of activity and interpretation. Before nature is penetrated it must be made to mean and work. That is, a stone can simply mean a small hard object which can be thrown, but it can also take on the broader meaning of being evidence of life 400 million years ago. This latter aspect opens up nature on a far more significant level. The stone is located within a far wider and richer field of intelligent activity.

In this sense, nature is "in" experience as much as experience is "in" nature. Experience can be considered as but one type of a number of events occurring in that realm of events called nature. Yet experience contains nature by being *of* it, by having events and their aspects as objects. Experience intends the world *because* it is in it. Experience is not only capable of responding to events as meaningful, or beholding an object *as* being a *what*, but it can also be a process by which an object can be related to other events and meanings, hence the "depth" and "elastic" nature of experience. In other words, the key to nature lies in the capacity of immediate experience to grow. As Dewey says, "The *intrinsic* nature of events is revealed in experience as the immediately felt qualities of things. The intimate coordination and even fusion of these qualities with the regularities that form the objects of knowledge . . . characterizes intelligently directed experience, as distinct from mere casual and uncritical experience" (*EN,* xii; *LW* 1:6). Immediacy reflects involvement in a situation which may be superficial or significant. The degree of continuity between experience and nature varies with how broad and deep the meaning of the situation is. But there must always be some degree of immediacy, for this is the *means* whereby the present experience can grow, develop or be related to others. We can go from perceiving an object *as* a rock to perceiving it *as* a fossil to perceiving it *as* proof of a special theory; in each case the object is in experience as what it is and as what it might become. The "rock" is not annihilated for the "fossil," nor does the simple fossil disappear for the "proof" anymore than the tapping noise disappeared for the blown window-shade. The experience grew in breadth and depth of meaning. The rock *became* the fossil which *became* the evidence for proof of a theory.

Experience and nature are related on the one hand by the fact that they function together in perspectives and on the other by the principle of continuity. Replying to Cohen and Hocking, Dewey emphasized the "importance of the category of perspectives" and stated that "this matter of perspectives is basic in the issue of the connection between nature and experience" ("Nature in Experience," in *ENF*, 245).[56] A perspective is simply the focused realization of articulation of an organized general, an interpretive stance of activity, or a "comportment toward the situation; it is a "seeing-as," the dawning of a significant aspect within a field of meaning. This is what is immediately perceived. It is a "take" on the world. It comprises the "what" and the "how" or the *way* the situation exists. Nature and experience, in other words, are dimensions of the structured transactions of organism and environment and of self and world which at each moment have a qualitative, organic continuity making it *that* situation. Experience and nature have a relational dynamic side, as well as a qualitative side, which are aspects of situations as functional wholes.

Dewey never fully developed his theory of continuity. But he constantly appeals to it at crucial moments in most of his writings. "Restoration of continuity is shown to do away with the mind-body problem," he claims at one instance, concluding that "the continuity of nature and experience is shown to resolve many problems that become only the more taxing when continuity is ignored" (*EN*, xiv-xv; *LW* 1: 8). Dewey in fact claims that it is the purpose of *Experience and Nature* to replace the traditional separation or opposition of experience and nature "by the idea of continuity" (*EN*, xvi; *LW* 1:9). In his essay, "The Inclusive Philosophical Idea," Dewey appeals to the principle methodologically. Referring to the traditional separation of the natural and the social (a dualism rejected by Dewey), he says, "A denial of the separation is not only possible to a sane mind, but is demanded by any methodological assumption of the principle of continuity—if that be termed a hypothesis which cannot be denied without self-contradiction . . ." (*PC*, 81; *LW* 3:45). Dewey accuses critics like Santayana of having "an underlying postulate that there is a breach of continuity between nature and man and hence between nature and human experience" ("Nature in Experience," in *ENF*, 248). For Dewey, the principle of continuity connects naturalism with emergentism, i.e., with the theory that higher forms or modes arise from lower ones but cannot be reduced to them:

> The term "naturalistic" has many meanings. As it is here employed
> it means, on one side, that there is no breach of continuity
> between operations of inquiry and biological operations and physical

operations. "Continuity," on the other side, means that rational operations *grow out of* organic activities, without being identical with that from which they emerge. . . . The primary postulate of a naturalistic theory of logic is continuity of the lower (less complex) and the higher (more complex) activities and forms. The idea of continuity is not self-explanatory. But its meaning excludes complete rupture on one side and mere repetition of identities on the other; it precludes the reduction of the "higher" to the "lower" just as it precludes complete breaks and gaps. The growth and development of any living organism from seed to maturity illustrates the meaning of continuity (*LTI,* 18-19, 23; *LW* 12:26, 30).

This passage is Dewey's most direct analysis of his principle of continuity, though one could argue that *Experience and Nature* itself constitutes a sustained inquiry into as well as application of this principle. Dewey is saying in the passage above that continuity refers to increasing levels of organic functioning which exclude either the possibility of being reduced to one identical type or of being utterly disconnected into self-enclosed, autonomous categories. The organic model, so important for Dewey from the start of his career, achieves mature expression in this theory. The example of the growth of a plant cited above demonstrates that Dewey is using continuity as the principle of organic development. As will be seen, this involves not only a naturalistic, functional teleology, but a reintroduction of Aristotle's fundamental concepts of actuality and potentiality. Continuity, for Dewey, also refers to the realization of newer, more inclusive types of order. Speaking of Merleau-Ponty's very similar views, John Wild described emergentism as an account of "how a higher order is founded on a lower and in a sense contains it, but at the same time takes it over and integrates it into new structures which cannot be explained by those that are taken over."[57] This clearly has echoes of Hegel, rather than Aristotle, in that for Hegel the later, "higher" stages do preserve the earlier *Aufhebungen.* But for Hegel, the radical indeterminacy of Spirit fundamentally projects itself toward becoming completely determined or "rational." As will be seen, Dewey's account of emergence of new types of order rejects the Hegelian belief that this emergence is dialectically necessary, that at each step there is presupposed a totally determinate resolution or comprehensive meaning—the "Absolute." Dewey's later doctrine of continuity is firmly grounded on the Aristotelian concept of real potentiality or real indeterminacy as an irreducible feature of nature.

That continuity must involve an element of novelty is essential to

Dewey's principle; yet, this novelty cannot be viewed as an extranatural "superject" (as in Whitehead's theory):

> What *is* excluded by the postulate of continuity is the appearance upon the scene of a totally new outside force as a cause of changes that occur. . . . On the other hand, should the consideration of scientific investigation be that development proceeds by minute increments, no amount of addition of such increments will constitute *development* save when their cumulative effect generates something new and different (*LTI*, 24; *LW* 12:31).

Continuity is more than sheer identity or sameness in repetition; it is less than a complete *saltus naturae*. There must be difference, but it must grow out of a prior condition, i.e. be a functional development of it.

To understand this idea, it is necessary to appreciate that Dewey was cutting against the grain of the Western tradition which either denied the potential equal ontological status with the actual, or eliminated it altogether from nature.[58] Dewey was, in effect, striving to reintroduce this idea, as were such thinkers as Peirce, Mead, and Whitehead. While the original sense of continuity as a "holding together" (Latin, *continuitas*; Greek, *synecheia*) clearly refers to a whole constituted out of or composed of parts, as Aristotle's discussion demonstrates, that is to a unity which has diverse parts and is involved in a process of development, the modern notion suggests mere numerical order or succession, an actual infinite series composed of atomic discreta.[59] While the later interpretation has labored toward the view of an "actual infinite," the former is firmly committed to the doctrine that continuity is potentiality. It is not the purpose of this essay to prove Aristotle's theory against that of the modern period; rather, it is simply to show to what extent Dewey's philosophy relies upon it and that this feature of Dewey's thought has caused the misinterpretations of his philosophy discussed above.

Peirce himself stated that "once you have embraced the principle of continuity no kind of explanation of things will satisfy you except that they grew."[60] This is not to fall back into the "genetic fallacy": it is to attempt to see things as temporal, organic beings in processes of development conditioned by actual and potential features. That Dewey shares this view is amply demonstrated by his unique article, "Time and Individuality." There Dewey stresses that time is not some actual, infinite substance in which everything exists (the old Newtonian view). It is a feature of the nature of individuals, from sub-atomic particles to human beings, and this always involves an element of novelty, the realization of some potentiality, or, in Dewey's words, "the principle of a developing career applies to all things in nature . . ." (*ENF*, 236).

Dewey like Peirce rejects the mechanistic theory of time because it regards time essentially as static, rendering evolution an appearance at best. To do this means to reintroduce potentiality, but not in the sense of an inner, unfolding "power"; potentiality is realized through interaction, according to Dewey.[61] In this same article he says:

> The idea of development applied to nature involves differences of forms and qualities as surely as it rules out absolute breaches of continuity. . . . If we accept the intrinsic connection of time with individuality, [developments] are not the mere redistributions of what existed before. . . . First and negatively, the idea . . . is excluded that development is a process of unfolding what was previously implicit or latent. Positively it is implied that potentiality is a category of existence, for development cannot occur unless an individual has powers or capacities that are not actualized at a given time. But it also means that these powers are not unfolded from within, but are called out through interaction with other things. While it is necessary to revive the category of potentiality as a characteristic of individuality, it has to be revived in a different form from that of its classic Aristotelian formulation (*ENF*, 236-37).

Dewey insists that "potentialities must be thought of in terms of consequences of interactions with other things. Hence potentialities cannot be *known* till after the interactions have occurred" (*ENF*, 238). Dewey rejects, therefore, the idea that potentiality implies a fixed or predetermined end in any absolute sense; potentiality simply refers to "a characteristic of change" (*ENF*, 220).

Dewey, again like Peirce, conceives of potentiality as the "tychistic" factor in nature, i.e., the domain of "the precarious," the aleatory and chancy, undetermined, brute, and contingent face of things which Plato called the Receptacle and Aristotle *hylē*. Individuals are realized by the different potentialities actualized:

> Individuality, conceived as a temporal development, involves uncertainty, indeterminacy, or contingency. . . . To say this is not arbitrarily to introduce mere chance into the world. It is to say that genuine individuality exists; that individuality is pregnant with new developments; that time is real. The mystery of time is thus the mystery of the existence of real individuals (*ENF*, 239-40).

Pragmatism is therefore grounded on an interpretation of nature in which consequences and possibilities are regarded as real factors of the world, and the present moment involves the issue of the future. A theory of action only makes sense in a world where time is real, that is, where experience is understood as fundamentally temporal, Nature is *phusis*, ordered processes, and is inclusive of its possibilities and potentialities as well as of its existent actualities.

In the same essay, Dewey explicitly relates creative emergence in nature to art. Art reflects the nature of things most completely in experience. "Genuine time," he states, "if it exists . . . is all one with the existence of individuals as individuals, with the creative, with the occurrence of unpredicted novelties" (*ENF*, 241). Art is this creative individuality at work in its most heightened form:

> Art is the complement of science. . . . Art . . . is not only the disclosure of the individuality of the artist but is also a manifestation of individuality as creative of the future, in an unprecedented response to conditions as they were in the past. . . . The artist in realizing his own individuality reveals potentialities hitherto unrealized. This revelation is the inspiration of other individuals to make the potentialities real. . . . Those who have the gift of creative expression . . . disclose the meaning of the individuality of others to those others. In participating in the work of art, they become artists in their activity. . . . The fountains of creative activity are discovered and released. The free individuality which is the source of art is also the final source of creative development in time (*ENF*, 242-43).

This is to say that participating in the creative discloses the meaning of individual activity. In human experience, process can develop into a creative expression, involving the individual in the active participation with the world which culminates in aesthetic meaning. Art and the aesthetic are therefore as "ontological" for Dewey as for Heidegger, since they can disclose the meaning of our existence and of the world's. In fact, Dewey argues that "it is reasonable to believe that the most adequate definition of the basic traits of natural existence can be had only when its properties are most fully displayed—a condition which is met in the degree of the scope and intimacy of the interactions realized" (*EN*, 262; *LW* 1:201). This of course is when experience itself is most fully realized in art, in *"an* experience." While Dewey would not go so far as to say that art reveals the *truth* of nature, it does reveal the possibility in nature for the fulfillment of value and meaning. It reveals, in short, nature's capacity to be ideally reconstructed. This has immense philosophical and practical significance—it provides the very basis on which directed or intelligent action makes sense. Art reveals that nature has potentialities which can be discovered and realized through guided action and that some of these potentialities lend human existence what meaning and value it has.

Thus principle of continuity is the key to understanding the relation of experience and nature. Experience emerges from nature but is continuous with it. We should expect there to be an irreducibly novel aspect of experience as well as a firm continuation of natural processes. Experience is the actualization of potentialities in nature and as such tells us something about nature. Nature is included within the scope of experience just as experience arises out of nature. This is what justifies experience as a methodological principle; it is an inclusive way of natural functioning. Thus the principle of continuity is *both* metaphysical and regulative.[62] The principle is regulative in the sense that it continually stresses the *possibility* of establishing understood relations; it is the antidote to those dogmas which, as Peirce says, block the path of inquiry. The goal of the principle is growth and gradual expansion of interpretation. This methodological attitude, which has become recently popular with the rise of hermeneutics, is clearly expressed in the following passage from Dewey's "Nature in Experience":

> There is a circularity in the position taken regarding the connection of experience and nature. Upon one side, analysis and interpretation of nature is made dependent upon the conclusions of the natural sciences. . . . The other aspect of the circle is found in the fact that it is held that experience itself . . . contains the materials and the processes and operations which, when they are rightly laid hold of and used, lead to the methods and conclusions of the natural sciences; namely to the very conclusions that provide the means for forming a theory of experience. That this circle exists is not so much admitted as claimed. It is also claimed that the circle is not vicious; for instead of being logical, it is existential and historic (*ENF*, 246-47).

No interpretation is absolute; likewise, there is no privileged a priori standpoint from which knowledge deductively follows. The situation of human experience is that it is "existential and historic," that is, it finds itself in an open-ended, temporal world and in a cultural tradition; involvement and meaning are with us before "knowledge" ever becomes a question. Instead of trying to escape the circle of our being, Dewey suggests that we operate within it so that meaning grows and deepens, so that continuity is realized. Hence, as Dewey states, philosophy's role is constructive criticism, interpretation, evaluation, and the "liberation of meanings." Philosophy is the way of meaning in experience and the way of experience in nature; it regards these from the standpoint of continuity.

V. Situations and Qualities

It remains to examine in what way experience and nature are continuous. Dewey understands this continuity in terms of his theory of situations. Situations are *ousiai* for Dewey; they stand for the primary realities, the basic ontic individuals from which philosophic understanding proceeds. Situations, moreover, provide the basis for understanding aesthetic meaning—they are the wholes in terms of which the context qualitatively defines and reveals itself. Aesthetic quality is a development or an emergent from the general qualitative aspect of situations.

Experience, like nature, grows together to form wholes. In Whitehead's word, it concresces. The wholes which it realizes are organic, that is, they are functional, composed of working parts, oriented toward an end (they have a teleological structure), and they have beginnings and endings, that is, they have histories or an implicit narrative structure. The parts or elements of situations Dewey calls "events," "*res*," "interactions," "states of affairs," and "transactions." Each situation is qualitatively unique, moreover:

> To insist that nature is an affair of beginnings is to assert that there is no single and all-at-once beginning of everything. It is but another way of saying that nature is an affair *of* affairs, wherein each one, no matter how it may be linked up with the others, has its *own* quality. . . . The phrase constantly in our mouths, "states of affairs," is accurately descriptive, although it is sheer nonsense in both the traditional spiritual and mechanistic theories. There are no changes that do not enter into an affair, *Res*, and there is no affair that is not bounded and thereby marked off as a state or condition. When a state of affairs is perceived, the perceiving-of-a-state-of-affairs is a further state of affairs. Its subject-matter is a thing in the idiomatic sense of thing, *res*, whether a solar-system, a stellar constellation, or an atom, a diversified and more or less loose interconnection of events, falling within boundaries sufficiently definite to be capable of being approximately traced (*EN*, 97-101; *LW* 1:83-85).

The unity of a plurality of events or interactions mark it out as an affair or "event." The various "parts" become aspects of a certain subject, organized so that they cooperate to realize an end—they *become* parts. In conscious experience, this unity is qualitatively apprehended in a prereflective manner, as Dewey insisted from early in his career. We have seen how this was a characteristic of his idealist view of experience, but it is strongly set forth in the *Essays in Experimental Logic* as well and becomes the cornerstone of his aesthetic theory:

Philosophers in their excessively intellectual preoccupation with analytic knowing are only too much given to overlooking the primary import of the term "thing": namely, *res*, an affair, an occupation, a "cause"; something which is similar to having the grippe, or conducting a political campaign, or getting rid of an overstock of canned tomatoes, or going to school, or paying attention to a young woman:—in short, just what is meant in non-philosophic discourse by "an experience." Noting things as if they were objects—that is, objects of knowledge—continuity is rendered a mystery; qualitative, pervasive unity is too often regarded as a subjective state injected into an object which does not possess it. . . . One advantage of an excursion by one who philosophizes upon knowledge into primary non-reflectional experience is that the excursion serves to remind him that every empirical situation has its own organization of a direct, non-logical character (*EEL*, 5-6, *MW 10* 322-23).

Special attention should be paid to this passage. Situations or "*res*" are primarily organized, active, lived experiences unified by a prelogical or pre-analytical qualitative unity which gives them their continuity and sense. With James, Dewey did not want to read experience from its analytical, cognitive post mortem, though he certainly did not dismiss the need for analysis or cognition. Throughout Dewey's philosophy, analysis and knowing only live within the greater events of life and only become intelligible themselves when relocated in this larger context. Art and aesthetic experience capture this sense of the lived qualitative unity of continuously developing experience and make us aware of its sense-giving character far better than cognition alone does. The connection of the passage above to Dewey's aesthetics is evident in the phrase "an experience," a term which was to signify the essence of the aesthetic in *Art as Experience*.

Situations grow; they have temporal thickness. They are "about" a subject matter, and they have a teleological focus, an "intentional" dimension, i.e., something toward which they are oriented dynamically. In a letter to his philosophical collaborator, Arthur Bentley, Dewey said:

A good deal of what I have done is in fact to show that words to which philosophers have given primary (or directly "existential") meaning really designate a function served by some primary "affair". . . . The Latin *res*, usually translated *thing*, is definitely *affair, Res publica*, etc.[63]

In this sense, then, Dewey claims that "Every existence is an event" (*EN*, 71; *LW* 1:63). Events, as noted, however, are parts of situations. That is, they are "open" toward the possibility of "growing together" to form a continuous whole. "That all existences are *also* events I do not doubt," asserts Dewey, "for they are qualified by temporal transition. But that existences are *only* events strikes me as . . . ignoring of the context. For. . . every occurrence is a *concurrence*. An event is not a self-enclosed, self-executing affair. . ." (*KK*, 60). This should distinguish Dewey's metaphysics from those which opt for monadologies, like those of Leibniz, Newton, or Whitehead. Situations always remain to some degree open-ended for Dewey.

As developing wholes, situations are always open to the possibility of failure as well as realization; they may disintegrate or dissipate or may simply fall short of their ideal unity and integration. They have, as Dewey says, "tighter and looser ties" (*EN*, 271; *LW* 1:207). Situations as wholes are immediate, in the sense of being to at least some degree actualizations and fulfillments which *exist*, which become manifest in the here and now. Yet, as inherently temporal and complex, they are "mediated," composed of functioning parts, having histories and projects or possibilities toward future developments. Dewey stated in one late article, "From one angle, almost everything I have written is a comment on the fact that situations are immediate in their direct occurrence and mediated and mediating in the temporal continuum constituting life experience."[64] In another response he said, "I point out that in my general doctrine about judgment and verification, *situation* is the key word, and that a situation is held to be *directly and immediately qualitative*" (*PM*, 257). To Pepper, Dewey emphasized this idea as well, "Mr. Pepper in his comments on my esthetic theory makes words like coherence, whole, integration, etc., the ground of his criticisms rather than *situation*."[65]

Situations have philosophical priority for Dewey. But what are they ontologically? The examples given by Dewey, like being ill with the grippe, are distinctively human situations. Also, the fact that Dewey locates the unity or wholeness of the situation in its qualitative aspect indicates that he is thinking of situations in terms of conscious, experiencing beings. There is a strong argument to be made that when Dewey speaks of situations he is referring solely to events with human participants. Gouinlock explicitly states, "It must be recognized that 'situation' always implies for Dewey conscious human participation. If there were no human beings (or comparably sentient creatures) there would be no situations in nature."[66] This would explain why Dewey included within his generic traits of "existence as existence" such categories uniquely applicable to human experience as meaning, the social, histories, etc. In this sense, situations are ways human beings are in the world.

But what does this do to Dewey's principle of continuity? Is man a rupture with nature, existing in an isolated human universe which renders the rest of nature inaccessible in the manner of Kant? Reflecting back on Dewey's emergentism, we recall that any newer, more complex, or higher level does have an aspect which is irreducible and inexplicable in terms of what has preceded it. On the human level, nature exhibits traits not present in immediately precedent lifeforms. Sensation becomes experience, a conscious awareness of meaning, realized through directed activity, which is expressed and shaped through symbolic interaction, social participation, or culture. Yet, there is also that aspect which keeps continuity with the rest of nature. In being cultured beings we do not cease being biological ones, nor do biological beings cease being physical ones. Though consciousness (which for Dewey is the immediate existent event of meaning) may be a novel trait of nature, it is also a reorganization and utilization of materials which had the potentiality of entering into meaning-events. Dewey himself states:

> It is a reasonable belief that there would be no such thing as "consciousness" if events did not have a phase of brute and unconditioned "isness," of being just what they irreducibly are. Consciousness as sensation, image and emotion is thus a particular case of immediacy occurring under complicated conditions (*EN*, 86; *LW* 1:75).

I would interpret this as signifying that when Dewey speaks of the generic traits as being of "existence as existence," he is referring to those features of situations which are exhibited in some form, more or less developed, in all levels of nature at large. "Immediate awareness of meanings"—consciousness—in human situations is "involvement" with the environment in simply biological situations, and "interaction" or "brute existence" in simply physical ones. *All* situations therefore have "immediacy," but only human situations have *qualitative* immediacy; likewise, all situations are mediated or related, but only human situations *mean* through their relations. This can also be applied, I think, to Dewey's category of "the social," which is the most inclusive category because it contains and realizes all traits of human experience insofar as it reflects the highest fulfillment of nature's potentialities. All situations are characterized by what might be called "field interaction;" i.e., they do not exist atomically unrelated to other events but interact as parts of a field. An atom is a cooperation of numerous particles which interact to form a relatively stable order. On the biological level, we see creatures involved in a number of complex patterns of behavior with other creatures as well as their own kind, some of which evolve into symbiotic relationships. Bees, fish,

wolves, apes—all have developed behavior which, by analogy, naturalists call social. Human beings exhibit this behavior in the most
complex way and have transformed original biological instincts into
cultured experience. New potentialities are realized; a hand, once
merely a means of assisting the organism for survival, a tool for
grasping, can evoke the subtlest shades of meaning in a Japanese No
drama.

Thus it is true that situations *primarily* refer to human situations
for Dewey, since these most fully realize and exploit the potentialities
of nature, but they do not *exclusively* refer to human situations. When
situations are spoken of, their primary sense is determined by reference to the world of human interactions. But, by virtue of the principle of continuity, we should not dismiss the rest of nature as a pure
"in-itself," as in much continental philosophy. To sever man from
nature, and make it a mystery as Dewey tirelessly insists, is thereby
also to render man a mystery. On the other hand, man is not to be
understood simply in terms of other natural situations which help
constitute his being. Though Dewey himself was careless and unsystematic about this point, I think it is far more consistent with the view
presented by his philosophy than that suggested by such critics as
Santayana or Thayer who regard him as an animist, ascribing human
traits to all nature, or, at the other extreme, that suggested by those
who would see Dewey trying to reduce all human existence to Darwinian or biological categories.

Situations are characterized by "transactions," as Dewey came to
call the distinctive type of interactions which successfully create a
whole. It is important that when Dewey refers to the "organism" or
the "individual" or the "self," he is *not* referring to a unity, a primary
"thing." He is referring to part of a whole process or transaction. In a
situation,

> No one of its constituents can be *adequately* specified as fact apart
> from the specification of other constituents of the full subject mat-
> ter. . . . Transaction regards extension in time to be as indispensable
> as is extension in space. . . . Transaction assumes no preknowledge
> of either organism or environment alone s adequate, not even as
> respects the basic nature of the current conventional distinctions
> between them, but requires their primary acceptance in a system
> (*KK*, 69-70).

In a letter to Bentley, Dewey explained this idea further:

> I think a word like "situation" may be safely used, provided its use is
> accompanied by a statement that it does *not* mean environment in
> the sense of "surroundings" of an organism . . . "Situation," is a

name for the field-event in its own diversified unity of qualities, qualifications. . . . What has influenced my use of "situation" is the necessity for the definite acknowledgment of the intrinsic variety of qualities in every event as a durational-extensional affair. . . . The situational aspect is that which makes possible and which invites or demands the analysis in consequence of which an *event* is capable of treatment as complex.[67]

One must not think of "organism" and "environment" or "self" and "world" as separate and separable entities which come together and then "interact" (it was over such confusions that Dewey adopted the term "transaction" for his more customary "interaction"). The biological organism is merely a locus where a number of different processes are organized and redistributed. Dewey and Bentley both made sport of those who viewed the epidermis as the barrier between internal and external relations. For the sake of pointing out, we "define" the cougar or mountain lion by its visible shape; but any biologist knows that the animal inhales, excretes, establishes territory, catches prey, mates, and occupies a position in the ecology of its environment. The term "cougar" simply signifies an organized integration of complex relationships, activities, and events which incorporate a whole transactional field. To understand the cougar is to understand it transactionally rather than simply as an individual thing which one can point out in a zoo. Dewey's is one of the first explicitly ecological views of nature and consequently of knowledge.

> The anticipated future development of transdermally transactional treatment has, of course, been forecast by the descriptive spadework of the ecologies, which have already gone far enough to speak of the evolution of the habitat of an organism as well as of the evolution of the organism itself. . . . Ecology . . . is still fuller of illustrations of the transactional . . . where the observer lessens the stress on the separated participants and sees more sympathetically the full system of growth or change (*KK*, 125-28).

According to one recent theory, the earth's primitive atmosphere had no free oxygen. Consequently, deadly ultra-violet radiation bombarded the planet, making life possible only in a limited area which received light but was shielded, the immediate off-shore zones. Here life began, developing into oxygen releasing life-forms like algae: the more oxygen in the atmosphere, the less radiation, and so the greater expanse of habitable area. Eventually land-based life forms became possible. Lovelock's "Gaia Hypothesis," which sees the earth as one transactional, self-regulating life-system might be another case. The transactional attitude here is evident; it is being applied today even to the evolution of the elements and the universe itself. This is Dewey's principle of continuity in action. His theory of situations is one with the theory of continuity, that is, situations are concrete instances or exemplification of continuity.

A final remark about the structure of situations must be made. Dewey generally discusses situations in terms of what they are not: they are not mechanical, not static, and so on. Positively, however, we can note a number of features: they are spatio-temporal, organically unified, and developmental; they have diversified parts and phases, and they are both immediate and mediated. All situations have at their center a tensive aspect. In conscious human behavior this can often be described as the "problematic" aspect, like the frightful noise which initiates an inquiry. It is important to note that Dewey's "problematic situation" and his description of intelligence as "problem solving" are really attempts to point out the underlying tensive nature of all experience rather than a naive effort to reduce all human experience and thought to deliberative calculation, like adding up a bill.

All situations are marked by a "stable" or formed and structured aspect and by a "precarious" or dynamic aspect. Every structure in nature exists in relation to variability; in fact, structures emerge as means of coping, striving for homeostasis but having to undergo and adapt. Dewey regards consciousness itself as having emerged from the tensive relationship organisms have with their environments; consciousness was the focus in experience through which the organism strove to reorganize or "reconstruct" the situation. Consciousness arises from fulfilling a functional need; it is not a pure given. Dewey states that "reflection . . . arises because of the appearance of incompatible factors within the empirical situation. . . . [It] appears as the dominant trait of a situation when there is seriously the matter . . .; when . . . a situation becomes tensional" (*EEL*, 9-11; *MW 10* 326).[68] The prereflective behavior and habits of the organism provide a structured basis against which consciousness functions and upon which it can draw. We are "in the world" in a variety of active ways long before we ever have to reflect consciously on how we are in a situation. "My thesis," says Dewey, is that "the intellectual element is set in a context which is non-cognitive and which holds within it in suspense a vast complex of other qualities and things that in the experience itself are objects of esteem or aversion, of decision, or use, of suffering, of endeavor and revolt, not of knowledge" (*EEL*, 4; *MW* 10:322).

Situations, then, are marked by a "focus area" which in human experience becomes the domain of consciousness, i.e., the domain of meanings. Within consciousness itself, deliberation marks only a phase of consciousness. Dewey is claiming, in other words, that situations are structured in terms of "foreground" and "background" and that even the most critical moment of rational thinking operates only as the center of a vast and dimly apprehended field of non-cognitive experience. When we select rational consciousness as the criterion against which all other experience is measured and set it apart from its functional locus in the world, not only is the world of meaningful but non-cognitive experience dismissed as "meaningless" emotive ejaculations, but the nature of reason itself is rendered opaque and mysterious. One can anticipate that Dewey will find aesthetic experience rather than cognitive experience capable of illuminating the field of non-cognitive meanings, the horizonal "wholeness" of the situation, within which reason functions and receives *its* meaning. Existence and meaning are contextual:

> Another trait of every *res* is that it has focus and context: brilliancy and obscurity, conspicuousness or apparency, and concealment or reserve, with a constant movement of redistribution. Movement about an axis persists, but what is in focus constantly changes. "Consciousness," in other words, is only a very small and shifting portion of experience. . . . *In* the experience, and in it in such a way as to *qualify* even what is shiningly apparent, are all the physical features of the environment extending out into space . . . and all the habits and interests extending backward and forward in time of the organism. . . . I . . . only point out that when the word "experience" is employed . . . it means just such an immense and operative world of diverse and interacting elements (*EEL*, 6; *MW 10*:323).

As the passage above says, conscious experience is "qualified" by the situation as a whole. This is no idle remark on Dewey's part; it is the solution to his troublesome "theory of quality" which, as we saw, caused so much misunderstanding. The function of consciousness is to grasp the problematic, tensive features of a situation and redirect them by intelligent reconstruction. In short, consciousness is the attempt to grasp a situation *as* a situation. It tries to bring the situation into focus. If we did not realize that we were in a situation that called for a definite response, e.g., braking to avoid a collision, we would not respond. We must, if the world is to make sense, be able in some way to see it contextually in terms of situations. The wholeness of the situation is extended in space and time and is an ongoing and developing affair. If it is to retain its unity as *a* situation, that wholeness must be sensed in the phase which is consciousness. In other words, consciousness is a response to the wholeness of the situation qualitatively at each moment and this sense of the situation as a whole is what determines the situation and directs it. The qualitative character of the situation, moroever, is fundamentally temporal and teleological.

The "quality" of the situation is neither "in" the sentient organisms nor "in" the object. The quality is only in the situation and is of it. The fallacy of simple location has plagued epistemology, in Dewey's opinion, especially since the rise of the modern period and its tendency to separate "minds" from the world and to regard them as things rather than as integrated activities. We are tempted to place consciousness and its modes in the mind (or, for the materialists, in the brain) because that is the place of control. That is, if a person has trouble with vision, we become concerned with his eye; a neurologist, concerned with the role of the nervous system, can locate key areas of the brain whose dysfunction results in cognitive, motor, or other defects. The epistemologist or the neurologist, selecting a phase of the whole situation and emphasizing it, disregards the other significant factors and so reifies the focus of his interest, treating the mind or the brain as a self-sufficient thing. The object, however, is merely an abstraction from its sense-giving context. This tendency is not uncommon; the average person, who locates objects of control in the world, just as readily assigns qualities to them; the redness is in the apple for all ordinary practical purposes. The criticisms of the skeptics are addressed to such naive realism. The whole point of Dewey's philosophy is that when such problems are regarded functionally, when we cease turning subjects and objects into fixed and distinct things, these problems disappear. This is why Dewey stresses the situation:

> The qualities never were "in" the organism; they always were qualities of interactions in which both extraorganic things and organisms partake. . . . Hence they are as much qualities of the things engaged as of the organism. For the purposes of control they may be referred specifically to either the thing or the organism or to a specified structure of the organism (*EN*, 259; *LW* 1:198-99).

Quality is not just of the situation but serves to mark out, define and distinguish one situation from another. In situations where there are sentient beings, Dewey states that feeling operates to discriminate situations:

> "Feeling" is in general a name for the newly actualized quality acquired by events previously occurring upon a physical level, when these events come into more extensive and delicate relationships of interaction. More specifically, it is a name for the coming to existence of those ultimate differences in affairs which mark them off from one

another and give them discreteness. . . . Thus qualities characteristic of sentiency are qualities *of* cosmic events (*EN*, 267; *LW* 1:204).

It is important to note in this passage that Dewey describes feeling as
an actualization of a physical event, i.e., it is an emergent, the realization of a potentiality. As I noted before, though "situation" is used
primarily for those interactions with human participants, by virtue of
the principle of continuity there would be comparable, but less actualized, types of interactions on the biological or physical planes. How
does this affect Dewey's claims about quality: are there "qualities" of
purely atomic events? Dewey was careless in addressing such problems with his theory. It can be solved, I believe, in the following way.
There is in all situations the character of immediacy, their immanent
wholeness which makes them unified. We should assume that as new
emergents transform situations, they display their unities in novel
ways. Living organisms, for example, do not simply act as physical
beings, but have a complex repertoire of behavior, eating, excreting,
reproducing, etc., which realizes new potentialities in nature. With
the emergence of conscious beings who experience with meaning,
"quality," or that realized through feeling, will stand for the wholeness, the immediacy of the situation as realized on that level. Likewise, the mediated and on-going aspect of the situation which calls
for acting and discrimination will exemplify itself in consciousness as
cognitive relations. Thus "immediacy" is mere "existence" on the
physical level, "behavior" on the biological and "quality" on the level
of meaning. These are continuous however. Had Dewey clarified his
emergentism more courageously, the problem of the status of quality
and the charge of animism would not have arisen.

This must be kept in mind when we note Dewey's significant
claim that every situation is unified and marked out by a "pervasive
quality":

> The pervasively qualitative is not only that which binds all constitu-
> ents into a whole but it is also unique; it constitutes in each situation
> an *individual* situation, indivisible and unduplicable. Distinctions
> and relations are instituted *within* a situation; *they* are recurrent and
> repeatable in different situations (*LTI*, 68; *LW* 12:74).

Situations are individuals for Dewey; each one is just that one and no
other and as such will never be repeated. Yet situations are not atomic;
they have relations with each other and with the past and future;
there may be traits appearing in a uniquely qualified way in one
situation which appear in a differently qualified way in another. Here,
as noted, critics try to set up a dualism between "quality" and "relation" and between the individual and the general. If each situation is

unique, how can it have universal features? If it has universal features, how can it be qualitatively unique? If situations develop and have temporal thickness, how can they "immediate"?

Two answers can be made here. Dewey's individual situations are more like Aristotle's individuals than like Newton's. That is, each individual is a process, an activity, which always has potentialities to act and be acted upon. It is not self-sufficient from the universe; it is only distinguishable. Presumably, for Newton, one atom does not need or depend on any other to exist.[69] Modern physics has dismissed this notion for one in which events are seen as inextricably connected with each other. Again, the tendency to regard an individual as a self-contained *thing* with no potentialities for interation is part of the seventeenth-century world view Dewey rejects. Dewey's individuals are organic wholes which have both an immediate aspect and a mediated one, an actual and a potential side, a radically unique and a formal or general character, just as did Aristotle's *ousiai*. Unlike Aristotle's *ousiai*, however, Dewey's situations have no fixed or essential endstate toward which they are heading. They are creative and complex affairs, not easily discriminable, though, to be sure, they have general dispositions. They are certainly not to be thought of in the typical manner one conceives of Aristotelian objects, such as cattle, tables, planets, or human beings, which are understood to be complete, self-contained activities which display their essential features in spite of their individualizing accidental traits—the traits which would make them genuinely contextual and historical. Dewey sees these as events to be understood functionally within their contexts or environments.

The second answer is that Dewey agreed with James that unless relations had a qualitative or felt side to them, they would be forever divided from concrete experience, i.e., we *experience* relations before we "know" them. Views which try to impose the universal from without upon experience inevitably end up by calling upon "transcendental" powers which accomplish their task through the mystery of a "synthetic imagination." This was the consequence of "the phsychologist's fallacy" for James, taking a distinction consequent to an experience and reading it back upon it as a primordial condition of it. As Dewey says:

> Were it true that only qualities coming to us through the sense-organs in *isolation* are directly experienced, then, of course, all relational material would be super-added by an association that is extraneous—or . . . by a "synthetic" action of thought. . . . The psychology underlying this bifuration was exploded by William James when he pointed out that there are direct feelings of such relations

as "if," "then," "and," "but," "from," "with." For he showed there is no relation so comprehensive that it may not become a matter of immediate experience. Every work of art that ever existed had indeed already contradicted the theory in question. It is quite true that certain things, namely ideas, exercise a mediating function. But only a twisted and aborted logic can hold that because something is mediated it cannot be immediately experienced (AE, 119; LW 10:124-25).[70]

Elsewhere, Dewey illustrates that the temporality of the situation is immediately felt or had. That is, since every situation is ongoing, it must be oriented to past and future, it must have a sense of whence and of whither. This is what gives the present its "place" and helps it develop with a sense of continuity and direction:

> Such interception and coalescence of qualities hitherto distinct characterize anything that may be called emergent. Put in a slightly different way, an event is both eventful and an eventuation. Since every event is also an interaction of different things, it is inherently characterized by something from which and something to which. . . . The "from which" and the "to which" qualify the event and make it, concretely, the distinctive event which it is ("Context and Thought" ENF, 97; LW 6:10).

The fact that situations are unified through a "pervasive qualitative whole" which is present throughout their development provides the underpinning for Dewey's theory of aesthetic meaning. "An experience" is just that: an organically inter-related situation which is unified throughout by a pervasive quality which gives it meaning.

VI. Conclusion

The role of quality and of immediacy is central in Dewey's theory of situations. It has been seen that Dewey's "Postulate of Immediate Empiricism" relied on this full and total experiencing of the world. It will be shown in the next chapter how Dewey's theory of meaning is a development of this. For now, it must be noted that "the situation" provides the non-cognitive, qualitative context for meaning. Dewey explicitly argues this in his important essay, "Qualitative Thought": "The situation as such is not and cannot be stated or made explicit. It is taken for granted, 'understood,' or implicit in all propositional symbolization. It forms the universe of discourse . . ." (PC, 97-98; LW 5:247). All cognitive or discursive thinking operates as but the center, the tensive focus, of the field of experience. As in his earliest idealism with the "psychological standpoint," Dewey constantly tries to regard experience in its fullest and richest way. This means that prior to the universe of explicitly, consciously used meanings, there is a vast, dynamic structure of prereflective involvement with the world which forms the tacit order against which consciousness emerges and which it uses as its material.

Situations of course may be regarded and discussed—else Dewey's own discussion would contradict itself with its first breath. This is done, however, only within the context of another situation. The minute we try to objectify and analyze a situation, we must place it within some larger universe of discourse. Dewey claims, "it is a commonplace that a universe of discourse cannot be a term or element within itself. One universe of discourse may, however, be a term within *another* universe" (*LTI*, 68-69; *LW* 12:74). One situation may develop into another and continuity be maintained. This means that the quality which unified the previous situation is now a discriminated part within a situation pervaded by another distinctive quality, the way concentric ripples in a pond contain further ripples.

This leads to the problem of how *a* situation, characterized by *a* quality, *also* contains many discriminated qualities. A mountain at sunset is not just *that* experience, but contains an indefinite number of discriminable features: colors of blue, magenta, azure, red; "things" like the mountain, trees, the sky, etc., "thoughts" and feelings and so on. Every situation, as organic, must have functioning parts. Many of these parts are picked out and highlighted because they have meanings which go beyond the moment or the immediate situation; i.e., they are relations. No two experiences of red are identical, yet we can respond to each as red. When we respond to things not simply as "had" but as "known," for Dewey, this connotes our active effort to establish continuity and meaning in experience and to control it. By using the abstract sign "red" we learn to *see* reds. This does not change the fact that we always see a particular shade of red in a context which engulfs it, grounds it, and gives it meaning. "Situations" themselves, as concepts, however, are intellectually discerned only within a context of general reflection and speculation.

Situations are fundamental for Dewey's "denotative method"; if experience is to have meaning, that meaning must be found in the nature of situations. Dewey's attempt to point out "generic traits" of nature was primarily an attempt to show that situations are complex conditions for meaning. Critics like Garrett or Rorty, who want to dismiss either the "ineffable" or qualitative side of Dewey's theory or to dispense with the role of the generic traits altogether, miss the fact that without these elements, meaning, evaluation, reconstruction, aesthetic appreciation, and other articulate types of experience would disappear. When Dewey set himself the task of treating experience in the fullest and richest way, of remaining faithful to experience as lived and encountered, he discovered that to achieve this end he had to rethink the relationship of man and nature, and to do this he had to come to grips with the hardest of all questions: What is real? Though Dewey professed that he was "describing" traits of situations, he realized that he was also presenting a theoretical interpretation subject to evaluation and criticism. Dewey, of all thinkers, never tried to present his ideas as settled candidates for dogmatic allegiance.

To say situations are qualitative and also relational is, however, no more "contradictory" than it is to say both "Dewey is grey" and "Dewey is in Columbia, less than six feet tall, and older than Randall." To understand the wholeness of the situation we obviously need both. When we get to the subject of art and of aesthetic meaning, it is just as important to point to the unique, integrated, and non-discursive aspect of aesthetic meaning as it is to point to the communicable, the inter-related, and the discursive side. Attempts to make the aesthetic one or the other do a disservice to experience. Conversely, the aesthetic experience itself contains a clue to the relation of man and nature. We are in the world situationally, and this means that we are in it qualitatively as well as relationally. Nature is disclosed in the aesthetic and moral as well as in the cognitive modes of experience. Indeed, the aesthetic, as it blends into "the religious,"[71] for Dewey, becomes the most inclusive, integrated and meaningful way man can be in nature or nature can disclose itself to man. To repeat Dewey's statement, "we are brought to a consideration of the most far-reaching question of all criticism: the relation between existence and value, or, as the problem is often put, between the real and the ideal" (EN, 415; LW 1:310). The possibilities of experience are as real as its existential actualities, and it is because we can grasp certain possibilities as possibilities for fulfilled experience that experience can be intelligently directed and realize those ideals concretely. In this way, experience becomes both meaningful and aesthetic—an experience.

To conclude, Dewey's general philosophy or metaphysics of experience can provide a coherent, organized and defensible theory. The problems detected by the critics are at the very least based on complex ideas ambiguously expressed in Dewey's work. Nevertheless, upon examination, most of the central ideas stressed by Dewey such as quality, continuity, generic traits, and so on, cannot be dispensed with for the sake of superficial simplicity. If they were, then deep contradictions would appear in Dewey's philosophy. Crucial in understanding Dewey's analysis of experience are the ideas of potentiality and of emergence as well as his view of the transactional nature of situations. These, in turn, must be regarded as concepts which

Dewey arrived at methodologically to serve his original and ultimate end of providing an account of experience which preserved its lived organic wholeness, richness, and diversity.

Meaning, the subject of the next chapter, is grounded upon experience as situational. Meanings are emergent functions of situations and consequently display continuity with nature. We must expect that meanings will reflect the complexity of situations as both immediate and as mediate, as qualitative and as relational. Meanings function within wholes or contexts and exhibit the full interactional human involvement with the world. When meanings are thoroughly integrated with their media of expression and are intensely organized so as to effect experiences which stand out because of their depth, continuity, and texture, they become art. Art and aesthetic meaning mark the fulfillment of nature in experience and of experience in meaning. It is there that the capacities of the world to achieve the interpenetration of sense and value in human life are realized.

Chapter 4

The Embodied Mind

The systematic examination of the structures of experience has provided us with the basis for approaching Dewey's theory of meaning. We can expect that meaning will exhibit in its own distinctive way the transactional and situational features of the world in which it arises and operates. Although our century has been preoccupied with the question of meaning, perhaps because so much of modern life threatens to be meaningless, many of the dominant theories would have done well to begin where Dewey did and reflect deeply about the nature of experience and the relation of human beings to the world before elaborating their conceptual refinements. Dewey's views on the nature of meaning will strike many contemporary readers as too general and unsystematic, given the sophisticated competing theories. No doubt Dewey's views, radical enough for the first quarter of our century, need development. But in many fundamental respects, Dewey is still ahead of his time. What I believe his theory of meaning offers is a general theoretical framework for much of the work recently begun. It may yet provide a fruitful arena where the valuable insights from both the analytical and phenomenological-hermeneutical traditions can come and work together. That task, however, lies far beyond the scope of this book. It will be enough here to sketch the outline of Dewey's theory and to see it as establishing grounds for the claim that aesthetic expression presents us with a *paradigmatic* case of meaning rather than a peripheral one, as it has so often been regarded.

Dewey's theory of meaning is a vital link connecting his aesthetics to his general philosophy of experience. Yet while Dewey's views on experience raised a storm of critical dust, his theory of meaning has barely received any attention at all. The work of Everett Hall, Max

Black, and Victor Kestenbaum stand as lonely exceptions to this rule.[1] To the extent, however, that the work of George Herbert Mead can be regarded as the development of a project which he shared with Dewey, one can easily begin to grasp some of the contemporary as well as historical implications of the theory. Indeed, this approach has much in common with the diverse (but, possibly, converging) disciplines of speech-act theory, semiotics, hermeneutics, and theories of metaphor. This is not to mention its relevance to work done in cultural anthropology, socio-linguistics, and sociology.

Dewey's approach to the subject of meaning has an amphibious quality. On the one hand Dewey is strongly committed to approaching the issue from the standpoint of behavior. Meaning, after all, is something that occurs under specific organic conditions. Dewey is therefore careful, on the basis of his principle of continuity, to see meaning as emerging out of our biological activity. On the other hand, still in accordance with the anti-reductionistic corollary of the principle of continuity, Dewey treats meaning as an emergent, as a new manner of existence which cannot be reduced to its component units of biological acts. Thus meaning must also be approached from the standpoint of the novel situation which it constitutes, that is, culture. In both instances, Dewey will strive to avoid the fallacy of treating meaning as primarily cognitive. Long before meaning becomes a topic for questions about verification, grammatical syntax, logical structure, or categorial analysis, it is an affair of stories, lullabies, games, expressions of feeling, social interaction, religion, education, and art. Language, in this all-inclusive sense is the medium in which human beings participate in culture. To live a human life is to live in a world permeated by meaning and value. This rich domain of cultural life not only is the material upon which art draws but is also the soil from which art grows.

Dewey is interested from the start, then, in avoiding two extremes in dealing with the topic of meaning. The first extreme might be called the mechanistic theory of meaning. This essentially views meaning as a precise code of signals. While such an approach might include a wide array of contemporary theories, ranging from reductionistic psychologies to structuralism, a simple and obvious instance is the classic statement of language in the third book of Locke's *Essay*. (Although this part of the *Essay* tends to be ignored, I think it could be shown that Locke's theory of ideas is in fact an elaboration of his views about language.) For Locke our ideas arise from the powers of substances to affect the mind or from its own powers of activity. In either case, ideas arrive or are produced as complete and final on their own, or, as Dewey puts it, "ready-made." All that is needed is a conventional system to represent our ideas to each other: "God, having designed man for a sociable creature . . . furnished him also with language, which was to be the great instrument and common tie of society. Man, therefore, had by nature his organs so fashioned, as to be fit to frame articulate sounds, which we call words" (*Essay*, III. i, 1). Locke always had trouble with his double attempt to think of man as discretely individual and also as a social being, as much so here as in his political theory. He continues:

> Man, though he have great variety of thoughts, and such from which others as well as himself might receive profit and delight; yet they are all within his own breast, invisible and hidden from others, nor can of themselves be made to appear. The comfort and advantage of society not being to be had without communication of thoughts, it was necessary that man should find out some external sensible signs, whereof those invisible ideas, which his thoughts are made up of, might be made known to others. . . . Thus we may conceive how *words*, which were by nature so well adapted to that purpose, came to be made use of by men as the signs of their ideas; not by any natural connection . . . but by a voluntary imposition, whereby such a word is made arbitrarily the mark of such an idea (III.ii.1).

Language is conceived of as a system of names conventionally agreed upon for commonly held, but subjective, ideas. It is a social agreement, soberly and practically entered upon by thoughtful creatures. The notions of "agreement" and "convention" still plague anthropology textbooks, even though both these terms clearly presuppose a social context of interaction already existing. Language is then seen as a cultural, hence *artificial*, superimposition upon a system of natural relations. Nature and culture are dualistically opposed.

At the other extreme, we might locate the idealist theories of language which see communication as the realization of Spirit's self-consciousness through a concretizing medium. Hegel's whole *Phenomenology of Spirit* can be read as the (torturous) history of the languages whereby Spirit expresses and thereby comes to know itself. From the human standpoint, it certainly presents a more dynamic and problematic account of language than Locke's. For example, we read:

> Language and labour are outer expressions in which the individual no longer retains possession of himself *per se*, but lets the inner get right outside him, and surrenders it to something else. For that reason we might as truly say that these outer expressions express the inner too much as that they do so too little: too much—because the inner itself breaks out in them, and there remains no opposition between them and it . . .: too little—because in speech and action the inner turns itself into something else, into an other, and thereby

> puts itself at the mercy of the element of change, which transforms
> the spoken word and the accomplished act, and makes something
> else out of them than they are in and for themselves as actions of a
> particular determinate individual.[2]

Hegel makes the point that language is the active working-out, the expression, of something "inner," but this inner is not determinate until it *is* expressed or embodied in some objective medium. But then it is no longer inner or private. In becoming objective, the expression unsuccessfully tries to freeze what is, after all, a living, self-transcending process. Eventually, of course, Spirit will overcome its self-alienation through its historic embodiments and become one with its expression, history, in one luminous moment of self-understanding.

Here it would seem that the Lockean tension between nature and language or culture disappears in the resolution of the Absolute. In the last analysis, however, I think Hegel succumbs to the subjective romantic view (which he strove to reject) whereby expression is the externalization of an inner self—the Absolute ultimately speaks only to itself about itself and realizes it is nothing other than this process of making Byronic stories about who it is. Another way of putting this is that whatever else we may think we are talking about, we are always, even if obliquely, referring to the Absolute. There is a final organizing teleology of speech which is the basis for making sense; the Absolute is the ultimate condition for the possibility of meaning at all.

Dewey and Mead, who both set out as Hegelians, had the intention of trying to naturalize what they considered the excesses of idealism while preserving its valuable insights. This does not mean, as Richard Rorty thinks, that they merely tried to hybridize Locke and Hegel, ending up with some sort of philosophical centaur. The problem was to come up with a model which could explain meaning as the development of symbolically mediated social interaction growing out of the conditional structures of biological activity. We have seen how Dewey grew dissatisfied with idealism and labored long and hard to compromise it with a more naturalistic perspective, a process which also involved a rethinking of naturalism. Whereas James' *Principles of Psychology* had been a guiding beacon in working out Dewey's theory of experience, it was singularly unhelpful on the subject of language or meaning, having in its 688 pages of text only two devoted to the subject. Experience and meaning were connected issues, however. Charles Peirce's early articles had introduced pragmatism essentially as a method of clarifying meaning through experimental inquiry.[3] If James' biological and teleological view of the mind could be connected with Peirce's view of inquiry as a method of determining, and thus settling, a disturbed or troubled situation through clarifying the practical consequences involved, then the basis for a theory of meaning as action could be established. This was essentially achieved in Dewey's breakthrough article of 1896, "The Reflex Arc Concept in Psychology." This article left the status of the social or the cultural rather indeterminate with respect to the questions of meaning. It was not really until *Experience and Nature* that Dewey came to work out the corresponding social dimension of his theory, which involved an application of the same model of action to the subject-matter of culture and meaning. Throughout this time Dewey and Mead mutually influenced each other, and their respective theories of meaning are quite complimentary. Dewey was tremendously aided by the articles of Mead, who in turn, based much of the lectures published as *Mind, Self, and Society* upon the less specific but synoptic theory of *Experience and Nature*. Meaning was to be understood as the symbolic *use* of biological gestures toward the end of coordinating social action. The individual needed to be able to take a social standpoint or perspective in order to interpret himself. Symbols provided just such a means: one could respond to them as others did and so use them with intent in regulating interaction. In this process, the individual realized his "social self."[4] Meaning had to be understood in terms of its functional and creative uses in cultural action.

This chapter will take the following path over this complex and rugged terrain. First, Dewey's crucial article on the reflex arc concept will be analyzed. This reveals that the unit of behavior, the act or the total action, determines the elements which fall within it and guides them as mutual coordinations. Two important phases of the act will then be discussed, emotion and habit. Every act is tensive and coordinating, having thereby emotional tone or depth as well as structure in action. Experience embodies this intrinsically dramatic and rhythmic quality, and art arises from the conscious exploitation of these features. In other words, experience is potentially expressive, and aesthetic expression is a natural realization of this capacity. But expression requires embodiment in a medium whereby it can become consciously, that is symbolically, appropriated. Communication relies upon the establishment of shared symbolic structures, i.e., culture. Communication relies upon a prereflective context of social action which lends itself to mutual articulation and thereby also makes possible a vast refinement and development of symbolic activity itself. A tacitly shared lifeworld expands into all facets of culture. Through communication as an ongoing process we can become significantly or meaningfully present to each other and thereby to ourselves. The presence of an articulated lifeworld leads to the development of experience as a self-reflective or conscious enterprise, spanning the range from non-cognitive feeling to immediately apprehended sense to cognitive signification. The analysis of Dewey's theory of cognitive significance is beyond the range of this book, being nothing less than his instrumentalism. Here it will be enough to see that experience naturally has the capacity to have immediately embodied meaning that is not explicitly cognitive but which expresses everything which makes shared life human and worthwhile. Meaning is a contextually determined social process which is structured but creative and dramatic and in which *participation* rather than decoding or autonomous self-realization is the key idea. The inhabitation of the lived body is our first work of art. But it is only as we strive to transform the body into a participant in community that it acquires a significant or expressive life.

I. The Act as the Unit of Meaning

The act is for the universe of meaning what the situation is for experience. It is a term which refers to that concrete, functioning, transactional whole through which the various phases are understood as integral organic parts and which, in turn, is realized by them. In spite of the inevitably Hegelian ring to this theory, it is emphatically naturalistic in the sense that it accounts for behavioral actions as well as cultural expressions by an appeal to the concept of organic activity. Instead of a transcendental Absolute, there is a natural organizing teleology to biological activity. In the context of culture, a number of individuals must be able to acquire a shared social perspective which can determine and coordinate their actions and forms the basis for the recognition of intent.

Working together at Chicago from 1894 to 1904, Dewey and Mead developed a biosocial theory of behavior which was ahead of its time, especially in its criticism of reductionistic S-R behaviorism. While Dewey laid the foundation in a brilliant series of articles on psychology, the most famous of which is "The Reflex Arc Concept in Psychology," Mead was the one who refined the theory, making it the cornerstone of his theory of social gesture.[5]

Before examining the theory of the act per se, the question must be asked, what sort of a world is it in which meaning arises? To this, Dewey answers, one in which there is structure and destruction; one in which action matters because it can effect a reconstruction; one, in short, in which there are both stable and precarious features so that *growth* rather than static, bare existing is the mark of life. The central fact of any life-form is that it has an environment. It is bonded to that environment in a stable way through its own internal adaptation and through the external support of the environment itself, or implementation.[6] To be in an environment through structured or ordered activity is to be open to those features which can be destablizing as well. The environment includes agents which may weaken or destroy the structures supporting an organism's existence. This may range from the microscopic wars of viruses, bacteria, and protozoa to the collapse of entire ecosystems. Were the universe simply fixed and predetermined in *all* respects, if, in other words, pure unperturbed mathematical harmony governed, meaning would not arise.[7] Not only would consciousness itself have no role to play, other than that of a ghostly spectator, but time itself would not exist. From this perspective one could not even perceive the *necessity* of the order. As Dewey notes, "A world that was all necessity would not be a world of necessity; it would just be" (*EN*, 64; *LW* 1:59).[8] Likewise, a world of pure flux would also be one of pure absurdity, utter meaninglessness. Even Heraclitus' cosmic flux had the hidden order of the "Logos," and Hume had his laws of association for the rhapsody of impressions.

The basic condition for meaning, then, is a world which has both the features of "the stable," the regular supportive order, and "the precarious," the adventitious, problematic, and aleatory disruption of that order. Here we should recall Aristotle's insistence upon both form and matter, actuality and potentiality as basic traits of the world. Dewey himself acknowledges that in his concept of matter Aristotle "came the nearest to a start in that direction. But his thought did not go far on the road. . . . Aristotle acknowledges contingency but he never surrenders his bias in favor of the fixed, certain and finished," (*EN*, 48; *LW* 1: 47). Most philosophies in Western civilization, says Dewey, are really "recipes for denying to the universe the character of contingency which it possesses so integrally . . ." (*EN*, 46; *LW* 1:46). The previous chapter argued that Dewey's understanding of experience and nature called for a reintroduction of the notion of genuine potentiality. It now will become evident that this concept is significant for understanding the topic of meaning as well. If meaning is a process of communication in which there is an on-going interplay of the determinate and the indeterminate, of the actual and the possible, this will illustrate its continuity with Dewey's general theory of experience and nature. Most theories of meaning have attempted to comprehend the subject strictly in terms of the formal, structured aspect. Hence logic came to be regarded as the appropriate manner of approach for handling the meaning of meaning. The result was the detemporalization of meaning; logic achieved its clarity by being timeless and empty. Dewey argues that meaning is only *possible* in a world which can be disrupted, in which ambiguity, change, and destruction play a role. This fissure in the world is essential to understand meaning. Meaning cannot be successfully abstracted from the world as *phusis*, as a temporal, generative process.

Thus Dewey approves the pluralism of Aristotle's natural philosophy, but rejects Aristotle's bias toward static classification. The plurality of nature also reflects nature's capacity toward dispersion, disorganization, and the gradual effacement of form. Order for Dewey is a dynamic and precarious process. It should be evident that the metaphysical issues raised in the previous chapter have a direct bearing on the question of meaning. Philosophies which view the real world as essentially static or purely actual with, at best, absolute mechanistic change from one atomic instant to the next will regard meaning as a question of simple logical correspondence or mirroring.[9] Though examples are rare of philosophies which go to the other extreme of advocating pure flux, one can note that in those cases meaning itself dissolves into pure random perception. Cratylus, we recall, ended up by only pointing at the flux, much as do the Zen Buddhists. Bergson saw language as inherently deceptive.[10]

Since nature is an on-going affair of stability and change, experience will reflect this on the organic level. Experience arises from the interaction of the organism with the environment, and as such involves the action of that environment upon the organism (and hence its capacity to be acted upon) and the action of the organism on the environment (its capacity to act upon the world and the capacity of the world to be acted upon). Dewey simply refers to this as "undergoing and doing." Now this process of interaction, of doing and undergoing, may follow a largely stable, routine pattern, such as one often sees in complex mating rituals between animals. It may, however, suddenly involve novel or threatening elements which either alert and warn the creature or inhibit and destroy it if unheeded. While other theories may either posit experience as originating in the world as a noetic spectator or as a mere epiphenomenal by-product, Dewey's view sees experience as arising from a functional need to interact effectively with the world, restoring stability by means or action. Certainly Dewey never intended for all experience to be reduced to a crude level of survival behavior or even to simple problem-solving like repairing a leak or trapping food. But historically and genetically from the Darwinian view, all the fundamental biological processes, the organs of perception, the complexities of the nervous system, and the structures of the human brain itself were selectively developed in the course of adaptation to an exploitation of the means of survival.[11] To whatever philosophical and poetic heights experience may take us, it also is there to help us get around.

Experience emerges from interaction; this origin provides the basis for intelligence, meaning, and the consummatory or appreciative phase of experience. There is, first of all, an inherent rhythm or shape to life as it oscillates between phases of stability and of instability. Any moment in the life of a creature is always situational and transactional. It is a moment of a process which has a past and a future, whether the organism is conscious of that process or not. When sensation and conscious experience occur, they may be seen as a broadening and deepening of this character. Significant too is Dewey's observation that growth and development are intrinsic to interaction. Growth is the establishment of continuity. Since organism and environment are mutually implicated at each moment, "It follows that with every differentiation of structure the environment expands" (*LTI*, 25; *LW* 12:32). There is, in short, a dynamic, rhythmic and growing nature to all interaction; experience exemplifies this in a heightened degree, and this aspect of experience itself becomes the basis for aesthetic experience and art.

Before examining how this rhythmic structure is possible and how it manifests itself in human experience, two further comments should be made. First it is not enough simply to assert that because experience has phases of doing and undergoing it thereby has structure. These phases must be *related* to each other or coordinated, and this relation itself must be recognized before meaning can arise. To adapt to an environment is not just to have a variety of responses, but is to have these responses *organized* into an overall unity of behavior. "Each particular activity prepares the way for the activity that follows. These form not a mere succession, but a series" (*LTI*, 27; *LW* 12:33). It is imperative for experience to be whole as well as diverse. The act of coordination or adjustment is teleological and temporal, and it establishes continuity.

The second point to keep in mind is that the structure of experience will be developmental, from a state of wholeness to a state of wholeness by way of an intervening phase of reconstruction or readjustment. The model of experience which Dewey presents is not a simple progression from a condition of routine, automatic behavior which is suddenly disorganized by a "problematic situation" leading to mechanical analysis, experimentation, reorganization and reintegration with a consummatory kick closing it off. There are a number of phases or functionally diverse parts operating at each moment. It is true that there is a temporal overall structure to *an* experience, and Dewey does tend at times to simplify this structure, so that one might get the impression that every significant moment of human existence follows the pattern of a motorist driving along, oblivious to the world, having a flat tire, being awakened to the need, fixing the tire, and merrily going on his way with the satisfaction of having gotten out of a jam. Balancing this teleological dimension of experience is Dewey's conception of experience as a total *field* of action which has a complex structure at each and every moment and different degrees of focus, clarity, obscurity, and organization. It is *this* which changes from one moment to the next, not by a jerky series of mechanical actions, but by increasing articulation, illumination, meaning, and apprehension. To summarize: one must keep vividly in mind that experience for Dewey is *both* process and field—a "field-process" if you will. Structure is temporally *dynamic*; activity is *ordered*.

We must also recall Dewey's contention that the cognitive phase of experience occupies only a portion of the field. Both prior to and posterior to any knowing of the world, the world is encountered as something "suffered and enjoyed" (*EN*, 1st, 12; *LW* 1:372) so that "the difference between the esthetic and the intellectual is thus one of the place where emphasis falls in the constant rhythm that marks the interaction of the live creature with his surroundings" (*AE*, 15; *LW* 10:21). This aspect of experience is "had" rather than known. For example, he says, "There are two dimensions of experienced things: one that of having them, and the other that of knowing about them so that we can again have them in more meaningful and secure ways" (*EN* 1st, 21; *LW* 1:379). Elsewhere, Dewey refers to "the universe of nonreflectional experience of our doings, sufferings, enjoyments of the world and of one another" (*EEL*, 9; *MW* 10:326). As experience becomes more organized, the qualitative immediacy does not retreat before a spectral world of relations. Rather, both the immediate or qualitative side and the mediate or rational side become more articulate and interwoven. The present moment, by being *part* of a whole developing situation, becomes suffused with the apprehension of the significance of the event, or "funded" in Dewey's term. Art itself, for Dewey, is the prime example of the power of experience to intensify and yet be meaningful. In other words, to understand Dewey's theory of meaning one must not lose sight of the world within which meaning occurs, nor of its inherently reconstructive and hence consummatory possibilities.

In the late 1890s Dewey at last hit upon an explanatory model of experience which satisfied his organic conception of experience, his attempt to have Hegel and Huxley at once. This model is most comprehensively presented in the article which stands as one of the major contributions to psychology, "The Reflex Arc Concept in Psychology," which appeared in 1896. Details of the view were worked out in a number of insightful articles, the most important of which are "The

Theory of Emotions" (1894-95), *Interest in Relation to the Training of the Will* (1895; 1899), "Imagination and Expression" (1896) and "The Interpretation of the Savage Mind" (1902). The essays printed in *Studies in Logical Theory* (1903) and Dewey's subsequent development of pragmatism would have been impossible without the basic ideas developed during this time. It is ironic that not only have Dewey's ideas been unprofitably ignored by philosophers and psychologists, but that his basic model has been used independently by thinkers as diverse as Maurice Merleau-Ponty, Jean Piaget, and Susanne Langer.[12]

The problem dealt with in "The Reflex Arc Concept in Psychology" is typically Deweyan: traditional dualisms (here that between stimulus and response in the peripheral and central nervous system) prevent a comprehensive, organic and functional account of behavior and experience. "As a result," states Dewey, "the reflex arc is not a comprehensive or organic unity, but a patchwork of disjointed parts, a mechanical conjunction of unallied processes," (*EW* 5:97). Instead of a mechanical cause-effect arc of stimulus and response, Dewey offers an idea which he calls "circuit co-ordination." What Dewey proposes, in other words, is to *start* with the idea of the organism already dynamically involved with the world and aiming toward unified activity. Since the organism is not self-contained, it must direct this impulsion toward an environment. Because the environment contains random, novel, and potentially disruptive elements, the activity must be one of continued readjustment and modification, that is, growth.

Take the old example of the child reaching for the candle and being burned. Whereas the old psychology sees a series of S-R actions and reactions (e.g., stimulus of bright-light; response of action-of-reaching; stimulus of pain; response of action-of-withdrawal), Dewey places these discrete actions within a whole context of developing activity, of exploration and coordination, in which the "stimulus" *can appear as such and so have meaning*. The same is true of the "response." First, the overall activity of the child is prior to any specific act of seeing. Dewey's infant is a bundle of out-going energies rather than a passive Lockean wax doll. Second, the *act* of seeing is prior to any "stimulation" of the retina; there is an elementary level of total sensorimotor coordination which organizes light into a visual field of "objects." Seeing is a general possible mode of organizing activity for the child. "In other words," says Dewey, "the real beginning is with the act of seeing; it is looking, and not a sensation of light" (*EW* 5:97). There is a "sensory quale," or a sense of the situation as a whole which is in process at the moment, which gives the particular moment its "value." Likewise there is of course the physical movement, "but both sensation and movement lie inside, not outside the act" (*EW*

5:98). Of course, beyond the simple act of looking lies the general coordination of looking and grasping. In this both the seeing and the reaching regulate and modify each other. The hand and the eye work together mutually supporting and coordinating each other in one activity directed toward an end. The experience in which they function widens and grows naturally.

> In other words, we now have an enlarged and transformed coordination; the act is seeing no less than before, but it is now seeing-for-reaching purposes. There is still a sensori-motor circuit, one with more content or value, not a substitution of a motor response for a sensory stimulus (EW 5:98).

When, in this simple example, the moment of the hand being burned is reached, it also falls within the circuit of the whole act and cannot be treated as mere sensation or abstracted stimulus. Dewey observes:

> It is worth while, however, to note especially the fact that it is simply the completion, or fulfillment, of the previous eye-arm-hand coordination and not an entirely new occurrence. Only because the heat-pain quale enters into the same circuit of experience with the optical-ocular and muscular quales, does the child learn from the experience and get the ability to avoid the experience in the future (EW 5:98).

The burn is interpreted or *seen as* the result of the action; if it were simply an isolated, brute sensation, unrelated to anything else, it would be a mindless, meaningless experience and would in no way enlarge one's perception or understanding of the world or change behavior at all. The original experience is "enlarged and transformed in its value." The various phases must be *seen as* parts of one whole act; the "feel" or "quale" of the beginning of the act and that of the end must be seen as termini of the same act, or, as Dewey puts it:

> The fact is that the sole meaning of the intervening movement is to maintain, reinforce or transform (as the case may be) the original quale; that we do not have the replacing of one sort of experience by another, but the development (or as it seems convenient to term it) the mediation of an experience. The seeing, in a word, remains to control the reaching and is, in turn, interpreted by the burning (EW 5:99).[13]

Experience has the capacity to grow, for moments to fuse together and become meaningfully related parts of an overall action. Continuity can be established so that experience becomes surcharged with meanings at issue. This is nothing else than what is perhaps the most important and distinctive human trait: the capacity to *learn*. It is no accident that at the time Dewey developed this theory he was engaged in his work on education at Chicago. Whatever else may have resulted from Dewey's research into education and the psychology of learning, perhaps the most crucial result for philosophy was Dewey's shift in epistemology away from "the problem of knowledge" toward the more important "problem of learning."

This analysis led Dewey to formulate the model of the circuit of coordination to replace the arc of previous psychology. What has been described is a circuit of "continual reconstruction" (*EW* 5:99). The emphasis is on the whole as well as the part. Dewey states that "what precedes the 'stimulus' is a whole act," and adds, "What is more to the point, the 'stimulus' emerges out of the coordination; it is born from it as its matrix; it represents as it were an escape from it" (*EW* 5:100).

> This circuit is more truly termed organic than reflex, because the motor response determines the stimulus, just as truly as the sensory stimulus determines movement. Indeed, the movement is only for the sake of determining the stimulus, of fixing what kind of stimulus it is, of interpreting it (*EW* 5:102).

A part of behavior can play either the role of stimulus or response "according to the shift of interest." "It is a question of finding out what stimulus or sensation, what movement and response mean, a question of seeing that they mean distinctions of flexible function only, not of fixed existence" (*EW* 5:102), claims Dewey. Particular note should be given to Dewey's use of the word "mean" here. The old model, in fact, has an inexplicable jump from physical agitation to psychic event and back again, which Dewey views as "a survivor of the metaphysical dualism, first formulated by Plato" (*EW* 5:104). For Dewey, stimulus and response are "teleological distinctions, that is, distinctions of function, or part played, with reference to reaching or maintaining an end" (*EW* 5:104).[14]

Dewey distinguishes two stages of teleological behavior: The first is the case where the means are comprehensively adapted to the end (such as in the instance of instinctive or thoroughly habitual behavior); the second is the case where consciousness itself arises as an attempt to define and mediate both stimulus and response. In the first example, "The end has got thoroughly organized into the means" (*EW* 5:104), so that there is no need for conscious behavior: the act is definite from the start. In the second case, there is the need to render the situation definite, and this means articulating the stimulus as well as the response. As Dewey points out:

> Neither mere sensation, nor mere movement, can ever be either stimulus or response; only an act can be that; the *sensation* as stimulus means the lack of and search for such an objective stimulus, or orderly placing of an act; just as mere movement as response means the lack of and search for the right act to complete a given coordination (*EW* 5:106).

For example, take the case of a child who is sometimes delighted by and sometimes hurt by bright objects. Whenever he encounters a bright object, the outcome is doubtful: a "problematic situation" occurs. Dewey says, "*Now the response is not only uncertain, but the stimulus is equally uncertain; one is uncertain only in so far as the other is. The real problem may be equally well stated as either to discover the right stimulus, to constitute the stimulus, or to discover, to constitute, the response*" (*EW* 5:106). Is the bright object a mirror or a flame? To determine which it is at once determines what consequences follow and which actions are appropriate. The doubtfulness of the end will call for the discrimination of the object in conscious perception.

Dewey summarizes this significant article the following way:

> The circle is a co-ordination, some of whose members have come into conflict with each other. It is the temporary disintegration and need of reconstruction which occasions . . . the conscious distinction into sensory stimulus on one side and motor response on the other. The stimulus is that phase of the forming of co-ordination which represents conditions which have to be met in bringing it to successful issue; the response is that phase of one and the same forming co-ordination which gives the key to meeting these conditions, which serves as instrument in effecting the successful co-ordination. They are therefore strictly correlative and contemporaneous. The stimulus is something to be discovered; to be made out. . . . As soon as it is adequately determined, then and then only is the response also complete. . . . It is the co-ordination which unifies that which the reflex arc concept gives us only disjointed fragments (*EW* 5:109).

To understand the ideas presented above is to grasp the underlying dynamism of Dewey's mature philosophy of experience. In itself, to be sure, it addresses only a portion of experience, the psychology of behavior. It provides, however, a broad basis for interpreting and integrating the other dimensions, such as meaning, inquiry, and art.[15] In addition, it effects continuity between Dewey's metaphysics of situations as transactional events and his theory of conscious, significant experience. The act is the genesis of a transactional situation on the level of organic behavior. Insofar as consciousness emerges from the act, it operates within it as an integral functional part. Yet, as will be seen, consciousness also brings with it the awareness of meaning.

To understand the act, it is necessary to go beyond the limited but central issue of simple sensorimotor coordination. Three important factors must be noted: first, because the whole act can be seen as the search for the proper stimulus to free action and unify the situation, the act is inherently selective; second, selectivity, which is a feature of all natural situations,[16] is manifested in experience as interest; and finally, selectivity and interest create the basis for an organized context of meanings and activities. While interest itself refers to the whole way the organism is implicated in its environment, its "intentional" involvement with a world, it also reflects the fact that every situation is relational: it is actively related and bound up with interactions, but it articulates a limited perspective. This does not mean all perspectives are of equal worth. Some are broad, generous, flexible, and profound while others are arbitrary, shallow, impulsive, and narrow.

A further basic observation can be made. Environments are not prior to organisms. That is, both are dynamically interdependent and are understood in terms of the other. George Herbert Mead offers the following simple illustration:

> It is a difficult matter to state just what we mean by dividing up a certain situation between the organism and its environment. Certain objects come to exist for us because of the character of the organism. Take the case of food. If an animal that can digest grass, such as an ox, comes into the world, then grass becomes food. . . . In that sense organisms are responsible for the appearance of whole sets of objects that did not exist before.[17]

The organism determines its environment—it literally transforms a physical context into an environment. In this sense, acts radically transform the world, for they mark the release of new potentialities for existence. This is especially true of acts which occur within the universe of significant or symbolic experience. An environment then becomes a meaningful world.

Selection as part of the act is the determination of an attitude or perspective. It becomes the basis for forming an attitude, which, to recall, was the main point of Dewey's postulate of immediate empiricism. In other words, acts involve the determination of a field of action which includes the possible range of stances one can take to the field. In his article "Perception and Organic Action," Dewey offers an insightful criticism of Bergson's theory of immediate, intuitive selection based largely upon the model worked out in "The Reflex Arc Concept in Psychology." For Bergson selection is not only preconscious but primarily negative; i.e., it screens or ignores stimuli, subtracting rather than adding. For Dewey, "perceived objects present our *eventual* action upon the world . . ." (*PC*, 213; *MW* 7:13).

> *What* we perceive, in other words, is not just the material upon which we *may* act, but material which reflects back to us the consequences of our acting upon it this way or that. So far as the *act* of perception is concerned, we are led to substitute an act of choosing for an act of accomplished choice. Perception is not an instantaneous act of carving out a field through supressing its real influences and permitting its virtual ones to show, but is a process of determining the indeterminate (*PC*, 214; *MW* 7:13).

The act of perception, for Dewey, is no more just a censor than it is a mere spectator of appearances. It is an actor-writer; it is involved in transforming and participating in the ongoing events.

Because acts involve a structure, they involve the participant, be it mute organism or conscious "self," in its entirety. "The whole organism is concerned in every act to some extent and in some fashion" (*HNC: II: vi*, 150; *MW* 14:105). This point is emphatically repeated throughout Dewey's writings, and has far-reaching implications for his aesthetics:

> It is not just the visual apparatus but the whole organism that interacts with the environment in all but routine action. The eye, ear, or whatever, is only the channel *through* which the total response takes place. A color as seen is always qualified by implicit reactions of many organs, those of the sympathetic system as well as touch. It is a funnel for the total energy put forth, not its well-spring. Colors are sumptuous and rich just because a total organic resonance is deeply implicated in them (*AE*, 122; *LW* 10:127).

Dewey is not just saying that the body is "implicated in perception" (*PC*, 226; *MW* 7:25), he is saying that the whole field of meanings is implicated as well. We do not perceive that shade of red because of some "simple idea" of red. In another essay, Dewey refers to this Lockean doctrine as "pure superstition." Instead, we perceive it as occupying a place on a continuum of discriminated colors. Even seeing something *as* a "color" is learned; originally we encounter total experiences from which "things" emerge. As Dewey points out, "a child recognizes its dresses long before it identifies colors . . ." (*PC*, 197; *LW* 2:51). The context of perception and meaning, then, must be conceived to be a whole field of sense and action which reverberates at each moment to the degree it is organized.

Therefore, in addressing the problem of meaning, Dewey does not start off by isolating the discussion to rules of linguistic usage. He begins by taking on a tradition deeply committed to mind-body dualism, to the separation of thought and action and to a pre-existent world of atomic objects, whether material atoms, Platonic Forms, Aristotelian individuals, or Lockean simple ideas, which provide the ultimate referents of meaning. Against these prejudices, Dewey tries to create a model of total organic coordination, the "psycho-physical" or "Body-Mind" as Dewey came to refer to it. The organism and its environment are mutually implicated at each moment; they are aspects of one situation fundamentally related through the act. The organism is just this ability to draw on a range of material in the world and transform the energy in that material into an organized pattern of activity. An environment is in turn that range of energy which is available to the organism and necessary for its survival.

To conclude, experience is part of a process of interaction. The organism-in-its-environment is the basic fact which any attempt to understand experience or meaning must confront. Too often philosophical theories of experience seek to ground themselves on an abstract, unitary *ego cogito* or *Ich denke*. As Dewey observes, originally it is much more accurate to say experience begins with "It experiences." Only when one is ready to take on responsibility for the consequences of action is it legitimate to say that "I experience" or "I think." The self emerges by committing itself to its future as a project.[18] To put it another way, the "identity" sought in experience will be found in the process of selecting and appropriating a course of action. Identity comes with identifying, and this presupposes the context of situational involvement. The unification or organization of experience, instead of being founded on an a priori given, is the inherent problematic side of experience for Dewey. That experience *is* capable of such integrity is revealed most vividly through the aesthetic or artistic, through *an* experience. But the overall continuity of experience is a perpetual problem for action, something which calls forth the need for care, intelligence, responsibility and meaning and which raises the question of value.

II. The Relation of Emotion and Impulse

The act arises from two basic conditions. The first is the ground of the biological structural functioning of the organism. While this area is properly the subject of biology and physical psychology, it does carry important implications for a theory of experience and meaning. The second condition is the social and cultural world into which each human is born. Not only are we intrinsically social creatures, depending on others for survival and fulfillment, but we interact with others and through this interaction come to realize ourselves as expressive, communicative beings who must mean what they say.

Let us look first at the biological aspects. The circuit of coordination described in the previous section provided a model of learning behavior. Dewey expanded his analysis in later works, most notably in *Human Nature and Conduct*, with increasing emphasis upon the role of impulse and habit in structuring our world into coherent, premeaningful patterns. Habits provide a stable repertoire of responses; impulse provides the dynamic impetus for immediate reconstructive focus in which the fixed, acquired pattern of behavior, the habit, gets re-enacted and adapted to fit the situation. In this latter case, not only is the old habit immediately involved, relived as it were, but it provides an interpretive structure or context to the immediate moment, raising the experience to a level of complexity and integration which it otherwise would not possess. In this process, the habit itself expands and grows as it tries to adapt to the new circumstance so that the domain of organized responses develops, a premonition of the growth of meaning in experience.

To put the issue into extreme cases, a world governed by pure routine habit is basically a non-conscious world. The repeated actions of an assembly-line worker dull consciousness to the point where a free-floating and diffuse day-dreaming may be most of what occupies attention. There is structure to the world—so much structure that automatic reflexes almost suffice. To take the opposite case, a world lived almost with pure impulse alone—the experiment of a Rimbaud for example—never acquires much meaning. Though consciousness may be raised to a pitch of frenzy, to the degree that structure is absent there is no meaning in the experience (other than, perhaps, the sense of confusion). In an ideal learning situation, however, not only is the present experience informed and interpreted through the past acquired habits, but the past, brought to bear on the novelties of the present, is revived and colors the experience with significance. Both the stable and the precarious are necessary preconditions for a consciousness which learns and grows. In addition, the present is informed with emotion and interest because of the role of the novelty of the impulse.

This third sort of experience is as much tinged with emotion as with meaning. As Dewey points out, "Habit is energy organized in certain channels. . . . Emotion is a perturbation from clash or failure of habit, and reflection . . . is the painful effort of disturbed habits to readjust themselves" (*HNC*, I:v, 76; *MW* 14:54). Emotion is not an internal state simply corresponding to an external condition, which is mysteriously projected onto the world. It is the tone of the world or of one's "attunement" to the situation. Dewey sees emotions as "intentional": "an emotion is *to* or *from* or *about* something objective, whether in fact or in idea. An emotion is implicated in a situation . . ." (*AE*, 67; *LW* 10:72). Or, as Victor Kestenbaum says, "Emotions are a particular reflection of the irreducible implication of self and world."[20]

Emotion plays a revealing role in Dewey's theory of experience. It reflects the importance of the prereflective dimension not only in sensing the structure, but in anticipating organizing action. A major example of this is the selective power Dewey accords emotions. Emotion is from the start a response in activity and reflects the underlying dynamics of interaction. In its shock, it evokes the *need* for organized activity. It mirrors a fracturing of action and mutely but effectively points out the crisis in the field of experience, demanding direction and selection of foci of importance.[21] As will be seen later, this is achieved primarily through the "pervasive qualitative whole" which guides the sense of the situation. For now, it should be noted that this unifying, expanding power of emotion accounts for the inherent expressive power of experience.

Dewey's important article, "The Theory of Emotion," which antedated "The Reflex Arc Concept" by a year, supplements the latter's account of learning behavior with an analysis of the role of emotion and expression in experience. There, Dewey tries to mediate between the Darwinian theory and the James-Lange theory. While Darwin tended to regard expression as the externalization of a preexistent internal emotion, originating in acts useful for survival, James, along with Lange, argued that "the bodily manifestations must first be interposed . . . we feel sorry because we cry, angry because we strike, afraid because we tremble, and not that we cry, strike, or tremble because we are sorry, angry, or fearful, as the case may be."[22] In other words, for James, the attempt to abstract all the *felt* physical symptoms associated with strong emotions results with nothing being left over; there is no "psychic" or mental entity existing apart, an "idea" or "impression" of "sadness," "anger," "fear," etc. "What kind of an emotion of fear would be left," argues James, "if the feeling neither of quickened heart-beats nor of shallow breathing, neither of trembling lips nor of weakened limbs, neither of goose-flesh nor of visceral stirrings, were present, it is quite impossible for me to think."

As in the article dealing with the reflex arc, Dewey sees that problem here is with the remnants of the old dualistic view of mind and body: either a psychic "feeling" with a physical reaction or a physical cause with a psychic effect. Dewey's solution here is similar also: If we look at the whole situation first, before breaking it up, both physical action and feeling have integrated functional roles. Dewey's major point is that "all 'emotional expression' is a phase of movements teleologically determined, and not a result of pre-existent emotion. . . " (*EW* 4:169). How are movements "teleologically determined"? Again, this refers to the act as the whole unit of behavior. Dewey states that "the situation clears itself up when we start from the character of the movement, as a completed or disturbed coordination, and then derive the corresponding types of normal and pathological emotion" (*EW* 4: 163). Normal emotion is that which has an object; pathological emotion, for Dewey, is "the objectless emotion," or rather, one which supplies its object and imposes it on the situation. In the normal case, though, there is a genuine response to the object; it "'sets trains going'—these are revivals of motor discharge and organic reinforcement. Upon such occasions thinking becomes really whole-hearted; it takes possession of us altogether, and passes over into the aesthetic" (*EW* 4: 157).

Here we see Dewey beginning to connect the aesthetic with a total, meaningful response to an object in a situation which involves the reintegration of a "disturbed coordination" in which both intelligence and emotion are interrelated and fulfilled. Expression is not the simple transit of a complete inner feeling out into the world by a mechanical action; nor is it just an accompanying inner response to physical conditions. It is the meaningful outcome of a process which has both phases of organic coordination and of emotional and conscious response and control. Thus Dewey says, "To an onlooker, my angry movements are expressions—signs, indications; but surely not to me" (*EW* 4: 154). Dewey repeats the same point years later in *Art as Experience*:

> At one extreme, there are storms of passion. . . . There is activity, but not, from the standpoint of the one acting, expression. An onlooker may say, "What an expression of rage!" But the enraged being is only raging, quite a different matter from *expressing* rage. . . . Again, the cry or smile of an infant may be expressive to mother or nurse and yet not be an act of expression of the baby (*AE*, 61; *LW* 10:67).

As will be discussed later, this is an important distinction for Dewey: the difference between a mute, uncontrolled "seizure" and the fully controlled and funded expressive gesture which realizes the aesthetic. To anticipate, they are parts of the evolving situation, the seizure coming first (like fear of a rattlesnake in the path), the phase of deliberation which tries to reconstruct the situation (e.g., to run, kill the snake, go around it, etc.), action and resolution. The original emotion of terror may be entirely transformed. From fearing the snake, we may develop an interest in snakes and their behavior and the role they play in desert ecology. We may even come to derive great satisfaction from observing them and, as naturalists do, seek them out. In the last case especially, the emotion has been transformed and made expressive because it has become connected with intelligence and meaning. It has been transformed by education. Instead of being eradicated, it has been given intelligent direction.

Emotion naturally arises in experience because experience is in a rhythmic alteration from stable to precarious and back. As a stable situation (like walking) is suddenly transformed into a precarious one (like running across a snake), the emotional seizure marks the inhibition of habits, and announces the phase of readjustment; it is the tension of object and response. "The emotion," asserts Dewey, "is, *psychologically, the adjustment or tension of habit and ideal . . .*" (*EW* 4:185). Emotion is properly considered a phase of the ongoing situation, and to the extent that experience is dramatic, intelligent, and informed, it will also have a depth of emotion to it and be expressive.

Here is one illuminating point where Dewey and Plato are in some agreement. Plato is often misunderstood as seeking to suppress desire. But for anyone who has read *The Symposium* or the central books of *The Republic*, it is evident that the good life for Plato does not involve the eradication of desire, or eros, but the education of desire. Eros mediates the world of ideal reality and the world of change, binding them together. Only those who feel this drive most have truly philosophical natures, says Plato. Philosophy, in other words, becomes the education and fulfillment of eros. However blind emotion may be as it awakens in the process of life, Dewey also argues that it becomes the impulsive force whereby we seek the ideal of reintegration and discover the paths of intelligence. The integrated experience, which Dewey sees exemplified in the aesthetic, will be alive with mind and feeling thoroughly interwoven. In its own way, the aesthetic experience will be that vision of the sea of beauty described by Plato. Only, for Dewey, this reflects the realization of the ideal possibilities of nature rather than the transformation of our natural origins in a moment of celestial homecoming. For both, however, one can state that human experience is a nisus toward a determining, meaning-giving horizon aesthetically apprehended, a drive which is the offspring of need and resource.

Dewey describes two further constituent factors of the act. These are impulse and habit. Impulse refers to the spontaneous, "plastic," and creative phase of the act in which the need for reconstructing the situation is apparent, and one seeks the best response, the "search for the correct stimulus." "Impulses are the pivots upon which the reorganization of activities turn, they are agencies of deviation, for giving new directions to old habits, changing their quality" (*HNC*,II:i, 93; *MW 14*:67). In broader terms, impulses reflect the possibility of creative response opened up in the tensive nature of the situation, and thus are vital for genuine growth and continuity. They mark the interface between the stable, structured world of habit and the immediacy of the present, which grabs us with emotional seizure.

Dewey distinguishes impulsion from impulse. The former term is the "movement outward and forward" of the "organism in its entirety." It is the general organizing activity of the living being rather than any specific action. "Impulsions are the beginnings of complete experience because they proceed from need . . . that belongs to the organism as a whole and that can be supplied only by instituting definite relations (active relations, interactions) with the environment" (*AE*, 58; *LW* 10:64). This is nothing less than the origin of the possibility of aesthetic experience. It indicates why Dewey will acknowledge the significance of *an* experience because of its capacity to satisfy the impulse for wholeness and integrity. The act is built upon this premise: significant experience is the striving toward fulfillment. When this striving is thwarted, the impulsion or demand tacitly operating becomes consciously revealed. Recall Heidegger's famous example of becoming aware of the essence of a hammer because of its breaking during routine activity, thereby suddenly leaping to attention. It goes from being merely "ready-to-hand" (the preconscious world of automatic habit, in Dewey's terms) to being "present-at-hand" (a tensive focus of consciousness for Dewey).[23] The moment the world is raised to awareness, as it were, is the moment it threatens to fall apart. The world as *object* arises from the world as action. If the sense of the original prereflective wholeness of experience is lost, we may settle upon any number of "dualisms" to account for the problematic world which sets consciousness its tasks: subject and object, mind and body, theory and practice, and so on. The broken hammer, originally part of a unified field of activity, is suddenly set off against "me" with my desires and purposes as a "thing" or "object."

To the extent the situation is reintegrated, meaning is added: "Blind surge has been changed into a purpose; instinctive tendencies are transformed into contrived undertakings. The attitudes of the self are informed with meaning" (*AE*, 59; *LW* 10:65). The carpenter with the broken hammer is suddenly aware of who he is, what he is doing, what role he plays in the entire project. He also is capable of being aware, as Heidegger points out, of the whole "world" involved in his simple activity: the hammer relates to nails, wood, building, living in houses, social occupations, and so on. For Dewey, the sense of the meaning of the situation becomes expressive as it is reconstructed:

> Impulsion from need starts an experience that does not know where it is going; resistance and check bring about the conversion of direct forward action into re-flection; what is turned back is the relation of hindering conditions to what the self possesses as working capital in virtue of prior experiences. As the energies thus involved reinforce the original impulsion, this operates more circumspectly with insight into end and method. Such is the outline of every experience that is clothed with meaning (*AE*, 60; *LW* 10:66).

It is essential, then, for there to be "working capital" for the situation to transcend merely impulsive reaction. But before the reconstruction of the situation through awareness of ends and means can be achieved, there must be this impulsion in experience.

Impulse, as distinguished from impulsion, stands for that particular phase of the act in which a specific tension is established which incites the search for the stimulus, i.e., which has a drive toward reintegration. We act "impulsively" when we try to mediate the situation on the basis of uninformed desire. Impulse naturally encounters the novel because it has no means-end relationship clearly in view. Artists, for this reason, may often seek to stimulate their imaginations through actions or drugs which randomize experience. The Dadaists, for example, "wrote" poetry by cutting up words, shaking them in a bag, and pulling them out one by one to form a poem. In seeking to become aware of a fresh, spontaneous image, one has to break with conventionalized, routine association. But, of course, pure impulsive action is not only a poor substitute for art, it is impossible. We find Dadaists, like Arp, admitting to rearranging "chance" patterns of fragments of paper. But even had he not rearranged the patterns, his method of determining the random pieces, his selection of materials, and so on, would be examples of order.

III. The Habitual Body and the Structure of Action

The role of structuring experience falls to habit. This concept, so central in pragmatism, received extensive treatment from Peirce and James before Dewey. For James, habit could denote both the rigidity and plasticity of behavior. Arising to meet the demands of a novel situation, habit could also become a set, repeated response. Habit, noted James, is at once the means of growth and "the enormous flywheel of society, its most precious conservative agent. It alone is what keeps us all within the bounds of ordinance, and saves the children of fortune from the envious uprisings of the poor."[24] For Peirce, habit was the basis of inference and action. "That which determines us," he says, "from given premises, to draw one inference rather than another is some habit of mind." Habits were the general structures of belief and were reflected in action as the meaning-giving interpretants of specific events. Through habit, the brute immediacy of experience could become a sign for a general objective reality. Indeed, for Peirce, "the whole function of thought is to produce habits of action."[25]

Dewey's account of habit proceeds from James' biological version on the one hand and Peirce's pragmatic version on the other, relating the two through the concept of the act. With James, Dewey sees habits arising from the nature of biological adjustment; with Peirce, Dewey asserts that they are the basis of the possibility of meaning and intelligent action. Habit, however, thus comes to have a notoriously broad range of meanings for Dewey. Kestenbaum observes that, "Habits are what Dewey variously calls 'accepted meanings,' 'funded meanings,' 'acquired meanings,' and 'organic meanings.' "[26] Dewey's use is even broader than this list suggests. Habits are "adjustments," "means," "organizations of energy" and "social modes of interaction" as well.

This is not to admit that Dewey is confused in his use. Habits primarily refer to the organizing abilities of the organism to reconstruct its environment; they "incorporate an environment within themselves. They are adjustments *of* the environment, not merely *to* it" (*HNC*, I:iii, 52; *MW* 14: 38). They are not "inner forces" or powers of an autonomous organism so much as dynamic, structured processes integrating the organism-environment field. They are general paths of integration and interpretation. As such they express continuity; in fact, they become the basis for the continuity between the biological and social worlds. Prior to any existing individual, there are those "definite modes of interaction of persons with one another" (*HNC*, I:iv, 59; *MW* 14:44) which are the "given" ways of interpreting and acting in the world. The symbolic universe of a culture, in other words, lies ready to shape the new impulsive lives born into it. Habits, then, are *situational* structures rather than individual reflexes, psychic associations or repeated actions.

Habits are therefore general dispositions or tendencies. This means two things for Dewey: "one that habits have a certain causal efficacy, the other that their outworking in any particular case is subject to contingencies" (*HNC*, I:iii, 49; *MW* 14: 37). More specifically, "all habits are affections . . . all have a projectile power. . . . All habits are demands for certain kinds of activity; and they constitute the self" (*HNC*, I:ii, 25; *MW* 14: 21). As Kestenbaum explains, habits are "dramatic" and "creative" prereflective, "sense-producing" aspects of experience. One culture's "way of life" may be quite different from another's such that given the same circumstances entirely different attitudes, meanings, and responses may be evoked. A mountain may evoke a religious, ceremonial attitude in an American Indian while to a mining geologist it may initiate exploration for coal and shale deposits. The point here is not "relativity of perception," it is rather that the whole world-view, the way of being in the world, for each individual not only structures the moment, but has that "projectile power" toward very different consequences. The Indian and the geologist do not see different mountains; they live different lives.

Though habits may incline us to act in certain ways in certain situations, no two situations are identical, and the differences from one situation to the next may not only determine the success or failure of that habitual way of acting, but may affect the habits themselves. In other words, the past is no absolute guarantor of the future, and habits, like rules, must ever be confronted with exceptions.

Habits have this general or universal character, as Peirce noted. This means they are capacities for treating different situations similarly in terms of relevant similar features. They constitute a complexly structured reservoir. Therefore, Dewey observes, "Repetition is in no sense the essence of habit." Repetition is not what makes habit possible; habit is what makes repetition possible.

> The essence of habit is an acquired predisposition to *ways* or modes of response, not to particular acts except as, under special conditions, these express a way of behaving. Habit means special sensitiveness or accessibility to certain classes of stimuli, standing predilictions and aversions, rather than bare recurrence of specific acts (*HNC*, I:iii, 42; *MW* 14:32).

Habits are the constitutive structures of organized responses. Any particular adjustment in one part of the field may mean a transformation of the whole system. Dewey is insistent on this point that "The whole organism is concerned in every act to some extent and in some fashion. . ." (*HNC*, II:vi, 150; *MW* 14:105). There is what Merleau-Ponty has happily called the "habitual body" which makes the world visible, i.e., to appear *as* a world; he says it is:

> By giving up part of his spontaneity, by becoming involved in the world through stable organs and pre-established circuits that man can acquire the mental and practical space which will theoretically free him from his environment and allow him to see it. . . . It is an

inner necessity for the most integrated existence to provide itself with an habitual body.[27]

Later on, Merleau-Ponty says that our habits "weave an environment" about us; Dewey would certainly agree.[28]

Habits are means of mediating situations; they are "active means, means that project themselves, energetic and dominating ways of acting" (*HNC*, I:ii, 25; *MW* 14:22). They are those tools which lie closest to hand, so close, as already noted, as to constitute the self. Habits are not to be thought of as purely means outside of ends; they determine, select and are immanent in those ends. Means, says Dewey, are everywhere in a process—ends are really just "terms" or limits of that process: "'End' is a name for a series of acts taken collectively— like the term army. 'Means' is a name for the same series taken distributively—like this soldier, that officer" (*HNC*, I:ii, 36; *MW* 14:28). The relation of ends and means via habits establishes the continuity of the act. Habits provide the conditions for meaning by not only creating the structured side of the situation, but by being the dynamic tools for transforming it. Dewey asserts that "habits are arts. They involve skill of sensory and motor organs, cunning or craft, and objective materials. . . . They require order, discipline and manifest technique" (*HNC*, I:i, 15; *MW* 14:16). Art is present with our most intimate and immanent way of being in the world.

The habitual body is the primary means and material of expression; it is the primary medium of meaning. The first characteristic of a "world," of a domain of significant experience, is the expressive gesture. While this idea will be discussed later, for now it can be observed that habit, infused with emotion and alive with impulse to the immediacy of the situation, is not only intelligent but potentially expressive. The simple, unconscious act of walking may tacitly embody a sense of pride, shame, indifference, or a host of other attitudes. The anthropologist Elizabeth Marshall Thomas says of the Kalahari Bushmen, "They are handsome because of the extreme grace in their way of moving, which is strong and deft and lithe; and to watch a Bushman walking or simply picking up something from the ground is like watching part of a dance."[29] While such habits alone do not constitute expression (except, as mentioned, in the derivative sense of a child's cry "expressing" pain to an onlooker or a gazelle "expressing" grace in running), they do provide the material for expression. The Bushmen easily transform their workaday habits into expressive actions, dances, and song.

While habit is thus the means toward expression and intelligent action, it is also capable of ossification into dead routine. This happens when habit loses its contact with emotion and impulse, in short, with the variety and immediacy of the situation. As Dewey illustrates:

> The difference between the artist and the mere technician is unmistakable. The technique or mechanism is fused with thought and feeling. The "mechanical" performer permits the mechanism to dictate the performance. It is absurd to say that the latter exhibits habit and the former not. We are confronted with two kinds of habit, intelligent and routine. All life has its élan, but only the prevalence of dead habits deflects life into mere élan (HNC, I:iv, 71; MW 14: 51).

Habits, being dynamic structures for Dewey, connote flexible means of enlarging or expanding the situation; habit as mindless repetition is a decayed, derivative mode. As Merleau-Ponty states, "Habits express our power of dilating our being in the world, or changing our existence by appropriating fresh instruments."[30] Dewey not only would agree with this but insist that habits form the basic tools of learning or of expanding the meaning of a situation. Dewey insists, "Habits enter into the *constitution* of the situation; they are in it and of it, not, so far as it is concerned, something outside it" ("Epistemological Realism" in *EEL*, 277; *MW* 7:120).

The immediate moment or phase of a situation is responded to *as* part of a situation because of this constitutive connective power of habit. Habits, in other words, frame or establish a temporal *context*, a referential basis of interpretation and action. To refer again to optical illusions like the Muller-Lyer diagram or Zöllner's lines, or even to visual puns like Jastrow's duck-rabbit, we see immediately how a habitual way of reading the world is brought up short, as it were, and made conscious. There are numerous examples to illustrate Dewey's thesis that our very way of perceiving the world, much less our ways of understanding it, depend upon the informative nature of habit. Bedouins living in an isolated culture which rejects pictorial images cannot intuitively see lines as representing a man or camel, nor can they see photographs as images of nature. Canadian Indians who live in circular, domed huts have a very different sense of spatial relationships and aesthetic balance than someone growing up in a modern city which is based on the grid and line. Again, visually oriented Eskimos incorporate numerous subtle "pun-drawings" into their art which we do not even notice. On a different scale, Kuhn's study of scientific revolutions points out how deeply this selective, prejudicial power of habit may influence primary data of research. Kuhn remarks that Western astronomers only began detecting change in the heavens after Copernicus had questioned the Medieval paradigm which thought of the heavens as progressive orders of changeless perfection: "The Chinese, whose cosmological beliefs did not preclude celestial change, had recorded the appearance of many new stars in the heavens at an earlier date. Also, even without the aid of the telescope, the Chinese had systematically recorded the appearance of sunspots centuries before these were seen by Galileo and his contemporaries."[31] Habits predispose use actively, they determine what we see, what we focus upon, and how we may respond.

There are several implications to note. First, "There is no immaculate conception of meanings or purposes" (*HNC*, I:ii, 30-31; *MW* 14:25). Not only are we always "in the world," but we are in it in certain active *ways* which respond and discriminate divergently. Habits are not "inner drives" or "powers" latent in us like the "seminal reasons" of the Stoics; they are not "things." They are dynamic and structuring aspects of those "field-events" called situations. The more complex and discriminating we are is due to the habitual ways we have of interpreting and responding to a situation; indeed, it refers to the very possibility of certain situations coming to be at all. Therefore, the more numerous our habits the wider the field of possible:

> Observation and foretelling. The more flexible they are, the more refined is perception in its discrimination and the more delicate the presentation evoked by imagination. The sailor is intellectually at home on the sea, the painter in his studio, the man of science in his laboratory. These commonplaces . . . mean nothing more or less than that habits formed in this process of exercising biological aptitudes are the sole agents of observation, recollection, foresight and judgment. . . . Concrete habits do all the perceiving, recognizing, imagining, recalling, judging, conceiving and reasoning that is done (*HNC*, III:i, 175-77; *MW* 14:123-24).

The point is not just that the sailor, artist, or scientist each has his own environment in which his skilled habits come into refined play; for the sailor a storm at sea *becomes* a situation which is more stable than precarious, possibly even an aid in speed; for the artist the storm *becomes* a situation which may eventuate in a painting or poem; for the scientist the storm *becomes* a situation in which meteorological phenomena may be studied. The habits of each person realize different potentialities in nature and create different situations.

Habits fused with emotion and impulse constitute objects of experience or "perceived meanings" and these meanings involve a "dramatic" or participatory attitude. An object reflects taking a determinate response to part of the world. These aspects are fundamental for the capacity of experience to achieve artistic expression and aesthetic enjoyment. Habit is kept alive through the roles of impulse and emotion. These signify a "break" with the homeostasis of the environment in some ways. This may be purely biological, as in the case of pain, hunger, or any reflex. It may also be an "imbalance" in the cultural environment, the world. A swastika on a synagogue, a parent's command, the cry of an injured child—all these evoke meanings which arrest and focus attention. The situation must be "minded"; its meaning discovered. This, according to Dewey, is the origin of consciousness. But why is consciousness a continuous phenomenon? Dewey's answer is that "in every waking moment, the complete balance of the organism and its environment is constantly interfered with and as constantly restored" (*HNC*, III:i, 178-79; *MW* 14:125). A consequence of this is that the more refined and diverse our responses are, the more there is to respond to, i.e., the more "attention" will be needed. In other words, more complex behavior can *create* problematic situations which would not exist on simpler levels. Because we live in a world of symbols, beliefs, and meanings, a falling star may initiate elaborate rituals to placate gods and set the world aright, whereas for a herd of cattle the event passes without concern. The more complicated our modes of being in the world are, the more intelligence is needed.

The question is, however, how do habits create "perceived meanings"? Keeping in mind that for Dewey the situation always operates with a number of phases or aspects functioning together, a schematic outline may help. Because the world always has some aspect of novelty to it, habits are, more or less, always in the process of readjustment (and this may involve *ignoring* novel features of the environment as well as paying attention to them). Because habits integrate and unify situations, they tend to project a context, to structure a situation around any immediate object, both spatially and temporally. We see a wheel as part of the car rather than as part of the ground, and we see space itself as having depth and direction because of habit. We also see things temporally as processes: we see the car's movement as part of one process, the growth of a child as another. We may interpret the process in terms of its future outcome, "going home," "growing vegetables," "discovering a solution," etc. The present moment comes to inhabit a spatio-temporal field of meaning and action, a context, and it is shaped by that context. Dewey avoids the transcendental-immediate dualism by beginning with a concept of the situation as a temporally developing whole, a "field-process."

As a situation develops, a "tensive" or "problematic" phase may arise. As mentioned before, "problematic" is not necessarily a happy term, connoting as it does simple, technological practical action in the crudest sense, like fixing a tire. *All* experience is problematical in some degree. By this term, Dewey was trying to refer to the tensive focus of a situation.[32] Lying down after a heavy meal is hardly the problematic situation that the lean hunter faces trying to snare today's food. It is for convenience that we call the latter problematic and not the former, but both are modes of adjustment.

Keeping in mind that situations are more or less secure or precarious rather than absolutely one or the other, when a problematic moment in the situation arises, habits are, as Dewey puts it, "turned inside out," i.e., stable habits become "reflected in remembered and perceived objects having a meaning" (*HNC*, III:ii, 182; *MW 14*: 127-28). More directly, objects are perceived meanings arising from the shock of world and habit:

> Thus out of shock and puzzlement there gradually emerges a figured framework of objects, past, present, future. These shade off variously into a vast penumbra of vague, unfigured things, a setting which is taken for granted and not at all explicitly presented. The complexity of the figured scene in its scope and refinement of contents depends wholly upon prior habits and their organization. . . . [Consciousness's] occurrence marks a peculiarly delicate connection between highly organized habits and unorganized impulses. Its contents or objects, observed, recollected, projected and generalized into principles represent the incorporated material of habits coming to the surface, because habits are disintegrating at the touch of conflicting impulses. But they also gather themselves together to comprehend impulse and make it effective (*HNC*, III:ii, 182-83; *MW 14:128*).

Among these discriminated aspects of the situation are those meanings which constitute the "self." The phase of deliberation or the adjustment of the immediate problem into a resolved context is characterized by Dewey as a "dramatic rehearsal in imagination" and as an "experiment" with ideas (*HNC*, II:iii, 190-91; *MW 14:132-33*). Clearly, what Dewey has in mind is simply that before we remove a rattlesnake from our path we try to imagine how we will do it, rehearsing possible avenues, trying to see what likely consequences might arise with each possible action. But, contrary to Dewey's language at this point, subjective speculation is secondary to the primary power of social deliberation. We debate with ourselves because we have debated with others. Discussion of how to deal with a problem in a social context, for Mead as well as Dewey, is what teaches us to deliberate privately. On a more elementary level, we are *taught* to be mindful and thoughtful. Mind is social and situational, and our efforts at "working" the immediate problematic phase involve organizing dramatic, dynamic habits of action and meaning into a coherent field. From being read as a brute object inhibiting action, the focus of perception is read against a number of possible contexts which reveal aspects of its meaning. The environment, so to speak, widens with this play of habits interpreting the object. "We do not act *from* reasoning;" claims Dewey, "but reasoning puts before us objects which are not directly or sensibly present, so that we may then react directly to these objects, . . . precisely as we would to the same objects if they were physically present" (*HNC*, III:iv, 200; *MW* 14:139).

The dramatic nature of this must be emphasized to contrast it with the utilitarian theory of reasoning as calculation. Dewey himself significantly chooses the metaphor of the actor—the artist—over against that of the accountant.[33] The purpose of foresight is not prediction but "to ascertain the meaning of present activities and to secure, so far as possible, a present activity with a unified meaning" (*HNC*, III:iv, 205-06; *MW* 14:143). Only rarely do we treat situations for the possible cumulative amount of pleasure or pain or even happiness likely to be obtained. The task is to reconstruct the present toward its ideal, realizable possibilities. The future consequences of the utilitarian never arrive; there is an infinite arithmetical sum to be computed. For Dewey, the utilitarians enslaved the present to the intangible future forever. It is the precise point of Dewey's approach to invert this priority and make the present the question for action. When, however, one sees the present as part of a *meaningful action*, as something which can contribute toward the meaning and value of our lives, then the present can be critically reconstructed in terms of future consequences. These consequences are dramatically enacted *ideals* of life. We participate in the meaning of the world dramatically. Tribal rituals and ceremonies point directly to this: before the world is quantified and measured it is inhabited. This underscores Dewey's central thesis that the question of "meaning" is vitally linked to growth of experience:

> We have to be always learning and relearning the meaning of our active tendencies. . . . [The] continual search and experimentation to discover the meaning of changing activity keeps activity alive, growing in significance. . . . Imaginative forethought . . . keeps that act from sinking below consciousness into routine habit or whimsical brutality. It preserves the meaning of that act alive, and keeps it growing in depth and refinement of meaning. There is no limit to the amount of meaning which reflective and meditative habit is capable of importing into even simple acts . . . (*HNC*, III:iv, 208-09; *MW* 14: 144-45).

Because there is habit in the situation, the field of experience is a structured context capable of further organization and wholeness. In fact, "habit" is just this capacity of experience to become a rich, connected field through participation and action. The whole precedes the part, but is realized through it. This, in brief, is the force of Dewey's emphasis on situation, act, and context. Because habit establishes the context, it transforms the basic biological nature of the act into a situation capable of taking on meanings.

One final characteristic of habit should be mentioned, one which links the subject directly to Dewey's aesthetics. Part of the meaning of a situation involves this drive toward wholeness, the attempt to mediate the problematic and transform it into the consummatory. This only happens because the immediate aspect of the situation in its problematic phase reveals itself as a means toward reintegrating the field. The present, in other words, becomes interpreted in terms of its ideal significance and so *becomes* a means of reconstructing itself.[34] In the deliberative phase of experience, after possible ways of reconstructing the situation have been imaginatively entertained, a specific course of action or mediation is selected. To the extent every experience has a mediated, reconstructive value, it has a potential end-in-view which "constitutes the meaning and value of an activity as it comes under deliberation" (*HNC*, III:vi, 225; *MW* 14:155). In art, the end-in-view becomes so wholly integrated with the act from beginning to end that the "meaning" of the work is the work itself. The guiding sense of the whole is immanent throughout, making it *an* experience.

The end-in-view organizes the field-process of experience; it gathers the whole context into itself as it functions, and in so doing is both immediately present and mediating, making the field present also. The end-in-view actively mediates between the real and ideal. The way this happens will be discussed later, but essentially it is through qualitative sense and feeling that the situation is immanent in the present moment:

> The "end" is the figured pattern at the centre of the field through which runs the axis of conduct. About this central figuration extends an infinitely supporting background in a vague whole, undefined and undiscriminated. At most intelligence but throws a spotlight on that little part of the whole which marks out the axis of movement. Even if the light is flickering and the illuminated portion stands forth only dimly from the shadowy background, it suffices if we are shown the way to move. To the rest of the consequences . . . corresponds a background of feeling, of diffused emotion (*HNC*, III:vii, 262; *MW* 14:180).

Thus the body, which will become the medium of expression and communication, is a prefigured, teleological and dynamic field. It incorporates luminous and horizonal features and is deeply implicated in the world as process. The capacity of the body to respond and act, to be disturbed and to organize, to feel itself threatened with disconnection and to generate strategies of reconnection with the world provides the condition from which communication emerges. In itself, however, embodied life is mute and unavailable, an event in the world but not in possession of itself as expression. Only when this embodiment is a socially shared event does it become used and so available for self-interpretation and expressive enactment. Only as the body becomes a symbolic medium does the self-other relationship emerge at all. A lived body is not necessarily anyone's body because it is not for someone other. Therefore, an analysis of the body alone will not give us the mind.

IV. Social Mind: Gesture, Expression and Participation

The dominant fact of human existence is the inhabitation of a world of meaning and value. This world lives in all those symbols through which we actively share or create our existence with others. Culture is the activity of communication. Ultimately, culture is nothing else than all those symbolic modes of shared participation which constitute the world. In one respect, culture simply is a general body of shared habits which make coexistence possible. Culture is rooted in the lived body. But it reflects powerful generalized habits which appropriate the body and make it part of a complex event, the traditions which bind the community. The body's very capacity to be involved and to adapt flexibly, makes it easily available to pre-existent determinate actions, the structures of the culture into which it is born. And these begin shaping it at once until eventually the body is attuned to the life of symbols so that they gain operative power and guide the body throughout most of its life. The root of "religion," *religio*, meant "to bind," no doubt because religion was what bound the community into a whole. It made one a member with duties, privileges, and commitments.

Dewey's emphasis on the organic basis of experience was necessary because of the dominant tradition which opposed the natural to the mental or understood it at best as a lower, degraded expression of Spirit's self-knowledge. For this Dewey was often regarded as a "naturalist" in the tradition of Darwin or Spencer. When Dewey developed his theory of culture, which saw mind as constituted through the shared participatory act of communication, an act which surpassed the biological body, he was regarded as a crypto-Hegelian.

This problem in interpretation should be familiar by now. Dewey was trying to keep faith with his principle of continuity, which was the essence of his naturalism, and so he seemed a materialist to the idealists, an idealist to the materialists, or something both at once to anyone who was a "nothing-butter" in the tradition of Hobbes. Dewey does regard the social as something more than what can be accounted for by biology or genetics, though these are factors which should not be considered irrelevant any more so than the physical environment itself. If it makes sense to see the Kalahari Bushmen, the Pygmies of Africa, the Eskimo, and the Polynesians in terms of their physical environments, it should also make sense to see culture in terms of the biological environment as a whole. Reductionisms like sociobiology or structuralism must be avoided, first because they are unnecessary, given Dewey's principle of continuity, and second, because in their desire to explain everything by a single principle they make mysteries of what they cannot account for. In *Experience and Nature*, Dewey had labelled his philosophy "naturalistic empiricism" or "naturalistic humanism." "To many," he added, "the associating of the two words will seem like talking of a round square, so engrained is the notion of the separation of man and experience from nature" (*EN*, 1a; *LW* 1:10). Later, in *Logic: The Theory of Inquiry*, Dewey transforms this name for his philosophy to "cultural naturalism" (*LTI*, 20; *LW* 12: 28), reflecting his growing dissatisfaction with "empiricism" as well as "humanism" as illuminating terms. I think this should be the term under which Dewey's philosophy is presented, showing as it does his interests ranged far beyond those of "instrumentalism."

Cultural naturalism regards the social as a new mode of functioning which arises naturally in the world by utilizing available structures and potentialities in novel and more inclusive ways. Life is transformed from mere copresence or coexistence into an interactive, participatory event in which there is meaning. Association or interaction is one of the generic features of existence. We see various forms of it from the subatomic level to the human. What differentiates these levels is the type of interaction which occurs. On all levels there is organization of parts into wholes, but these wholes realize different ends; they accomplish different things. Clearly, what human coexistence accomplishes is something more than physical interaction or even mere survival. As the Greeks saw, human beings are capable of pursuing "the good life," the life where intelligence realizes a variety of worthwhile ends, of which shared experience is paramount.[35] But for Dewey this is not to be accounted for by a preordained end shaping the restless matter of nature from above. It comes about with the accomplishment of communication. While communication may have originated in aiding our species to survive, given that coordinated group action was necessary to a creature of our individual weakness, once present it set the stage for the realization of an untold number of *new* ends, a range of possibilities recorded in our histories and cultures and which have not yet been exhausted.

In *Experience and Nature,* Dewey's discussion of communication follows his analysis of experience as situational, nature as precarious and stable, ends as naturally suffered, enjoyed, or "had" events, and means or instruments as active "doings" whereby we undertake to reconstruct the world. The placement and sequence of the chapters in this book follow a hidden but very profound dialectic. A world in which experience played no role nor which had any function to realize in its environment would not interest us. A world without change would not generate desire or intelligence just as a world without structure would eternally frustrate them. A world in which there were no moments undergone and enjoyed for their intrinsic qualities would not establish the quest for obtaining those experiences when they vanished. The search for means of stablizing and directing the world sets one on the path of action, which is to eat of the fruit of the tree of knowledge. Action in turn creates the possibility of interaction with others of our kind as well as with other objects in the world. But when we interact with those who deal with the world as we do, new possibilities are opened which are not present in our transactions with fire, stone, or even animals. We come to grasp that the other is another like us, and we are like him. There is a common, shared experience which makes communication possible and mutual interaction far more flexible, far more rich in its possibilities than anything ever seen before. Thus Dewey begins his discussion with the quiet understatement, "Of all affairs, communication is the most wonderful" (*EN,* 166; *LW 1:* 132). It is in his subsequent chapters that we see all which it leads to: the realization of individuality and creativity, meaningful experience, conscious deliberation, the arts of intelligence, and critical wisdom.

What makes communication possible and what is it? In one sense, it makes itself possible simply because we are born into a world where there already is a system of communication which is progressively directed toward us. But it would be more accurate to say it makes *us* possible. We gesture, talk, and express ourselves because we were taught to. What is artificial is to try to project ourselves back to a state of nature, as did Locke or Rousseau, and then see communication as an artifice built upon the artifice of our social existence. Communication should not be understood by opposing it to the natural; instead it should be regarded as a transformation of it.

The question then comes down to: *how* does communication utilize and transform the biological structures so that something entirely new, meaning, comes to characterize the world? That human beings have an unusual capacity to form and reform habits is noteworthy, but not enough to indicate the radical sort of change brought about by language and culture. But if we start with the recognition that from the beginning human beings are involved in complex social relationships in which mutual action, recognition, bonding, and the prolonged raising of children are facts, the capacity for emotional response and habitual development is part of a much more complex environment. Our first emotional responses are less likely to be the familiar Lockean ideas of red, sweet, round, and so on than those of dependence, love, separation, anxiety, and others which probably have no name. Our first acts of genuine communication are more likely to be cries for food or demands for attention than naming indifferent objects.

The social context, as anyone who grew up in a family can tell, is not by and large a tranquil one. Problematic situations seem rather the order of the day. This is especially true of the young, who have not mastered that mysterious and difficult medium whereby they can express needs, wants, or desires. In order for expression to occur, something must be utilized as a medium, some public event which can be shared and responded to. The first thing at hand, so to speak, is that most available means of organizing the world about us, the body. Our first years are spent mastering its possibilities. But to use one's body as a means to something else, such as using one's arm and hand as a means to reaching a toy, is not the same as using one's arm and hand as a means for someone else to do something, such as indicating that one wants the toy. The former is simply using the body; the latter is to make use of it, to apprehend it as the initiating part of an action which requires for its completion the responsive participation in that action by another for whom the gesture is a *gesture*. Communication begins in the event of participation in a social situation where the interaction between the participants realizes some end. We may be creatures with a flexible range of habitual responses—the human palate and throat can make an amazing variety of sounds. But by the time we are two or three we have settled down to concentrating on just those sounds which define the tonal range of our linguistic group, its aesthetic contours, so to speak. The reason for this is obvious—these are the tones we need to use to be understood; these are the tones which signify words.

Dewey and Mead thus see the origin of communication in two events. The first is simply the capacity to appropriate the body and its talents as a means to an end. The second event is to regulate action from the concept of symbolic mediation and mutual participation. Dewey observes:

> Gestures and cries are not primarily expressive and communicative. They are modes of organic behavior as much as are locomotion, seizing and crunching. Language, signs and significance, come into existence not by intent and mind but by overflow, by-products, in gestures and sound. The story of language is the story of the *use* made of these occurrences; a use that is eventual, as well as eventful. . . . If the mere existence of sounds . . . constituted language, lower animals might well converse more subtly and fluently than man. But they became language only when used within a context of mutual assistance and direction. The latter are alone of prime importance in considering the transformation of organic gestures and cries into names, things with significance, or the origin of language (*EN*, 175; *LW* 1:138-39).

Later on, Dewey adds, "The heart of language is not 'expression' of something antecedent, much less expression of antecedent thought. It is communication; the establishment of cooperation in an activity in which there are partners, and in which the activity of each is modified and regulated by partnership. To fail to understand is to fail to come into agreement in action; to misunderstand is to set up action at cross purposes" (*EN*, 179; *LW* 1:141).

This bears a good deal of consideration. Dewey had resolved the dualistic reflex arc by showing that sensorimotor coordination was a mutual adjustment of one whole act. The child reaching for the candle guided his reaching by his seeing and his seeing by his reaching. The phases interpreted each other because they were part of one continuous activity. It was the continuity of the activity which allowed for the further interpretation of the heat and pain to be responded to by withdrawing the burnt hand. Dewey is using the same model here, but on the scale of social participation. The act is now one shared by several members instead of being that of one organism. If the act is to be accomplished, there needs to be a means of communication because there is the need of *mutual* ongoing coordination. The participants in the act need to know what the others are doing so that they can determine their own conduct, and vice versa. Above all, there must be some mutual agreement on the end of the action, that is, on what the action is. A symbol system arises when such available material as cries or movements of the arms or head can actively mediate action between several participants. In other words, the meaning of a symbol lies not in its capacity to create similar images in different people's minds nor simply in its capacity to fall under a semantic rule.

It lies in the capacity to coordinate action toward a commonly undertaken end. Syntactics and semantics exist because of their pragmatic value. To see meaning as grounded in the act of communication, moreover, is to see it as a problematic process of mutual interpretation in which there is a constant interplay between clarity and ambiguity.

Meaning is as temporal as it is social. To see language or meaning as a code is to see it in terms of defining a settled or unproblematic situation. Such rigid codes do exist, from the elaborate codes used in logic and mathematics to the kinship relations of tribal cultures. These reflect highly stablized modes of interaction. If mathematicians could not agree on the use of rules governing their symbols, or if a tribe could not agree on kinship patterns, little further work could be accomplished. While such rigidly organized structures do exist and provide a reassuringly exact body of data for the investigator, there is little reason to regard them as paradigmatic instances of meaning or culture. Their very lawlike nature leads to the tendency to regard language or culture as a synchronic structure, when the obvious fact is that both have evolved. If life had gone on in such a precise environment where ambiguity played no role, neither mathematics nor structuralism would have come to be.

Therefore Dewey chooses to look at *communication* as the key to meaning, and this is to be understood as a transactional event in which structure and ambiguity, actuality and possibility, order and disorder are present. The temporality and teleology of the event cannot be safely ignored. On the one hand, Dewey sees communication emerging from tools and on the other from signalling events. Both these subjects must be approached cautiously. By pointing to tools, Dewey is attempting to show that it is through a particular objective mode of conduct that we begin to appropriate the very *idea* of action, which in turn reveals our temporality and our situationality. A tool is a means of grasping the future through control of the present.

> The first step away from oppression of immediate things and events was taken when man employed tools and appliances, for manipulating things so as to render them contributory to desired objects. In responding to things not in their immediate qualities but for the sake of ulterior results, immediate qualities are dimmed, while those features which are signs, indices of something else, are distinguished. A thing is more significantly what it makes possible than what it immediately is (*EN*, 128; *LW* 1:105).

The immediate is not ignored so much as reinterpreted. We do not infer fire by not seeing smoke nor do we drive a nail by not using the hammer. We could not escape the immediate if we wanted to. A "tool" is a transformation of the immediate in terms of its possibilities toward the future by using it to integrate or organize conduct. The present becomes seen in terms of the possibilities it contains rather than purely in terms of its actualities, its purely had or undergone qualitative ends. Tools are instrinsically temporal and situational structures.

> Man's bias toward himself easily leads him to think of a tool solely in relation to himself, to his hand and eyes, but its primary relationship is toward other external things, as the hammer to the nail, and the plow to the soil. Only through this objective bond does it sustain relation to man himself and his activities. A tool denotes a perception and acknowledgement of sequential bonds in nature (*EN*, 123; *LW* 1:101).

A hammer refers to the hardness of nails, the softness of wood, the drive of force and friction, the need for shelter in a world of cold and rain as well as to the being who holds the hammer and drives it with skill and art, who needs the shelter and from this need has devised a plan. To grasp the hammer is to grasp a project. A hammer is only metal and wood otherwise. In grasping the project, we undertake the *present* as the *material* for the basis of action. The immediate moment is no longer had but used and directed. Tools are transcendentals for Dewey:

> The invention and use of tools have played a large part in consolidating meanings, because a tool is a thing used as a means to consequences, instead of being taken directly and physically. It is intrinsically relational, anticipatory, predictive. Without reference to the absent, or "transcendence," nothing is a tool. The most convincing evidence that animals do not "think" is found in the fact that they have no tools, but depend upon their own relatively-fixed bodily structures to effect results. . . . Anything whatever used as a tool exhibits . . . an existence having meaning and potential essence (*EN*, 185-86; *LW* 1:146).

Tools reveal the world in terms of its relations, bonds, conditions, or structures because they also reveal the user in terms of his projects. Man himself stands forth as an agent, as a being with a temporal existence which is purposively involved with the world in terms of its portents and possibilities. To set upon the path of action is also to set upon the path of self-transformation. For when man undertakes to reconstruct the world, he reveals new ends as well securing old ones. Originally, the domestication of grain or cattle may have been seen as supplementing the needs of a nomadic existence. But gradually man's discoveries transformed him into a farmer and town-dweller, a builder and a planter, a creator of social structures more complex than the loose democracies of the hunter. Fire warmed at first, but it became the means to pottery, metallurgy, steam-power, and petroleum energy.

But in discussing tools we have jumped ahead of ourselves, for most tools are cultural instruments. That is, they "are bound up with directions, suggestions and records made possible by speech; what has been said about the role of tools is subject to a condition supplied by language, the tool of tools" (*EN*, 168; *LW* 1:134). The hammer also refers to the refining of metal, the shaping of wood, the toolmakers, the carpenter who learns his trade from the master carpenter and who may come to pass his knowledge on. The hammer exists in a context of contracts and payments, boom times and bust; it is used with reference to blueprints, to shouts of orders and requests. But the central point remains: tools are extensions of the projects of the body and it is because they reveal the present in terms of its possibilities that the biological individual can undertake the most important task, the active participation in the social project itself.

As already indicated, communication *is* just that activity of co-ordinating social action. Like any other project, it requires instruments, tools or a medium. Thus a very special and unique tool is called for which allows for *mutual* coordination. It must allow for the members to participate in one action, to share ends and apprehend possibilities together. Thus, the major achievement of communication will be its intrinsic capacity to make action intelligent through making it social.

> When communication occurs, all natural events are subject to reconsideration and revision; they are re-adapted to meet the requirements of conversation . . . . Events turn into objects, things with a meaning. They may be referred to when they do not exist, and thus be operative among things distant in space and time, through vicarious presence in a new medium. . . . Events when once they are named lead an independent and double life. In addition to their original existence, they are subject to ideal experimentation: their meanings may be infinitely combined and rearranged in imagination and the outcome of this inner experimentation—which is thought—may issue forth in interaction with crude or raw events (*EN*, 166; *LW* 1:132).

The presence of communication makes the immediately lived moment fraught with meaning. "Even the dumb pang of an ache achieves significant existence when it can be designated and descanted upon; it ceases to be merely oppressive and becomes important . . ." (*EN*, 167; *LW* 1:133). From comforting and tendering a small, sick child to holding the hand of a dying friend or parent, a mere organic event is transformed into something significant because it is shared and participated in by others. Heroic, even if lonely, deaths can become significant actions. While Heidegger is right that "death" forms the ultimate horizon of my possibilities as an individual, defining "my life" and "my actions," it is not true that death is necessarily an isolatingly absurd event, as many existentialists have understood. I may also grasp my death as an event *for* others; but for Dewey this would make all the difference. It can be a mode of meaningful participation. The finality of individual death opens up the possibility, even the necessity, of participating in a shared social project which transcends individual lives—culture. Everyone dies, but the culture continues.[36] As Dewey observes in *Democracy and Education*:

> Every one of the constituent elements of a social group. . . is born immature, helpless without language, beliefs, ideas, or social standards. Each individual, each unit who is the carrier of the life-experience of his group, in time passes away. Yet the life of the group goes on. . . . If a plague carried off the members of a society all at once, it is obvious that the group would be permanently done for. Yet the death of each of its constituent members is as certain as if an epidemic took them all at once (*DE*, 2-3; *MW* 9:5-6).

Education and enculturation are necessary means of establishing continuity of action and meaning. The process of coming to be a member of a group is the primary and omnipresent fact of human life. It should not be unnatural to discover in the activity of learning a better and truer model for meaning and communication than those based on the notions of static, atemporal structures. The arts of social life transcend the biological limit of death, and this has meaning for human existence as it is lived. Through culture, the individual life can be taken up into a transindividual project.

The key to communication is how we come to participate in the life of others and they with ours. Once this is possible, the mutual coordination of action, the common appropriation of projects also is possible. Dewey finds the key in that of learning or dramatic participation. To be born into a society is to be born into structured patterns of activity. What one learns in education is to participate in these roles; to become a member of the group is to know one's range of actions which have significance for the group. To learn to be human involves learning how to play by rules. There are many early instances of this in the miniature games we play from peek-a-boo to knocking down towers of blocks. But the supreme game of course is language; it is the game of games, the one which opens up the avenues to all the rest of the culture's activities through education. Language is the "tool of tools" becuase of its orchestral power in coordinating our varieties of projects into one culture, one community.

> The importance of language as the necessary, and, in the end, suffi-
> cient condition of the existence and transmission of non-purely or-
> ganic activities and their consequences lies in the fact that, on one
> side, it is a strictly biological mode of behavior, emerging in natural
> continuity from earlier organic activities, while, on the other, it com-
> pels one individual to take the standpoint of other individuals and to
> see and inquire from a standpoint that is not strictly personal but is
> common to them as participants or "parties" in a conjoint undertak-
> ing. But it first has reference to some other person or persons with
> whom it institutes *communication*—the making of something com-
> mon (*LTI*, 46 *LW* 12:52).

The essence of language is that there is always a "one" and an "other" who interact. It is not an impersonal system of difference because it has a participatory structure reflected in the very number and persons of verbs not to mention in the cases of pronouns. Other modes of cultural participation are also deeply reflected in the varieties of lan-guages. The plurality of forms of address in Japanese and other Asian languages forces awareness of the social hierarchies involved. The word for "I" is often a mode of the form "your subject." In English, the use of "man" to refer to men and women has come to be seen as part of a social problem. Thus, learning a culture is learning the roles we can take and this in turn comes to define who we are. The underlying problematic of the social encounter may be this very tension in testing our self-understanding or self-image. Only through social participa-tion do we acquire a self, yet this is ever at risk, as Erving Goffman has shown.[37]

From birth on, we are involved in more and more activities; as we master the elementary roles we are pushed on to more difficult ones. From being the mere recipient of attention, we are asked to give attention, from being treated as not responsible for our actions, we are progressively treated as more and more responsible. We are espe-cially asked to participate as communicants.

> If we had not talked with others and they with us, we should never
> talk to and with ourselves. Because of converse, social give and take,
> various organic attitudes become an assemblage of persons engaged
> in converse, conferring with one another, exchanging distinctive
> experiences, listening to one another, over-hearing unwelcome re-
> marks, accusing and excusing. Through speech a person dramatical-
> ly identifies himself with potential acts and deeds; he plays many

roles, not in successive stages of life but in a contemporaneously enacted drama. Thus mind emerges (*EN,* 170; *LW 1:*135).

By "mind," Dewey is not referring to personal self-consciousness but to the general modes of conduct which create the possibility of the self along with the role of the other. Mind appears or is appropriated by individuals in a culture, but "is in itself a system of belief, recognitions and ignorances, of acceptances and rejections, of expectancies and appraisals of meanings which have been instituted under the influence of custom and tradition" (*EN,* 219; *LW 1:* 170). Mind is a way of referring to the possibilities an individual may act on in terms of culture. Cultures are just these generalized tendencies for structuring, interpreting, and responding to the world. As one is involved in participating in shared activity, one becomes aware that it is "I" who is asked to do something, that it is "I" who must respond, that there is someone here who is within my sphere of action—which is to say that the act called for is to be *my* act. There must be some way, some means of responding which fulfills the request for participating.

The means for doing this is through symbolic action. Symbolic action is to be distinguished from signalling, though it utilizes signalling. Most animals exhibit signalling behavior: the waving of fins, the rustling of feathers, the bristling of hair, the arching of the back. While such acts bring about consequences, they are done without intent. As Dewey notes, "Primarily meaning is intent and intent is not personal in a private and exclusive sense" (*EN,* 180; *LW 1:*142). In other words, the act of the peacock or the cat is not "expressive"—except in a derivative sense to an onlooker. The animal is not using the gesture to stand for the activity, even though the result may be accomplished through the immediate act. For example:

> By habit, by conditioned reflex, hens run to the farmer when he makes a clucking noise or when they hear the rattle of grain in a pan. When the farmer raises his arms to throw the grain they scatter and fly, to return only when the movement ceases. . . . But a human infant learns to discount such movements; to become interested in them as events preparatory to a desired consummation; he learns to treat them as signs of an ulterior event so that his response is to their meaning. He treats them as means to consequences. The hen's activity is egocentric; that of the human being is participative. The latter puts himself at the standpoint of a situation in which two parties share. This is the essential peculiarity of language, or signs (*EN,* 177-78; *LW 1:*140).

In one of his less dramatic illustrations, Dewey gives the instance of one person asking another to bring her a flower, say by pointing.

The proper response is not to the movement of her arm, but to its intent, that is, to see it *as* "pointing to something." How is this possible? The person responding must, as it were, try to become the first person and see the situation from that person's standpoint—to try to see what the situation *is* for her, that of wanting the flower and for him to get it. In seeing the object of the gesture, the flower, he must see the relationship between the flower and the desire of the other, with the additional component of seeing the role he plays in this. He will bring her the flower only if he can integrate himself into a shared response, namely that she should have the flower. The "stimulus" to his act of bringing the flower is his "anticipatory share in the consummation of a transaction in which both participate" (*EN*, 179; *LW 1*: 141). They must both share the common possibility of the situation and define their roles within it for communication to occur. The first person must point with the intent that the act be seen-as the *beginning* of an uncompleted act, as a request *for* the other. She must take his standpoint, she must see him as a respondent to her gesture just as he must see her in terms of her perspective, the initiator of an action. There is a double sharing of perspectives here to define the roles in which each looks at him or her self from the other's standpoint as well as their own. This is what makes the gesture a symbol which coordinates action. It has the same intent for both parties—they can both respond to it from a *common* standpoint. Communication is the elucidation of this common standpoint, a making common. "Such is the essence and import of communication, signs and meaning. Something is literally made common in at least two different centres of behavior. To understand is to anticipate together, it is to make a cross-reference which, when acted upon, brings about a partaking in a common, inclusive undertaking" (*EN*, 178; *LW 1*:141).[38]

The gesture which is used may have originated with the impulse simply of reaching to get desired objects. This was its preintentional use. But such an act could easily become associated with others bringing that which was out of reach. It is when the child *uses* the reaching or pointing gesture in order for the other to bring the flower that a common perspective has been established. A signal has then become a symbol, though perhaps not a well-defined one. The child may point to get the object pointed at; she may point simply to say "there!" or "Go away!" or any other number of meanings. Because the symbol is indefinite, and thus creates misunderstandings, it may be limited and supplemented by other symbols to express the necessary differences of action. But even in the use of complex symbol systems, there is the constant possibility of misunderstanding (indeed, the complexity of a system invites this because of the potentially creative range of its use). Thus the act of communication is often one of each party mutually supplementing, checking, and modifying their actions or interpretations. A Platonic dialogue can be just an exhibition of "mutual coordination" in which each party genuinely participates with the other in trying to define the object of the quest, such as the definition of courage, justice, or friendship.

Communication is defined by symbolic interaction, the mutual capacity to respond to the meaning of the tool used as a symbol. Language is the most efficient and creative of the symbol systems invented, for it readily passes from one user to another and back. At one moment I can be the "I" and at the next moment the "you" or the "he," and I have no difficulty sorting these out or placing them together. I became your "you" and someone's "he." The identity here is functional. The dynamics of the situation are grasped. To be involved in communication, then, is for there to be an interplay not only between various parties, but between the present, the past, and the future. As Dewey puts it, "If we consider the *form* or scheme of the situation in which meaning and understanding occur, we find involved simultaneous presence and cross-reference of immediacy and efficiency, overt actuality and potentiality, the consummatory and the instrumental" (*EN*, 181; *LW 1:* 143). To discover the situation we are in is to discover the action which is being undertaken. This is why ostensive definitions, like the case of Malinowski asking for the word for the object he was tapping, are context dependent. One must see the situation, and the situation is grasped through its possibilities, and possibilities are hard things to point at. Education is largely the attempt to make us easily grasp the likely range of possible meanings of a situation. As Dewey said, we must learn to anticipate together.

> What a physical event immediately is, and what it *can* do or its relationship are distinct and incommensurable. But when an event has meaning, its potential consequences become its integral and funded feature. When the potential consequences are important and repeated, they form the very nature and essence of a thing, its defining, identifying, and distinguishing form. To recognize the thing is to grasp its definition. Thus we become capable of perceiving things instead of merely feeling and having them. To *perceive* is to acknowledge unattained possibilities; it is to refer the present to consequences, apparition to issue, and thereby to behave in deferrence to the *connections* of events (*EN*, 182; *LW* 1:143).

Essences for Dewey are thus the commonly recognized possibilities or modes of interaction events have. We call the table a table because that is what it functions as for the most part—it's predominant function is denoted. And if we should use it momentarily as a stage or stepping stool, we still call it a "table" because that is what it "really" is (that is what we use it for most of the time, and this common use is what allows us to refer to the object). When we come to asking about Reality, the essences we come up with will be the preferred modes of interaction. Hence for Dewey "reality" marks a predominance of bias or preferrence, an evaluation, and this is why it is such a dangerous word to use *apart from* the activity of critical evaluation, as most metaphysicians have done. But the capacity of the immediate to become fraught with the portent and meaning of the future has the utmost significance for the question of "immediate meaning." The futurity of the act, its possibilities, can be apprehended in the present through symbols. Symbols literally embody meaning because they work in coordinating attitudes or organizing experience. "Essence is never existence, and yet it is the essence, the distilled import, of existence; the significant thing about it, its intellectual voucher, the means of inference and extensive transfer, and object of esthetic intuition. In it, feeling and understanding are one; the meaning of the thing is the sense it makes" (*EN*, 183; *LW* 1:144). To this Dewey adds that we should not be surprised that "the very essence of a thing is identified with those consummatory consequences which the thing has when conditions are felicitous." The history of metaphysics is written in that sentence.

Communication easily becomes the means whereby the goods of life are realized and appropriated and so itself becomes consummatory. It realizes all those goods which involve being with others. Participation is naturally that activity whereby we realize and use our participatory roles, our selves. Most conversation is not the utilitarian conveying of practical information; it is simply a means of being with others and being present to them. Dewey chides the nominalist theory of meaning primarily because it is antisocial. Nominalist theories, like Locke's, miss the main point of communication—that it reveals man as a participant prior to being an individual. Although language is instrumental, by its very power to make present those goods of shared life, to create shared life in doing so, it is supremely consummatory as well. "For there is no mode of action as fulfilling and as rewarding as is concerted consensus of action. It brings with it the sense of sharing and merging in a whole. Forms of language are unrivalled in ability to create this sense, at first with direct participation on the part of an audience; and then, as literary forms develop, through imaginative identification" (*EN*, 184; *LW* 1:145). Art appropriates this capacity directly. It can already be seen that aesthetic meaning for Dewey is a participatory event in which communication is a primary and not a secondary feature. It is founded in and also is the realization of social life, culture.

Language is communication and communication is culture. Though the verbal tools we call languages are paradigmatic means for cultural participation, they are not the only means. Thus, properly speaking, language is culture at large:

> Language, in its widest sense—that is, including all means of communication such as, for example, monuments, rituals and formalized arts—is the medium in which culture exists and through which it is transmitted. . . . It includes . . . not only gestures but rites, ceremonies, monuments, and the products of the industrial and fine arts. A tool or machine . . . is also a mode of language. For it *says* something, to those who understand it, about operations of use and their consequences. To the members of a primitive community a loom operated by steam or electricity says nothing (*LTI*, 20, 46; *LW* 12: 27, 51-52).

The world of primary experience, which Dewey describes at the beginning of *Experience and Nature* as the basis for all our secondary, refined or reflective experience, is just this lifeworld of culture, of embodied goods, participation, action and interaction, in which meaning is transmitted through communiation. Our reflective enterprises are only possible because they appropriate a symbolic and shared material. Reflective thought will mark a transformed *use* of this material. It has the capacity to be the genuine liberator of meaning for Dewey—unless, of course, it forgets its humble origin.

There is always a tension in meaning, then, between the rules of custom and the innovations of creative use. "Meanings are rules for using and interpreting things; interpretation being always an imputation of potentiality for some consequence" (*EN*, 188; *LW* 1:147). If meaning did not have this rule-like nature, it could not bind or generate a community of action. But as we saw with habit, no two events are the same. Rules must be applied to them to mean, and their application always is a challenge to their *traditional* meaning. Those theorists which see in "ordinary language" the paradigm of meaning ignore the creative demands each situation of life presents. They would be the tribal elders who repeat something because "it is the way of the ancestors." To be sure, one cannot legitimately create a private language. It is amusing to remember that Tolkien's original desire was to write an account of the Elvish language, but in order to do so he had to create a world and a history for it, even a theology. But in the creative exploration of meaning lies the secret of communication. Meanings almost demand to be played and experimented with, as Dewey observes: "Meaning, fixed as essence in a term of discourse, may be imaginatively administered and manipulated, experimented with. Just as we overtly manipulate things, making new separations and combinations, thereby introducing new things into new contexts and environments, so we bring together logical universals in discourse, where they copulate and breed new meanings" (*EN*, 194; *LW* 1:152). Meanings evolve, and much under the conditions that Darwin's pigeon breeders raised pigeons.

There is a tremendous force present in the life of symbols which needs to be recognized. "Language is. . . not a mere agency for economizing energy in the interaction of human beings," asserts Dewey, "It is a release and amplification of energies that enter into it, conferring upon them the added quality of meaning. The quality of meaning thus introduced is extended and transferred, actually and potentially from sounds, gestures, and marks, to all other things in nature (*EN*, 173; *LW* 1: 137-38). We learn meanings by using them, and this means that we must apply them in a variety of contexts and situations. Dewey observes, "A newly acquired meaning is forced upon everything that does not obviously resist its application, as a child uses a new word whenever he gets a chance or as he plays with a new toy" (*EN*, 188; *LW* 1: 147-48). On a general level, one may think of the various creative meanings the word "god" or "divine" has had in history. Dewey points to the broadening of the legal term "jurisdiction," which evolves from meaning simply the place of the crime, to right of extradition, to location of the crime in the event, to legal power of action defined with respect to desirable consequences. The development of meaning thus has a dynamic quality which is realized through the social medium. Even one's own utterances take on new significance as others interpret them or use them. "All discourse, oral or written," says Dewey, "which is more than a routine unrolling of vocal habits, says things that surprise the one that says them, often indeed more than they surprise any one else" (*EN*, 194; *LW* 1: 152). Writers and poets are those who try to say such surprising things and discover what they mean. They must play the role of speaker and auditor at once (hence, perhaps, the tendency to speak of "muses" or the subconscious as a source for creativity). The successful poem or work of literature will impart that surprising utterance so that it comes to inhabit the living language of the culture and mark a new occasion for shared experience. "The level and style of the arts of literature, poetry, ceremony, amusement, and recreation which obtain in a community . . . do more than all else to determine the current direction of ideas and endeavors in the community. They supply the meanings in terms of which life is judged, esteemed, and criticized" (*EN*, 204; *LW* 1:159).

Ideals or visions of life have directive power because they illuminate the possible. Our world-views given in culture determine the meanings and values of our lives. The living body of a culture is the community.

> Communication is uniquely instrumental and uniquely final. It is instrumental as liberating us from the otherwise overwhelming pressure of events and enabling us to live in a world of things that have meaning. It is final as a sharing in the objects and arts precious to a community. . . . communication and its congenial objects are objects ultimately worthy of awe, admiration, and loyal appreciation. They are worthy as means because they are the only means that make life rich and varied in meanings. They are worthy as ends, because in such ends man is lifted from his immediate isolation and shares in a communion of meanings. . . . When the instrumental and final functions of communication live together in experience, there exists an intelligence which is the method and reward of the common life, and a society worthy to command affection, admiration, and loyalty (*EN*, 204-05; *LW 1*: 159-60).

V. The Sense of Context

Meaning arises from the mutual effort to communicate. It is a process in which the members are participants trying to adjust and adapt to each other through symbolic action. Each is trying to determine through the other and himself what the meaning of the situation is. The situation is one of mutual, constant interpretation. Both the temporal dimension and the contextual structure of the situation are significant factors in meaning. Not only is meaning primarily an ongoing process of interpretation, but this process is one of trying to render the significant context of the situation determinate. There is in the meaning-event an interplay between the indeterminate and the determinate, and the development of the interpretation is largely that of the participants progressively eliminating those possible alternative interpretations which are not features of the situation, as well as articulating and exploring those features which have bearing and are relevant. In short, the participants are trying to determine *what* the situation *is*, and the resulting meaning of the situation will be seen-as the outcome of the process of interpretation. The task of communication is that of finding a common situation whose meaning can be shared. The interpretive horizon or context of the situation will be the same for the participants. Significant action is that in which the members are all responding to the *same* situation or interpretive context. They will be able to interact and communicate with the least amount of misinterpretation allowable.

But ambiguity can never be eliminated. Not only is there always a vast amount of inarticulate tendencies, assumptions, or possible deviations from what is explicitly shared, but the very fact that situations are always developing in time means that further interpretive responses may break down and that the shared situation is no longer shared, at which point there is a fracture in the community. The Protestant Reformation represented just such a fragmentation in the history of European Christianity. Once the common context of the interpretive authority of the Church disappeared, there emerged a veritable babel of new communities of theological languages, which gradually defined their own interpretive contexts, as, for example, in the works of Luther or Calvin. The constant thrust of the possibilities of the future into the present and the emergence of new events marks the need for continual interpretation. Organized situations may become disorganized, even because of the activity of new interpretations. Likewise, the automatic repetition of a past interpretation in a new event may render the present entirely problematic or reduce it to minimal significance, ignoring its creative potential. Meaning reflects a permanent problematic of situations.

Communication and meaning are for Dewey a genuinely dialogical process of mutual exploration, discovery, growth, and learning. The paradigmatic instance of meaning is to be found in the active participation of members in learning about the world and each other. The essence of meaning, in other words, lies in significant growth, and growth involves creativity as well as order. Meaning is most fully exemplified in this sort of continuity. Views which seek to understand meaning primarily in terms of a static synchronic system of signs and rules will be faced with the paradoxical intrusion of the temporal and concrete contextual use of the system, and elaborate conjurations will be needed to exorcise the Cartesian demon. Meaning is a shared project of the human condition, something to be mutually undertaken. Meaning is something we must constantly strive for, discover, and seek out together.

We encounter the world as a structured and significant place. The world of ordinary experience is not one of sense data or internal hypotheses about external states of affairs. We meet people, sit in chairs, sip coffee, discuss politics and movies, fall in love, have disagreements, and worry about death and taxes. The meaning of these events is encountered or had. But obviously it is only because we have spent a great deal of time organizing our responses to the world that it has taken on the configuration that it has. The structured and significant world of our immediate experience is the product of a long art. The organization of the visual field is based on a complexly integrated body of sensorimotor responses. These responses represent capacities of the living organic body as well as structures of the environment. Language furthers our ability to organize experience and activity so that we can respond to the sense or meaning of an event above and beyond what we realize in terms of its place in the field of sensorimotor activity. The world, then, has levels of tacit interpretation in it as it is directly or immediately encountered.

This is not to suggest that the world in itself is unstructured or that its structure is noumenal. Order, for Dewey, is neither autocratically imposed on a chaotic manifold of sense nor is it passively received and imprinted on us like a stamp on wax. Order arises from the possible conjunctions of the organism and its environment realized through interaction. There must be a world with a certain order to it and an organism with a certain order to it prior to any activity which may be undertaken. A body is an implicit range of interpretation and that structured range of objects to which it can respond marks its environment. A body which could not read its environment would die. But it does not have to read all the features of the world, only those which are relevant for it to carry on its activity. Nor is it necessary for the organism to duplicate those features of the environment which are significant. Thus I think it is best that we understand Dewey's view as one in which there are a plurality of possible interpretive contexts or situations. As the range of possible functions increase in the situation, the range of possible interpretations expands. There are a plurality of possible worlds to the extent that there are a plurality of possible universes of action.

Dewey's analysis of meaning as had or undergone is important because it provides the basis for his theory of aesthetic meaning. Aesthetic meaning is but the capitalization of the fact that the sense of the world is directly encountered or had in ordinary experience. The world has sense, according to Dewey. But obviously this is not to be taken as implying that there is but one true way of interpreting the world. The world may have many senses. The sense of the world refers to the immediately had or undergone coordination of the organism to an environment. We encounter the world as a structured field because of our continual and organized responses. The sense of the world arises from transactional activity. It is for this reason that we see chairs and people instead of indeterminate masses. The meaning of these objects is directly had as part of the experience. Experience has a range of possible ways of encountering the world, extending from the highly indeterminate, unlocalized feelings we have to the highly articulate symbolic manipulations of cognitive experience. These might be seen as extremes of the continuum of sense. In distinguishing these aspects, it should not be forgotten that they may *all* be copresent in experience, functioning together:

> The qualities of situations in which organisms and surrounding conditions interact, when discriminated, make sense. Sense is distinct from feeling, for it has a recognized reference; it is the qualitative characteristic of something, not just a submerged unidentified quality or tone. Sense is also different from signification. The latter involves use of a quality as a sign or index of something else, as when the red of a light signifies danger. . . . The sense of the thing, on the other hand, is an immediate and immanent meaning; it is the meaning which is itself felt or directly had. . . . The meaning of the *whole* situation as apprehended is sense. . . . Whenever a situation has this double function of meaning, namely signification and sense, mind, intellect is definitely present (*EN*, 260-60; *LW* 1:200).

Here Dewey explicitly asserts that meaning can be "immediate." It must be recalled that in Dewey's metaphysics of situations, immediacy in no way excluded mediacy: situations were at once both immediately existing and processes of development. At any moment a situation "exists"; it has an immediate degree of its realization, and this stage reflects the whole of the process in its own way. Dewey argues that the total act of behavior is immanent in and determining of the various sensorimotor coordinations at each moment. The *whole* act was present in the part. This feature will also be present on the level of meaning. Dewey distinguishes three plateaus of existence, the physical, the psychophysical and the mental or the level of meaning.[39] Through the principle of continuity, although each level will display its own irreducible features, there will be generic traits linking them. Just as Dewey proposes a field-theory of nature and a transactional view of life, exemplified in his theory of the act, so, too, will he give a transactional analysis of the experience of meaning.

Dewey does seem to contrast the "immediate meaning" of sense with the discursive or mediate meaning of signification and the immediate but unmeaningful presence of feeling. This has created a difficult problem in understanding Dewey's central thesis, since one is likely to be at a loss as to exactly how one shifts between these phases or how brute immediacy and relational mediacy can fuse together to create "sense." When Dewey comes to speak of quality, which stands for the immediate, felt aspect of experience, he says, "Quality is quality, direct, immediate and undefinable"; elsewhere he asserts that "Immediacy of existence is ineffable" (*EN*, 110, 85; *LW* 1: 92, 74). It might be inferred from these passages that any talk of "immediate meaning" is contradictory. Meaning seems here to be a matter of relations. The previous chapter noted how critics like Garrett and Bernstein were led to conclude that Dewey's theory was gangrenous and needed amputation. I argued against these critics that Dewey's principle of continuity and theory of situations does present a coherent alternative.

Though Dewey was undeniably careless, even negligent, in formulating certain parts of his philosophy, I don't think this is a difficult problem to unravel. First, one must constantly return to what Dewey means by "experience"—something very different from what someone like Hume does. Experience for Dewey cannot be reduced to "elements" which must be classified rigorously as "qualities" or "relations." These terms are at best abstractions made to clarify and organize experience in certain situations, and as such should be regarded functionally as the tools they are. We learn to use terms like "red," "sweet," "hard," or "disgusting" to focus on aspects of certain situations and terms like "before," "next to," "taller," and so on to focus on other aspects. But these sets of terms do not exclusively refer to simple qualities or relations. "Red" can refer to a variety of hues, no one of which we ever see twice, but which are *related* for us by the term, which thereby helps us organize our general experience. Likewise, we can pick on so-called relational aspects and take them as qualifying the situation. "Tallness" easily can be seen as a quality, but so can "next-to-ness" or "beforeness." Experience, according to Dewey, can be taken qualitatively or relationally, depending on how we are using it. Primary experience is malleable, and we may focus on the intrinsic aspects of the immediate moment or we may try to relate the immediate phase into a larger process or context. In short, there is only a problem connecting "qualities" and "relations" when the psychologist's fallacy has been committed and these abstractions are mistaken for pre-existent constitutive elements. It is of historical note that the term "quality" appears with Plato's effort to distinguish subject and attribute (along with his apology for coining such a "bizarre" word), and Aristotle originates the term "relation" also in connection with philosophical problems in metaphysics and logic.[40] "Qualities" and "relations" were inventions of philosophic analysis.

Secondly, if we look at how experience functions, we see that both qualities and relations are fully compatible, and are, indeed, necessary for each other. Take once more the example of hammering. A hammer, nail, and board may all be taken for their immediate qualities, or they may all be taken relationally, say in terms of purpose or cause and effect. But if we start with the basic *action* of hammering we see that it would be impossible unless both aspects were in the experience. If we tried to hammer a nail solely by considering the relational aspects, disregarding the color, shape, heft, force and so on, the job would be botched if it ever could begin (for how could we identify the hammer or nail without their telltale qualities?). Likewise, by regarding only the qualities, we could not integrate them into a meaningful, continuous action. In primary experience, we "sense" what the hammer is and how we are using it; we tend to discriminate qualities or relations as problematic situations arise, e.g., this hammer feels "too heavy" or one has to change the angle at which one is driving the nail. It is the whole situation, however, which makes these distinctions meaningful, not vice versa.

On this analysis, I believe that it would be better to regard Dewey's distinctions of feeling, sense and signification as matters of *degree* along a continuum rather than as three separate modes of experience. At one extreme, as we focus more on the immediate aspects, we tend toward "feeling," losing sight of the unrealized potentialities of the project at hand. We pay attention to the present on its own account and ignore the future. At the other extreme, we can become absorbed in trying to mediate or locate the immediate in a future-oriented process, operation or context. We may become solely concerned with the final outcome of an action and its significance so that the immediate loses its qualitative luster in anticipation of those to come and becomes a bare sign. It is at these extremes of feeling and signification that experience is likely to fall apart and the means-end relationship become divided. We may come to view all mediation, relation or cognition in experience as solely "practical" or significant. All qualitative feeling may be consigned to sheer emotional reaction or detached, "purely aesthetic" attitudes. This is the state of affairs, of course, which Dewey decries and against which his philosophy of experience is directed. For this reason, then, it is best to regard "pure feeling" and "pure signification" as limiting terms, and, in fact, bizarre extremes impossible in themselves, of the continuum of "sense." The ideal to which Dewey points is the continuous interplay of sense and signification so that the immediate is taken up into a broad and deep context which in turn is realized and brought to light in immediate experience. This is exactly what Dewey means by *an* experience.

Feeling, then, denotes the qualitative or immediate side of experience, the part which is "had" or undergone. It still exemplifies the immediacy of existence, but now consciously, while also remaining grounded in the situation. To repeat Dewey's important discussion of this idea:

> The most that can be said about qualities in the inanimate field is that they mark the limit of the contact of historical affairs, being abrupt ends or termini, boundaries of beginning and closing where a par-

ticular interaction ceases. . . . In life and mind they play an active role. . . . For in feeling a quality exists as a quality and not merely as an abrupt, discrete, unique delimitation of interaction. . . . "Feeling" is in general a name for the newly actualized quality acquired by events previously occurring upon a physical level, when these events come into more extensive and delicate relationships of interaction. More specifically, it is a name for the coming to existence of those ultimate differences in affairs which mark them off from one another and give them discreteness. . . . Thus qualities characteristic of sentiency are qualities *of* cosmic events (*EN*, 266-67; *LW* 1:203-04).

For every situation in experience there is an underlying sense or feeling of the "pervasive qualitative whole" which makes everything experienced *as* belonging or not belonging, *as* making sense or not of *that* situation. It is this feeling of the whole context which marks off "aesthetic experience" as the consummation of a whole process.

Though feeling may be immediately had or undergone, Dewey notes that "it is capable of receiving and bearing distinctions without end" (*EN*, 257; *LW 1:* 198). This is what communication and language exploit, for they transform a quality into a bearer of meaning.

As life is a character of events in a peculiar condition of organization, and "feeling" is a quality of life-forms marked by complexly mobile and discriminating responses, so "mind" is an added property assumed by a feeling creature, when it reaches that organized interaction with other living creatures which is language, communication. Then the qualities of feeling become significant of objective differences in external things and of episodes past and to come. This state of things in which qualitatively different feelings are not just had but are significant of objective differences, is mind. Feelings are no longer just felt. They have and they make *sense*, record and prophesy (*EN*, 258; *LW 1:*198).

Qualities are capable of functioning in meaning situations through their power both to be immediately had and to have, as part of their immediate aspect, the sense of the larger situation in which they function. Because immediate experience can conserve "within itself the meaning of the entire preparatory process," says Dewey, means and ends can be discriminated and intelligence ceases to be a matter of instinct or sheer habit. "The result is nothing less than revolutionary. Organic activity is liberated from subjection to what is closest at hand in space and time. Man is led or drawn rather than pushed. The immediate is significant in respect to what has occurred and will occur. . ." (*EN*, 269; *LW* 1:206-07).

This is a highly crucial observation. The immediate sense of experience may be *had as* the consummatory outcome of a process—its *meaning* may be that of completion or fulfillment, and that meaning will be directly embodied *in* the object of experience. The origin of aesthetic feeling is to be found in learning to enjoy the presence of sense. Dewey notes that when language is used so that an "emphatic immediate presence of sense occurs" it becomes poetry (*EN*, 293; *LW* 1: 223). In such moments, there is a qualitatively enjoyed meaning to the situation which is not a purely monochrome or simple feeling. Indeed, the contrary seems to be the case: there is the sense of richness, texture, variation, and complexity which have been successfully organized. This is what Dewey says reflects a completed or total organic response. In less biological terms, there is an integrated and consummatory moment in which one's interpretive responses are called forth and fulfilled in the object. A coordinated perspective is realized which brings the sense of the situation alive to consciousness.

Experience is a field-event incorporating the horizons of feeling, the objects of sense, and the foci of consciousness. Dewey's analysis of consciousness is one of the most interesting topics in *Experience and Nature*. It is important here because aesthetic meaning is meaning realized in conscious appropriation. In fact, for Dewey, the aesthetic and artistic phases of experience mark the highest realization of consciousness. Dewey begins by distinguishing two types of consciousness, consciousness which simply is the having of experience and consciousness which is the having of meaning or meaningful experience. In the latter case there is awareness of objects or events in terms of their sense. Consciousness is an event for Dewey, and therefore to be distinguished from mind or the total system of meanings, the cultural background of consciousness:

> The relation of mind to consciousness may be partially suggested by saying that while mind as a system of meanings is subject to disorganization, disequilibration, perturbation, there is no sense in referring to a particular state of awareness *in its immediacy* as either organized or disorganized. An idea is just what it is when it occurs. . . . Immediately, every perceptual awareness may be termed indifferently emotion, sensation, thought, desire: not that it *is* immediately any one of these things, or all of them combined, but that when it is taken in some *reference* to conditions or to consequences or to both, it has, in that contextual reference the distinctive properties of emotion, sensation, thought or desire (*EN*, 304-05; *LW* 1:230-31).

As immediately undergone, consciousness simply is that totality of experience which is qualitatively had. But taken in its temporal reference its meaning becomes part of the way it is undergone, i.e., it is had as desire or thought. And it is precisely this capacity of consciousness to embody within itself at the moment how functions in the temporal structure of the situation which allows it to become the occasion of a complex variety of meaningful experiences. Indeed, on further analysis, consciousness is not a timeless, static moment but a volatile, transitional nexus in the field of meaning. "Consciousness," Dewey says, "an idea, is that phase of a system of meanings which at a given time is undergoing re-direction, transitive transformation" (*EN*, 308; *LW* 1:233). Later, he adds, "The *immediately* precarious, the point of greatest immediate need, defines the apex of consciousness, its intense or focal mode. And this is the point of *re*-direction, of *re*-adaptation, *re*-organization" (*EN*, 312; *LW* 1:236).

Consciousness is a reconstructive activity. But it is reconstructive of a field of meanings. In other words, consciousness for Dewey has an intrinsic dramatic and narrative structure which operates within a web of meanings which provide the sense-giving felt context:

> Every case of consciousness is dramatic; drama is an enhancement of the conditions of consciousness. . . . It seems to me that anyone who installs himself in the midst of the unfolding of drama *has* the experience of consciousness in just this sort of way; in a way which enables him to give significance to descriptive and analytic terms otherwise meaningless. There must be a story, some whole, an integrated series of episodes. This connected whole is mind, as it extends beyond a particular process of consciousness and conditions it. There must also be now-occurring events, to which meanings are assigned in terms of a story taking place. Episodes do not mean what they would mean if occurring in some different story. They have to be perceived in terms of the story, as its forwardings and fulfillings. At the same time, until the play or story is ended, meanings given to events are of a sort which constantly evoke a meaning which was not absolutely anticipated or totally predicted: there is expectancy, but also surprise, novelty (*EN*, 306-07; *LW* 1:232-33).

This is essentially the structure of *an* experience, as will be seen in the next chapter. Consciousness is the event which realizes meaning. It is the tensive focus as well as the temporal enactment of a dramatic or narrative world. Just as time has meaning as a dramatic or narrative event, so dramatic or narrative meaning is inherently temporal.

There are two implications to be drawn from this analysis of consciousness. The first is that every conscious event is part of a larger situation in which there is a supporting context, an interpretive world in terms of which the event of consciousness takes on meaning. This environment is present in or had in experience as the sense of objects and the horizons of feeling. Although, Dewey insists, there are no meanings without language, any linguistic event has a substructure of "an immense multitude of immediate organic selections, rejections, welcomings, expulsions, appropriations" and so on:

> We are not aware of the qualities of many or most of these acts. . . .Yet they exist as feeling qualities, and have an enormous direc- tive effect on our behavior. . . . In a thoroughly normal organism, these "feelings" have an efficiency of operation which it is impossi- ble for thought to match. Even our most highly intellectualized operations depend upon them as a "fringe" by which to guide our inferential movements. They give us our *sense* of rightness and wrongness, of what to select and emphasize and follow up, and what to drop, slur over and ignore among the multitude of inchoate meanings that are presenting themselves (*EN* 299-300; *LW* 1: 226).[41]

As the previous chapter showed, this qualitative feeling which binds and organizes the situation is precisely what determines the situation as such. It is the integration of the total coordination of interpretive responses; it is a genuinely binding or organizing event which actual- izes the possibilties of the situation toward significant mutual support and action. Because consciousness is always intentional of an object located within an event or ongoing situation, the present moment is both a case of and a problem for interpretation:

> "This," whatever *this* may be, always implies a system of meanings focussed at a point of stress, uncertainty, and need of regulation. It sums up history, and at the same time opens a new page; it is record and promise in one; a fulfillment and an opportunity. . . . It is a comment written by natural events on their own direction and ten- dency. . . . The union of past and future with the present manifest in every awareness of meanings is a mystery only when conscious- ness is gratuitously divided from nature, and when nature is denied temporal and historic quality. When consciousness is connected with nature, the mystery becomes a luminous revelation of the operative interpenetration in nature of the efficient and the fulfilling (*EN*, 352- 53; *LW* 1: 264-65).

The second implication to be drawn from Dewey's analysis of consciousness is the significance he attaches to having a civilized or uncivilized subconscious. It is evident that by the "subconscious," Dewey is referring to the whole tacit dimension which undergirds interpretation and meaning. But this dimension is not to be thought of as the reservoir of irrational drives which contort the conscious life toward their darker ends. This of course is possible. But to the extent that one lives a life which is the product of an intelligent culture, there will be an integration and productive relation between the conscious and unconscious phases of experience:

> The deification of the subconscious is legitimate only for those who never indulge in it—animals and thoroughly healthy and naive children—if there be any such. The subconscious of a civilized adult reflects all the habits he has acquired. . . . It is most reliable in just those activities with respect to which it is least spoken of, and least reliable with respect to those things where it is most fashionable to laud it (*EN*, 300-01; *LW 1:* 228).

By the last remark, Dewey means that it is in our most fully alert and consciously intelligent moments, such as in mathematics, philosophy, or "in a highly cultivated fine art" that the civilized subconscious is most fully praised and realized. To see the paradigm of the subconscious in neurotic cases is much like identifying the characteristics of health from a ward of the sick and dying. Art, then, is truly capable of expressing the subconscious through conscious articulation. This expression may even be said to be the realization of the implicit meaning of the field of experience. In the work of art, there is a provocative power which is capable of probing deeply into the psychic life of man. The dynamisms and tensions it incorporates may not be resolved, for there may be no final resolutions of the basic tensions which are life except death. But the work of art may be able to evoke, illuminate, and give catharsis to such tensions. Furthermore, as the psychic life of man, the universe of mind, develops and modifies, as the underlying interpretive worlds which guide meaning change, works may wane and die or suddenly spring to life after centuries to reveal something about ourselves long forgotten. For the Christians of the fifth century, the poems of Sappho revealed nothing more than unlicensed pagan sexuality, and were systematically destroyed. Today, the trash heaps of Roman Egypt are sifted in the hopes of bringing them to light. Sappho understood the beauty of the flesh, the lived, passionate body which felt and saw everything intensely and clearly. When the early Christians rejected the world, it was this very capacity to celebrate, affirm, and enshrine the flesh which was denied. Thus Sappho's works were annihilated while Plato's were copied and preserved. The Platonic Eros is, after all, a heavenly directed one even if it must climb the ladder of the body's passions as well as the passions of the intellect.

One of the central problems for the narrative of consciousness, then, is the establishment of context. To inhabit the world is to inhabit it through an organized manner of response. It is to be able to fit in with a universe of discourse grounded on a universe of shared life.

Truly to grasp the sense of an event is to grasp it in terms of a form of life. This is precisely the anthropologist's problem. For not only does he try to inhabit the world of another people, he must yet remain a Western anthropologist, someone who identifies himself within the context of science. On the one hand, the anthropologist must try to encounter the world of the culture he studies as it is lived, or, in Dewey's expression, as it is had. On the other hand, it is his job to bring to light the whole tacit dimension of the world he is studying through the critical and analytical tools of his science. The tension between these rival tendencies has been dramatically illustrated in the writings of Carlos Castaneda and the controversy surrounding them. Castaneda believed that to understand the world of the Yaqui medicine man Don Juan he had to accept it on its own terms. His effort to live within that world directly meant, however, he could no longer study it. To inhabit a world in one sense is to be able to respond to the symbols of that culture as the people do and without a constant accompanying detachment. Yet, one does not achieve understanding by abandoning the need for critical interpretation. The anthropologist who remains totally detached from the culture he studies, however, may achieve objectivity at the cost of rendering his subject matter, the life of a people, completely opaque. The ambiguity of the human situation cannot be evaded either in the blind acceptance of a culture's symbols or by their suppression. The need for interpretation is obliquely acknowledged by the very fact Castaneda transformed the world of the Yaqui shaman into literary books—something the Yaqui do not need to do.

We may see an internal instance of this paradox in Thomas Kuhn's theory of the nature of scientific revolutions. During a scientific revolution, such as the period when the Ptolemaic and Copernican models or paradigms were competing, there is a problem in going from one interpretive context to the other much like that of the member of one culture trying to inhabit the world of another. Nevertheless, although Kuhn seems to regard the leap from one paradigm to the next almost as an instance of existentialist choice, the process he describes is more like one of *learning* to shift one's contextual perspective. In other words, human beings are primarily capable of learning to participate in a shared social perspective, of making experience continuous as well as progressive. We can learn someone else's worldview because we have learned our own, as it were. When, as in the case of a scientific revolution, there is a radical shift in assumptions, these shifts are nevertheless interpreted as due to the conflict of rival theories and definite problems with evidence. In learning someone else's culture, the anthropologist has available to him precisely what the members of the culture lack, methods of illuminating the tacit meanings of their world. It should be no surprise that the encounter would also throw the assumptions of the anthropologist's world into relief as well. To the extent that philosophy itself exists as a critically interpretive and evaluative enterprise, as one which seeks to become self-reflective and self-critical within its own culture, it must find methods of detachment in the very process of creating tools of analysis. In other words, philosophy needs its speculative moments to reveal its own possibility as an analytical enterprise. One doesn't simply criticize ideas; one criticizes ideas in terms of other ideas. This naturally leads to the projection of new interpretive horizons which have been specifically created for the purpose of illuminating a critical issue, that is, the creation of metaphysical systems.

Human experience is a process of learning contexts. There are no neutral or absolute reference points from which we may speak or interpret. In his essay, "Context and Thought," Dewey says:

> We grasp the meaning of what is said in our own language not because appreciation of context is unnecessary but because context is so unescapably present. It is taken for granted; it is a matter of course . . . Habits of speech, including syntax and vocabulary, and modes of interpretation have been formed in the face of inclusive and defining situations of context. . . . We are not explicitly aware of the role of context because our every utterance is so saturated with it that it forms the significance of what we say and hear (*ENF*, 90; *LW* 4:4).

The human project and problem is always that of learning the sense of the world.

But the sense of the world depends ultimately, in whatever context we are in, upon the felt, qualitative, and non-cognitive dimension. This theme is the central topic of Dewey's highly significant essay, "Qualitative Thought." Without the role of quality to create the sense of the situation, inquiry would be impossible. By "quality" Dewey is referring not primarily to particular discriminated qualities *within* a situation, but to the distinctive, unnameable uniquely characteristic feel of *that* situation. The qualitative sense of the whole situation provides the fusion of part and whole in experience which, in terms of meaning, is the integration of "text" and context.

> By the term situation in this connection is signified the fact that the subject-matter ultimately referred to in existential propositions is a complex existence that is held together, in spite of its internal complexity, by the fact that it is dominated and characterized throughout by a single quality . . . The situation as such is not and cannot be stated or made explicit. It is taken for granted, "understood," or

implicit in all propositional symbolization. It forms the universe of discourse of whatever is expressly stated or of what appears as a term in a proposition. The situation cannot present itself as an element in a proposition any more than a universe of discourse can appear as a member of discourse within that universe. . . . The situation controls the terms of thought; for they are *its* distinctions, and applicability to it is the ultimate test of their validity (*PC*, 97-98; *LW 5*: 246-47).

It is this sense of the whole situation which allows it to be regulated. It is evident that what is right or fitting, that is, what is rational, is for Dewey ultimately determined by the situation as a whole, and how this whole is felt or enters into conscious experience. Does this make Dewey in the last analysis an intuitionist like Bergson? Definitely not. To be sensitive to the controlling quality of the context is to embark upon the path which intelligently explores nature. Although the focus of consciousness may depend upon the tacit horizon or fringe, it is capable of controlling and interpreting the situation so that it realizes those meanings and values which fulfill and do not frustrate human existence. Furthermore, it is possible for there to be better and worse determining contexts. A civilized context, one which is deeply interwoven with the world and which allows for the development and growth of experience through means, is far better than an impulsively and irrationally guiding context or one which is deadingly mechanical and routine. The cognitive and the non-cognitive can, for Dewey, enter into a mutually supportive and creative relationship, and this is exemplified in the thinking of the artist. Art has the unique capacity to present the rich suggestiveness of meaning; the horizon of indeterminate meaning becomes revealed in its positive role. "The full content of meaning," says Dewey in the essay referred to, is best apprehended" in the presence of the work of art." He adds that "Language fails not because thought fails but because no verbal symbols can do justice to the fullness and richness of thought" (*PC*, 102; *LW 5*:250).

Genuine works of art are "intellectual and logical wholes" because "the underlying quality that defines the work, that circumscribes it externally and integrates it internally, controls the thinking of the artist his logic is the logic of what I have called qualitative thinking" (*PC*, 103; *LW 5*:251). Dewey, in fact, goes further and maintains that artistic thought is merely a paradigm of intelligent, meaningful human experience, which is the central thesis of *Art as Experience*:

> The logic of artistic construction and esthetic appreciation is peculiarly significant because they exemplify in accentuated and purified

form the control of selection of detail and mode of relation, or integration, by a qualitative whole. . . . Artistic thought is not however unique in this respect but only shows an intensification of a characteristic of all thought (*PC*, 103-04; *LW* 5:251-52).

The question of meaning for Dewey cannot, therefore, evade the importance of the "lived experience," since it is a prime example of what meaning is. From the start of his philosophical development, Dewey had found the ultimate significance of experience to lie both in its capacity for richness and in its sense of wholeness. Gradually, however, Dewey ceased to find an idealist metaphysics a proper account for this. Instead, he located the aesthetic as the most descriptive category, by which he referred not to some museum experience of works of fine art but to life organized into a creative, dramatic and expressive situation. To understand this dynamic whole, Dewey used such concepts as we have seen in this chapter: impulse, habit, the act, emotion, gesture, sense, and context. But in the last analysis, Dewey wished to point to the whole in which these were but abstracted features, phases playing different roles. If Dewey's theory lacked the logical rigor of other philosophies of meaning, it had what they so often conspicuously lacked, namely, a vision of the human world within which logic and language occur. Because art pointed to this world in such a dramatic way, Dewey came to view it not as a pleasant theme for a philosophical pastime, but as a central subject which constantly demanded philosophical investigation.

VI. Conclusion

It should be evident now why Dewey's discussion of meaning is a vital link between his metaphysics of experience and his aesthetic theory. Art is not casually proclaimed by Dewey to be a subject of central significance for philosophy: "To esthetic experience, then, the philosopher must go to understand what experience is" (*AE*, 274; *LW* 10:278). The topic of meaning is a fairly neglected area of Dewey's philosophy, and it has been for that reason I have taken some time in examining it. Dewey rejected the idea that meaning could be profitably confined within the parameters of logic or linguistics, for what was to be the explanation of *their* meaning. The approach which sought to interpret meaning ultimately in terms of atomic self-evident truths had been tried, and Dewey found that instead of illuminating experience, such an attitude only succeeded in mystifying it. Dewey therefore undertook to see meaning in terms of that complex totality of the ways we are in the world, both as biological creatures and as cultural beings.

On the level of the body, Dewey sees in its primary structures and modes of response the basis for the emergence of the significant gesture.[42] The reconstruction of the reflex arc into the circuit of coordination provided him with the basic model which would guide his understanding of activity as a process of constant adaptation and organization within one whole act. This allowed him to analyze the respective functions of emotion and habit. Emotion is that feature which reveals our tensive, problematic involvement with the world and which becomes capable of transformation into an expressive consummatory feeling. We are linked to the world primarily through emotion. But we are also inhabitants of the world; that is, we have woven a complex network of possible responses which provide structure and method to our actions. It is the habitual body which grounds the further organization of experience in the context of social communication. Meaning emerges from communication, from the effort of participants to modify and interpret a situation through a shared set of symbols in virtue of which the situation becomes common or takes on a common meaning for the participants. Language is the highest development of such a common symbol system and largely functions to coordinate other activities. But language creates new modes of shared life which it can directly embody. Language succeeds in so restructuring our world, that the world is encountered on the level of sense. Sense is continuum of experience, ranging from feeling at one extreme to cognitive signification at the other. When sense is realized in conscious experience it is just that immediate, qualitative sort of meaning which becomes the possibility of aesthetic experience. Experience can become the immediately sensed consummation of a process. In this sort of conscious experience the non-cognitive and indeed subconscious context are fully operative. Sense can become a revelation of the way we are in the world and so can express its meaning. Dewey explicitly points to the example of the artist and the method of artistic thinking as a paradigm for intelligence. Art as a process is the civilization of experience; it is the struggle to embody meaning and value in terms by which we are humanly realized.

Chapter 5

The Art of Experience

In 1931 John Dewey delivered the first of the William James Lectures at Harvard; the subject was to be the philosophy of art. The book which grew from these lectures did more than commemorate James in an oblique way, for if any book fulfilled the promise of James' late-blooming radical empiricism it was *Art as Experience*. At the same time, this work marked the culmination of Dewey's struggle to articulate what "experience" is in its fullest and richest sense. Although the book is still one of Dewey's most popular, it is often regarded as a tangential, if happy, addition to the mainstream of his thought, the part covered by the rubric of "instrumentalism." The other tendency, as noted, was to see his aesthetic theory as simply inconsistent with his philosophy altogether. For those who regarded pragmatism and its heirs as the hard-headed kitchen drudge's philosophy, the grasping child of utilitarianism and positivism, *Art as Experience* would have appeared anomalous indeed. The alternative was to force upon it an interpretation consistent with the prejudices of a reductionistic naturalism. Susanne Langer took this option, describing the book as an application of the sort of doctrinaire behaviorism which reduces all higher human values and ideals to questions of "animal psychology."[1] Others criticized Dewey's effort to approach aesthetic experience as a development of ordinary experience for blurring or removing exactly those distinguishing features which made the aesthetic unique. Particularly troublesome were Dewey's organic metaphors which were indiscriminately used with both the biological and aesthetic associations. Finally, there was the questionable view which Dewey espoused that the aesthetic was instrinsically an act of expression or communication. The inherent difficulties of the expression theory seemed to be combined with the dubious claim that art had some sort of syntactic or semantic structure.[2]

Since Dewey had spent his career commenting on the dualistic habits of thinking which pervaded modern philosophy, he should not have been surprised to see his one book which went directly to the heart of the problem systematically misinterpreted and subjected to outlandish accusations. It is a pity that he did not more strenuously and lucidly present his ideas or defend them. What was needed most of all was an analysis of the relationship between his description of aesthetic experience and his instrumentalism. The same theory of experience underlies both aspects of his philosophy, but instrumentalism only gains its significance because of the aesthetic possibilities of experience to have directly funded consummatory meaning and value. The fundamental condition for instrumentalism is that experience is capable of integrated fulfillment which is the result of intelligently directed human activity. It is the very possibility for experience to take on this satisfying quality which determines the evaluation of so much of our ordinary experience as unfulfilling, fragmented, problematic, or meaningless. If human experience reached its possible limits in mindless routine or disconnected activity, not only would Dewey's aesthetics be superfluous but his instrumentalism as well. Human culture, according to Dewey, is permeated with indications that such is not the case. Aside from the active cultivation of the practical arts of survival, most human activities are directed toward achieving and sustaining experiences which make life an integrated, significant, and organized whole. The fact that experience is often fractured or seems opposed to the fulfilling ends of human life, whether through war, famine, disease, or sudden death, leads to the tendency, in Dewey's eyes, for men to seek some sort of explanation for their sufferings. Often the symbols of human frustration become erected into powerful cultural beliefs which assuage despair by confirming as eternal truth the inherently fractured nature of human life. Instead of circumscribing life with a tragic consciousness, such beliefs reinforce either a passive fatalism or a rigid moralism and so become self-fulfilling prophecies.

Dewey did not approach the subject of aesthetic experience, then, simply to "round out" his philosophy. Dewey explicitly stated in the book that the test of any philosophy's ability to understand experience is to be found in its treatment of the aesthetic dimension. Presumably this should apply to Dewey's own philosophy. In this light, *Art as Experience* must be read as a central and crucial text. Experience for Dewey is most fully comprehended from the standpoint of art. Art reveals that experience is capable of being intelligently and creatively appropriated and transformed. Through art man is able to realize the potentiality for meaning and value to be directly embodied in the world. The moral taught by the arts is that when the self-conscious attitude of the artist toward his material has been extended to all experience, to the whole range of human life, then life itself is capable of becoming an art. When such an attitude prevails, the aesthetic dimension of experience will not be regarded as a special, limited, or effete kind of experience. The task of Dewey's philosophy is to bring this moral home.

This chapter will examine the central concepts of Dewey's analysis of experience which has been aesthetically shaped. After examining the origin of art from the general conditions of experience, I will turn to the most significant idea in Dewey's aesthetics, having *an* experience. The nature of aesthetic experience to be expressive will be discussed next. Dewey's theory of expression will be contrasted with the more traditional understanding of this concept, which has received a good deal of serious criticism in recent years. After evaluating whether Dewey's theory is open to these criticisms, I will discuss the nature of aesthetic form as the temporal development or articulation of care for a subject. Form, as the on-going organization of the elements of *an* experience, gradually exposes or reveals a horizon of human care. In other words, form is the way *an* experience shows what it is about. Throughout the development of *an* experience, there is the pervasive sense of the regulating but nondiscursive quality which provides the context of meaning in the situation. While this quality remains tacit in ordinary experience, it is explicitly felt in aesthetic experience. This is what allows for meaning to be concretely embodied or directly funded in experience. Because art heightens this feeling, the experience is immediately felt to be developing in an intelligent and consummatory manner. It becomes alive with the sense of its own progressive realization of meaning and value. Aesthetic quality thus becomes one with the capacity of experience to open up toward those ideal ends which give significance, direction, and fulfillment to human action. While these are topics more appropriately discussed in Dewey's philosophy of religion and his analysis of the democratic life, there is a close and natural progression to these themes from his description of aesthetic quality. Art reveals the possibility for experience to be illuminated with consummatory ideals which genuinely bind human beings together in the shared pursuit of the good life, a life which is expressive, creative, committed to freedom, and intelligently directed. The democratic community is the community which has undertaken the liberating responsibility of the art of experience. The human project is a constant imperative to expand and explore the horizons of meaning. Both the self and the community emerge and determine their significance within these horizons. Because aesthetic experience is distinctively capable of grasping experience in general as a process of articulation or growth, it succeeds in providing the basis for overcoming any dualism which separates man from the world or from his fellow human beings. Art, in this sense, unites the metaphysical and political aspects of Dewey's philosophy.

While the conclusion of this book will briefly touch on such themes, this chapter will remain confined to discussing the aesthetic features of experience. Dewey selects his description of *an* experience as providing a paradigm for all experience. *An* experience is one which has been successfully transformed through intelligent action so as to be an inherently complete and dynamically moving whole which realizes the sense of meaning and value as deeply as possible. Although knowing may play a significant role, *an* experience is not primarily cognitive. Nor is it "practical," in the utilitarian sense of the word, although it surely involves activity. It is more complete and inclusive than either of these types of experience, the intellectual and the practical, taken in isolation. This is a very radical feature of Dewey's philosophy. Philosophy has remained satisfied with treating experience primarily as cognitive. Not only has this affected theories of meaning, but it has pushed art and the aesthetic to the penumbra of philosophical concerns. Dewey opts to select aesthetic experience as his primary instance of meaning and to determine affairs of knowing and action in relation to it. If we begin with the sorts of experiences where cognition or action are central features, we are focusing upon instances where the problematic has intruded, where experience has fallen apart or threatens to disintegrate. If such experiences are taken as primary, then "epistemology" will end up as the sum and substance of human self-understanding. For Dewey, this is much like selecting to study human beings under extreme crisis situations, such as famine or war, and from this making generalizations about what we are "really" like under normal circumstances. Such conditions do exist from time to time, and it is important to study them. But they provide a poor model for understanding human beings as homemakers, parents, friends, teachers, scientists, or artists. If one selects the principles of a moral theory by how well they deal with absurd life-boat situations one ends up with an ethics that, at best, is useful in a life-boat. The same is true of a theory of experience. From the beginning, Dewey wished to avoid any approach to philosophy which manages to gain conceptual certainty and a false clarity by commencing with arbitrarily and narrowly defined problems. Dewey's own philosophy can be criticized for being hazy and general at times, but certainly not for being trivial or narrow-minded.

I. The Origin of Art in Experience

We have seen that Dewey looked to art to illuminate the meaning of "experience." Given that, the beginning of *Art as Experience* is strangely oblique and problematic, for Dewey says that if we are to understand the nature of art it is necessary to avoid the tendency to think of objects primarily encountered in museums. On reflection, however, this is understandable. The meaning of "art" in a culture which is accustomed to separating the aesthetic from the normal course of human experience can only mislead philosophical inquiry. Although art has the capacity to reveal experience in its most living and significant moments, when it is pushed to the fringes of society it is predictable that it will reflect this displacement. When it does not become an art of criticism or an art of alienation, it will become an art of seclusion, introversion, and opacity. The very presence of an "artworld," with its dealers, fadists, intellectual czars, bohemian eccentrics, and even aestheticians should not simply be accepted as empirical data upon which to construct a theory, but should occasion critical reflection instead. An "institutional theory of art" is the predictable outcome of a society that institutionalizes art.[3] Because the artwork is capable of being treated like an object or thing, a physical entity which can be stored in a basement, we are apt to understand the *work* of art to *be* a thing, an object which is consummated in its sheer physical presence or its functional utility.[4] A museum reinforces this attitude, for decontextualized works of art are liable to be understood as "pure" objects, things which have no natural relation to ordinary life. A Greek statue of a god may easily be placed next to a modernist canvas, and both will be understood to be instances of "works of art," objects for a special "aesthetic attitude." Instead of engaging and developing experience with a sense of meaning, the work of art closes in upon itself and remains a mere thing. For Dewey, as for Heidegger, the work of art is an event and cannot be innocently confused with the physical object which is a condition for the experience. There is no work of art apart from the human experience. The object, suggests Dewey, is more properly termed the "art product" while "the actual work of art is what the product does with and in experience" (*AE*, 3; *LW* 10:9).

This step radically recontextualizes art as a process within experience, which is to say within culture and history. "Art" ceases to refer to a fixed class of objects or to a detachable essence, and the "aesthetic" ceases to refer to a peculiar type of subjective experience. It is much more illuminating to see cultures as on-going efforts to give shape and significance to the human encounter. Cultures frame universes of sense and meaning which give order and value to life; works of art thus become significant explorations in the consummatory possibilities of meaning. The realm of art stands for all the possible human articulations of life; instead of being merely an object, the work of art comes to be the project of sharing an organized response to the universe, of discovering a consummating meaning. Works of art are inescapably located within the historical and cultural contexts of their appreciators as well as of their creators. Instead of pointing to a timeless realm, they reveal human historicity.

Dewey finds in the work of art the distinctive ability to bridge the dualism of modern culture which seeks to separate the aesthetic from the world of ordinary experience. The task of the aesthetician is "to restore continuity between the refined and intensified forms of experience that are works of art and the everyday events, doings, and sufferings that are universally recognized to constitute experience. Mountain peaks do not float unsupported; they do not even just rest upon the earth. They *are* the earth in one of its manifest operations" (*AE*, 3; *LW* 10:9). The "earth" to be recalled in thinking about art is the natural capacity of human experience to become significantly and vividly imbued with funded interest. Dewey cites the examples of "the fire engine rushing by; the machines excavating enormous holes in the earth; the human fly climbing the steeple-side; the men perched high in air on girders, throwing and catching red-hot bolts." He points to "the tense grace of the ball-player" and the "delight of the housewife in tending her plants" (*AE*, 5; *LW* 10:11).

When he was 25 in 1884, Dewey had speculated about a "new psychology" which would be based on "that rich and varied experience" which included all "the unwritten tragedies and comedies of daily life" (*EW* 1:48). In one sense, *Art as Experience* is the fulfillment of that youthful project. But there is one important difference: the abandonment of "the psychological standpoint." The origin of art is not to be accounted for by the workings of Spirit. Instead, Dewey locates the emergence of the aesthetic in the natural human capacity to celebrate life through a community of meaning. To understand the experience embodied in the Parthenon, Dewey comments, at some point we must take into account "the bustling, arguing, acutely sensitive Athenian citizens" and attempt to connect them "with people in our own homes and on our own streets" (*AE*, 4; *LW* 10:10). The ability of the Greeks to give expressive shape to their art arises from the same human ability to take sensual delight in the world. Whatever the differences in the culture of fifth century Athens and twentieth century America, which Dewey certainly does not ignore, his point remains that expressively organized works of art are developments of general habits of perception connected with a world of cultural meanings. Cultures teach us to see and respond to the world in a variety of ways. Art is simply an intensification of this process. The different needs and habits embodied in different cultures will generate different aesthetic forms. Chartres Cathedral or the World Trade Center arose from radically different needs and desires than the Parthenon and express different forms of human life. Nevertheless, because they have drawn on the expressive possibilities of perception, we can find them to be aesthetically engaging as well as statements of their cultures. Such objects gain expressive power by drawing on the habits of perception and meaning of their cultures rather than by ignoring them.

To grasp the origin of art it is also necessary to grasp the origin of the community of shared experience. Art forces us to think about how human beings are related to the world and to each other. It is because the world is not only genuinely inhabited by the human organism but because it is communally, that is, symbolically appropriated that art is possible at all. Such a theory may be contrasted briefly with one like Kant's aesthetics which builds on his dualistic assumption that man is primordially cut off from nature and his view that human beings are primarily related to each other by an abstract respect for each other's rationality. Aesthetic experience seems paradoxical and problematic to Kant for it is neither cognitive nor ethical. It struggles to be subsummed under our cognitive judgments, but its objectivity, universality, and necessity turn out to involve subjectivity, particularity, and contingency. Art seems to appeal to human desire, but only in a strange disinterested manner. The work of art marks the random occasion for man to enjoy the abstract harmony of his own faculties. In the case of the sublime, Kant shows that we are in fact enjoying a vicarious moral drama. The awesome power of brute nature recalls to us our own unassailable moral worth. Any attempt to locate these expressive features in the basic ways man is actively connected to the world are shown by Kant to be projections of our own human subjectivity. It was only natural for romantic idealists like Schelling to attribute subjectivity to reality in order to overcome these paradoxical conclusions in the Kantian philosophy.

Nature turned out of the door will come back through the window. Dewey proposes that, instead of appealing to the artifice of an idealist metaphysics, we begin by seeing art as an activity grounded in man's social transactions and his transactions with nature. Whereas the Kantian view is plagued by not really being able to account for why human beings create art in the first place, from the Deweyan perspective it is the most natural thing that they do. Our museums are full of objects from other cultures which were never created for the sake of being seen in a museum. They were produced to participate in the cultural and practical needs of human life. The carvings of the gods, the ornaments for clothing, weapons, bowls, and ceremonial objects directly participated in the dramatic activities of the group—they were all parts of "the significant life of an organized community" (*AE*, 7; *LW* 10:13). A community which is threatened with disorganization, which threatens to cease being a genuine community, will have difficulty establishing a significant shared life. Under such circumstances, Dewey suggests, art will become problematic. The ideal of "art for art's sake" would be unintelligible to most human cultures throughout history. This was an attitude generated in the nineteenth century under the rising influence of an industrial bourgeois society which no longer found a place for the artistocratic justification of the arts. The artist could not justify himself to his utilitarian society except by appealing to *its* aesthetic standards. If he refused to compromise his art, he tended to starve. Artists came to see themselves as opposed to their society, outcasts or "poètes maudits." The ideal of "pure art" was consciously espoused as a direct challenge to the bourgeois demand that the artwork be practically useful or comprehensible on the most rudimentary level. At odds with society, the artist justified his activity by regarding himself as a spiritual aristocrat, like Baudelaire, an aesthetic anarchist, like Rimbaud, or as a reactionary mystic in a spiritually unenlightened age, like Yeats. Dewey's point, in any case, is that the ideal of art for art's sake is only possible when art has ceased to play a direct and vital role in organized community life; it is, in other words, a symptomatic response to a disorganized society which cannot grasp itself as an aesthetic project.

For this reason, Dewey sees the modern predicament of aesthetics as embodied in the museum. He is not suggesting that museums are intrinsically bad; Dewey certainly recognized their role not only in preserving works of art otherwise threatened with destruction but the public function of making works generally accessible whereas before they had often been the private possessions of the aristrocracy. Dewey's own connection with the Barnes Foundation shows that he saw the potential educational function of such institutions. Dewey's essential point remains, however, that the "museum attitude" toward art has infected aesthetic theory, and the result has been that theory has been unable to fulfill its primary function of connecting works of high artistic achievement with the natural aesthetic demands of human experience. When objects from widely different contexts are relocated next to each other, such as a Greek statue and a modernist canvas, it will be difficult to see what they have in common. Because both works of art will be capable of being classified as "formed objects," one will be tempted to interpret them as having only "aesthetic form" in common. The original context will be forgotten and lost. One of the results of the institutionalization of art, then, is the formalist interpretation of art. This attitude has been brilliantly analyzed by André Malraux, who realizes that the process of decontextualization has proceeded one step further: the modern museum is a "museum without walls," a museum of the imagination, that is, the book. Photographs not only decontextualize a painting or sculpture, but they make them all virtually the same size. "A Romanesque crucifix was not regarded by its contemporaries as a work of sculpture; nor Cimabue's *Madonna* as a picture," Malraux begins, "Even Pheidias' *Pallas Athene* was not, primarily, a statue."[5] Malraux, unlike Dewey, takes this positively: decontextualization has allowed works of art to be regarded not just as formed objects but as "representatives of a style." *This* is where human creativity is to be found: in the creation of styles. "It is hard for us clearly to realize the gulf between the performance of an Aeschylean tragedy, with the instant Persian threat and Salamis looming across the bay," he remarks, adding "All that remains of Aeschylus is his genius."[6] It is almost as if the task of the artist is to create a pure style which will reveal nothing except his genius. Malraux even speculates that the final liberation of art, as it confronts the traditions of the Orient and "peoples to whom the very idea of art meant nothing," will be from the idea of art itself. Art, in other words, will achieve some sort of cultural nirvana.[7]

It would be unfair to leave the impression that Malraux espouses an empty formalism. In response to the question which naturally arises in formalism, why do human beings create art or what is the meaning of artistic activity, Malraux gives an existentialist answer: art is a defiant gesture against human mortality. "All art is a revolt against man's fate," he claims; the creative act is the "eternal victory over the human condition" which "affirms man's victorious presence,"[8] Art becomes for Malraux an abstract act rather than a specific contextual response; whatever the actual historical circumstances behind the creation of a work of art, there is really only the paean of heroic humanity establishing itself in the void.[9]

Dewey would regard such an explanation as an unnecessary and abstract, if noble, salvaging of meaning in art in the face of formalism. Art for Dewey begins with the existential and historical response to the human condition, which is not so much the Promethean effort on man's part to leave his signature on the universe as the inner consummatory value of responding to the world with articulate sharable meaning.

The danger of losing the concrete event of art has become even more pronounced in recent literary criticism. Here, too, formalism has been the predominant attitude from the New Critics to Northrop Frye and the Structuralists. The excesses of the latter have led to the shipwreck of Deconstructionism. Edward Said aptly describes the general attitude of current theory:

> "Textuality" is the somewhat mystical and disinfected subject matter of literary theory. Textuality has therefore become the exact antithesis and displacement of what might be called history. Textuality is considered to take place, yes, but by the same token it does not take place anywhere or anytime in particular. It is produced, but by no one and at no time. It can be read and interpreted, although reading and interpreting are routinely understood to occur in the form of misreading and misinterpreting. . . . As it is practiced in the American academy today, literary theory has for the most part isolated textuality from the circumstances, the events, the physical sense that made it possible and render it intelligible as the result of human work.[10]

Said contests this view: "My position is that texts are worldly, to some degree they are events, and, even when they appear to deny it, they are nevertheless a part of the social world, human life, and of course the historical moments in which they are located and interpreted." It may seem strange that such points must be argued for. I simply bring them up to show that Dewey's problematic which begins *Art as Experience* seems to be grounded in the tensions and paradoxes surrounding aesthetics in this century. Said himself provides an interesting analysis of the social and political context in which such extreme theories become possible.[11]

Dewey chooses to begin the search for the origin of art in aesthetic events rather than in those objects which try to cultivate and control those events. If the art object is a development of experience, one should ask what sort of experience it is the development of. "The first great consideration is that life goes on in an environment; not merely *in* it but because of it, through interaction with it" (*AE*, 13; *LW* 10:19). Life is an activity, a temporal process of adjustment and readjustment, which has intrinsic to it qualities of struggle, victory, and defeat. Not only are we woven into a dynamic world, but as participants we are characters in its drama. This fundamental organic activity, as has been shown, shapes the very structure of the world we come to inhabit with a temporal and dramatic dimension. In short, the structure of life is growth. "Life itself consists of phases in which the organism falls out of step with the march of surrounding things and then recovers unison with it. . . . And, in a growing life, the recovery is never mere return to a prior state, for it is enriched by the state of disparity and resistance through which it has successfully passed" (*AE*, 14; *LW* 10:19). These "biological commonplaces," Dewey adds, "reach to the roots of the esthetic in experience." The work of art has its ultimate origin in the tensive drama of the lifeworld; it reflects its rootedness in the moment of reconstruction or recovery, in the activity which is a temporal process of transforming the problematic and indeterminate into a sustaining, organized relationship. The outcome of such a process will be more than a restoration of the balance of the previous state because the new harmony will be *seen as* the result of struggle, tension, and activity. "Equilibrium comes about not mechanically and inertly, but out of, and because of, tension," Dewey observes, adding that even below the organic level "form is arrived at whenever a stable, even though moving, equilibrium is reached." Order is the dynamic resolution of energies into a moving organized structure; it "is not imposed from without but is made out of the relations of harmonious interactions that energies bear to one another" (*AE*, 14; *LW* 10:20).

Dewey is not reducing the aesthetic to organic struggle. But he is identifying the nature of organic form as the *roots* of the aesthetic. Form by its nature is tensive, developmental, temporal, and includes within it the elements of activity, involvement, and growth. It cannot exclude the problematic or indeterminate, but must incorporate these. It cannot be self-enclosed, for it is called forth by being open to the world. The origin of art in tensive form has several important implications. First, to the extent there is tension underlying the achievement of form there will be emotional involvement. Emotion, as the previous chapter showed, results from our tensive relations in the situation. On the aesthetic level, says Dewey, the artist's concern for organized form may actually lead him to experiment with moments of "resistance and tension"—indeed, he "rather cultivates them, not for their own sake, but for their potentialities, bringing to living consciousness an experience that is unified and total" (*AE*, 15; *LW* 10:21). The achievements of aesthetic order are the result of explorations of aesthetic disorder. Organic order is not the result of Platonic timelessness. It is a general capacity to guide change; it is implicated at each moment in the possibility of change.

This leads to the second implication: that the nature of tensive form is both temporal and rhythmic, that is, developmental. Form is "ordered change." It is an inherently temporal and rhythmic pattern in experience. The underlying problematic tension of artistic-aesthetic experience achieves expression in and through an interactive process of development. All works of art are temporal, and form is the guiding structure of the experience which reveals the work. Not only does form originate from the tensive dimension of experience, it also originates from the capacity of experience to be integrated and whole. Indeed, it is the very possibility for experience to be whole which reveals the tensive *as* tensive in the first place. The roots of satisfaction, resolution, completion, of closure and wholeness are to be found in the aboriginal ability of an organism to come successfully to terms with its environment. Happiness and delight, says Dewey, "come to be through a fulfillment that reaches to the depths of our being—one that is an adjustment of our whole being with the conditions of existence" (*AE*, 17; *LW* 10:23). The highest expressions of religion are rooted in this desire to adjust the whole of our being to the universe as a whole in a satisfying and meaningful manner. Thus even through moments of struggle or bare endurance, Dewey notes that "there abides the deep-seated memory of an underlying harmony, the sense of which haunts life like the sense of being founded on a rock" (*AE*, 17; *LW* 10:23).

Most conscious life is lived with vivid awareness of regrets and the disparity between our ideals and the real world, of roads not taken and roads that could have been travelled better. But the past need not merely be a burden to us—it may offer hope, guide our present actions, and provide reassurance that life need not be what it presently is. The present is a lived moment in time. This means the presence of what Santayana calls the "hushed reverberations" of the past and the orientation toward the possibilities of the future. "To the being fully alive," says Dewey, "the future is not ominous but a promise; it surrounds the present as a halo" (*AE*, 18; *LW* 10:24). The origin of art lies ultimately in this very moment of being fully alive, where the word "fully" is not to be taken lightly but in the sense of fulfillment. Dewey sees the immanence of the aesthetic in any creature which is living at the pitch of its senses. "The activities of the fox, the dog, and the thrush may at least stand as reminders and symbols of that unity of experience which we so fractionize. . . . The live animal is fully present, all there, in all of its actions: in its wary glances, its sharp sniffings, its abrupt cocking of ears. All senses are equally on the *qui vive*" (*AE*, 19; *LW* 10:24). This is not merely living fully in the present, but living in the present as process: "The past absorbed into the present carries on; it presses forward" (*AE*, 19; *LW* 10:24). One is connected to the world in the living moment. To be so totally integrated in the moment is just what the Zen Buddhists call "enlightenment." It is simply "being-*there*"—that instant of complete awareness in which subject and object disappear, in which one doesn't so much see the Buddha as become him.[12] The haiku strives to reveal, through its concrete but suggestively minimalist technique, the immediate vitality of the moment. Take, for example, a haiku by Tantan (1674-1761):[13]

> On the rock
> waves can't reach,
> fresh snow.

Three condensed images, rock, waves, snow, are dramatically fused and interrelated; we are given a moment, but a moment which has tensions seen and unseen. Aside from the sense of the snow being threatened by the waves, the sense of contrast between the action of the waves, the endurance of the rock, and the fragility of snow, we may also locate hidden suggested transformations: the snow comes from water, and the water eventually wears away even the rock. In its very immediacy, the world of the haiku is revealed in its transiency. The poem brings these suggestions into an intensely sharp and heightened focus. "Experience in the degree in which it *is* experience is heightened vitality," Dewey observes, "it signifies active and alert commerce with the world" (*AE*, 19; *LW* 10:25).

By grounding the aesthetic in the life of the flesh in the world, Dewey recognized that he was setting himself against a moral tradition which had opposed flesh to spirit. In this opposition, Dewey sees the underlying rift which tears the fabric of all contemporary living, which compartmentalizes to no end and murders to dissect. "Only occasionally," Dewey comments, "in the lives of many are the senses fraught with the sentiment that comes from the deep realization of intrinsic meanings" (*AE*, 21; *LW* 10:27). We seek stimulation and excitement without coming in touch with the world. "We see without feeling," notes Dewey, and our senses become a barrier between us and the world, superficial and unfulfilling. They are no longer the doors of true perception but are narrowly used only for entertainment value. There is no passion in the intellect either, he complains, just as there is no insight in perception. It should be recalled, therefore, that in writing a book on art, Dewey is presenting a radical theory of human life and conduct; the artistic use of experience marks a principle for ethics and social theory which cannot be ignored. The Puritan, Dewey wryly comments, is more in touch with the sensual nature of experience than the epistemologist who sees the eye only as "an imperfect telescope designed for the intellecutal reception of material to bring about knowledge of distant objects" (*AE*, 21; *LW* 10:27). For Dewey, the eye is an organ of desire, a means which can connect us sensually and immediately with the world.

Dewey reiterates a point I mentioned in the previous chapter, that "sense" is the apprehension of the embodied meaning of the world and as such cannot be sharply separated from intellect:

> "Sense" covers a wide range of contents. . . . It includes almost everything from bare physical and emotional shock to sense itself— that is, the meaning of things present in immediate experience. Each term refers to some real phase and aspect of life of an organic creature as life occurs through sense organs. But sense, as meaning so directly embodied in experience as to be its own illuminated meaning, is the only signification that expresses the function of sense organs when they are carried to full realization. The senses are the organs through which the live creature participates directly in the on-goings of the world about him. In this participation the varied wonder and splendor of this world are made acutal for him in the qualities he experiences (*AE*, 22; *LW* 10:27-28).

The emphasis on realization and participation in this passage should be noted. Sense is a realization both of the world and the organism because it is the mode of their interaction. Sense carries with it both the elements of activity and intelligence, hence any effort to contrast it or separate it from faculties of will or intellect are misguided from the start. Even in Dewey's early *Psychology*, as was seen, he was forced to speak of feeling in terms of willing and thinking. The artificial faculties of that work have now been thoroughly naturalized so that Dewey can say that sense cannot be opposed to action for it *is* action; nor can it be opposed to mind, for "mind is the means by which participation is rendered fruitful through sense" (*AE*, 22; *LW* 10:28). Sense establishes the continuity of organism and environment rather than separates the two. It is perfectly natural, then, for Dewey to add that experience, "when it is carried to the full, is a transformation of interaction into participation and communication" (*AE*, 22; *LW* 10:28).

The world realized through sense is dramatically complex, moving, and articulated. The more complex the organism-environment relation, the more experience will reflect this complexity in "an endless variety of sub-rhythms." Even "fulfillment is more massive and more subtly shaded" (*AE*, 23; *LW* 10:29). Space is not encountered as an empty void of coordinates, but as the dramatic possibility of movements. Time is not a mechanical counting, but full of the "ebb and flow of expectant impulse" (*AE*, 23; *LW* 10:29). This overall complexity is a precondition for highly significant experience, even if that experience is momentary. Dewey gives the example of a room suddenly lit brightly for an instant or of a landscape revealed by a bolt of lightning. Although the moment of perception may have been swift, the ordered whole was revealed through the focusing of previously developed organized responses. And this is exactly how art works. Art marks the occasion where the possibilities for the significant configuration of the world are actualized. The moment of genuine perception, which should be the beginning for any adequate theory of experience, cannot be confused with the passively undergone, mindless sensations or feelings to which there is no intelligent response nor with the cold, swift act of bare identification and categorization. Much epistemology, however, takes these minimal moments of experience as paradigm. Perception, on the other hand, is the active exploration of the world. It meets sensation not only with a coordinating response but with a question; curiosity and interest are there from the start. The senses are *used* intelligently to discover a world which is apprehended *as* worthy of interest and care. A sensation which is simply "had" or undergone remains uninformed, ignorant, blind, and without issue. Not even the skeptic's question would arise as a significant response if such were experience. Likewise, where the world presents us with nothing new except the boring repetition of the same, the dogmatic nod of simple identification suffices. Classification is a helpful servant but a tediously dull master. Perception advances; in it experience grows and consciousness comes to inhabit the world rather than pass over it. Whereas other theories of experience often sound as if they were long explanations of why we shouldn't encounter the world with wonder and curiosity, Dewey's approach treats these aspects as of utmost significance. It is with this in mind that Dewey asserts, "Art is thus prefigured in the very processes of living (*AE*, 24; *LW* 10:30). The living moment, when perception is exercised at its fullest, is the origin of art. Art is experience directed toward the intelligent exploration of the senses of the world, and it takes as its theme the rich and varied possibilities of response which stimulate involvement and discovery. "The senses of the world," Dewey would say that the ambiguity in this phrase is illuminating. Sense is the sense of meaning. Life prefigures art because art articulates or is a figuration of life.

The arts of experience give the world significant embodiment. And the fully embodied mind inhabits the world sensitively, intelligently, artistically. Dewey takes Keats' famous stanza from the "Ode on a Grecian Urn" as illustrative:

> Beauty is truth, truth beauty—that is all
> Ye know on earth, and all ye need to know.

Truth for Keats, Dewey points out, did not mean intellectual correctness, the correspondence of proposition and fact; "It denotes the wisdom by which men live, especially 'the lore of good and evil' (*AE*, 34; *LW* 10:40). All such wisdom depends on the capacity to envision ideals and bring them about. The imagination, the mind raised to its aesthetic and artistic pitch, gives reasoning what meaning it has. "Man lives in a world of surmise, of mystery, of uncertainties," states Dewey, " 'Reasoning' must fail man . . ." (*AE*, 34; *LW* 10:41). Dewey finds in the meaning of the phrase "on earth" the scene of the perennial problematic of the human condition, where the "irritable reaching after fact and conclusion" (to use Keats' phrase) by itself "confuses and distorts instead of bringing us to the light" (*AE*, 34; *LW* 10:41). Those who regard Dewey simply as an instrumentalist should consider this passage well. "There are but two philosophies," he says, "One of them accepts life and experience in all its uncertainty, mystery, doubt, and half-knowledge and turns that experience upon itself to deepen and intensify its own qualities—to imagination and art. This is the philosophy of Shakespeare and Keats" (*AE*, 34; *LW* 10:41). And, one must add, of Dewey too.

II. The Fruits of Intelligence: "An Experience"

If the first two chapters of *Art as Experience* are an investigation into the roots of art, the third and most famous chapter of the book, "Having an Experience," is a discussion of art and the aesthetic as the cultivated fulfillment of experience. Dewey casually introduces the distinction between those ordinary moments of life characterized by "distraction and dispersion," where the projects and plans are left unfulfilled because of the discord of thought and action or due to failure of will, and those moments, however rare, in which "the material experienced runs its course to fulfillment" (*AE*, 35; *LW* 10:42). This latter is "*an* experience." The distinction is worth reflecting on, especially for those who have characterized Dewey's as an optimist's philosophy.[14] *Most* experience, at least in our day and age, is *not* "*an* experience." Dewey finds this the human tragedy, for it signifies that most experience is unconsummated in its meaning, divided against itself and paralyzing further action, often needlessly so at that. There is a remarkable discussion in *Experience and Nature* in which Dewey attacks the utilitarian attitude that eulogizes means in light of a completely indefinite conception of ends.

> The existence of activities that have no immediate enjoyed intrinsic meaning is undeniable. They include much of our labors in home, factory, laboratory, and study. By no stretch of language can they be termed either artistic or esthetic. Yet they exist, and are so coercive that they require some attentive recognition. So we optimistically call them "useful" and let it go at that, thinking that by calling them useful we have somehow justified and explained their occurrence. If we were to ask useful for what? we should be obliged to examine their actual consequences, and once we honestly and fully faced these consequences, we should probably find ground for calling such activities detrimental rather than useful (*EN*, 363; *LW* 1: 271-72).

To think instrumentally is to take ends into account first, not last. This is the point Thoreau makes at the beginning of *Walden* in the chapter ironically called "Economy." "How many a poor immortal soul have I met well-nigh crushed and smothered under its load, creeping down the road of life, pushing before it a barn seventy-five feet by forty, its Augean stables never cleansed, and one hundred acres of land, tillage, mowing, pasture, and woodlot!" To which Thoreau adds, "But men labor under a mistake. The better part of the man is soon plowed into the soil for compost." Thoreau undertook his "experiment" in the middle of society, "a mile from any neighbor," to illustrate the point that life is the end which unintelligent "practical" action often converts into a means. (Those who criticize Thoreau for not really "roughing it" like the pioneers may be said to have missed the point of the whole book.)[15] To call something useful, says Dewey, just because it is good at "bringing into existence certain commodities" is to forget "their effect upon the quality of human life and experience," which in fact may be quite undesirable. "What they also *make* by way of narrowed, embittered, and crippled life, of congested, hurried, confused and extravagant life is left in oblivion. But to be useful is to fulfill need. The characteristic human need is for possession and appreciation of the meaning of things, and this need is ignored and unsatisfied in the traditional notion of the useful" (*EN*, 362; *LW* 1:272). To miss this point in Dewey is likewise to miss the point of his whole philosophy.

Therefore, in drawing attention to those occasions when *an* experience is realized, Dewey is pointing to something which at once illuminates most of human life for what it is as well as presents the concrete possibility of what it might be. In *an* experience the conclusion is not merely a terminus or an ending, but a moment which brings a process to fulfillment: it is the outcome of a guided process of action which organizes and unifies the experience. "Such an experience is a whole," remarks Dewey, "and carries with it its own individualizing quality and self-sufficiency. It is *an* experience" (*AE*, 35; *LW* 10:42). Such experiences are the realization of a temporal process and are unified by a distinctive quality, but they are not necessarily happy or pleasurable. Dewey points to rather innocuous examples, such as playing a game of chess or dining at a fine French restaurant. But he also, significantly, includes experiencing the fury of an Atlantic storm while at sea as well as a rupture of friendship. Elsewhere, he mentions being sick with the grippe.[16] Any experience, to the extent that it becomes so organized as to exhibit in a consciously intense manner an integrating quality, becomes *an* experience and reveals a dimension of the meaning of the human encounter of the world. Such experiences may not always be of a world or of a creature who is happy, pleasant, or at harmony. The quality of such an experience is not only undergone intensely, but it is seen to be the quality of *that* situation and expressive of its meaning in a directly embodied way. These experiences may enter into life so as to become touchstones of our understanding, foci in terms of which we interpret other experiences. But often the situation so directly embodies its meaning that our attempts to relate or describe it fail and end with the frustrated remark, "You had to be there!"

This is a point worth remembering for Dewey's account of *an* experience: art represents the most successful effort to control the chance conditions by which such experiences are had. By subjecting a medium to the forms of the art, *an* experience becomes sharable among many. Art not only comes to be a potential ground for the shared experience of a community at a particular moment in time, but it continues to have power in the historical life of the culture. Art provides, then, a reservoir of shared experience vital in the exploration of the meaning of existence. It should not surprise us that many of these experiences reveal that existence has its dark, tragic, irrational, or fractured dimensions.

One may recall the friendship-rupturing argument in childhood which revealed in the playmate the sudden meaning of racism or remember being desperately sick to the point where the body seemed in the total grip of an alien, malevolent power, where all sense of autonomy was lost to the blind authority of the disease. A nightmare may run its course to fulfillment and thereby come to be *an* experience of nameless childhood terror. Often such experiences remain only at an inchoate level, tacitly shaping our world and its meanings, dimly informing them, if consciously at all. So much of human existence is shaped by such conditions, it is natural that they should become the subject matter of art. Tragedy represents a continued effort to come to terms with the destructive collisions of human life. The plays of the South African playwright Athol Fugard are a painful, masterful probing into the meaning of racism. In Camus' *The Plague,* the question of the meaning of human existence is posed by a sudden mortal disease. Kafka's *Metamorphosis* exploits the power of the nightmare to reveal a dehumanizing world. Works like these affect us and do so directly because they draw upon genuine elements of human experience and succeed in articulating them into a meaningful whole.

There can be an organizing unity even to experiences which have as their subject matter disturbing or even tragic themes. In *an* experience, then, there will be a continuity which coherently relates and connects the phases so that the outcome will be the end of a process and not an isolated, meaningless event.

> In such experiences, every successive part flows freely, without seam and without unfilled blanks, into what ensues. At the same time there is no sacrifice of the self-identity of the parts. A river, as distinct from a pond, flows. But its flow gives a definiteness and interest to its successive portions greater than exist in the homogeneous portions of a pond. In an experience, flow is from something to something. As one part leads into another and as one part carries on what went before, each gains distinctness in itself. The enduring whole is diversified by successive phases that are emphases of its varied colors. Because of continuous merging, there are no holes, mechanical junctions, and dead centres when we have *an* experience. There are pauses, places of rest, but they punctuate and define the quality of movement. They sum up what has been undergone and prevent its dissipation and idle evaporation (*AE*, 36; *LW* 10:43).

The primary feature of *an* experience is that it is an affair of *temporal* development. Not only is there progression, but there is progressive integration which gathers the temporal phases together as belonging, relating to each other, sustaining and interacting with each other in a tensive, dramatic unity so that there is a cumulative sense of an overall event being accomplished or brought to completion. Each phase or moment must be grasped *as* a phase or part of a larger whole; the sense of the whole must be present in the part. While in most experiences the unifying qualitative sense of the whole, which ultimately constitutes the horizon of meaning, is left tacit, in *an* experience this is consciously apprehended and realized so that the *sense* of the experience is the presence of its meaning, felt as a guiding, controlling qualitative unity pervading all the various parts in their variety. "An experience has a unity that gives it its name, *that* meal, that storm, that rupture of friendship. The existence of this unity is constituted by a single *quality* that pervades the entire experience in spite of the variation of its constituent parts. This unity is neither emotional, practical, nor intellectual, for these terms name distinctions that reflection can make within it" (*AE*, 37; *LW* 10:44). In *an* experience, the non-cognitive suffuses all the conscious moments of transition in a sustaining manner. The experience has an intrinsic *sense* of depth and order as well as mystery, but this sense is present in the surface and is realized through it. One can always reflect on a good work of art, for there is much more in it than is ever immediately or initially apprehended. But one reflects *on* the work because it is only through the textured surface of the work that its world is revealed.

An experience also marks a moment of genuine thinking. In most thinking the conclusion is simply arrived at, and the process of thought is a troublesome means to that end. Yet even there the conclusion must be realized *as* the conclusion *of* what precedes if it is to make sense. But such cases are not paradigmatic moments of thinking, according to Dewey. They are mechanical and utilitarian rather than artistic. "In fact," says Dewey, "in an experience of thinking premisses emerge only as a conclusion becomes manifest" (*AE*, 38; *LW* 10:44). Heidegger observes that we try to think the thought of a thinker so that we can come to ask the question he asked.[17] Even in Dewey's "Reflex Arc" article, he noted that intelligent action was the *search* for the proper stimulus, that is, it was the effort to determine the *meaning* of the situation, to grasp the present in terms of its possibilities and histories. We cannot understand another philosopher or the history of philosophy as a set of answers to questions posed clearly and distinctly from the outset. Exploring the "arguments of the philosophers" will miss what is philosophical about them unless one also tries to comprehend what is the origin and intent of their thinking, what questions they *tried* to ask—and what questions they did not try to ask. To arrive at the moment where thought is completed, one must grasp the tensive problematic which set it going and in terms of which it is a possible meaningful response. To get the sense of someone's thought, one must try to determine the context in terms of which it makes sense. To do this successfully will be to realize the unifying qualitative aesthetic of the thought. Hence, Dewey says, "no intellectual activity is an integral event (is *an* experience), unless it is rounded out with this quality. Without it, thinking is inconclusive. In short, esthetic cannot be sharply marked off from intellectual experience since the latter must bear an esthetic stamp to be itself complete" (*AE*, 38; *LW* 10:45).

Dewey also applies the characteristics of *an* experience to the question of action, of genuine *praxis*. Most so-called practical activity is not practical, as already noted. That is, it either achieves nothing or it achieves its ends automatically, without care, attention, or involvement. "Obstacles are overcome by shrewd skill, but they do not feed experience" (*AE*, 38; *LW* 10:45). Between this form of arid utilitarianism and sheer romantic impulsiveness, "there lie those courses of action in which through successive deeds there runs a sense of growing meaning conserved and accumulating toward an end that is felt as accomplishment of a process" (*AE*, 39; *LW* 10:45). Thus, genuine moral and political action is deeply aesthetic in character. Dewey blasts most morality for its "anaesthetic quality," its "grudging piecemeal concessions to the demands of duty" where it should exemplify "wholehearted action" (*AE*, 39; *LW* 10:46). Action which realizes and fulfills the human need for meaning and value, for living a significant life in the world, is as aesthetic and intelligent as it is revolutionary. "Social reform,"' Dewey remarks elsewhere, "is conceived in a Philistine spirit, if it is taken to mean anything less than precisely the liberation and expansion of the meanings of which experience is capable" (*EN*, 411; *LW* 1:307). To which he adds, "Nothing but the best, the richest and fullest experience possible, is good enough for man." This experience is "the common purpose of men." Thus, thinking and action come together in the arts of experience which must be the arts of meaning and value realized in human life.

To repeat, according to Dewey human life stands in need of liberation; most of our experience, if not totally anaesthetic, is far from meaningful or fulfilling. It falls toward either of two extremes, to simple, loose disorganization which neither commences nor completes anything or to rigid, lockstep mechanical routine which deadens the mind due to the absence of intrinsically fulfilling ends. "There exists so much of one and the other of these two kinds of experience," asserts Dewey, "that unconsciously they come to be taken as norms of all experience" (*AE*, 40; *LW* 10:47). When the aesthetic appears, it is perceived as unnatural, as artificial, or as the magnificent, erratic product of genius. While the extraordinary talent and creative power of certain individuals is undeniable, the possibilities for their accomplishments are determined by genuine cultural conditions. Bach born into an Amazonian tribe would not have been Bach; Beethoven born in the fourteenth century would not have been Beethoven. To regard such men and women as heavensent exceptions to the rule is only appropriate when the conditions of existence have been taken in hand and guided toward ends which incorporate the genuine creative possibilities of experience. The denaturalization of art is the dehumanization of man.

The possibility of art lies in the effort to keep experience from falling toward meaningless ritual or yawning chaos. Plato introduces Eros as the cosmic intermediary, the spirit which bridges the eternal gods and the transient mortals and thereby "prevents the universe from falling into two halves."[18] The result is creation. So, too, for Dewey, the human impulsion toward meaning gives birth to the arts by which blind impulse and dead habit are fused into creative spirit. "The enemies of the esthetic are neither the practical nor the intellectual. They are the humdrum; slackness of loose ends; submission to convention in practice and intellectual procedure. Rigid abstinence, coerced submission, tightness on one side and dissipation, incoherence and aimless indulgence on the other, are deviations in opposite directions from the unity of an experience" (*AE*, 40; *LW* 10:47). An experience is motivated throughout by spirit, by Eros, in which life comes to new and creative birth.

Having emphasized the movement and unity of *an* experience, Dewey comments on three important characteristics or phases within it: closure, emotion, and structure or form. These will be addressed later on more extensively, but it is necessary to comment on how these function together to create authentic perception. "Closure" is another way of referring to the sense of intrinsic completion arrived at through *an* experience. It is, first of all, a dynamic resolution, a coordination and harnassing of the tensions within the experience which threaten to disintegrate it. "This closure," says Dewey, "of a circuit of energy is the opposite of arrest, of *stasis*" (*AE*, 41; *LW* 10:47). There can only be closure on completion where there has been profound struggle and conflict; otherwise there is no movement, no perception, no action, no completion. Without tensiveness there "would be no taking in of what preceded" (*AE*, 41; *LW* 10:48). "Taking in" is what opens the world to perception, and for perception to occur the world must open tensively and problematically. Dewey adds, "It involves reconstruction which may be painful." Thus, closure refers to something much deeper than a terminus, an ending which brings a process to a stop. It is a closing together which holds within it the opening of the world. Through this opening, experience has grown and developed, but only because it has also been controlled and constrained. For closure is also the closing out, the exclusion of possibilities which would have deadened or dissipated the experience. *An* experience comes to be only because of its inherent finitude. From the moment of commencement, closure must be present as the very possibility of meaning. Indefinite and unending experience means nothing because it accomplishes nothing. It can neither gather elements together nor exclude what does not belong; such experience is "unowned" because no decisions are made within it. For experience to speak, there must be a pervasive sense of belonging and not-belonging, of what is appropriate and fitting and what is not. For *an* experience to be realized there must be the sense that the parts fit and are appropriated; they are owned and belong to the experience. The closure of *an* experience reflects the presence of care, of controlling interest, which has entered the world through its tensive opening. And through this entry, the world has come to be itself as the lived material of experience.

Because of the elements of struggle and control, the experience is highly emotional. The experience is undergone. Dewey remarks that "there are few intense esthetic experiences that are wholly gleeful. They are certainly not to be characterized as amusing, and as they bear down upon us they involve a suffering that is none the less consistent with, indeed a part of, the complete perception that is enjoyed" (*AE*, 41; *LW* 10:48). The emotion of *an* experience is not to be confused with the ordinary, nameable emotions of non-aesthetic experience—emotions which may be used as material or subject matter for aesthetic exploration. Emotion is not an instantaneous, locateable feeling; it is the total undergoing of the experience, thereby binding the self and the world in the temporal dimension of the event. It is thus "the moving and cementing force" among the parts of *an* experience. "It selects what is congruous and dyes what is selected with its color, thereby giving qualitative unity to materials externally disparate and dissimilar. It thus provides unity in and through the varied parts of an experience" (*AE*, 42; *LW* 10:49). In the course of *an* experience there may be a variety of different emotions. As the material has variety and complexity it will evoke complex responses. But these various responses will nevertheless belong to the tapestry of the whole and be undergone in terms of it. The response to the overall experience determines not only its significance but how each part is felt. The themes of a mad old man judicially trying a foot stool in place of his ungrateful daughter or of a blind man being told he is standing at a cliff's edge when he is not in themselves may strike us as comic themes, even if somewhat pathetic or cruel. But in *King Lear*, Lear's mad trial court has an outraged nobility to it which hints that *all* justice is absurd convention in a world without law. Edgar's jest with his blinded father is a wrenching lesson in fortitude. (Gloucester steps over the imagined "edge of the cliff" and passes out; his son revives him, persuading him he has fallen but has been miraculously saved. "Thy life's a miracle," he says, "Bear free and patient thoughts.")

The form of *an* experience is the pattern of events, the structure of the interaction, through which the experience develops. All experience, of course, has interaction. But "An experience has pattern and structure, because it is not just doing and undergoing in alternation, but consists of them in relationship" (*AE*, 44; *LW* 10:50-51). Action and reaction are woven together into one continuous experience whose subsequent meaning develops out of the precedent events, and this connection is consciously realized. "The action and its consequence must be joined in perception. This relationship is what gives meaning; to grasp it is the objective of all intelligence" (*AE*, 44; *LW* 10:51). *An* experience, because it is guided by art, is the education, the leading forth, of perception. The parts lead to and reinforce each other so that there is an intelligent structure, that is, meaning. It is this which provides the basis for interpreting or perceiving a particular phase or part in terms of how it fits into the whole, which is the job of criticism.

Perception is this effort to "take in" experience in a concrete, emotional, but intelligent, way. Perception tries to grasp just this relation of doing and undergoing in a meaningful fashion. It is for this reason that Dewey is willing to say that in some respects the artist exhibits intelligence in a more exacting, intent, and penetrating manner than the scientist. "A painter must consciously undergo the effect of his every brush stroke or he will not be aware of what he is doing and where his work is going," says Dewey. "To think effectively in terms of relations of qualities is as severe a demand upon thought as to think in terms of symbols, verbal and mathematical. Indeed, since words are easily manipulated in mechanical ways, the production of a work of genuine art probably demands more intelligence than does most of the so-called thinking that goes on among those who pride themselves on being 'intellectuals'" (*AE*, 45-46; *LW* 10:52). Perception is the struggle to make sense of the world; it involves not only the exploration of the world as medium but the disclosure of our possible responses to it. Possibilities must be brought to light and control the action for the world to take on meaning.

Perception links creation and appreciation, art and the aesthetic. These demands are not two separate or disjointed acts, but reciprocal and mutually sustaining phases of one experience. To be sure the creator of the work of art and the one who discovers it and enjoys it may be different individuals. Dewey's point, however, is that the artist embodies in his artistic creation the attitude of the appreciator and that the appreciator must try to adopt the stance of the creator to see what the work is attempting to reveal. "Art," says Dewey, "denotes a process of doing or making," the active work executed or achieved through a medium; "aesthetic" tends to refer simply to passive appropriation. But when art ignores how the product looks, it becomes mechanical, just as appreciation which is purely passive is titillation at best. "Craftsmanship to be artistic in the final sense must be 'loving'; it must care deeply for the subject matter upon which skill is exercised" (AE, 47-48; LW 10:54). From this we may infer that what the artist seeks to reveal in the work and make available for others is just this care for what matters in the work. To evoke aesthetic concern, the work must be able to guide and cultivate perception so that it becomes directly involved in what the work is about. A work which ultimately does not care for what it is about, its "substance," as Dewey calls it, reveals itself as careless. The material is ultimately not about anything worth caring for. The medium may be handled in a facile, slick fashion; there may be overwhelming technique. But the total effect may be to block perception, to stop an experience from developing. From the cheap "original oil paintings" one may buy in department stores to the brittle technic of a pianist who records, for example, all of Beethoven's piano works, the effect is that one passes over the material quickly. If one tries to concentrate and work with the work, there is nothing there with which to work. Such works are efficient, mechanical, and lifeless. Compare, for example, a well known photograph of Gertrude Stein with Picasso's famous portrait of her. The photograph shows a heavy old woman in her apartment. The apartment is cluttered, there are paintings on the wall, and she is beside her poodle. No doubt this is how Stein looked but the photograph is taken in a matter of seconds. The Picasso, on the other hand, conveys immediately a compact, yet complex sense of directed force and power; we sense the sort of elemental yet keenly intelligent personality Stein was. The warm browns and blacks throw the luminous face and hands into dramatic relief. The displaced eyes seem to capture a movement of the head, going from a position of leaning forward with wide-eyed concentration to being tilted back, the eyes half-narrowing in critical judgment. The whole effect is a magical fascination with an enigmatic, attractive, but threatening character. (To those who said that Gertrude didn't look at all like her portrait, Picasso aptly responded, "She will.")[19]

An experience embodies intelligently controlled action; it leads to involvement with the subject matter through care. To create this, the artist must take on both the role of maker and viewer and integrate these activities so that they control his action. Dewey puts it succinctly, "The artist embodies in himself the attitude of the perceiver while he works" (AE, 48; LW 10:55). This signifies a total integration of the powers of perception. We do not see just with the eyes, as Dewey insisted from the time of his early psychological studies; rather the *whole* organism sees. Dewey developed this point from the "Reflex Arc Concept" article and draws the following conclusions:

> As we manipulate, we touch and feel; as we look we see; as we listen, we hear. The hand moves with etching needle or with brush. The eye attends and reports the consequenes of what is done. Because of this intimate connection, subsequent doing is cumulative, and not a matter of caprice nor yet of routine. In an emphatic artistic-esthetic experience, the relation is so close that it controls simultaneously both the doing and the perception. Such vital intimacy of connection cannot be had if only hand and eye are engaged. When they do not, both of them, act as organs of the whole being, there is but mechanical sequence of movement, as in walking that is automatic. Hand and eye, when the experience is esthetic, are but instruments through which the entire live creature, moved and active throughout, operates (*AE*, 49-50; *LW* 10:56).

Merleau-Ponty has made much the same point. In "Eye and Mind," he says, "It is by lending his body to the world that the artist changes the world into paintings. To understand these transubstantiations we must go back to the working, actual body—not the body as a chunk of space or a bundle of functions but that body which is an intertwining of vision and movement."[20] In *an* experience, there is the accomplishment of an integrated coordination.

The continuity of interaction creates a dynamic, growing experience in which the relationship between the parts is perceived. This leads to the overall sense of the elements of the experience as "fit" or "harmonious"—or, if the work is unsuccessful, as jarring or fumbled. The successful work of *an* experience is dominated by the sense of accomplishment or achievement. An *action* has been completed. There is the sense of control and cooperation, even in those works which may appear to be uncontrolled. A Jackson Pollack may at first seem entirely random, but gradually there emerges a sense of basic rhythms and richness of texture. "In as far as the development of an experience is *controlled* through reference to these immediately felt relations of order and fulfillment," states Dewey, "that experience is dominantly esthetic in nature. The urge to action becomes an urge to the kind of action which will result in an object satisfying in direct perception" (*AE*, 50; *LW* 10:56). Dewey gives here the example of a potter who, in making a bowl, "makes it in such a way so regulated by the series of perceptions that sum up the serial acts of making."

The integration of the activity, in other words, will be reflected in the object. The object which is the condition of aesthetic perception, the product which engenders the "working of the work," will have the living form of an act. Susanne Langer has provided a fascinating study of this idea in her *Mind: An Essay on Human Feeling*. There she says:

> If feeling is a culmination of vital process, any articulated image of it must have the semblance of that vital process rising from deep, general organic activities to intense and concerted acts, such as we perceive directly in their psychical phases as impacts of felt actions. Every artistic form reflects the dynamism that is constantly building up the life of feeling. It is this same dynamism that records itself in organic forms; growth is its most characteristic process and is the source of almost all familiar living shape.[21]

"Elements in art," she adds later, "have not the character of things, but of acts."[22] Though Langer still insists on her isomorphic symbolism and the analogy of art to logical projection where Dewey would emphasize interaction and participation, the point made here is quite compatible. More interesting is her use of the morphologist D'Arcy Thompson's concept of "phase beauty." Thompson, in studying the structure of organisms, showed that the form cannot be analyzed apart from the temporal process of growth and that indeed it can embody the growth process in its gradated structure. "A flowering spray of Montbretia," he says for example, "or lily-of-the-valley exemplifies a growth-gradient. . . . Along the stalk the growth-gradient falls away; the florets are of descending age, from flower to bud; their graded differences of age lead to an exquisite gradation of size and form; the time interval between one and another, or the space-time relation between them all, gives a peculiar quality—we may call it phase-beauty—to the whole. A clump of reeds or rushes shows this same phase-beauty, and so do the waves on a cornfield or on the sea."[23] The various stages of the temporal process are captured in the present structure, giving in the present the sense of growth. Langer applies this to a number of examples with her characteristic sensitivity for the concrete.

> In a Cambodian Buddha statue, for instance, there is usually a perfect elaboration of the head, and a flowing line to the hands, which are given slightly less articulation; the torso and crossed legs are very simply treated as large surfaces and opposed curves. There is a gradient of development toward the head, culminating in the face, and a lesser one toward the hands, that leads up to their delicate form and gesture. Such a figure has the living stillness of a plant; its "inward action" is concentrated in its apex, the head. . . . Its expressiveness suffuses the figure. . . the traditional lotus pedestal repeats the theme of slow and gradual efflorescence.[24]

Likewise, she compares Egyptian sculpture with Greek art. In the former she sees "the growth impulse spent" or "grown form, not growing." Thus even a statue of a child will have a fixed, eternal quality. "Greek sculpture, by contrast," she says, "seems in the process of individuation. . . . If Greek art. . . makes an impression of perfection, it is different from the perfection of great Egyptian works; it reaches a perfect moment, like an eternalized act of coming into its own."[25] The Egyptian statue inhabits a universe in which order is complete; it thus does not seem to be in time at all. The Greek presents the vital accomplishment of order in which the sense of the process of perfection is felt. To stress Dewey's point, in *an* experience there will be the progressive organization of acts into one completed act. Unlike Langer, however, Dewey will not be forced to rely on the notion of an external form which somehow mirrors an inner feeling. The interaction of the organism with the object will generate an organic experience which is not the mirror of life, but is life.

Just as the creator must embody within himself the attitude of the appreciator, so too the appreciator must take an active, creative role for perception to occur. Perception is receptive, yes, but receptivity, notes Dewey, is not passivity. "It, too, is a process consisting of a series of responsive acts that accumulate toward objective fulfillment. Otherwise there is not perception but recognition" (*AE*, 52; *LW* 10:58). Recognition, like mere identification, does not become involved with the object more than to classify it. Perception must "develop freely." Where there is perception, "There is an act of reconstructive doing and consciousness becomes fresh and alive" (*AE*, 53; *LW* 10:59). Thus, perception must arise from an intrusion of the world, a sense that experience *needs* reconstruction rather than identification. Perception, in short, begins with provocation, and provocation calls for active response. "Perception is an act of the going-out of energy," insists Dewey, "in order to receive, not a withholding of energy. . . . We must summon energy and pitch it at a responsive key in order to *take* in" (*AE*, 53; *LW* 10:60).[26] We must *learn* to see. Seeing—perception—in turn comes about only in a developing experience:

> For to perceive, a beholder must *create* his own experience. And his creation must include relations comparable to those which the original producer underwent. They are not the same in any literal sense. But with the perceiver, as with the artist, there must be an ordering of the elements of the whole that is in form, although not in details, the same as the process of organization the creator of the work consciously experienced. Without an act of recreation the object is not perceived as a work of art. The artist selected, simplified, clarified, abridged and condensed according to his point of view and interest (*AE*, 54; *LW* 10:60).

This is not the place to enter the controversial topic of whether one must or can experience what the creator of the work experienced.[27] What Dewey is saying is that for *an* experience to occur, we must develop an organized, integrated response to the work; presumably the form of the work helps us do this, and the form is the dynamic structure of the work which the artist actively realized through his art. To encounter a work of art is to engage in a dialogue of perception. As Nathan Knobler puts it, speaking of the visual arts:

> The appreciation of art results from an *active* participation on the part of an observer. The work of art and the person who stands before it take part in a *dialogue,* in which each contributes a portion of the whole experience. This dialogue has its counterpart in the studio, for the creation of the work of art frequently results from a process in which the artist acts upon the work and is in turn acted upon by it. . . . The production of a work is a dynamic activity, in which the artist acts and then responds to each act as the process continues to the next step in the sequence that eventually brings forth the completed work. . . . The work of art exists as a completed physical entity when it is presented to view, but it becomes an object of aesthetic value only when it causes a response in the observer, and the nature of that response is dependent upon an active participation in the aesthetic experience. The work of art has a statement to make, but it is the observers of the work who shape that statement into a personal communication by committing themselves to the experience.[28]

An experience comes to be in the development of perception which takes an interactive approach to the material of experience, the world. The artist may (or must) create from his or her moments of solitude—the creative need as well as the act arises, we have seen, from a moment of division and separation from the world which is at once a love of and abiding care for the world. The work may be privately enjoyed (only eight of Emily Dickinson's poems were published in her lifetime; Van Gogh died owning most of his works), but in every instance there is a minimum audience of one. Every artist must harbor a discerning critic or create by luck alone. Dewey laments that there is no word in English to unite artistic and aesthetic into one process which culminates in the consummatory, the culturation or cultivation of experience which is rooted in nature. "The consummatory" was, perhaps, a homely term even for Dewey. It is meant to connote that the experience consummates the ideal possibilities of experience. There is an immanent sense of accomplishment in *an* experience, though that sense may be one of tragic resolution. There is, even so, the awareness of a process brought to fulfillment so that the capacity of experience to mean has been realized through a medium of activity.

The sense of the consummatory, therefore, is present throughout *an* experience and is felt intensely in the guiding, unifying, organizing quality through which all the parts belong and cooperate toward the overall end. The sense of the consummatory is gradually transformed from a feeling of immanent possibility, of the ideal capacity of the experience, to one of progressive realization. The end of the work does not lie outside it but within it as a moving force, the entelechy rather than the terminus. "A drama or a novel," Dewey dryly observes, "is not the final sentence" (*AE*, 55; *LW* 10:61). "That which distinguishes an experience as esthetic," he continues, "is conversion of resistance and tensions, of excitations that in themselves are temptations to diversion, into a movement toward an inclusive and fulfilling close" (*AE*, 56; *LW* 10:62). The consummatory is what brings the work forth as well as what guides it, selecting which possibilities to realize and which to exclude, integrating all elements in terms of the idea of the experience as a completed whole.

Malcolm Cowley writes of Whitman's "Song of Myself" in his introduction to *Leaves of Grass:*

> The true structure of the poem is not primarily logical but psychological, and is not a geometrical figure but a musical progression. As music "Song of Myself" . . . comes closer to being a rhapsody or tone poem, one that modulates from theme to theme, often changing key or tempo, falling into reveries and rising toward moments of climax, but always preserving its unity of feeling as it moves onward in a wavelike flow. It is a poem that bears the mark of having been conceived as a whole and written in one prolonged burst of inspiration, but its unity is also the result of conscious art. . . . He did not recognize all the bad lines. . . . , but there is no line in the first edition that seems false to a single prevailing tone. . . . Whitman was not working in terms of "therefore" and "however." He preferred to let one image suggest another image, which in turn suggests a new statement of mood or doctrine. His themes modulate into one another by pure association, as in a waking dream, with the result that all the transitions seem instinctively right.[29]

This is a precise example of what Dewey takes to be the characteristic features of *an* experience. As *an* experience grows, it reveals its material and the possibilities of that material for being expressive and belonging together. The material is gathered together as it becomes evident or established in the work. The work is the process, the demanding enactment binding creator and appreciators through the care for the subject matter. Thus art can reveal the human inhabitation of the world as a genuine possibility, and through this art also leads to the shared world which organizes and integrates, indeed makes possible, the genuine community.

III. Expression: The Articulation of Emotion

Experience which is artistically shaped becomes expressive. In the course of this process, emotion becomes articulate. For this reason, art not only has meaning and communicates, but has form. To grasp the work of art is just this effort to find the expressive ground. Dewey sees expression as a crucial means of approaching the question of artistic-aesthetic experience. Because of his direct use of terms like "expression" and "emotion," Dewey's theory has often been connected with those other theories which hold some form of the view that the essence of art is expression, such as Santayana's or Croce's. Moreover, because the expression theory has received a good deal of criticism by such rigorous thinkers as Bouwsma, Hospers, and Beardsley, it becomes necessary to take Dewey's approach with some wariness. If Dewey's aesthetics relies on the idea of expression, and his aesthetics represents the articulation of his general theory of experience, then any problems with the idea of expression must be taken seriously. At best, Dewey is congenially given credit for formulating an aesthetic theory which is more concerned with the artist's production or creation of the work and which must, therefore, expect to have problems when it applies these ideas to the audience's response. Yet, as we have seen, it was the very intent of Dewey's theory to break down the rigid distinction between artistic and aesthetic experience which this concession requires. If Dewey's theory of expression is inappropriate for the appreciator of a work, it should also be questioned in terms of its fitness for the creator.

While such an attitude may seem too all-or-nothing, it is safe to say that the purpose of Dewey's approach in aesthetics and in philosophy in general was to get around the sort of divisions and distinctions which have generated fruitless controversies and even more fruitless solutions. If his theory has anything to offer at all, it is a bypass for prefabricated dilemmas. It is a great mistake to associate Dewey's views of expression with either Croce or Santayana since they both adhere to the sort of dualisms Dewey rejected. Croce, on the one hand, grounds his analysis of expression firmly upon the metaphysics of absolute idealism. The work of art for him is primarily the intuition, not the physical object, as the first chapter revealed. Spirit literally creates an object out of itself. Santayana, on the other hand, was a materialist. Though Dewey was particularly impressed with Santayana's *Life of Reason,* he set himself firmly against Santayana's views on the relationship of experience and nature.[30] In *The Sense of Beauty,* Santayana regards beauty or aesthetic quality as a projection or objectification of a subjective state. The sense of beauty was an inner phenomenon, the product of associations and feelings, and the subject matter for psychology. Both Croce and Santayana, in the last analysis, hold to the division between inner and outer, subject and object, association and intuition that Dewey questions. Instead, Dewey begins with art arising from the natural interaction of an organism with the world and from the cultural interaction of members in a society. Art and expression are to be interpreted from this standpoint, and this, I believe, makes a great deal of difference.

It will help first to examine briefly some of the traditional assumptions and criticisms of the idea of expression. Throughout most of Western civilization, art was interpreted to be *mimesis,* an imitation or representation of some object or action. This object could exist externally in a variety of ways: as a natural being, as an historical or mythological character, or as a divine being. The artists were mainly regarded as craftsmen who worked within the cultural tradition and who sought to render through intensely controlled images a heightened awareness of the underlying values and meanings of the culture. In most cases, works of art were evaluated in terms of how well they served this function. With Plato, the whole enterprise of art is thrown into question because of its very inability to escape the particular, concrete, sensuous, and conventional modes of depicting the world. Plato's objections to art are not so much that it only presents a copy of a copy, but that it lacks any critical self-awareness of what its true objects are. Plato's criticism of the poets is at heart the same as his criticism of the sophists who confused perception with knowledge: both end up being committed to the demos, to becoming, and to serving rather than educating the desires. In reaction, Plato creates his new poetry, which takes as its theme the self-critical method of Socrates. Plato's myths and dialogues are meant to sustain the dialectical nature of inquiry rather than silence it.[31] The extension of the mimetic theory by Aristotle and Plotinus corrects Plato's censure, Aristotle by his naturalism (art can give us ideal types and thus be "more philosophical" than history), Plotinus by his supernaturalism (the artist can transcend the forms of nature and give us *higher* sensuous representations of the Forms).[32]

The transition from viewing art as *mimesis* to viewing it as expression comes through the romantics, though it presupposes the Enlightenment's emphasis on history, the individual, and the nature of the mind as an artful power in the construction of perception and knowledge. The theoreticians of romanticism, like Schelling, Schopenhauer, and Coleridge, were strongly influenced by their version of Neo-Platonism.[33] The artist, by opposing himself to convention which was an artifice for man's practical needs, an economical and political affair rather than a moral one, was reaffirming his connection to the true sources of being, namely, Spirit. In the *Critique of Pure Reason*, Kant had precariously shown that the possibility of knowledge lay with the productive power of imagination (or, as Kant redrafted it in the second edition, with the power of the understanding itself). This in turn revealed that the a priori synthetic unity of all experience was one and the same with the activity which constituted the self, the "act of the self-activity of the subject."[34] This opened the path for the idealists: experience was the creative product of an activity which was the self—not the empirical ego, but the transcendental Self. The primary nature of the self was not to receive impressions from the external world and simply perceive or recombine them; nor was it to abstract from these images universal essences. The self being a creative power grasped or knew itself only through its creations which it had to recognize *as* products of *its* inherent activity. Not only was the activity of the self regarded as its essential characteristic, but this activity was creative rather than reproductive. Spirit was less like the good craftsman receiving material and plans elsewhere and working according to social conformity; rather, it was like the artist who produced from himself a novel, unique object. Thus, while many of the romantics like Schelling were Platonists of a sort, the act of creation was vital rather than merely mimetic. The poet might, through genius or inspiration, come in touch with the realm of Spirit and its archetypal Forms. But to do so was also to be imbued with the creative source, the Self, which demanded externalization or "ex-pression." A great demand was laid upon the artist, for this Self was infinite and all expression by nature had to be finite. Hence art had to seek to express the infinite in the finite, the sense of power which exceeded the measures and rules of man's finite intellect. Emotion, not reason, must be used.

We therefore find a guiding metaphysical concern in the romantics when they assert, to use Wordsworth's famous statement, that "all good poetry is the spontaneous overflow of powerful feelings."[35] This does not mean going to extremes—Wordsworth protests the use of "gross and violent stimulants" to produce excitement. These are only necessary, he argues, to minds which have been reduced to a "savage torpor" by the numbing effects of urbanization and industrialization. The *Lyrical Ballads*, Wordsworth suggests, was written with a therapeutic aim: to recover "the great and simple affections of our nature." It was only through the development of man's natural feelings that he could once again come in touch with the spiritual sources of his being. The book contained, as it were, a double critique of urban, conventional, industrial, "rational" man: Wordsworth turning to scenes of rustic life, Coleridge to the supernatural.[36] The poet is the healer; through his own recovered feelings he may educate the feelings of his audience so they may regain a spiritual stance toward the universe. Therefore, Wordsworth adds:

> I have said that Poetry is the spontaneous overflow of powerful feelings: it takes its origin from emotion recollected in tranquillity: the emotion is contemplated till by a species of reaction the tranquillity gradually disappears, and an emotion, similar to that which was before the subject of contemplation, is gradually produced, and does itself actually exist in the mind. In this mood successful composition generally begins. . . . Now. . . the Poet ought to profit by the lesson thus held forth to him, and ought especially to take care, that whatever passions he communicates to his Reader, those passions, if his Reader's mind be sound and vigorous, should always be accompanied with an overbalance of pleasure. . . . the human imagination is sufficient to produce such changes even in our physical nature as might almost appear miraculous.[37]

Elsewhere, Wordsworth says that poetry "proceeds whence it ought to do, from the soul of Man, communicating its creative energies to the images of the external world."[36] As M. H. Abrams observes, for romanticism, the criterion of a work of art is no longer its fidelity to the original or its social utility, but whether it is sincere or genuine: "Does it match the intention, the feeling, and the actual state of mind of the poet while composing?"[39] Not only was art given the duty of externalizing a subjective, inner landscape, but it had to do this by rejecting conventions and establishing its own laws.

The problems such a theory has are evident: how can something inner be externalized and yet be the same, how can the appreciator be sure he has responded with the appropriate emotion, how can there be a correlation between subjective feelings and certain tones, shapes, colors, or rhythms? The difficulties of using the term "expression" with reference to works of art has been particularly well discussed by O. K. Bouwsma and John Hospers. Bouwsma especially succeeds in clarifying the various senses of the term "expression." He describes the different contextual usages to reveal their "family resemblances." We are tempted to say, "The music expresses sadness" for a variety of reasons. We speak of people being sad and distinguish those who "express" their feelings from those who do not. The behavior of someone who expresses sadness, the slow movements, the look in the eyes, the tone of the voice, may be extended to animals which display similar characteristics. A pet dog may "express" sadness at being left behind. We also speak of various objects being sad, like "a sad book," because they make us feel sad, although we recognize that there is nothing in the book which is the sadness. The view that a work of art expresses sadness, says Bouwsma, rests upon the confusion of the idea of a person openly expressing feelings with the idea of a sentence expressing meaning. But one doesn't have to *be* sad to write a sad poem or piece of music, nor does one have to be sad to understand it. A sentence does not express meaning, Bouwsma continues, by having to be spoken in a certain way, with a certain tone, or with a certain rhythm. Should I respond to a sentence by asking, "What are you trying to say?" it would be possible for you to rephrase the sentence or expand it. This cannot be done with aesthetic expression; when one doesn't understand a poem or a piece of music there is no such alternative, according to Bouwsma: "There will be only one thing to do; namely, read the verses again, play the music once more."[40] A work of art is expressive, he concludes, only in the sense in which a face with character is expressive. "Words have character," he says, and adds that all sorts of things, lines, letters, even numbers, "have their peculiar feel."[41] Everything has a certain "physiognomy" about it, and works of art have a physiognomy which is expressive. "My only point is that once the poem is born it has its character as surely as a cry in the night, " says Bouwsma. "The light of the sun is the sun, where you see it. So with the character of a poem."[42] On this basis we may legitimately assert that "The music is sad," but we shall not be tempted to understand by this locution that the music *expresses* sadness. "And above all we shall not, having heard the music or read the poem, ask, What does it express?"[43] The physiognomy of a sad poem is similar to the physiognomy of a sad person. But there is no necessity for a work of art to have a character which reminds us of anything else. The fact that a work may seem expressive in this sense is in any case no guarantee that it is aesthetically enjoyable.[44]

Such an analysis is certainly useful in removing some rather simple-minded notions about expression. But the conclusion leads to an intuitionistic theory of aesthetic experience: either you see the character or you don't. Dewey would criticize an approach like Bouwsma's, then, for ending too abruptly. One does not teach someone the meaning of music or poetry simply by repeating the notes or the words until the person "gets it." It is possible to analyze images and relationships, to connect elements of the work with one's experience, or to repeat the performance with a *different* emphasis. It may be that after these alternatives have been exhausted, the recalcitrant appreciator may still not "get it." He may still find Wagner tedious and unbearable whereas his friend is transported into a heaven beyond description. But then it is also possible that one may not "get" the meaning of a complicated idea which is syntactically well-expressed. This is where Dewey's analysis of *an* experience as a gradual, developmental, or growing process of articulation is helpful. It isn't that we either get a work or don't; it's that we are trying to *learn* the work. A cubist painting may look like a mixed-up jumble to someone whose idea of a picture comes from the family photo-album. One could endeavor to make the person understand what cubism was reacting to and why it chose to do what it did. Due to the invention of photography, artists came to question whether the canvas had to be a window portraying objects set in a fixed, one-eyed perspective. If one learns to grasp the context and the problems, the cubist painting begins to take on sense as an exploration of new possibilities. At first, one may not like or understand a Japanese garden or a Gothic cathedral, Indian ragas or atonal music, Shakespeare or Joyce, but the important fact is that one can learn to like them. These objects can *become* expressive. In the same manner, no one originally begins by being able to express himself either in a particular artistic medium or in the languages of the culture in general. But one can come to master a medium so that one can use it expressively. To live in a culture means having to master many media of expression. This is why it is wrong to see Dewey's theory of expression as a theory about how a particular artist at a particular moment creates a particular work. It is part of his general theory of how we are constantly learning the sense of the world.[45] We have an impulsion toward experiencing the world with meaning and value.

"Every experience," Dewey says (and the emphasis on "every" should be noted), "of slight or tremendous import begins with an impulsion, rather *as* impulsion" (*AE*, 58; *LW* 10:64). As discussed previously, by "impulsion" Dewey is referring to an overall drive for organized activity. It is "a movement outward and forward of the whole organism" (*AE*, 58; *LW* 10:64). Impulsions "are the beginnings of complete experiences." In other words, Dewey is saying that impulsion for complete experience, for *an* experience, is to be found at the root of *all* experience. And the only way that impulsion can be realized is "by instituting definite relations (active relations, interactions) with the environment" (*AE*, 58; *LW* 10:64). The impulsion is a general, undefined activity at the source of experience, but it can only be fulfilled in a particular concrete manner by actively appropriating and modifying a medium, by interacting with a definite environment. It is only natural that impulsion, even though it is directed toward the world through action in its essence, must run into checks and frustrations. The drive toward the consummatory, which may now be understood to be the very heart of experience for Dewey, thereby creates the possiblity for lack of fulfillment. It is because human beings can live meaningful lives that they can also suffer the fate of leading lives which are broken or unrealized. Because blind impulsion is checked, the search for means occurs, eventuating in the arts of intelligence. Experience thereby acquires conscious purpose and expands through the articulate network of habits and symbols. This moment when experience stands in need of reconstruction and the task is undertaken is "the outline of every experience clothed with meaning" (AE, 59; LW 10:66). There is an assimilation of present experience to past; responses are generalized and socialized; the future becomes a guiding presence in controlling the immediate direction of action. There is a crucial connection between the fixed past and the oncoming novelty of the future in the living present. "The junction of the new and the old is not a mere composition of forces," Dewey insists, "but is a re-creation in which the present impulse gets form and solidity while the old, the 'stored,' material is literally revived, given new life and soul through having to meet a new situation. It is this double change which converts an activity into an act of expression" (AE, 60; LW 10:66).

To recall, the conversion of activity into expression is more than mere discharge; the baby does not express pain, though it may be in pain, whereas the actor may express pain. Wordsworth's addition of "recollected in tranquillity" is the necessary counterbalance to "the overflow of powerful feelings," at least for there to be expression. Otherwise there is mere discharge and no meaning. "To discharge is to get rid of, to dismiss; to express is to stay by, to carry forward in development, to workout to completion" (AE, 62; LW 10:67-68). Expression is the result of sustaining the impulsion toward complete experience; it not only strives to meet the world, but to carry the situation forward. For this to happen the world must be explored and rendered articulate. A mere act of discharge, Dewey states, differs from an expressive act in that it has no medium. Pain may involve tears and sobs, but these are not used with the intent of expressing pain when they are simply physical reactions. They may, of course, come to be used to express pain, and may succeed because they are common responses and as such readily offer themselves to the interpretation of others. To express means to undertake the problematic task of using a medium which is socially available, or which is by nature open to public response and interpretation. Whenever there is a medium, experience has been undertaken as an artistic project. The world has been interpreted as *material*, as something which is potentially capable of successful organization. The present becomes understood *as* action, and this involves not only an awareness of the need for complete experience, but of the need to care for the medium, since, as Dewey says, "Everything depends upon the way in which the material is used when it operates as medium" (*AE*, 63; *LW 10*:69). When one seeks expression, one must care for the medium and be mindful of it. *An* experience only comes to be expressive when it has been genuinely cared for, minded, and intelligently understood. A medium is revealed only when the task of art is also revealed.

Thus expression is not, for Dewey, externalizing the internal; it is not strictly "pressing out" what was present in complete, pre-existent form. Though every experience begins with a raw material, expression is realized only as that material ceases to be raw and becomes transformed, articulated, embodied, and directed in light of its possibilities for order. Expression does not arise from a subjective need but from a situational transformation. It is a phase of activity, not a static state or quality. As Dewey puts it, "Juice is expressed when grapes are crushed in the wine press. . . . Through interaction with something external to it, the wine press, or the treading foot of man, juice results. . . . It takes the wine press as well as grapes to ex-press juice and it takes environing and resisting objects as well as internal emotion and impulsion to constitute the *expression* of emotion"(*AE*, 64; *LW 10*:70). Emotion arises as a response to the checking of impulsion but it is by nature temporally and situationally intentional—it is emotion *about* and *of* and is directed *toward* or *away from* objects. "An impulsion cannot lead to expression save when it is thrown into commotion, turmoil," Dewey argues, "Unless there is com-pression, nothing is expressed" (*AE*, 66; *LW 10*:72). The world calls forth a response and emotion reveals both the concern about the world and the concern about how we are in it.

Expression does not seek an exact external correlate of some inner feeling. From the start the emotional involvement with experience asks to be developed and transformed through activity. The emotion begins as an indefinite need for response. It is not "the" feeling of sadness or joy. Much discussion of the expression theory tacitly (or explicitly) relies on just such a misleading notion of emotion as some sort of *nameable* generalized feeling. If emotion could be so easily defined and named, it would not *need* expression. Where there are easily implemented coordinated responses to a situation, emotion is readily channeled and released without further care or significance. We may say to an acquaintance, "I'm sorry" on hearing of his misfortune and this may be said to "express concern." But it is the friends who stand by that person in the hour of need, who listen to, talk with, or just have time for that individual, who genuinely express concern. For these people, there are no easy responses to the problem, and the complexity and depth of the situation comes home to them. Only someone who was insensitive to the differences between these two situations could maintain that the meaning of "I'm sorry" in both cases was the same. Yet a number of aestheticians try to treat the question of expression in art by seeing it as analogous to the formula "x expresses y."[46] The theory that emotions are preformed, definite, identifiable entities infects our theories of art, says Dewey, without in the least illuminating them. "Save nominally," he asserts, "there is no such thing as *the* emotion of fear, hate, love. The unique, unduplicated character of experienced events and situations impregnates the emotion that is evoked. Were it the function of speech to reproduce that to which it refers we could never speak of fear, but only of the fear-of-this-particular-oncoming-automobile" (*AE,* 67; *LW* 10:73). The problem of expression, then, is one with the problem of the "individualization of works of art," that is, how experience becomes *an* experience. The problem begins just where Bouwsma's analysis stops. How does the experience become expressive so that it has a pervasive quality which gives it its "physiognomy"?

The task of the artist is to make the medium expressive so that the appreciator who encounters it will interact with it in such a way as to have an organized as well as emotional response—the emotion must be articulated as well as evoked by the medium. This is probably best achieved by *not* trying to focus on a preconceived, general, nameable feeling or quality. Merleau-Ponty tells the following story of Cézanne:

> In *La Peau de chagrin* Balzac describes a "tablecloth white as a layer of newly fallen snow, upon which the place-settings rise symmetrically, crowned with blond rolls." "All through youth," said Cézanne, "I wanted to paint that, the tablecloth of new snow. . . . Now I know that one must will only to paint the place-settings rising symmetrically and the blond rolls as they are in nature, then you can be sure that the crowns, the snow, and all the excitement will be there too."[47]

Any number of bad works have started out by trying to portray "bravery" or "beauty." A purely abstract feeling is not evoked from the material but imposed on it; hence, it cannot act as a guide and control of the expressive possibilities of the material. Expressiveness is achieved through feeling the relationships of the interacting parts so that the phases of doing and undergoing are present in the experience. Emotion is crucial for expression as the organizing force. As Dewey puts it, "It reaches out tentacles for that which is cognate, for things which feed it and carry it to completion" (*AE*, 67-68; *LW* 10:73). But emotion is not what gets expressed; it is the manner of expression:

> Yes, emotion must operate. But it works to effect continuity of movement, singleness of effect amid variety. It is selective of material and directive of its order and arrangement. But it is not *what* is expressed. Without emotion there may be craftsmanship, but not art; it may be present and be intense, but if it is directly manifested the result is also not art (*AE*, 69; *LW* 10:75).

Emotion, in other words, is essential for expression; it is the capacity to become involved with a subject matter or a medium. It directs action toward something which will render our responses articulate and continuous so that *an* experience occurs. This means that we must develop concern for the possibilities inherent in the world for meaningful response. If the emotion is lacking, there is no involvement, no care, and so no deep or significant response; if the emotion is discharged, the meaning of the response is not even an issue. Emotion is crucial in making experience both continuous, so that development occurs, and intelligent. But the result will be that the experience or work as a whole will embody its pervasive qualitative unity and meaning. The emotion will not be represented by the work but will be the very power of the work to become a theme or project for experience. To say that *King Lear* expresses the feeling or emotion of "King Lear," is not to answer a question, but to raise one. It calls for a patient and detailed experiencing of the work, the revelation of character through language and action, the relationship of the events, awareness of the underlying themes and the ambiguities, and an envisagement of the whole as dramatically enacted. The emotion evoked by the work will be about the work; the work will not be about the emotion in any other sense.

For a work to become expressive, emotion needs to be articulated through a medium. This requires a certain deflection of emotion because the work must not reach its goal too quickly or it will lack depth and interest. The major problem in creating or encountering a work of art is sustaining and rewarding interest. If in writing a story, the goal were to get to the last word as soon as possible, the world's literature could be read in a dictionary. The writer may want to close the story with a particular line, but that line must culminate an experience or process and its meaning and effect come through encountering the development as a whole. In order to accomplish this, the work must create a tensive, dynamic world, full of novelty, ambiguity, contrast, and suggestive connections. The task of writing a good haiku is to achieve the revelation of a world through a minimum of words. It may take seconds to read, but it must sustain a meditative response. Writers like Hemingway have sought a spare style in order to evoke a vivid, brilliant, luminous world which hovers above a hidden, darkly moving undercurrent.

One might take as an example Hemingway's well-known story, "Big Two Hearted River." On the surface very little that is dramatic happens. Nick Adams has hitched a ride on a train to go fishing; he jumps off and passes through a town which has burned down, probably due to a forest fire. He looks at the trout in the stream, then hikes into the woods beyond the burned country. He takes a nap, comes to the meadow and makes camp, setting up his tent and then fixing dinner. The next day he wakes up, catches grasshoppers, makes breakfast, gets his fishing rod and goes down to the stream where he catches a small trout and throws it back, hooks a big one which gets away, then finally gets two others. Afterwards, he cleans the fish and returns to his camp. That's all. But the story is written with intensity; every image is exact and there is an underlying sense of anxiety and ritual so that gradually it becomes evident that the story is about a rebirth, the reconnection of a wounded human being with the healing forces of nature. The powerful use of symbol and the luminous natural prose create the sustained double image of reality and dream. It surely is a story about a man who goes fishing; but the seemingly innocuous images build in intensity and suggested meaning, flowing like the river with a brilliance and necessity. We are never told in the story that Nick has sustained a dark injury, but the feeling of the need to escape the world, reflected in the burned and blackened landscape which suggests the battlefields of Europe after the war, pervades the story. Indeed, if we look at its position in Hemingway's In Our Time or connect it with the other Nick Adams stories, we see that Nick's life is surrounded with darkness and horror. In contrast with the ominous blackness of the burned village and forest inhabited by black grasshoppers, Nick looks into the stream:

> Nick looked at the burned-over stretch of hillside, where he had expected to find the scattered houses of the town and then walked down to the railroad track to the bridge over the river. The river was there. It swirled against the log spiles of the bridge. Nick looked down into the clear, brown water, colored from the pebbly bottom, and watched the trout keeping themselves steady in the current with wavering fins. As he watched them they changed their positions by quick angles, only to hold steady in the fast water again. Nick watched them for a long time.[48]

In this paragraph a number of highly emotional images are evoked. The surprisingly burned town and the sinister countryside are contrasted with the clear, moving river which abides the destruction without change: "The river was there." The living force of the river opens up before Nick's prolonged gaze: it is clean, clear, and contains colored stones and moving fish. The fish themselves seem vitally in contact with the force of the river itself; their every movement is an exact yet delicate response to the flowing water enveloping them. The scene is clearly depicted, yet there is movement, tension and ambiguity throughout. The prose is pointing insistently to the river, saying that it is important and that, like Nick, we should look at it a long time. There is also something suggested by the repeated emphasis on the movement and clarity of the water, suggesting purity and purification (but, as Cézanne said, without using the words "purity" or "purifying"). There is a repeated emphasis on the trout which "hold steady." These themes come with redoubled force in the next paragraph:

> He watched them holding themselves with their noses in the current, many trout in deep, fast moving water, slightly distorted as he watched far down through the glassy convex surface of the pool, its surface pushing and swelling against the resistance of the driven piles of the bridge. At the bottom of the pool were the big trout. Nick did not see them at first. Then he saw them at the bottom of the pool, big trout looking to hold themselves on the gravel bottom in a varying mist of gravel and sand, raised in spurts by the current.

Twice more we are told how the fish hold themselves in the current; a moral is being revealed. The preceding images of the swiftness and clarity of the river are also repeated here. The river, seemingly transparent in the preceding paragraph, takes on even more transparency in the second as its true bottom is revealed, showing the large trout, which almost seem to be in direct contact with the earth. The repeated use of the verbs "look," "watch," and "see" indicate that the event is something highly significant for the one who looks. We recognize that this is no idle glance, but is the prolonged look arising from a deep emotional need or thirst which is being slaked at long last. The whole scene sustains a complex but very expressive quality. The story continues in this manner so that, at the end, when Nick is himself in the river, there is the abiding sense of resolution and final purification, consummated by the religious sense of the catching and cleaning of the fish. The meal is not described, but it can be felt to be a eucharist. We suddenly understand the ritual importance Nick places on doing everything right, from setting up the tent to making coffee. As he prepares the tent, we get a sudden transference. The word "smooth" which has been repeatedly used for the river ("The river made no sound. It was too fast and smooth"), is shifted to Nick's own actions:

> He smoothed out the sandy soil with his hand and pulled all the sweet fern bushes by their roots. His hands smelled good from the sweet fern. He smoothed the uprooted earth. He did not want anything making lumps under the blankets. When he had the ground smooth, he spread his three blankets. One he folded double, next to the ground. The other two he spread on top.

The action of spreading the blankets is done carefully and exactly, as is the splitting of the wood for tent stakes and the pitching of the tent. As Nick crawls inside the tent, "Already there was something mysterious and homelike." Hemingway uses short repetitive sentences to emphasize the completion of this act and that it has been done right:

> Now things were done. There had been this to do. Now it was done. It had been a hard trip. He was very tired. That was done. He had made his camp. He was settled. Nothing could touch him. It was a good place to camp. He was there, in the good place. He was in his home where he had made it. Now he was hungry.

The short, almost panting sentences emphasize the completion of action, the finality as well as the realization of what he was doing: coming home. Nick has achieved this by doing everything smoothly and precisely, like the trout in the river. This marks the unifying theme, the underlying pervasive quality of the story, and gives the ending its sense of completion or closure. In this way, "Big Two-Hearted River" is an experience of how two hearts, Nick's and the river's, come together; the homecoming is realized and achieved. This story might be contrasted with one Hemingway wrote of an unsuccessful homecoming, "Soldier's Home," which, significantly, is not a Nick Adams story (and which was included along with "Big Two-Hearted River" in *In Our Time*). Krebs, the character of "Soldier's Home," cannot come home from the war, for his home has not changed and cannot understand that he has. But in "Big Two-Hearted River," the last paragraph has Nick climbing up the bank, going back to camp, looking over the river and thinking of the days ahead.

The expressiveness of the story lies in taking a situation which is ambiguous at the start. When the story begins, we do not know immediately *what* it is about; our response is as yet undefined, though there is the incipient expectation as to how the subject matter will be revealed. The progress of the story is just this gradual elucidation of the subject matter *and* the emotion at the same time. Expression lies in the articulation of emotion through the medium. The emotion must be completely worked into the material. "The sculptor conceives his statue, not just in mental terms, but in those of clay, marble or bronze" (*AE*, 75; *LW 10*:81). Originally, says Dewey, "we should find at the beginning an emotion comparatively gross and undefined," but the artist's talent lies precisely in his ability "to work a vague idea or emotion over into terms of some definite medium" (*AE*, 75; *LW 10*:82). Therefore, he concludes, "Expression is the clarification of turbid emotion" (*AE*, 77; *LW 10*:83). Aesthetic emotion occurs when the vague feeling has been rendered articulate—or, more accurately, it is this sense of gradual articulation and definiteness progressively realized throughout the course of *an* experience so that the sense of pervasive quality and closure is present from the start.[49] Expression is the significant ordering of feeling through a definite medium. The internal theme of Hemingway's story is an instance of this. Nick gradually attains a sense of detachment through a ritual of homecoming. By treating his hike and fishing as art, he lives through *an* experience. The story can also be viewed from the external standpoint of Hemingway's own effort to transform his shattering experiences through the exacting rites of his art, a struggle which is also the theme of *The Old Man and the Sea.*

Emotion which has been thus objectified is aesthetic, but this is not the projection of emotion onto an object, as Santayana held. By objectification, Dewey means the process of becoming an object for emotion. The term applies equally to the appreciator as to the creator. The task of the artist is to produce an object which can, through its own structured material, guide the responses of the participants toward a consummatory end; it is the task of the participants to respond appropriately to the work—to work with the work. It is an artificial dilemma, says Dewey, to separate the expressiveness of the work from either the transformation wrought upon a public material by the artist or from the response to it by the appreciators. The work has a novel or unique characteristic, but its "material came from the public world and so has qualities in common with the material of other experiences"; in this way the aesthetic object "awakens in other persons new perceptions of the meanings of the common world" (*AE*, 82; *LW 10*:88). If the art object had nothing in common with the world at large, it would never be experienced at all. Its expressive power lies in this ability to take something from the public realm, such as experiences of hiking or fishing, and transform our ordinary, nonaesthetic modes of perception of them.[50]

The essence of the aesthetic event is the reconstruction of perception so that the sense of meaning becomes immanent in the material. While the meaning of the sign is external to the particular medium (the yellow of a road sign does not have to be exactly *that* shade of yellow), the meaning of the work of art is one with the manner of its expression. Signification represents a general mode of possible response. The caution needed on twisting roads is capable of generalization so that the sign makes sense in a variety of contexts. But the work of art individualizes experience into *an* experience. Meaning is, as Dewey puts it, given a "local habitation" (*AE*, 91; *LW* 10:96). A map of a city presents a schema of general movements possible within the context, just as the rules of chess give a system of possible moves. But using the map to see the city or using the rules to play a game produce an individualized, concrete experience. "An intellectual statement is valuable in the degree in which it conducts the mind to many things all of the same kind," while the "meaning of an expressive object . . . is individualized" (*AE*, 90; *LW* 10:96). Dewey even goes further and argues, "Meaning is more fully expressed, even in its essential nature, in an individualized form than in a diagrammatic representation or in a literal copy. The latter contains too much that is irrelevant; the former is too indefinite" (*AE*, 92; *LW* 10:97-98). The portrait of the artist outdoes either the photograph or a topographical diagram simply because it "says more."

It may be helpful here to note Leonard Meyer's interesting discussion of meaning in music.[51] Why, asks Meyer, does a Bach fugue strike us as better or more significant than "Twinkle, Twinkle Little Star"? Both pieces have unity, variety, and style. The Bach is more complex and longer, true, but these qualities are not necessarily conditions for greatness—some of Brahm's shorter works are better than his symphonies. Meyer contrasts a Bach fugue with a piece by Geminiani, similar in structure. Both begin by creating a "structural gap" which gives a "sense of incompleteness" that we expect to be filled in. "This melodic incompleteness," Meyer notes, "is complemented by the ryhthmic instability of this first musical shape."[52] This is analogous to the beginning of Hemingway's "Big Two-Hearted River" with the "gap" or symbolic tension it presented between the river and the town. The "instability" to be overcome was to mediate this tension by connecting the character of Nick meaningfully with the elemental, purifying image of the river. In the musical compositions, the openings "have established musical goals to be reached."[53] The question is *how* those goals will be reached. Expectations of possible resolutions have been generated; but the Geminiani reaches the goal in a fairly predictable and direct manner. The Bach fugue, however, "moves down slowly with delays and temporary diversions through related harmonic areas. It establishes various levels of melodic activity with various potentials to be realized. Furthermore, these delays are rhythmic as well as melodic," Meyer adds.[54] The Geminiani turns its ending into a cliché or platitude; it doesn't set up resistances to be overcome. From this example, Meyer suggests that "value has something to do with the activation of a musical impulse having tendencies of a more or less definite goal and with the temporary resistance or inhibition of these tendencies."[55]

Meyer explains this feeling by appealing to information theory. The relation of value and resistance in goal-oriented activity lies in the probability of one event following from another. "Musical events," he says, "take place in a world of stylistic probability."[56] From one note, any number of other notes may follow with equal probability. But as the key and themes are established, the probability of certain notes and sequences is increased and others are decreased. "As more tones are added," Meyer observes, "and consequently more relationships between tones are established, the probabilities of a particular goal become increased." According to information theory, a highly organized situation is one in which, given A, B follows with very high probability. In such a case, minimal information is communicated. The less predictable the situation, the less certain the antecedent-consequent relationship is and so more information is conveyed when B follows A. In the story of the lady or the tiger, there is more information where the possibility is that there will be either a beautiful woman or a tiger behind the door than there would be if the possibility were that behind either door the young man was certain to find a tiger. Meyer quotes Norbert Weiner's saying, "the more probable the message, the less its information. Clichés, for example, are less illuminating than great poems."[57] Disturbances or deflections from goal-oriented action, says Meyer, "lower the probability not only of the particular consequent but of the musical situation as a whole. And it does not seem a rash step to conclude that what creates or increases the information contained in a piece of music increases its value."[58] Or, to use Gregory Bateson's expression, it's the difference that *makes* a difference which counts.[59]

Meyer continues to distinguish desirable from undesirable probabilities: the desirable probabilities arising from the inherent structures of the musical style, the undesirable simply being meaningless "noise." There must be an exploitation of the probabilities which can organize the experience into a whole. A series of random notes doesn't overcome any difficulty or end up with a structured response. There is a range of creative deviation, in other words, which can be used to make the work inherently *interesting*. The fact that there is a limit to the probabilities keeps us involved to see what follows. In a totally random series, the lack of predictability makes it pointless to try and organize our responses just as in a highly controlled and predictable series, boredom quickly sets in. The good composition exploits possibilities and overcomes the tendencies to dispersion by bringing them together into a pattern in which their capacity for successful integration is realized. Thus the work as a whole is necessary for these possibilities to coexist and the necessity of the work is the realization of their coexistence. The work is generated as an individualized and expressive event. As Dewey puts it:

> The impulsion is modified by collateral tendencies; the modification gives it added meaning—the meaning of the whole of which it is henceforth a constituent part. In esthetic perception, there are two modes of collateral and cooperative response which are involved in the change of direct discharge into an act of expression. These two ways of subordination and reenforcement explain the expressiveness of the perceived object. By their means, a particular incident ceases to be a stimulus to direct action and becomes a value of a perceived object (AE, 97; LW 10:103).

The expressiveness of the object also relies on the habits of the one who encounters it. The expressiveness is not strictly in the object just as the emotion does not pre-exist fully complete in the artist prior to creation. Expression refers to an interaction; it is an event which becomes *an* experience. Though the artist strives to render the object as structured as possible, so that it may guide the experience of the appreciators, there must be responsive habits for the appreciators to encounter the object aesthetically. The aesthetic encounter with the object will evoke emotion and transform or reconstruct the habits of perception of the appreciators. In this sense, then, the function of art can be said to be representation—not as formally translating an exact image or idea but as "re-presenting" the *world*, as giving the world back to us in its freshness and novelty. Representation, says Dewey, "may also mean that the work of art tells something to those who enjoy it about the nature of their own experience of the world: that it presents the world in a new experience which they undergo" (AE, 83; LW 10:89). In other words, art gives us a new ability to respond to the world, a new organized habit of coordination. The appreciator uses the work to take on this general, new, integrated manner of interpreting and organizing experience as a whole. As we experience the work of art, we begin to sense the overall patterns and connections of its world. This is what is meant by a "world" being given through a work; and the work, the *working* of the work, is achieved as this new horizon gradually becomes perceived and is sensed as guiding the experience. Van Gogh, for example, teaches a new manner of seeing. Understanding or appreciating a work of art does not add arithmetically to our total fund of experience, except in a trivial sense. Art changes the qualitative way we experience; it marks genuine growth in the meaning of our world. The aesthetic object is seen as expressive because this new manner of perception is arrived at through direct interaction with the formed medium. The art object functions as the source and organizer of our significant responses. We interact with the physical poem or painting. Our responses are occasioned by the object so that they become intentional of *it*. Hence, we respond to the *object* as being expressive. The object marks the focus of our action.

Arguments about whether the expressive quality is in the object or in us are the result of a gratuitous dualism. By relocating art as an event in which there is genuine interaction, in which the object is intended for aesthetic response and the appreciator is oriented toward the world, the problem of expression becomes a question of the conditions and contexts which bring it about. Dewey points to formalists like Roger Fry who try to read paintings exclusively in terms of the relations of shapes and lines and colors. These alone have "meaning," says Fry, for the pure artist. But, Dewey points out, shapes, colors, and lines are expressive only because they are integrated into a general body of coordinated, funded responses. Curves look smoothly flowing or turbid, limp or dynamic, and shapes can seem balanced or tottering, simple or complex. "The painter did not approach the scene with an empty mind," states Dewey, but with a receptive mind, and this implies that there is "bias and tendency" at work. The work which results is "a function of what is in the actual scene in its interaction with what the beholder brings with him" (*AE*, 87; *LW* 10:93). Cézanne and Monet, set before the same landscape, will respond to different elements and achieve different effects. Had Monet painted Mont St. Victoire, we would have seen it as though glimpsed in a fleeting, shimmering movement of light rather than as Cézanne's solid assertive region where force defines space. "No matter how ardently the artist might desire it," Dewey adds, "he cannot divest himself, in his new perception, of meanings funded from his past intercourse with his surroundings. . . . If he could and did, there would be nothing in the way of an object left for him to see" (*AE*, 89; *LW* 10:95). This is as true for the appreciator as the creator of a work. There must be a body of coordinated responses for the appreciator even to grasp the object as a work; the more refined and complex one's body of responses, the more expressive the work can be. Not only will there be a more complex reading of the work, but the more complex the means of discrimination and perception, the more there will be to react and respond to. The experience is thereby capable of having an emotional range and depth otherwise impossible.

It is not enough, however, simply to have an articulate, sensitive manner of response. Trained, coordinated habits left on their own operate mechanically—thus a critic may have a less involved response to a work than someone who is less educated. When this happens, says Dewey, the critic only cares for "*how* things are done, he does not care for *what* is expressed. The other factor that is required in order that a work may be expressive to a percipient is meanings and values extracted from prior experiences and funded in such a way that they fuse with the qualities directly presented in the work of art" (*AE*, 98; *LW* 10:104). The encounter with the work of art constitutes a moment of genuine growth in experience where the process of response and active perception fuses together. This necessarily involves the awakening and lively use of a great body of our habits which become intensely focused on the luminous moment of consciousness. In other words, habits become involved with or care about the subject matter of experience. As Dewey puts it, "when excitement about subject matter goes deep, it stirs up a store of attitudes and meanings derived from prior experience. As they are aroused into activity they become conscious thoughts and emotions, emotionalized images" (*AE*, 65; *LW* 10:71). This goes beyond mere external association to constitute "a fusion so complete as to incorporate both members in a single whole" (*AE*, 99; *LW* 10:104). Fusion marks the realization of *an* experience due to the powerful confluence of perceptive responsiveness and articulate activity; there is transaction in the fullest sense between world and self so that quite literally they grow together. Expression is this concrescence which becomes individualized as *an* experience. "The expressiveness of the object of art is due to the fact that it presents a thorough and complete interpenetration of the materials of undergoing and action, the latter including a reorganization of matter brought with us from past experience. . . . The expressiveness of the object is the report and celebration of the complete fusion of what we undergo and what our activity of attentive perception brings into what we receive by means of the senses" (*AE*, 103; *LW* 10:108). There is a fusion of the complex structure of the work and the perceptive body achieved through activity; the horizons of the world of the work and of the interpretive self fuse in the work as process, that is, as the working of the work. This creates an intensification of the sense of life, where "sense" is to be understood in its full, pregnant ambiguity as that which is sensed and that which makes sense.

This experience marks the inhabitation of the world. "Through habits formed in intercourse with the world," says Dewey, "we also in-habit the world. It becomes a home and the home is part of our every experience" (*AE*, 104; *LW 10*:109). *An* experience is this process of coming to inhabit the world. Our habits creatively work themselves into the object, and the object becomes our perception. In this integrative moment it can most fully be said that man is a being in the world and realizes consciously the meaning of his being. At the same time, the meaning of the world is revealed through experience. Dewey claims that:

> Art throws off the covers that hide the expressiveness of experienced things; it quickens us from the slackness of routine and enables us to forget ourselves by finding ourselves in the delight of experiencing the world about us in its varied qualities and forms. It intercepts every shade of expressiveness found in objects and orders them in a new experience of life (*AE*, 104; *LW 10*:110).

Because of this, Dewey adds, works of art communicate, whether public expression is part of the artist's original intention or not. There is in the experience of the work a communicating between self and world by expressive activity. The artist may be indifferent to his immediate audience, but the work may eventually "create an audience to which he does communicate" (*AE*, 105; *LW 10*:110). The promise of the work is met with the shared, appropriative response, and in that dramatic moment meaning blossoms forth. Thus, Dewey asserts, "In the end, works of art are the only media of complete and unhindered communication between man and man that can occur in a world full of gulfs and walls that limit community of experience" (*AE*, 105; *LW 10*:110).

The concept of expression is vital to an understanding of art and the aesthetic experience—indeed, it is vital to understanding Dewey's theory of meaning and community. The criticisms levelled against traditional expression theories are inapplicable to Dewey's because of the radical transformation his theory of experience achieves. Experience is a total situational event which involves biological interaction and cultural interpretation. It is a temporally developing process of articulation rather than a brute, subjectively enjoyed, isolated mental event which is the product of a mysterious spiritual activity. Because experience is developmental, it is potentially expressive. It can be directed toward moments of meaningful integration. But this requires an emotional response to the world, an organized repertoire of structured activities or habits, and a definite medium of reconstruction. This marks a significant break from the romantic theory of expression as the externalization of an inner aesthetic vision. The task for emotion is to become integrated with an object, and this is only achieved by becoming concerned with the content or subject matter of experience so that an articulate, structured, creative activity ensues. In short, emotion is not what gets expressed—it is not denoted by the work—it is *how* something gets expressed, the organization of an attitude. It is the deep, impassioned involvement with the world which undertakes the project of becoming integrated through interaction. To describe the various phases of artistic and aesthetic activity as expressive is not to make a misleading or trivial claim. It is, for Dewey at least, the key to overcoming partial and inadequate interpretations of this process. Such views either confine expression to the psychology of the creator or reduce it to the intuitive physiognomy of the work. Artistic-aesthetic activity is a conjoint and unified activity founded in our commerce with the world and each other. Expression, in other words, is nothing less than the task of life, standing as it does for the fulfillment of our human impulsion for meaning and value. Expression is realized only through an active process of articulation which depends upon a concrete medium or material to give it embodiment and make it definite. Because expression is a process, it is an activity characterized by a certain manner of realization. It is experience which has been ordered, shaped, or given form. Aesthetic form, then, marks the next significant subject in need of reinterpretation by Dewey's transactional account of experience.

IV. Form and Process

Since art is an intensification of ordinary experience, it will exemplify the general features of experience: situationality, transaction, reconstruction, and temporality. This has tremendous consequences for Dewey's treatment of form. For expression to be realized, the material of the work must be successfully organized. Form is the crucial means whereby this is achieved. Traditional views of form have treated it as some sort of timeless, static essence underlying the work like an ontological skeleton, waiting to be intuited in an act of aesthetic apprehension. The familiar discussion by Clive Bell is a case in point. Bell begins by asking what is it that all aesthetic objects have in common (by which, of course, he means objects which are the occasion of a distinct, unique "aesthetic emotion"); the answer is "significant form." "The starting-point for all systems of aesthetics must be the personal experience of a peculiar emotion," he claims. What do Chartres and Mexican sculpture have in common which generates this? "Only one answer seems possible—significant form.

In each, lines and colours combined in a peculiar way, stir our aesthetic emotions. . . . 'Significant Form' is the one quality common to all works of visual art."[60] How contrary this approach is from Dewey's may be grasped by the inferences Bell draws from this assumption. For example, Bell asserts, "to appreciate a work of art we need bring with us nothing from life, no knowledge of its ideas and affairs, no familiarity with its emotions. Art transports us from the world of man's activity to a world of aesthetic exaltation. For a moment we are shut off from human interests; our anticipations and memories are arrested; we are lifted above the stream of life."[61] "To appreciate a work of art," he concludes, "we need bring with us nothing but a sense of form and colour and a knowledge of three dimensional space." The task art demands is congruent with the implicit Platonism Bell advocates: one must be a "perfect lover" and rise above anything muddied with human concerns which contextualizes art so that one at last grasps a pure universal. "Great art remains stable and unobscure because the feelings that it awakens are independent of time and place, because its kingdom is not of this world."[62]

Dewey repudiates such a view. From his naturalistic and historical standpoint, form is the active temporal continuity of interaction which the work brings about so that *an* experience is achieved. It is thus more like the life of the work, its *psyche* in the Aristotelian sense, than a ghostly, Platonic presence. Form is the energetic process of organizing the material of experience into a funded, meaningful, consummatory event which does not transcend life but fully actualizes it. Form is the dynamic process of shaping experience by means of a medium so that it becomes expressive. It emerges in context and in time with an appropriative act: the material is taken *as* material *to be* formed. Form projects a teleology for the material which can only be realized through the material. Throughout the process, the teleology of the experience is immanent, emphatically present, and sensed as a guiding movement. At the commencement of an expressive act, self and world hang tensively poised; the field of possibility opens and the need for definite, organized activity, of controlled response, is revealed. Action and response, exploration and adjustment, discovery and integration initially display experience as a rhythmic field, as yet indeterminate, but insistently pointing toward a determinate, organized individual experience. This is as much true for the appreciator of a work as for the creator. As a composition begins, we prepare to listen; we open a book with the anticipation of responding to the world it will offer; we begin by looking at a painting by marking its details and patterns. Form can only emerge with the on-going organization of experience, but what it reveals is the capacity of the material to be significantly appropriated. Form doesn't illuminate itself or point to a timeless Platonic object; it illuminates the material, that is, the world. It achieves this through the unfolding of a history; form reveals the ways the various parts of phases temporally work together so as to establish a meaningful whole. Form is the "energy" of the work, so to speak—it is the *ergon*, the working of the work, which becomes realized as an engergetic, structured activity, or *energeia*.

Dewey's analysis of form is complex because form stands for the way the various elements of the work become discriminated as well as integrated. It is helpful to note first that one significant contrast between Dewey's approach and one like Bell's is that for Dewey form is what individualizes rather than universalizes experience—or rather it universalizes through individualizing experience. It is the "material" which provides the connection with the world of common experience. This is the public world of nature and culture which must be reconstructed for *an* experience to occur. Expression is the creative renewal of experience; it must appropriate the public world as material but also transform it by achieving an individual, coordinated, articulate response. Thus by "material," Dewey refers to the whole domain of biological activity, habit, and organic responses as well as to the domain of culture, the symbol systems, values, beliefs, and histories which define a community. If a work achieves a uniquely powerful integration of such materials, it becomes universal in the sense of providing an enduring basis for renewed experience. "The *material* out of which a work of art is composed belongs to the common world," says Dewey, "rather than to the self, and yet there is self-expression in art because the self assimilates that material in a distinctive way to reissue it into the public world in a form that builds a new object. The new object may. . . come to be established as part of the acknowledged world—as 'universal'" (*AE*, 107-08; *LW 10*:112). If the material were private rather than public, the work would be inaccessible—it would be like the art of the insane.[63] What the creative work offers is a new way of organizing the material of the common world so that its meaning becomes freshly present; this manner of organization can be learned by the audience of the work. The form, then, is a transitive as well as transformational activity which passes from the interaction of the creator and his material to the interaction of the work and the audience. The form is no more in the object than in the mind—it is the organization of response to a material.

This presents Dewey with the paradox that the form, as the creative renewal of experience residing in the process of the various encounters, has no fixed and final essence. There is no specific end to the work as such, nor is there any one specific way for the work to work, so to speak. That is, there may be a number of genuine responses and interpretations to any individual work, and these responses will themselves be historically and contextually determined. Dewey puts it, "A new poem is created by every one who reads poetically. . . . every individual brings with him, when he exercises his individuality, a way of seeing and feeling that in its interaction with old material creates something new, something previously not existing in experience" (*AE*, 108; *LW* 10:113). Dewey's emphasis on individuality and the self in this and the previous passage should be noted. Individuality is the creative response to the world; the reader who reads creatively will encounter the same work differently throughout his or her life. One can never experience a work the second time exactly as one did the first (for at the very least, one would recognize it—or fail to). *King Lear* may have been an assignment in high school, then later in college. One may experience it through several productions in a lifetime. Reading the play as an aging parent will certainly be different from encountering it as a struggling student. Even if one could exactly duplicate one's first experience of it, this would not be a genuine encounter with the work. The value of rereading a great play like *King Lear* will be in the discovery of new elements and ways of understanding it. Thus, according to Dewey's approach, we should not regard the variety or even divergence of interpretations as a logical difficulty in a great work—indeed, these may be indications that it is a masterpiece.

The question may be raised, however, whether Dewey has made the work dissolve into the infinity of subjective responses, placing the refined interpretations of the scholar and the actor on the same level as the freshman. What is denoted, after all, by the title of a work? Isn't there a *King Lear* to which "King Lear" refers? To this, Dewey's response is that "Titles are, so to say, social matters. They identify objects" (*AE*, 112; *LW* 10:117). That is, they are practical tools which direct us to certain discernible objects, like a particular text or a canvas, which is the condition for the work of art. To recall, Dewey radically distinguishes the event of the encounter, the work of art, from the "art product." The latter is "physical and potential," he says, while the work is "active and experienced. It is what the product does, its working" (*AE*, 162; *LW* 10:167). The work of art is not a physical object; it is an event, or, perhaps even better, a project. *King Lear* denotes more than a text (and even here which text is problematic); it also refers to a history consisting of the conditions of its origin, its various renditions, problems, ambiguities, and the responses and interpretations these have called forth (such as the eighteenth century's need to rewrite the ending of *Lear* so that the tragedy is averted). This history is still on-going to the extent that the work continues to call attention. What is denoted by *King Lear* is an event which lies even *more* in the future than in the past. It is the task of undertaking a genuinely sensitive, responsive interpretation. *King Lear* points to a possible experience, an encounter with the work which asks us to understand it passionately and comprehensively.[64]

The well-formed work will be one which establishes continuity in experience. Form marks the creative renewal of experience so that it dynamically grows or develops. The greatness or universality of a work indicates its capacity to enter into a variety of contexts and significantly shape them:

> The "works" that fail to become *new* are not those which are universal but those which are "dated." The enduring art product may have been, and probably was, called forth by something occasional, something having its own date and place. But *what* was evoked is a substance so formed that it can enter into the experiences of others and enable them to have more intense and more fully rounded out experiences of their own. This is what it is to have form. It marks a way of envisaging, of feeling, and of presenting experienced matter so that it most readily and effectively becomes material for the construction of adequate experience on the part of those less gifted than the original creator (*AE*, 109; *LW 10*:114).

Form reflects the capacity of the art product and the responsive perception of the appreciator to work successfully together. Dewey is arguing that those products which can enter into a variety of contexts and powerfully interact so as to generate the consummatory renewal of experience—which provide enriching channels for complex but organized responses—explain our sense of the timeless quality of great art. This is less like the timelessness of a Platonic essence than the timelessness of a species which is highly adaptable to a variety of environments. Form is the creative growth of the work through its encounters or enactments; it is fundamentally historical and dynamic. Ironically, Dewey sees such objects which are capable of generating future consummatory experience as well as present consummatory experience as the most instrumental. As he puts it in *Experience and Nature*, a genuinely aesthetic object "that is not also instrumental turns in time to the dust and ashes of boredom. The 'eternal' quality of great art is its renewed instrumentality for further consummatory experiences" (*EN*, 365; *LW 1*:274). Art, for Dewey, is the highest form of the instrumental. This reveals how contrary most interpreters of Dewey take his meaning. Dewey was usually understood to say that art which was not *also* useful for some limited practical purpose was not art in its highest sense. What this passage shows is that instrumentalism must be understood ultimately in terms of the goal toward which it aims: aesthetic experience.[65]

The strict utilitarian concept of practicality for Dewey is based on a narrow, abstract view of experience. Most tools are instruments to a fixed range of predetermined ends or functions, but art exists to fulfill experience as a whole.

> Mutual adaptation of parts to one another in constituting a whole is the relation which, formally speaking, characterizes a work of art. Every machine, every utensil, has, within limits, a similar reciprocal adaptation. In each case, an end is fulfilled. That which is merely a utility satisfies, however, a particular and limited end. The work of esthetic art satisfies many ends, none of which is laid down in advance. It serves life rather than prescribing a defined and limited mode of living (*AE*, 135; *LW* 10:140).

In the response to the work, says Dewey, "The entire organism with all its charge of the past and varied resources operates, but it operates through a particular medium, that of eye, as it interacts with eye, ear, and touch" (*AE*, 195; *LW* 10:199). Art is the process by which experience as a whole is served; it has become integrated but luminous with value and meaning because it has been mediated by active intelligence. The otherwise partial and separate ends of action become fused into one developing integrated acitvity, *an* experience. "Perception that occurs for its own sake," Dewey insists, "is the full realization of all the elements of our psychological being" (*AE*, 256; *LW* 10:261). Human experience hungers for the realization of meaning and value directly in experience as it is lived and undergone, and not in the infinitely evanescent future of the utilitarians. While Dewey denies that art is a mode of knowledge, it is through art that we have a "sense of increase of understanding, of a deepened intelligibility on the part of the objects of nature and man" (*AE*, 288; *LW* 10:243). Crucial to art is this "sense of disclosure and of heightened intelligibility of the world" (*AE*, 289; *LW* 10:294). In art, "knowledge is transformed; it becomes something more than knowledge because it is merged with non-intellectual elements to form an experience worth while as an experience." He continues:

> I have from time to time set forth a conception of knowledge as being "instrumental." Strange meanings have been imputed by critics to this conception. Its actual content is simple: Knowledge is instrumental to the enrichment of immediate experience through the control over action that it exercises. . . . Tangled scenes of life are made more intelligible in esthetic experience: not, however, as reflection

and science render things more intelligible by reduction to conceptual form, but by presenting their meanings as the matter of a clarified, coherent, and intensified or "impassioned" experience (AE, 290; LW 10:294-95).

Experience is formed when it achieves this end. This provides the necessary context to understand Dewey's often repeated definition of form: "Form may be then defined as the operation of forces that carry the experience of an event, object, scene, and situation to its own integral fulfillment" (AE, 137; LW 10:142). This is only possible if the specialized, limited end has become surpassed for the sake of satisfying experience as a whole. "Only when the constituent parts of a whole have the unique end of contributing to the consummation of a conscious experience, do design and shape lose superimposed character and become form," Dewey reasserts, "They cannot do this so long as they serve a specialized purpose. . . . This interfusion of all properties of the medium is necessary if the object in question is to serve the whole creature in his unified vitality" (AE, 117; LW 10:122). Form is the organization of the various phases and parts of experience toward the end of experience as a whole, which is the inherent sense of fulfillment in meaning and value. Experience is sensed as fraught with significance.

Form emerges as the course of experience fuses into a consummatory whole. Not only does this reveal the inherent temporality of aesthetic form, but it shows that form establishes dynamic, rhythmic relationships which move from the potential and ideal to the actual and real. On the initial level, form reveals the material as material, as the medium to be explored in perception. There is some ambiguity with this theme in Dewey's discussion, for material can be anything which is present in the work to be used or worked upon. This includes more than the physical medium, incorporating elements of perceptual organization and cultural interpretation. When we see Michelangelo's "Creation of Adam" from the Sistine Chapel, we see more than arranged planes of colored plaster—and we should, in spite of what Bell thinks. There is a question, therefore, between what is legitimately "in" the work and what is external to it. Dewey draws the distinction between the "subject" of the work and the "substance" which is revealed through form. The subject of the Sistine panel is the story of the creation as told in the Judeo-Christian tradition. It is present in a variety of works besides Michelangelo's, such as those by unknown Medieval sculptors, Byzantine ivory carvers, or the renditions by Ghiberti and Rodin, and it can be present in a variety of media, such as Milton's poetic version in Paradise Lost. The substance, on the other hand, is what the particular work is about—it is what is revealed through the work. It is what is encountered as inherently belonging to the work. It is obvious that no sharp line can be drawn between what is internal or external to any work at any time or in the course of its history. Dewey tries to illustrate the distinction with Matisse's famous reply to someone who criticized his painting for not looking realistic: "Madam, that is not a woman; that is a picture" (*AE*, 113; *LW* 10:118). One may also think of Magritte's picture of a pipe with the words painted below it, "Ceci n'est pas une pipe," which makes the same point: it's a painting, not a pipe. Nevertheless, this is where the temptation to a formalism such as Bell's originates and Dewey parts company with those who see art as supremely only about itself, as if it were some sort of temple to the principle of self-referentiality. From the Deweyan perspective, what the work is about is not fixed or frigidly unchanging for all who are perfect lovers. The boundaries of what is internal or external to the work may vary, and almost certainly will, as time and history affect the interpretive contexts. Material which was originally internal to the work may quickly become external. Dante wrote the *Divine Comedy* in the heat of religious conviction and political emotion. Today we must rely on scholarly recontextualization so that some of the internal substance of the work may be shown. But it is nonetheless true that we read the notes to the *Inferno* for the sake of the poem rather than reading the poem for the sake of identifying the historical characters in it, unless of course one is studying fourteenth century Florentine politics. It is conceivable that a work may become totally inaccessible at certain times and places or that after being dormant it may spring to life. One could not revive the ceremonials of Aztec human sacrifice today; an attempt to restore the bright, original polychrome of Greek statues would inescapably lose our aesthetic interest and strike us as vulgar. Thus the terms "subject" and "substance" should be read as signifying for Dewey a fluctuating boundary, a tensive penumbra surrounding every work. What is significant is that the encounter of a work which eventuates in *an* experience does establish such a tensive field in which there is a focal area where elements are sensed as inherently belonging together; this is what makes it *an* experience.

Form reflects the capacity of the material of experience to be revealed and as it is revealed to grow together. Dewey speaks of "the inherent tendency of sense to expand, to come into intimate relations with other things than itself, and thus to take on form because of its own movement—instead of passively waiting to have form imposed upon it. Any sensuous quality tends, because of its organic connections, to spread and fuse" (*AE*, 124; *LW* 10:129). In other words, the very sense of experience is organized development or growth which realizes a fused continuity. The dynamically integrated experience is full with its meaning; it is pregnant with its own unfolding future:

> As long as "meaning" is a matter of association and suggestion, it falls apart from the qualities of the sensuous medium and form is disturbed. Sense qualities are the carriers of meanings, not as vehicles carry goods but as a mother carries a baby when that baby is part of her own organism. Works of art, like words, are literally pregnant with meaning. Meanings, having their source in past experience, are means by which the particular organization that marks a given picture is effected. They are not added on by "association" but are either, and equally, the soul of which colors are the body or the body of which colors are the soul—according as we happen to be concerned with the picture (*AE*, 118; *LW* 10:122-23).

The meaning of a work of art is its very capacity to generate *an* experience. Experience does not simply randomly expand; it must expand so that it fuses. In this sense, while there is development in *an* experience, it must always be development *of* the substance of the work. Form, or the organization of the substance, must be a constant gathering together as well as an opening up.

This is achieved through the relational, rhythmic structure of the work. Since the fusion of form and matter in the work is due to "the intimate relation of undergoing and doing in interaction of a live creature with the world of nature and man" (*AE*, 132: *LW* 10:137), Dewey pays special attention to the dynamic aspect of the relational feature of *an* experience. By relation, Dewey is not referring to a fixed or abstract property between two entities. He appeals to the idiomatic usage which "denotes something direct and active, something dynamic and energetic. It fixes attention upon the way things bear upon one another, their clashes and unitings, the way they fulfill and frustrate, promote and retard, excite and inhibit one another" (*AE*, 134; *LW* 10:139). The rhythmic structure of the work is that of continuity of action realized in and through intelligent perception. The primary structural feature of the work of art is that it is an organized material which is realized through activity; it is achieved in time. Dewey rejects utterly the idea that some forms of aesthetic experience are nontemporal, which is to say, nondevelopmental. This is saying something more than that it always takes time to perceive a work. It is saying that this perception has a developmental order to it; the experience has a cumulative effect in which the past is gathered up into the present and the present actively pushes toward the future. The tem-

poral expanse of the experience is "full," that is, it marks the fulfillment of a meaningful event rather than just the passing of mechanical
clock-time.

Thus, the interpretation of rhythm as mere recurrence miscon-
ceives the way rhythm shapes or organizes experience. A recurrence
which genuinely sums up previous experience and carries it forward
is not repetition but furtherance. A repetition in a progressively developmental epxerience marks either a weakening of effect or a
strengthening of it, as any composer knows. There is resolution of
tension as well as generation of new tensions. Therefore, Dewey
insists that "esthetic recurrence is that of *relationships* that sum up and
carry forward. . . . Recurring *relationships* serve to define and delimit
parts, giving them individuality of their own. But they also connect
. . ." (*AE*, 166; *LW 10*:171). The activity which characterizes the work
of art as fully lived experience is not that it simply escapes being static
but that it becomes characterized as having a career:

> Now that which marks off the living from the dead is not bustle and
> ado, nor does a picture literally move. The living being is character-
> ized by having a past and a present; having them as possessions of
> the present, not just externally. And I suggest that it is precisely
> when we get from an art product the feeling of dealing with a *career*,
> a history, perceived at a particular point of its development, that we
> have the impression of life (*AE*, 176; *LW 10*:180-81).

Once again it is important to recall the impact of James' theory of felt-
relations in considering Dewey's theory of experience. The rhythmic
quality of the present moment, the ability to experience it in terms of
its history or career, is due to how certain tensions, relations, and
incipient actions are funded in perception. Thus Dewey is being fully
consistent when he at once insists that *an* experience is inherently a
temporal, developmental affair and when he asserts that "what is not
immediate is not esthetic" (*AE*, 119; *LW 10*:123). The immediate is
experienced as or felt to be a phase of *an* experience. In short, the
immediate is both qualitative and rhythmic. As Dewey explains, "For
whenever each step forward is at the same time a summing up and
fulfillment of what precedes, and every consummation carries expectation tensely forward, there is rhythm" (*AE*, 172; *LW 10*:177).

The rhythmic dimension of *an* experience has several features.
First of all there is the dramatic commencement, the opening, of *an*
experience. Dewey calls this phase "seizure." In this moment the
immanent possibility of experience becoming *an* experience is actively
felt. "The total overwhelming impression comes first," Dewey says,
"perhaps in seizure by a sudden glory of the landscape, or by the

effect upon us of entrance into a cathedral when dim light, incense, stained glass and majestic proportions fuse into one indistinguishable whole. We say with truth that a painting strikes us. There is an impact that precedes all definite recognition of what it is about" (*AE*, 145; *LW* *10*:150). There is a sense of incipient wholeness of the experience which is beginning but which is as yet unfulfilled because the experience has not yet been actively mediated or discriminated. Dewey goes on to say, "Not only, however, is it impossible to prolong this stage of esthetic experience indefinitely, but it is not desirable to do so. There is only one guarantee that this direct seizure be at a high level, and that is the degree of cultivation of the one experiencing it. In itself it may be, and often is, the result of cheap means employed upon meretricious stuff. And the only way in which to rise from that level to one where there is intrinsic assurance of worth is through intervening periods of discrimination" (*AE*, 145; *LW 10*:150). In other words, for *an* experience to begin there must be this primary phase of seizure, the precritical or undiscriminated *sense* of an aesthetically organized whole. If this feeling is to be fulfilled, the perceiver must have critical habits of discrimination for perception to continue and develop. The experience must become articulate; otherwise there is a bare and relatively meaningless isolated moment which may in fact have very little ability to develop and continue experience. Criticisms such as Stephen Pepper's miss this point by simply identifying the moment of seizure with the whole aesthetic experience. Pepper's view, in short, ends up trying to prolong the initially inarticulate and undeveloped commencement of *an* experience.[66]

The phase of seizure is characterized by the dawning sense of "the promise of meaning." The experience is filled with portent of the consummatory. Perception is called forth, but underlying its activity is the abiding promissory sense of a genuinely fulfilling, whole experience in process. As perception begins actively to respond and work with the material, the rhythmic organization of the experience develops out of the ground of seizure. Tensions, anticipations, and resolutions are felt. Undergoing and doing weave together in what Dewey calls the "rhythm of surrender and reflection" (*AE*, 144; *LW 10*:149). In this process the various elements and relations of the work become articulate: we begin to discriminate the way the various parts are different and unique as well as how they relate to and support each other. The exploration of the work reveals how the material has been ordered so that "form" and "material" become distinct. In working with the work, there is also the perception of what is germaine to the work, what genuinely belongs to it and counts as substance, and what does not and is subject.

These functional distinctions amplify and organize the total ongoing experience. If the sense of wholeness is lost, the experience dissipates or collapses dramatically. Throughout *an* experience the sense of closure and the consummatory are counterpoised and tensively present. The work as a whole is realized and enacted at each instant, and each moment becomes a realization *of* a work. "The consummatory phase of experience—which is intervening as well as final—always presents something new," says Dewey, so that it "is recurrent throughout a work of art, and in the experience of a great work of art the points of its incidence shift in successive observations of it" (*AE*, 139; *LW* 10:144). Likewise, "Every closure is an awakening, and every awakening settles something" (*AE*, 169; *LW* 10:174).

An illustration of this can easily be found in Joyce's use of intensified moments or "epiphanies" in his *Portrait of the Artist as a Young Man*. The book is a masterful example of the creation of complex tensions and resolutions so that the cumulative process gives one the sense of the growth of a personality. As the story develops, minor themes and tensions begin to reveal larger ones, which in the end reveal the fundamental drama of the book: the tension between the artist's autonomous craft of celebrating the world and the snares laid to subvert his intelligence to other ends, such as the Church or the State. Connected with this are various symbolic constellations. Images of stagnant water gradually build up into an image of Ireland, while images of flowing water indicate freedom. The tension between the senses and the intellect develops into a radical division between sexuality and religion. The moment young Stephen Dedalus is able to overcome this division and to unite his spirit with his senses in the creative affirmation of the world occurs in the famous epiphany of the bird-girl at the end of the fourth chapter:

> A girl stood before him in midstream, alone and still, gazing out to sea. She seemed like one whom magic had changed into the likeness of a strange and beautiful seabird. Her long slender bare legs were delicate as a crane's and pure save where an emerald trail of seaweed had fashioned itself as a sign upon the flesh. Her thighs, fuller and softhued as ivory, were bared almost to the hips where the white fringes of her drawers were like featherings of soft white down. Her slateblue skirts were kilted boldly about her waist and dovetailed behind her. Her bosom was as a bird's, soft and slight, slight and soft as the breast of some darkplumaged dove. But her long fair hair was girlish: and girlish and touched with the wonder of mortal beauty, her face.
>
> She was alone and still, gazing out to sea; and when she felt his presence and the worship of his eyes her eyes turned to him in quiet

sufferance of his gaze, without shame or wantonness. Long, long
she suffered his gaze and then quietly withdrew her eyes from his
and bent them toward the stream, gently stirring the water with her
foot hither and thither. The first faint noise of gently moving water
broke the silence, low and faint and whispering, faint as the bells of
sleep; hither and thither, hither and thither: and a faint flame trem-
bled on her cheek.

　　—Heavenly God! cried Stephen's soul, in an outburst of profane
joy.[67]

The description of the girl at the seashore metamorphoses her into a
mythic creature, indeed a Siren with the head of a woman and body of
a bird. But there is a remarkable fusion of themes and images in this
one description. The colors previously associated by Joyce with the
Holy Virgin are presented now in the sensuous but innocent girl of
flesh and blood. In addition to the blue of the Virgin's robe (echoed in
the "slateblue skirts"), we can recall from Stephen's childhood the
litany of the Virgin in which she is called "Tower of Ivory" and "House
of Gold" (echoed here in the girl's ivory colored thighs and fair hair):

> Eileen had long thin cool white hands too because she was a girl.
> They were like ivory; only soft. That was the meaning of *Tower of
> Ivory* but protestants could not understand it and made fun of it. . . .
> She had put her hand into his pocket where his hand was. She had
> said that pockets were funny things to have: and then all of a sudden
> she had broken away and had run laughing down the sloping curve
> of the path. Her fair hair had streamed out behind her like gold in the
> sun. *Tower of Ivory. House of Gold.* By thinking of things you could
> understand them.[68]

The bird-girl at the seashore transforms the symbols of the Virgin into
those of the mythic siren; she does not demand Stephen to abjure his
senses as the Church had done. He can gaze worshipfully upon her
with a profane joy. The girl manages to synthesize the four elements
as well: she stands in the water, upon the shore, and there is a flame
upon her cheek—the bird imagery connotes the air. The use of the
images of moving water also fuses the contrast between the stagnant
pool which is Ireland and the creative freedom which the artist must
seek by flight. As a child at school, young Stephen is shoved into a
stagnant ditch: "And how cold and slimy the water had been! And a
fellow had once seen a big rat jump plop into the scum. The cold slime
of the ditch covered his whole body. . . . " Even the water of the bath
is a "warm turfcolored bogwater." In contrast, after his encounter
with the bird-girl Stephen looks out to sea: "A rim of the young moon
cleft the pale waste of the sky like the rim of a silver hoop embedded

in grey sand; and the tide was flowing in fast to the land with a low whisper of her waves, islanding a few last figures in distant pools."[69] The new moon, the source of poetry, seems to touch the earth and set the waters of life, imagination, in motion.

In this passage, then, there is at once a complex instance of what Dewey calls "summing up and carrying forward." The fusion of the themes in the epiphany of the bird-girl bring the story to a new resolution, but at the same time it opens up a new problem for the character: the implication of the image is that Stephen can only be free by leaving Ireland over the sea, as Daedalus escaped the Cretan Labyrinth. And this is in fact how the book ends, with Stephen Dedalus writing in his journal, "Welcome, O life! I go to encounter for the millionth time the reality of experience and to forge in the smithy of my soul the uncreated conscience of my race," after which he adds a prayer to the master artist, the maker of labyrinths, "Old father, old artificer, stand me now and ever in good stead."[10]

Form is this very working of the work, the definite, organized means whereby the work as a whole comes to be in experience. It is how the substance, what the work is about, shows itself in its temporal development. Dewey is able to assert that the "form of the whole is present in every member" (*AE*, 56; *LW 10:*62). The present moment is grasped as part of an overall process culminating in a funded, closed experience. Dewey's presentation of form as the way the substance of the work shows itself might also be illustrated by an example from the visual arts. In Michelangelo's "Creation of Adam" from the Sistine Chapel, we have one of the simplest yet most powerful works of art ever created. A formalist like Bell, however, is forced to begin by painfully abstracting out *only* the lines, shapes, and colors and then must contemplate only these lest he fail as a perfect lover and stain the experience with any human content. While the formal analysis of the implicit shapes and their relations reveals much of how the work achieves its effects and expresses itself, the greater part of the expressiveness of the work, its power and its enigma, are ignored because they have been shoved to the realm of the subject and not left as substance. From the Deweyan standpoint one begins with the initial seizure created by the work. We are confronted with human shapes in a very dynamic relation; one on the left lies passively slumped, barely propped up like a doll; in the floating figures on the right the dominant figure leans out of the swirling cloud of cloaks to touch the finger of the reclining figure on the left. There is a felt relation between the two main figures. Given that most observers of the work are familiar with the story of Genesis, it is apparent that what is represented is the creation of Adam by God. We understand that the basic tension in the

work is that between creature and creator. This is effectively rein-
forced by the asymmetrical balance of the composition. There is an
implicit sharp diagonal line running from the upper left corner down
along the slope of the earth to the bottom. We have the impression
that all of the force and energy is on the right hand side; it is "pushing" toward the left. The fact that the diagonal does not run from the
upper left to the lower right corner further establishes this. But such a
relationship can only be felt as dynamic, as potentially out of balance,
because the human eye is used to judging shapes in terms of their
weight, movement, force, and stability.

There is not a total cleavage between the two parts of the picture,
however. The almost-touching fingers counteract the division as a
tensive focal point. The effect is a sense of a dramatic temporal moment: the imminent future of the event, when the spark of life leaps
from God's finger to Adam, is immediately sensed. We now understand that Adam's body has everything except spirit, hence it's passive, flaccid and heavy posture. God, the creative force itself, is represented by a tautly poised figure, hanging like a gymnast in a moment
of supreme self-controlled movement. There is a further basic rhythm
in the picture: that between the bare, sharply slanting hill of the earth
and the crowded, billowing cloud from which God emerges. The
smooth shape of the cloak is felt to be blowing in the wind, and the
numerous, alert faces in it create the sense of a cluster of intently
active beings. Not only does this add to the sense of the creative
complexity of the right side, but it effectively weighs that side down
so that the immediate sense of imbalance is corrected further. A second relation between the two halves is realized when we notice that
God is looking directly into Adam's eye as he reaches out to him.

The basic rhythm of the work is emphasized by the simple shapes
dominating the two halves. On the left side the slope of the earth
marks a right-angle triangle (in fact a triangle whose sides form a 3:4:5
ratio, the "golden proportion"). This is a fundamentally inert or static
figure. On the other side, the cloak forms a loose oval, which is not
only a dynamic shape, but also suggests the form of the egg, a tacit
reference to the idea of creation. Further relationships can be discerned. Given the narrative of the picture there is some importance to
be ascribed to the woman's head emerging from under God's arm
looking with intent concern at the unfolding event. If Adam marks
the moment of Creation, this may be Eve, and the reference may be to
the Fall. Following this clue, we are drawn to the child below Eve who
looks away from the event, reading it as Jesus or the Salvation which
stands beyond history at the end of time (hence his looking away
outside the picture). In these relationships, then, the history of man is

symbolized. Nevertheless, we are brought back, again and again, to the dramatic focus of the work, the approaching fingers and the imminent moment when God's gaze will suddenly be met by a reply from man. The work includes a meditation upon the relation of man and God. It would have been traditional and natural for the relation between creator and creature to have been expressed entirely vertically, the creator above and dependent man below. But Michelangelo has them nearly meet eye to eye on the same level, Adam only being slightly lower than God. Such confident humanism is artistically softened by the numerous indications of the location of the creative energy—of that there can be absolutely no doubt from the first moment of beholding the work. The passive curve formed by Adam's body creates a line flowing down his torso and along his outstretched leg and quietly reflects the curve of the approaching oval of God's cloak, as if bearing its imprint. Finally, the figure of God forms a floating triangle, the slightly tipped base running from toe to outstretched hand.[71] The structural dimensions are thoroughly integrated into the human narrative, however, and operate to sustain it.

The form is the opening up or revealing of the world of the work; as long as the elements can be successfully integrated back into the whole experience, they are part of the substance rather than mere subject matter. Because the form of the work is due to the interaction of the appreciator and the product, it has a growing, developing, and experimental quality. One of the persistent tyrannies of Platonist aesthetics is the notion that there is a secret, fixed or complete essence standing behind the work as a self-same objective which every experience aims for but only duplicates in an incomplete manner. Dewey is not advocating the relativist attitude that all encounters with the work are of *equal* worth. Critical, intelligent, and educated perception by its very nature will be incapable of making such a naive pronouncement. A contextually grounded approach will seek to establish the work through interaction. There may always be an ambiguous, horizonal nature to this work. The work may achieve itself differently as its historical contexts differ. Nevertheless, it can establish a dynamic continuity within the experience of the culture so that its history as a work saves it from unintelligibility. In other words, the work will live a life in the world of the culture, and this life keeps the antihistorical attitudes of absolutism or subjectivism from enforcing upon the work a false clarity or a needless obscurity. Form, then, can be understood as the historical life of the work which provides continuity between the various consummatory encounters of it; it is a functional, cultural horizon which develops and grows (or which withers and dies). Because form can be understood in this manner, it is in principle something that can be learned and taught. As one encounters a work in experience one gradually comes to develop and articulate one's perception in terms of what the work reveals. On a primary level, the work itself teaches us how to respond. But because the work exists within a living cultural environment, one may also be able to learn how to encounter works through the participation of others. A musical friend may teach us how to appreciate Beethoven just as a music teacher may teach us how to play him. Form not only establishes continuity in one's individual experience but in social experience as well. Form, as the dynamic working of the work which articulates experience into *an* experience, is the realization of the potentialities of the work in time. For Dewey, the form is evoked from the material by interaction. This places Dewey's theory at odds with those that impose form on the work from without or that simply see the work as mirroring an inner form of feeling. Form is also the opening of the work which reveals what the work cares about: its substance. To encounter a work is not simply to acquire a technique of perception. One doesn't demonstrate that one understands Van Gogh by being able to paint a perfect copy or even to make a perfect forgery. It is possible to come to see what Van Gogh was concerned with by studying his technique, but the study of his technique itself belongs to art history and not immediately to the experience of his work as a work. *What* the work is concerned about is what is encountered directly in the experience through the organized medium. This "what" cannot be successfully transferred into discourse (to do so one would have to recreate the work itself). It is an integral characteristic in our progressive experience of a work of art that what it is about will be an affair which grows, changes, and takes on new life. It has all of the ambiguity and mystery of the world, as well as its light and clarity.

V. The Immanent Horizon: Qualitative Meaning

Clive Bell typifies the essentialist approach to the question of art: if there is such a thing as art, we must first distinguish it from everything which it is not, and then seek its uniquely defining characteristics. Such presuppositions naturally dispose the investigation to separate art from life and then force it to posit some instrinsic subject matter, such as a peculiar emotion about pure form, which is either intuitively grasped or not. The whole tenor of this strategy is that of retreat—art is something that must be marked off and enshrined behind impregnable definitions. It is not even questioned whether the sort of fragile, hot-house experience Bell takes as aesthetic is the natural starting point. At least, for Dewey, if we are to understand art, it must be seen in terms of its genesis from experience as a whole. The aesthetic for Dewey is not so much a special kind of experience as it is the realization of the impulsion of all experience toward significant integration. It is a kind of experience only in the sense in which the complete is different from the incomplete. Art is not a specific category of human experience to be set off and compared with our cognitive and moral experience. The aesthetic is a way of articulating experience so that it realizes expressive meaning and value. Since the subject matter of art is as broad as life itself and since form is simply the power of organizing a medium to reveal its substance, aesthetic form ceases to be understood as the common essence unifying all the arts. It is evident that form, which for Bell was what art was ultimately about, is for Dewey the differentiating principle, the distinctive manner of organized or articulate response to the expressive powers of the medium. The arts are connected because they share a common concern for rendering experience meaningful in a concrete way.

Works of art are significant for Dewey. While an inquiry into the origin and nature of the aesthetic can profitably begin by forgetting examples of fine art and focusing on the implicit aesthetic possibilities of our daily living, as Joseph Kupfer has shown,[72] such an inquiry must eventually recall and reflect upon truly great works of art. These reveal as almost nothing else can, says Dewey, the inherent possibilities of experience to realize expressive meaning. On what basis, though, does Dewey reintroduce instances of fine art when the whole thrust of his approach has been to show that such works have no unique binding essence and in fact may perilously reflect the inner dualism of a society which unpragmatically seeks to separate its utilitarian means from its subjectively enjoyed ends? There is, Dewey argues, a "common substance" to the arts. It is not form which joins those experiences or works which achieve expressive embodiment so much as what form shows or reveals about experience itself, namely, its capacity to become individualized in a consummatory manner—-to become *an* experience. In other words, works of art reveal that the pervasive quality, which provides the meaning-determining horizon of all experience, can become consciously realized or explicitly felt. This qualitative feeling can then be used toward the *further* integration of experience. The experience becomes framed by it so as to become the continuous manifestation of a binding qualitative sense of meaning. In art, experience grows through the exploration of the world so that a dynamic continuity is established on the level of consciousness, that is, on the level of mind or meaning.

It has already been indicated that the phase of seizure is the "opening up" of the work as work, as the felt promise of meaning or the immanent sense of possible fulfillment. What this moment establishes is not a discrete, subjectively felt state of consciousness but a whole organization of anticipatory attitudes and potential responses. It marks a genuine beginning in which one becomes oriented to the world through a definite medium whose specific determinations have yet to be worked out. But to the extent that these determinations or possibilities do become articulated, they will be regarded as developments of one continuous experience whose temporally related actions and responses will fuse together and become funded as they progress. The phase of seizure marks the anticipation of the possibility of *an* experience and this anticipation is so consciously present as to focus and direct activity *toward* the realization of that possibility.

> I have previously noted that artist and perceiver alike begin with what may be called a total seizure, an inclusive qualitative whole not yet articulated, not distinguished into members. . . . Moreover, not only does the "mood" come first, but it persists as the substratum after distinctions emerge; in fact they emerge as *its* distinctions. Even at the outset, the total and massive quality has its uniqueness; even when vague and undefined, it is just that which it is and not anything else. If the perception continues, discrimination inevitably sets in. Attention must move, and, as it moves, parts, members, emerge from the background. And if attention moves in a unified direction instead of wandering, it is controlled by the pervading qualitative unity; attention is controlled *by* it because it operates within it (*AE*, 191-92; *LW* 10:195-96).

We sense the possibility of a completed, coordinated response to the event; this sense of completion only comes about through a highly tensive and emotional involvement with the work. The work reveals a dramatic movement in which experience may grow and yet remain integrated. It is this possibility of *an* experience which both individualizes and articulates itself by controlling attention—we constantly evaluate whether the experience has "lived up to its promise," so to speak. This is not primarily done on a cognitive level, though intelligence certainly has an active, discriminating role to play. The determination of whether the whole is realized or achieved is something apprehended immanently in the phase of the work; if there is any sense to the use of the term "intuition," Dewey says, it is in reference to the pervasive sense of the possibility of the realization of a whole, aesthetically individualized promissory experience, is or is not realized through the working of the parts together:

> Not only must this quality be in all "parts," but it can only be felt, that is immediately experienced. I am not trying to describe it, for it

cannot be described nor even be *specifically* pointed at—since whatever is specified in a work of art is one of *its* differentiations. I am only trying to call attention to something that every one can realize is present in his experience of a work of art, but that is *so* thoroughly and pervasively present that it is taken for granted. "Intuition" has been used by philosophers to designate many things—some of which are suspicious characters. But the penetrating quality that runs through all the parts of a work of art and binds them into an individualized whole can only be emotionally "intuited." The different elements and specific qualities of a work of art blend and fuse in a way which physical things cannot emulate. This fusion is the felt presence of the same qualitative unity in all of them. "Parts" are discriminated, not intuited. But without the intuited enveloping quality, parts are external to one another and mechanically related. Yet the organism which is the work of art is nothing different from its parts or members. It *is* the parts as members—a fact that again brings us to the one pervasive quality that remains the same quality in being differentiated. The resulting sense of totality is commemorative, expectant, insinuating, premonitory (*AE*, 192-93; *LW* 10:196).

The last sentence quoted is particularly revealing about what Dewey is so tortuously trying to express. The pervasive quality is not a specific or absolutely identical quality which at any particular moment in the experience can be denotatively located or pointed out— the sort of thing that Hume thought the impression of the self must be. It is not a clear or distinct object in the experience occupying the focus of attention. Instead, Dewey is indicating that the organizing quality is nothing other than the temporality of the developing event as a whole. It is present throughout the phases either tacitly or explicitly as the guiding sense or context, the horizon of the event. An organism is not something distinct from all its parts; it is the integrating of those parts which allow them to function *as* members of an organized whole. Nor does an organism exist at one changeless instant but throughout a temporally extended period during which change and transformations constitute its activity. The qualitative horizon is present similarly in *an* experience as the temporal organization of each particular phase which establishes that phase as a development of a process. In the moment of seizure, the whole is only intuited or felt in an indeterminate manner. As consummatory funding and discrimination replace the indeterminacy of seizure, they are experienced as the developments *of* what was sensed as indeterminate before. As the experience is clarified, the clarification is of that which was in need of clarification. Thus seizure can be understood as the immanent sense of this need. From one point of view, the phase of seizure marks a significant break with the routine habits of ordinary perception, for we are suddenly aware of the possibility of *an* experience in a world where discontinuity and incompletion seem the rule. This is what gives force to those theories which seek to determine the aesthetic by its detachment from our practical or natural attitudes. To use the ideas of "disinterestedness," "psychic distance," or "bracketing" to describe *an* experience is much along the same lines as defining man as "not an ape," however. From Dewey's perspective at least, the work summons us toward a true interest, involvement rather than disinterest, in which the world is not bracketed out so much as opened up in light of its fecund possibilities for meaning. Aesthetic experience realizes on a conscious level our need for integrative experience. It focuses our attention and efforts; it summons us to a project.

The phase of seizure is marked by the impending sense of the as yet unarticulated richness of *an* experience or the sense of there being more to the experience than is immediately taken in. Fusion marks the confluence of the parts which have been discriminated. From a functional standpoint, seizure and fusion are alternating rhythms in *an* experience. To the extent that *an* experience has depth to it, the ever-present feeling that there is something more to articulate which eludes us at the moment, the sense of the "surplus" or "superabundance of meaning" which James called the sense of "the ever not quite," it will have a dimension of seizure which is the perpetual opening of the work. To the extent that the work dynamically moves from the mute realm of the potential to the actual and becomes a concretely achieved, organized whole, realizing certain possibilities at the expense of others *for the sake of* overall unity, there will be fusion or the sense of closure which individualizes the work. This is what makes the work stand forth as something *there,* something complete and self-contained. This is what gives the work its texture or its quality as surface available to sense. Seizure marks the anticipatory attitude that there remains further work; the exploration of the world of the work remains a future possibility. Fusion is retrospective, commemorating the work as accomplished, although it may also mark the realization of certain new ambiguities, tensions, and dimensions which stand in need of further resolution.

This progressive grasping of the whole through the part is what Dewey means by "intuition." It may be recalled that in this idealist period Dewey appealed to intuition as the capacity of Spirit to know itself as a whole, as an individual. It is helpful to see a connection here between his early and later philosophies only if the differences are kept in mind. This process is no longer understood in terms of an absolute self acting so as to know itself. The activity is one of a problematic progression from the indeterminate to the determinate realized through interaction with an object. Aside from dismissing the metaphysics of self-activity, Dewey no longer approaches art as a case of knowledge. Intuition here is precisely the non-cognitive dimension of experience made conscious and operative . It functions so as to realize the individuality of an experience which is also its sense of wholeness, integration, or self-belonging:

> There is no name to be given it. As it enlivens and animates it is the spirit of the work of art. It is its reality, when we feel the work of art to be real on its own account and not as a realistic exhibition. It is the idiom in which the particular work is composed and expressed, that which stamps it with individuality. It is the background which is more than spatial because it enters into and qualifies everything in the focus, everything distinguished as part and member (*AE,* 193; *LW 10*:197).

Dewey directly appeals here at the most crucial moment in *Art as Experience* to his field-theory of experience in which the distinct, sharp objects of the focus area of experience are set within a context which determines the focus though it remains undetermined itself. "We are accustomed to think of physical objects as having bounded edges," he remarks. "Then we carry over this belief in the bounded character of all *objects* of experience (a belief founded ultimately in the practical exegencies of our dealings with things) into our conception of experience itself. We suppose the experience itself has the same definite limits as the things with which it is concerned" (*AE,* 193; *LW 10*:197). The whole purpose of Dewey's mature philosophy is to question this assumption and provide an alternate theory of experience which successfully accounts for both the determinate clarity of some parts of the field and the indeterminate but conditional nature of other parts. Although *all* experience has this field structure, it is consciously revealed in artistic-aesthetic experience, in *an* experience:

> But any experience, the most ordinary, has an indefinite total setting. Things, objects, are only focal points of a here and now in a whole that stretches out indefinitely. This is the qualitative "background" which is defined and made definitely conscious in particular objects and specified properties and qualities. There is something mystical associated with the word intuition, and any experience becomes mystical in the degree in which the sense, the feeling, of the unlimited envelope becomes intense—as it may do in experience of an object of art (*AE,* 193; *LW 10*:197).[73]

This aspect is precisely what Dewey describes in *A Common Faith* as the religious *quality* which experience may have. Dewey thereby is able to distinguish "the religious," which is a non-cognitive quality, from the particular doctrinal beliefs which constitute religions. In this book, he describes experiences marked by such a quality as moments "having the force of bringing about a better, deeper and enduring adjustment in life" or "significant moments of living" (*CF*, 14; *LW* 9:11). Such moments are different from those which mark particular or limited accomodations of our attitudes. These latter sort of experiences, Dewey observes, do not involve "the entire self" and are "mainly *passive*" (*CF*, 15; *LW* 9:12). There are also particular active moments of readjustment where we readapt the environment rather than just our responses to it.

> But there are also changes in ourselves in relation to the world in which we live that are much more inclusive and deep seated. They relate not to this and that want in relation to this and that condition in our surroundings, but pertain to our being in its entirety. Because of their scope, this modification of ourselves is enduring. It lasts through any amount of vicissitude of circumstances, internal and external. There is a composing and harmonizing of the various elements of our being such that, in spite of changes in the special conditions that surround us, these conditions are also arranged, settled, in relation to us (*CF*, 16; *LW* 9:12-13).

Dewey's discussion of this reorganization (or "comportment") of our "being in its entirety" is a hidden but highly significant and crucial theme in his thought. We adopt an attitude which is not partial but which appropriates our life as a whole. This attitude constitutes the self who we are and establishes the horizons for the meaning and value of life. In presenting this thought Dewey appeals to art and imagination (the kind of imagination which "intervenes" rather than that imagination which "supervenes"):

> The connection between imagination and the harmonizing of the self is closer than is usually thought. The idea of a whole, whether of the whole personal being or of the world, is an imaginative, not a literal idea. The limited world of our observation and reflection becomes the Universe only through imaginative extension. It cannot be apprehended in knowledge nor realized in reflection. Neither observation, thought, nor practical activity can attain that complete unification of the self which is called a whole. The *whole* self is an ideal, an imaginative projection. Hence the idea of a thoroughgoing and deep-seated harmonizing of the self with the Universe (as a name for the totality of conditions with which the self is connected) operates only through the imagination. . . (*CF*, 18-19; *LW* 9:14).

The religious is the grasping of the aesthetic possibilities of life as a whole through an ideal. It is the realization of life as aesthetic project.

The "unification of the self" is the organization of a field of meaning and value which will not only determine activity in the present but its significance as well. This is a project in the richest sense possible (a pro-jection, a "throwing" of oneself forward or an understanding of oneself in light of one's futurity) because it is what realizes the sense or meaning of the *present*. This organization of the self through recognition of the ideal possibilities of experience is also an organization of oneself toward the world—it is a transactional event in the fullest sense. Dewey insists that such an organization is not something consciously chosen. "An 'adjustment' possesses the will rather than expresses its product," he states, adding, "It is pertinent to note that the unification of the self throughout the ceaseless flux of what it does, suffers, and achieves, cannot be attained in terms of itself. The self is always directed toward something beyond itself and so its own unification depends upon the idea of the integration of the shifting scenes of the world into that imaginative totality we call the Universe" (*CF*, 19; *LW* 9:14). This Dewey calls the authority of an *ideal*, not a fact, over choice. Our ideals are not cognitive claims; they are integrative projects of meaning and value; they constitute what Dewey calls a "moral faith" (*CF*, 21; *LW* 9:15). It is an ultimate condition *for* action rather than the acknowledgement of a fully actualized reality. At this point, however, where one might easily suspect Dewey of lapsing into unfounded idealism, he firmly rejects the idealist interpretation of such experience:

> All possibilities, as possibilities, are ideal in character. The artist, scientist, citizen, parent, as far as they are actuated by the spirit of their callings, are controlled by the unseen. For all endeavor for the better is moved by faith in what is possible, not by adherence to the actual. Nor does this faith depend for its moving power upon the intellectual assurance or belief that the things worked for must surely prevail and come into embodied existence. For the authority of the object to determine our attitude and conduct, the right that is given it to claim our allegiance and devotion is based on the intrinsic nature of the ideal. The outcome, given our best endeavor, is not with us. The inherent vice of all intellectual schemes of idealism is that they convert the idealism of action into a system of beliefs about antecedent reality. The character assigned this reality is so different from that which observation and reflection lead to and support that these schemes inevitably glide into alliance with the supernatural (*CF*, 23-24; *LW* 9:17).

To recognize an ideal *as* an ideal is to recognize it as a *possibility* for integrating experience rather than as the preestablished meaning of experience. Dewey realistically recognizes that the presence of a possibility is no guarantee of its realization—possibility is not necessity. Even the power to be affected by certain ideals rather than others may be something out of our control. Action relies on situational conditions, and these may fail to be sufficient or may be eroded by the intrusion of the precarious. Even the promissory truth of the ideal, its seeming capacity to integrate experience meaningfully, may betray us. The moment when experience is transformed in light of an ideal possibility marks the event in which human faith, courage, and tragedy also become possibilities.

When Dewey speaks in *Art as Experience* of the intuitive quality which pervades and unifies *an* experience, he is therefore pointing toward something of far deeper significance than just a continuous undergone or had feeling. It is an awakening to our fundamental orientation toward the world and ourselves. Moreover, it is the reconstruction of these orientations which constitute genuine growth of meaning. Dewey quotes Tennyson's "Ulysses,":

> Experience is the arch wherethro'
> Gleams that untravell'd world, whose margin fades
> Forever and forever when I move,[74]

and adds, "For although there is a bounding horizon, it moves as we move. We are never wholly free from the sense of something that lies beyond. . . . This sense of the including whole implicit in ordinary experiences is rendered intense within the frame of a painting or poem" (*AE*, 193-94; *LW* 10:197-98). The work of art makes dynamically explicit the situational nature of experience. It discloses a process of expanding or moving horizons which reconstruct and determine the sense of that which occupies the conscious focus of perception. It is because the horizon is immanently present that *an* experience has the integration and sense of coherence which make it whole.

> The undefined and pervasive quality of an experience is that which binds together all the defined elements, the objects of which we are focally aware, making them a whole. The best evidence that such is the case is our constant sense of things as belonging or not belonging, a sense which is immediate. It cannot be a product of reflection, even though it requires reflection to find out whether some particular consideration is pertinent to what we are doing or thinking. For unless the sense were immediate, we should have no guide to our reflection. The sense of an extensive and underlying whole is the context of every experience and it is the essence of sanity. . . . Without an indeterminate and undetermined setting, the material of any experience is incoherent (*AE*, 194-95; *LW* 10:198).

This paragraph is a highly condensed rendition of Dewey's philosophy of experience as discussed in the previous chapters. It is a manifest misunderstanding to argue that in such passages Dewey is being inconsistent with his general philosophy. In fact, I contend, Dewey is expressing in such passages the essence of his philosophical vision. It is evident, furthermore, that artistic or aesthetic experience constitutes the paradigmatic instance of these traits.

Far from being a completely indefinite or inarticulate sort of experience, Dewey is compelled to acknowledge the "exquisite intelligibility and clarity we have in the presence of an object that is experienced with esthetic intensity" (*AE*, 195; *LW* 10:199). Once again, Dewey points to the "religious" quality of such experiences, not because they reveal some supernatural realm, but because such moments mark the fulfillment of the impulsion of the self toward embodied meaning and value. The pervasive, sense-giving, qualitative whole:

> . . . explains also the religious feeling that accompanies intense esthetic perception. We are, as it were, introduced into a world beyond this world which is nevertheless the deeper reality of the world in which we live in our ordinary experiences. We are carried out beyond ourselves to find ourselves. . . . the work of art operates to deepen and to raise to great clarity that sense of an enveloping undefined whole that accompanies every normal experience. This whole is then felt as an expansion of ourselves (*AE*, 195; *LW* 10:199).

The "world beyond this world" is simply the possibility for fulfilled meaning present in *this* world. Because so much of human experience is fragmented and divided, however, such moments are interpreted as revelations of an entirely different metaphysical order. As a result, we fail to recognize our ordinary experience as the ground from which such fulfilling moments develop, that they are *its* possibilities. In short, the aesthetic experience presents Dewey's strongest basis for reconstructing other domains of human experience: his projects for reconstruction in philosophy, education, morals, and politics. *An* experience indicates the possibility for human beings to become involved with the world in such a manner as to realize and comprehend the growth of experience toward meaning and value. The development of the self is just this process of developing an increasingly articulate apprehension of meaning and value. Growth is not due to the simple aggregation of experience; it is a continuous reconstructive transformation and reorganization so that new interpretive horizons are revealed. Thus "intuition," or the apprehension of the pervasive qualitative whole as the immanent meaning of experience, is not a static or instantaneous insight but a process, a realization of the significant potentialities of experience. " 'Intuition,' " Dewey says, "is that meeting of the old and new in which the readjustment involved in every form of consciousness is effected suddenly by means of a quick and unexpected harmony which in its bright abruptness is like a flash of revelation; although in fact it is prepared for by long and slow incubation" (*AE*, 266; *LW 10:270*).

A significant reconstruction of experience is possible only if there is a rich background of meanings. This background is the cultural horizon of intelligence concretely embodied in our habits. Experience, to be free, must be educated, and its education must be an education for the end of freedom.

Such a background of meanings is what Dewey refers to as "mind." Mind is the vast encultured network of organizing interpretations. It is the range of ability to organize a field of experience so that it has focus and horizon mediately related. This does not mean, however, that experience is always "minded" in a completely successful or satisfying manner—indeed most of the time, according to Dewey, it is not. "Mind," he observes, "that is the body of organized meanings by means of which events of the present have significance for us, does not always enter into the activities and undergoings that are going on here and now. Sometimes it is baffled and arrested" (*AE*, 273; *LW 10:277*). Experience has an inherent capacity to fragment or break asunder, creating the sense of alienation and the loss of meaning. In *an* experience, however, mind succeeds in mediating the event, thereby giving it shape and direction. Mind is thus an inherent tendency to organize and be concerned with the meaning and value of experience. Dewey in fact sees this understanding of "mind" implicit in the popular (as opposed to the philosophical) use of the term. "For in its nontechnical use," he says, " 'mind' denotes every mode and variety of interest in, and concern for, things: practical, intellectual, and emotional" (*AE*, 263; *LW 10:267-68*). It includes memory, the act of recollecting the past in terms of its significant and valued sense. It signifies active attention, being "mindful." It signifies purposive action. "Nor is mind in these operations something purely intellectual," comments Dewey, "The mother minds her baby; she cares for it with affection. Mind is care in the sense of solicitude, anxiety, as well as of active looking after things that need to be tended. . . . In short 'to mind' denotes an activity that is intellectual, to *note* something; affectional, as caring and liking, and volitional, acting in a purposive way. Mind is primarily a verb. It denotes all the ways in which we deal consciously and expressly with the situations in which we find ourselves" (*AE*, 263; *LW 10:268*). As such, mind constitutes the possible meanings of the self, the horizonal possibilities of organized experience.

The use of mind in experience marks the actualization of possible fields of meaning and value. This individualizes mind. "Control of material by a self," Dewey asserts, "is control by more than just 'mind'; it is control by the personality that has mind incorporate within it" (*AE*, 277; *LW* 10:281).[75] Possibilities must be selected by a controlling interest. Such purposiveness gives a teleological or dramatic structure to experience which implicitly involves the role of the self and its history. In other words, the self is a mode of constitutive and interpretive involvement. The self is a means of organizing as well as understanding experience. In integrated action purposiveness becomes consciously revealed and the self becomes framed by the recognition of the purposes as *its* purposes. It appropriates or owns them through action. "Purpose is this identification in action. Its operation in and through objective conditions is a test of its genuineness; the capacity of the purpose to overcome and utilize resistance . . . is a disclosure of the structure and quality of the purpose" (*AE*, 277; *LW* 10:281). Once again, Dewey sees this as paradigmatically exemplified in the work of art. The self emerges through the tensive struggle between the range of necessary conditions and its impulsive tendency to individualize experience:

> For art is the fusion in one experience of the pressure upon the self of necessary conditions and the spontaneity and novelty of individuality. Individuality itself is originally a potentiality and is realized only in interaction with surrounding conditions. In this process of intercourse, native capacities, which contain an element of uniqueness are transformed and become a self. Moreover, through resistances encountered, the nature of the self is discovered. The self is both formed and brought to consciousness through interaction with environment. . . . From the first manifestation of a child of an impulse to draw up to the creations of a Rembrandt, the self is created in the creation of objects. . . (*AE*, 281-82; *LW* 10:286).

Individuality is the creative incarnation of meaning, of mind, into *an* experience. That is, the "self" marks the realization of a nexus of integrated events which belong together; they are all *of* an organizing process.[76]

Such experience is transfigured through imagination. It is through the imaginative appropriation of the possibilities of the present that the present takes on its ideal significance and can be integrated in a temporal process toward a consummatory closure. "Imagination" is not a faculty for Dewey but the active, reconstructive project itself. It is not only in aesthetic experience that imagination is present; all conscious experience must be imaginative to the degree that the past is used to interpret the present and its bearing toward the future. The roots of experience may lie with the interaction of the living organism with its environment, but "that experience becomes conscious, a matter of perception, only when meanings enter it that are derived from prior experience. Imagination is the only gateway through which these meanings can find their way into a present interaction; or, rather, . . . the conscious adjustment of the new and old *is* imagination" (*AE*, 272; *LW* 10:276). Imagination is not an abstract schematic power much less a faculty of fancy, of imaging. It is an activity which weaves the flux of experience into a meaningful continuity by constantly organizing and reconstructing the situational event so that it develops a horizon and focus which reveal its temporal possibilities for consummatory integration. Imagination grasps experience as *growth of meaning through action*. For this to be realized, however, the possibilities of the situation must be grasped as such, as ideals, and one must act on the faith of their ideal quality, and this involves more than a certain amount of risk. Dewey comments that there is "always a gap between the here and now of direct interaction and the past interactions whose funded result constitutes the meanings with which we grasp and understand what is now occurring. Because of this gap, all conscious perception involves a risk; it is a venture into the unknown, for as it assimilates the present to the past it brings about some reconstructions of that past" (*AE*, 272; *LW* 10:276). It is not just that we are always interpreting experience, but that our interpretations form the conditions for our range of possible actions and hence the range of the possible meanings and values which fund experience. To achieve the presence of meaning in experience, there must be a creative effort to grasp the meaning of the present. And this can only be achieved through imagination.

The importance of this theme for Dewey's philosophy cannot be over-estimated. In *A Common Faith* Dewey calls this imaginative reconstruction of experience "God"—to the dismay and confusion of his supporters as well as his critics. Dewey's own explanation of this is unusually clear, however:

> The idea that "God" represents a unification of ideal values that is essentially imaginative in origin when the imagination supervenes in conduct is attended with verbal difficulties owing to our frequent use of the word "imagination" to denote fantasy and doubtful reality. But the reality of ideal ends as ideals is vouched for by their undeniable power in action. An ideal is not an illusion because imagination is the organ through which it is apprehended. For *all* possibilities reach us through the imagination. In a definite sense the only meaning that can be assigned the term "imagination" is that things unrealized in fact come home to us and have power to stir us. The unifica-

tion effected through imagination is not fanciful, for it is the reflex of the unification of practical and emotional attitudes. The unity signifies not a single Being, but the unity of loyalty and effort evoked by the fact that many ends are one in the power of their ideal, or imaginative, quality to stir and hold us (*CF*, 43; *LW* 9:29-30).

Imagination is nothing other than the ability to grasp the meaning of the present in terms of a possible situation which may be realized *because* its ideal possibility has been grapsed and used to mediate the situation and direct action. This is only possible through an alert sensitivity to the pervasive quality of the situation. If the ideal simply remains ideal, a possibility unrealized, it fails to mediate the situation; it is then incapable of becoming the *meaning* of that situation or of any phase of it. To the extent that the ideal successfully establishes continuity, it marks the realization of *an* experience in which the qualitative character of the situation abides and determines the significance of the parts.

Dewey is somewhat vague about the ontological status of the domain of the possible, but he is firmly committed to interpreting it as grounded in the on-going events and histories of nature. Possibilities exist, in other words, as the possibilites *of* events; in themselves they are incomplete—they are not complete in a Platonic heaven nor is their completion guaranteed by world history as for Hegel. "The aims and ideals that move us," asserts Dewey, "are generated through imagination. But they are not made out of imaginary stuff. They are made out of the hard stuff of the world of physical and social experience. . . . The new vision does not arise out of nothing, but emerges through seeing, in terms of possibilities, that is, of imagination, old things in new relations serving a new end which the new aids in creating" (*CF*, 49; *LW* 9:33-34). "Moreover," Dewey adds, "the process of creation is experimental and continuous." It is only through interaction that possibilities become clarified as well as tested. The ideal itself may come to be modified or rejected on the basis of its ability to conduct and illumine experience. It is to this inherent capacity of experience to promote and generate ideals which transform the meaning of experience by recognizing deeper and broader ends that Dewey ascribes the name "God":

> For there are forces in nature and society that generate and support ideals. They are further unified by the action that gives them coherence and solidity. It is this *active* relation between ideal and actual to which I would give the name 'God.' I would not insist that the name *must* be given. . . . But the facts to which I have referred are there, and they need to be brought out with all possible clearness and

force. There exist concretely and experimentally goods—the values of art in all its forms, of knowledge, of effort and of rest after striving, of friendship and love, of growth in mind and body. . . . A clear and intense conception of a union of ideal ends with actual conditions is capable of arousing steady emotion. It may be fed by experience, no matter what its material (*CF*, 51; *LW* 9:34-35).

Another way of describing such a view is that one approaches experience from the attitude of the artist; life and the world itself can be creatively appropriated as material for consummatory meaning and value, but only by paying infinite care and attention to its qualities and by educating one's own powers of action and perception. Such an attitude obviously involves taking risks—for this is what it is to be genuinely moved by the power of an ideal—but it does not imply taking blind risks or dispensing with intelligent conduct, quite the contrary. If faith ultimately directs intelligence, then faith is only justified through intelligence. By "faith" Dewey means "the unification of the self through allegiance to inclusive ideal ends, which imagination presents to us and to which human will responds as worthy of controlling our desires and choices" (*CF*, 33; *LW* 10:23). Faith is the capacity to guide one's conduct in light of an inclusive ideal of human experience to be meaningful and funded with value. This ideal cannot be genuinely possessed in the abstract because there ultimately is no human existence in the abstract. The imaginative appropriation of the world—which is also the imaginative appropriation of the self—demands a progressive (and critical) articulation of the ideal. The only way this can be achieved is through action governed by an active awareness of the creative possibilities of experience. Such possibilities come to light only through exploratory action guided by critical intelligence. They are hunted out rather than received from above.

Philosophy for Dewey was just such an enterprise. The most "far-reaching question" with which philosophy is concerned is "the relationship between existence and value, or . . . the real and the ideal" (*EN*, 415; *LW* 1:310). Most philosophies have tried to force one term to be governed by the interpretation given to the other. For Dewey, however, philosophy must see the real and the ideal, the actual and the possible, as ever hung in a problematic tension, perpetually posing the question of the meaning of human existence. That such a problematic refuses to go away may lead some philosophers, like Rorty, to abandon the enterprise altogether. Philosophy then becomes concerned with aesthetics and criticism in a purely formal, negative sense, the pastime of academic intellectual czars and their faddists.[78]

It is in quite the contrary sense that Dewey states, "To esthetic experience, then, the philosopher must go to understand what experience is" (*AE*, 274; *LW* 10:278). In aesthetic experience one finds this genuine concern with the tensive problematic of experience to incorporate or exclude its ideal possibilities for meaning and value. Aesthetic experience as revealed through the fine arts uncovers this aesthetic nexus of experience as a whole:

> In art as an experience, actuality and possibility or ideality, the new and the old, objective material and personal response, the individual and the universal, surface and depth, sense and meaning, are integrated in an experience in which they are all transfigured from the significance that belongs to them when isolated in reflection. "Nature," said Goethe, "has neither kernel nor shell." Only in esthetic experience is this statement completely true. Of art as experience it is also true that nature has neither subjective nor objective being; is neither individual nor universal, sensuous nor rational. The significance of art as experience is, therefore, incomparable for the adventure of philosophic thought (*AE*, 297; *LW* 10:301).

Art as experience, in short, reveals the birth of meaning in the creative task of experience itself.

The social dimension cannot be forgotten. The exploration of the expressive significance of experience requires involvement in a social or cultural project. Art reveals the expressive capacity of experience, says Dewey, and because "the objects of art are expressive, they communicate. I do not say that communication to others is the intent of an artist. But it is the consequence of his work—which indeed lives only in communication when it operates in the experience of others" (*AE*, 104; *LW* 10:110). Dewey makes an even more extreme claim: "In the end, works of art are the only media of complete and unhindered communication between man and man that can occur in a world full of gulfs and walls that limit community of experience" (*AE*, 105; *LW* 10:110). This is a point repeated throughout Dewey's work: that communication, the basis of all social life, is most fully realized in art which reveals the latent ideality of experience in a concrete manner. Such experience allows for genuine participation in those inclusive ideals of life which provide the horizons of meaning and value in a direct and immediate transaction. The community comes to be in expressive activity; the world comes to mean through our shared encounter with nature and with each other.

> Every art communicates because it expresses. It enables us to share vividly and deeply in meanings to which we had been dumb, or for which we had but the ear that permits what is said to pass through in

transit to overt action. . . . Communication is the process of creating participation, of making common what had been isolated and singular; and part of the miracle it achieves is that, in being communicated, the conveyance of meaning gives body and definiteness to the experience of the one who utters as well as to that of those who listen. Men associate in many ways. But the only form of association that is truly human, and not a gregarious gathering for warmth and protection, . . . is the participation in meanings and goods that is effected by communication. The expressions that constitute art are communication in its pure and undefiled form. Art breaks through barriers that divide human beings, which are impermeable in ordinary association. (*AE*, 244; *LW* 10:248-49).

I do not think that Dewey is making the dubious claim here that we can grasp the meanings of works of art swiftly and surely or that fine art is the solution to alienation. Instead, Dewey is pointing to the capacity of human beings to be meaningfully present *to* each other and not merely alongside or proximate to each other, through participating in activity governed by the light of shared ends. Such activity *is* art and all fine art springs from this possibility. Such shared ends and goals allow for the very possibility of significant interaction or communication. One can come to interpret one's own activity from the standpoint of the whole shared activity; it is only such a perspective which gives rise to the idea of having "one's *own* activity" at all. There are progressively more general and inclusive ends from which one can determine what "one's own activity" is. There are richer and narrower conceptions of the meaning of human life. If one cannot grasp the larger or more inclusive ideals concretely in the present situation, they cannot operate as controlling and guiding ends-in-view. Such ideals can become immanently felt in experience only to the extent that they are capable of locating the immediate present in a pervasive qualitative horizon which controls and guides the present. In this manner they provide the moment with a temporal orientation and aim beyond immediate organic responses. They constitute the possibility of experienced continuity; the present can become part of a significant narrative project or it can desert that project, becoming a deviation rather than a development. When experience becomes genuinely expressive it becomes mediated by activity artistically executed. A wealth of possibilites have been successfully brought to light and integrated into *an* experience. Because such activity is supremely creative, it encounters risks, possibilities for failure, for disintegration. It is a genuine confrontation with the problematic dimension of experience because it is also a genuine confrontation with the ideal possibility of experience. The task of achieving expression is the task of realizing the community continuously; the community found-ed on creative experience must be made and remade *because* it faces the perpetual creative possibilities and the precariousness of the world. Dewey called the community which succeeded in understand-ing itself in this manner "democracy."

VI. Conclusion

I have tried to show in this chapter that Dewey was serious when he said that any philosophy of experience is consummated in its aesthetics—and there is no philosophy which ultimately is not a phi-losophy of experience, however it may ignore or abuse its origins. *Art as Experience* is not only the place where Dewey attempted to relocate works of fine art back in their social contexts, but it is to that work one must go to gain a complete understanding of what Dewey himself meant by "experience"—and thereby also what he meant by "nature," "method," "meaning," and "community." Contrary to those who see the work as an arbitrary or sentimental deviation of Dewey's old age from the robust instrumentalism and naturalism of his middle years, I maintain that it is here that we find the fruition of his lifelong quest for a comprehensive theory of experience. By refusing to understand the aesthetic as a form of cognitive experience, Dewey incorporates the richest and most fulfilling moments of human existence without sacri-ficing them atop the temples of our fear-born need for certainty. Dewey's analysis of aesthetic experience also provides the underlying explanatory context for understanding those parts of experience which *are* concerned with inquiry. The situational theory of expe-rience sees the cognitive as ever operating within the determining context of the non-cognitive. In most experience we are simply not aware of such a horizonal dimension to our immediate concerns and projects. Dewey regards such experience as potentially leading to a dualistic philosophy. If one commences philosophizing about the world by ignoring the temporal and horizonal nature of experience, the result will be any one of innumerable dualistic renditions: one may select as the paradigmatic moment of experience that of sudden arousal and alarm. Experience becomes interpreted as a disorganized, overwhelming bundle of impressions in desperate need of order by laws of association or powers of synthesis. Or one may select the moment when one resolves a problem and the latent rationality of the event becomes manifest. One can reside with the moment when one encounters a hard, fixed habit which meets the needs of a situation as a key fits a lock. The temptation here will be to become a realist of one sort or another. One can focus on the moments when the assured fixed habit crumbles away in the face of an overwhelming, pressing problem. If this sort of experience is taken as paradigmatic, one is inclined toward subjectivism of voluntarism. If one attempts to frame a theory of experience where these episodes still carry their weight of truth without forcing the others to conform to their structures, one must develop a functionalistic view of how they operate. But such a view only becomes possible when there is some sort of end-state around which these functions are integrated.

The end-state is the capacity of experience to be transformed so as to be wholly integrated, to be *an* experience. Such experience includes emotion, expression, form, quality, and communication. It also marks the moment when nature becomes culture, that is, nature's potentiality for embodying meaning and value have been consummatorily fulfilled through action. Such moments have high moral significance for Dewey because they indicate that nature contains these possibilities, if not as self-complete, autonomous entities, then at the very least as ideals which may be striven for by the arts of intelligence. Instead of "the world well lost" as a philosophical problem, aesthetic experience reminds philosophy of the world that is in need of reconstruction and care. This does not escape the inherent problematic structure of the world; indeed, it recalls this structure vividly, but not as a dualistic schema. A genuine recollection of the problematic is also a reminder to ourselves, of how we are in the world together, and how action is called for. If the tasks of experience are hard, it is easy to understand why many have chosen to symbolize human impotence and frustration in the false securities of fixed categories, eternal essences, logical universes, sense data, and so on. The power of experience to "boil over" (as James put it) such limits may incline others simply to see the world as nothing but boiling over and conceive the project of philosophy as nothing more than deconstructive cookery of its own past recipes. Set over against this, Dewey, however, would point to the presence of the aesthetic, the outcome of art, which genuinely retrieves the world through culture by exploiting its dynamism, its precariousness, its novelty, as well as its order, stability, and recurrence.

Such a recollection not only provides a recognition of the integrity of experience, but it establishes the possiblity for community. In seeking to express, we find the other; community is born of dialogue and of shared, participatory endeavor. We come to realize that we inhabit the world only with and through each other, and this is how it comes to mean and have value. Through the culture of nature the community appropriates itself as art.

Conclusion: Creativity, Criticism, and Community

Human beings inhabit a world. That is, we participate in shared universes of meaning and value which have been realized through human activity. This transformation of the powers of nature into expressive media giving shape and significance to human life is ultimately what Dewey means by "art." Art, in other words, is nothing else than the quest for concretely embodied meaning and value in human existence. The theme of art is life appropriated for its creative and expressive possibilities. The fine arts are but special instances of this fundamental human activity—special because they are highly successful. If the moral taught by the fine arts were applied to the entire range of our social and personal existence, the result would truly be "the light that never was on sea or land" to which Dewey frequently refers.[1] The art of life is the goal behind Dewey's ethics, his philosophy of democracy, and his theory of education. To treat life artistically is to exercise both imagination and reflection toward the exploration of the possibilities of the present.

The material out of which human life is built is "experience," understood in its Deweyan sense as that vast concurrence of natural events and cultural meanings in all their obscurity and power as well as in their focal clarity and luminosity. The tremendous task to be undertaken is to grasp the present—not as an immediate, isolated bare occurrence, as an indefinitely fleeting "now," but as the dynamically insistent occasion for establishing continuity or growth of meaning. Present experience stands for that whole complexity which establishes the human project as such. The "problematic situation" behind all problematic situations is just this ultimate task of creatively appropriating the ideal possibilities of the present which will illuminate action so that experience will consummately fulfill and enrich human existence. This is the problematic which calls forth reflective thinking, not just for now and again, but continuously. We are ever confronted with the question of the meaning of the present, to improve upon the nick of time as Thoreau said.

Experience is the on-going world of nature culturally inhabited. It is not therefore primarily either subjective or unshaped, a manifold of blooming, buzzing precepts. It is shaped and shaping, primarily cultural and therefore interactive. In the dynamic process of life, there is no pure moment when the slate is clean, ready for "experience" to begin like the hovering spirit of God above the waters of the deep. Life comes from life and is born to the world. Awaiting each new life there is a social world with its language, beliefs, rites, roles, legends, and histories. The physical environment is there too, with its rhythms of heartbeat and breath, the close darkness of night and the shining brilliance of day, its seasons of dust and drought, monsoon, snow, or spring. The world is not so much "interpreted" as it is inherited. Cultures are not to be understood as schematic systems of oppositions but as shared significant responses to the world.

Cultures are universes of activity through which members come to be present to each other and so present to themselves. Indeed, one could define a culture as that organized body of activities by which human beings are meaningfully present to each other. In this sense, cultures are fields of communication which realize shared, participatory ends. As Dewey points out in *Democracy and Education:*

> Society not only continues to exist by transmission, by communication, but it may fairly be said to exist in transmission, in communication. There is more than a verbal tie between the words common, community, and communication. Men live in a community in virtue of the things which they have in common; and communication is the way in which they come to possess things in common. What they must have in common in order to form a community or society are aims, beliefs, aspirations, knowledge—a common understanding—like-mindedness as the sociologists say. . . . The communication which insures participation in a common understanding is one which secures similar emotional and intellectual dispositions—like ways of responding to expectations and requirements (*DE*, 4; *MW* 9:7).

More is required for there to be a community than either mere physical proximity or working together toward a common end. Without the existence of a means of communication, two human beings can hardly be said to be significantly present to each other. Likewise, the parts of a machine work toward a common end, but do not constitute a community. If there were an activity in which all members were "cognizant of the common end and all interested in it so that they regulated their specific activity in view of it, then they would form a community. But this would involve communication. Each would have to know what the other was about and would have to have some way of keeping the other informed as to his own purpose and progress. Consensus demands communication" (DE, 5; MW 9:9).

To participate in a culture, then, is in some way to be able to envision imaginatively, that is emotionally as well as conceptually, the ideals which integrate and determine the fundamentals of the "way of life" of a people. How are such imaginative visions communicated themselves? The first and obvious answer is education. "Not only is social life identical with communication," says Dewey, "but all communication (and hence all genuine social life) is educative." Dewey could be accused of arguing in circles here—that education demands communication, which demands education—were it not for what he adds:

> To be a recipient of communication is to have an enlarged and changed experience. One shares in what another has felt and in so far, meagerly or amply, has his own attitude modified. Nor is the one who communicates left unaffected. . . . Except in dealing with commonplaces and catch phrases one has to assimilate, imaginatively, something of another's experience in order to tell him intelligently of one's own experience. All communication is like art. . . . In final account, then, not only does social life demand teaching and learning for its own permanence, but the very process of living together educates. It enlarges and enlightens experience; it stimulates and enriches the imagination; it creates responsibility for accuracy and vividness of statement and thought (DE, 5-6; MW 9: 8-9).

Art is this very process of imaginatively enlarging experience, thereby establishing communication through education. Culture is transmitted in its stories and ceremonies, its images and dramas, which form the prereflective tapestry of a people. From infancy on, these meanings and values gradually expand and take on further significance. They do not lie statically in the mind, but dynamically organize experience so that it gains in meaning and depth. To understand the political history of a nation one might well begin by examining the stories told to its children.

The primary factor in education is the culture itself, and this is by and large not a self-conscious or self-critical medium. As Dewey points out, "What conscious, deliberate teaching can do is at most to free the capacities thus formed for fuller exercise, to purge them of some of their grossness, and to furnish objects which make their activity more productive of meaning" (*DE*, 17; *MW* 9: 21). The unconscious influence of the environment, he adds, "is so subtle and pervasive that it affects every fiber of character and mind." Among the most potent factors in this tacit cultural environment are, according to Dewey, language, manners, aesthetic standards, and standards of values in general. This last, says Dewey, is less a separate issue than a fusion of the previous three. "We rarely recognize the extent in which our conscious estimates of what is worthwhile and what is not are due to standards of which we are not conscious at all," he concludes, "But in general it may be said that the things we take for granted without inquiry or reflection are just the things which determine our conscious thinking and decide our conclusions. And these habitudes which lie below the level of reflection are just those which have been formed in the constant give and take of our relationships with others" (*DE*, 18; *MW* 9: 22).

That culture is something within which we live, move, and have our very being is both liberating and binding, for as it establishes the very possibility of a shared life of meaning and value it also determines the range of values and options easily and manifestly available, obscuring alternatives. One cannot escape culture—as Dewey was fond of pointing out, no one was made free by being left utterly alone. The key is to develop a culture that is consciously aware of itself as a shaping and shapeable power. This is to say that culture must recognize itself as a creative project in which the need for critical self-reflection, reevaluation, and exploration of the possibilities of life are of utmost importance. Such a culture must see itself problematically rather than ideologically, and yet it will be consciously dedicated to the ultimate end of enriching life with its full aesthetic potential for meaning and value.

Democracy for Dewey is not a name for a special political institution so much as one for such a creative-critical culture. Political freedom is more the result of a free culture than the other way, Dewey insists. Only a democratic culture can be the safeguard of democratic government. In *Freedom and Culture*, Dewey says:

> The problem is to know what kind of culture is so free in itself that it conceives and begets political freedom as its accompaniment and consequence. . . . The problem of freedom and of democratic institutions is tied up with what kind of culture exists. . . . The struggle for democracy has to be maintained on as many fronts as culture has aspects: political, economic, international, educational, scientific and artistic, religious" (*FC*, 6, 13, 173).

In *The Public and Its Problems*, Dewey insists that "The idea of democracy is a wider and fuller idea than can be exemplified in the state, even at its best. To be realized it must affect all modes of human association. . . . Regarded as an idea, democracy is not an alternative to other principles of associated life. It is the idea of community life itself" (*PP*, 143, 148; *LW* 2: 325, 328). It is, in short, the community which realizes itself or comes into being through the very ideal of fulfilled human existence. To be sure, this ideal will always remain an ideal, says Dewey, and so "democracy in this sense is not a fact and never will be" (*PP*, 148; *LW* 2: 328). Nevertheless, ideals are the integrating factors of a community, and a democratic community is one which defines itself in terms of the democratic ideal.

The democratic community, through its very ideal of itself, must see itself as perpetually problematic. The "state" will be the particular organized and formally instrumental factor in realizing the community, but as history and circumstances change, as problems and new needs arise, the state will change. Hence it is that Dewey says, "By its very nature, a state is ever something to be scrutinized, investigated, searched for. Almost as soon as its form is stabilized, it needs to be remade" (*PP*, 31-32; *LW* 2: 255). The democratic community takes itself experimentally and therefore artistically and intelligently. It realizes that it is ever in danger of losing itself, of becoming hidden from the possibilities of the present or from its own inherently unfinished and problematic nature.

The vital question, then, is how the democratic community can keep itself ideally present to itself. Art, says Dewey, not only realizes the community in its fullest sense, as communication, but embodies in itself the very quest of the democratic community: the creative exploration of the fulfilling meanings and values of experience. In other words, through art, the democratic community discovers that task and the possibility of genuine communication:

> We have but touched lightly and in passing upon the conditions which must be fulfilled if the Great Society is to become a Great Community; a society in which the ever-expanding and intricately ramifying consequences of associated activities shall be known in the full sense of the word, so that an organized, articulate Public comes into being. The highest and most difficult kind of inquiry and a subtle, delicate, vivid and responsive art of communication must take possession of the physical machinery of transmission and circulation and breathe life into it. When the machine age has thus perfected its machinery it will be a means of life and not a despotic master. Democracy will come into its own, for democracy is a name for a life of free and enriching communion. It had its seer in Walt

Whitman. It will have its consummation when free social inquiry is
indissolubly wedded to the art of free and moving communication
(*PP,* 184; *LW* 2: 350).

The connection between the ideal of aesthetic communication in
Art as Experience and that expressed here is manifest. Although the
tone of rhapsodic intensity in such passages may lead one to conclude
that Dewey is indulging in utopian romanticism, the ideal of communication accomplished on the highest artistic levels is both a rigorously demanding and sobering project. Genuine communication is only
achieved through a creative transformation of experience which involves the combination of a rich cultural matrix, the critical use of
intelligence, and the active struggle to establish continuity or growth.
In other words, the full potential of experience to fund human life
with meaning and value is an ideal always at peril because it is the
highest ideal possible. It is much easier to frame a theory of society on
inherent, absolute moral rules or a theory of meaning on a formal
logical or syntactic structure. Both of these satisfy "the quest for certainty," the need for the sense of intellectual safety, which involves an
abandonment or even the repression of the perennial presence of the
problematic, the indeterminate, the aleatory, and the unknown.

To acknowledge these factors, then, is not to condone either a
utopian optimism or a romantic voluntarism. Such attitudes are at
best naive and at worst hubristic. The commitment to the aesthetic
possibilities of experience necessarily requires the active presence of
an alert, critical intelligence. If experience is to be most fully significant in its truly creative moments, these cannot be left to faith or raw
will for realization. A critical sense is needed in the first place for the
need of the creative act to be recognized. In ancient times, the act of
the artist was not to create new forms but to repeat and perpetuate
tradition. This was seen as having the magical property of renewing
the vitality of the culture. As with ancient Egypt, the aesthetic forms
of a culture could last for thousands of years—indeed, the culture
became the perpetuation of its traditions. But after its first flowering
in Old Kingdom art, Egyptian art only demonstrates its otherwise
suppressed power of expression when there has been a serious threat
to the culture itself. It is after the disruptive anarchy that the moving
Middle Kingdom portraits of the weary pharaohs are made; it is after
the expulsion of the foreign Hyksos that New Kingdom art blossoms
forth, culminating in the lyrical freedom of the Armarna period.

Criticism is not necessarily present in a new self-conscious fashion during vital or dynamic moments in a culture's life, but it is
implicit in all creative activity. Not only is it directed toward the
possibilities of the expressive potential of a medium or material, but it

stands in critical relation to tradition and the present. A critical or creative act can only seek to reintegrate a culture by also distancing itself from the authority and presence of what has been already accomplished. This paradoxical relation to tradition is more explicit in self-conscious critical activity. Edward Said has pointed out that criticism must always be grounded upon some cultural context, but that it also sets itself over against the mere acceptance of the dominant values and beliefs by which a culture identifies itself. It is neither strictly inside or outside culture but "close to" it:

> Criticism in short is always situated; it is skeptical, secular, reflectively open to its own failings. This is by no means to say that it is value-free. Quite the contrary, for the inevitable trajectory of critical consciousness is to arrive at some acute sense of what political, social, and human values are entailed in the reading, production, and transmission of every text. To stand between culture and system is therefore to stand *close to* . . . a concrete reality about which political, moral, and social judgments have to be made and, if not only made, then exposed and demystified. If . . . every act of interpretation is made possible and given force by an interpretive community, then we must go a great deal further in showing what situation, what historical and social configuration, what political interests are concretely entailed by the very existence of interpretive communities. This is an especially important task when these communities have evolved camouflaging jargons.[2]

It is an illusion of critical methodology, Said is saying, to believe that an ahistorical, pure, value-free, "unworldly" method is even possible for criticism. Not only the work of art but the act of reception, interpretation, and perpetuation of works are worldly, historical acts. Said thereby is calling into question all formal theories of criticism (such as "New Criticism" or structuralism) as well as "pure" anti-methodological strategies such as deconstruction. The problem of criticism, in other words, is to be critical of itself as well as of its subject-matter. The advantage of criticism is that by its very nature it opens itself to such self-reflective questioning. It contains the inherent ambiguity of human existence as an intrinsic element of its own practice. Another way of putting it is to say that when criticism takes itself in a purely "aesthetic" mode—"aesthetic" understood in its non-Deweyan sense here—it disconnects itself from the very source of art and of intelligence itself, the lifeworld, which is a scene of struggle, ambiguity, history, conflict, and creativity.

In many respects I think this approach is quite sympathetic to Dewey's own broad understanding of criticism, which he identifies with philosophy itself. But it applies also to the specialized tasks of aesthetic criticism. The task of critical intelligence is to explore and develop experience, not to terminate it. Criticism confronts the problematic relationship of man and the world and of man and history in undertaking the understanding of culture. It can then become the continuation of the project called forth by the creative act or object. Every work of art stands in a tensive, ambiguous relation with its substance, whether it has achieved a revelation of the substance and communicated care for it. Criticism, in its concern with the working of the work, is also sensitive to this tensive dimension; it must seek to establish the relation of the work and the world. That is to say, it must pursue the question of the creative continuity of the work. Criticism can be and is legitimately concerned with questions of form. But it is equally concerned with questions of content, of historical interpretation, of interpretation itself, and with the relation of the work in all its dimensions to the world. From a Deweyan perspective, then, criticism is a pluralistic enterprise having a number of tasks. Instead of seeking to provide fixed, pure methodologies, it can understand itself as genuinely experimental and hermeneutic. The final task of criticism is none other than the quest for community, for the elucidation of those values and ideals which create and bind a public together through a recognition of its fate and history as well as its inherent choices and possibilities. It is not so much that criticism is a function of "communities of interpreters" as it is the quest for community in which interpretation becomes a meaningful activity.

The ultimate task of human existence is the cultivation, the civilization of our natural capacities toward the fulfillment of life. This means to exist actively in a world of meaning and value. If we understand meaning and value as fundamentally divorced from nature, purely autonomous, fixed, and formal, the tensive ambiguities of life will be rendered opaque. When Dewey finally termed his philosophy "Cultural Naturalism," he was not speaking lightly: the cultivation of natural potentials has been the history of man. It has not, however, been generally recognized and so not approached either self-consciously or methodically, that is, experimentally. The quintessence of the scientific attitude for Dewey was not to be found in its results nor in its tendencies toward reductionistic thinking. Rather it was to be found in the cooperative spirit of exploration, creative speculation connected with practical action, which would thereby provide some basis for the further evaluation and understanding of the world. Science becomes most truly intelligent when it exhibits its creative and artistic side rather than its formalistic or materialistic side. The "experimental spirit" which Dewey often appeals to is the spirit of tentative exploration rather than technological manipulation.

The Greek theory of "science" as *theoria*, intellectual vision, still dominates the modern interpretation of science, even though its activity has changed from speculative to practical or experimental activity. In art however, we value the artist over the aesthetic spectator. The implications of this shift should be carried through:

> It would then be seen that science is an art, that art is practice, and that the only distinction worth drawing is not between practice and theory, but between those modes of practice that are not intelligent, not inherently and immediately enjoyable, and those which are full of enjoyed meanings. When this perception dawns, it will be a commonplace that art—the mode of activity that is charged with meanings capable of immediately enjoyed possession—is the complete culmination of nature, and that "science" is properly a handmaiden that conducts events to this happy issue. Thus would disappear the separations that trouble present thinking: division of everything into nature *and* experience, of experience into practice *and* theory, art *and* science, of art into useful *and* fine, menial *and* free (EN, 358; LW 1:268-69).

It has been a strange irony that so much interpretation of Dewey's own philosophy has been approached from just such prejudices. This has largely been due, I think, from the neglect of the centrality of Dewey's aesthetics in his general theory of experience. Nothing in Dewey's philosophy makes sense without understanding his philosophy of experience, and it is impossible to comprehend this without coming to full terms with the aesthetic dimension of experience. This is no external or superfluous part, but rather the innermost living heart of everything Dewey had to say. It has been the purpose of this study to attempt a steady and systematic interpretation of Dewey's philosophy from this standpoint. If it has been at all successful, we may have a legitimate basis for regarding Dewey, along with Wittgenstein and Heidegger, as one of the truly monumental thinkers of the century, not because of his negative "deconstruction" of "the tradition," but because of his courageous promise of a creative and yet critical vision of human life.

Notes

INTRODUCTION

1. Richard Rorty, *Philosophy and the Mirror of Nature* (Princeton, New Jersey: Princeton University Press, 1979), p. 368.

2. James Gouinlock, *John Dewey's Philosophy of Value* (New York: Humanities Press, 1972), Victor Kestenbaum, *The Phenomenological Sense of John Dewey* (Atlantic Highlands, New Jersey: Humanities Press, 1977), R.W. Sleeper, *The Necessity of Pragmatism* (New Haven: Yale University Press, 1986), Raymond Boisvert, *Dewey's Metaphysics* (Fordham, forthcoming). This last book was made available to me in manuscript form.

3. The term "idealism," which is used extensively in the first two chapters of this book, is obviously a name for a group of family resemblances rather than a precisely defined concept. The same holds true of "naturalism." By "idealism," I mean primarily any philosophical position which interprets reality ultimately in terms of the category of "self," or, more precisely, through a "self-activity" of perceiving or knowing. "Naturalism" is taken to mean any philosophy which attempts to connect the phenomena of human existence to the larger processes of the universe. It should be noted that this definition of naturalism is not committed to the more limited forms which argue that all human phenomena must be *reduced* to physical or biological events or that science constitutes the essential form of human experience. Under those criteria, Dewey could not be classified as a naturalist.

4. See Rorty's article, "Dewey's Metaphysics," in *New Studies in the Philosophy of John Dewey,* edited by Stephen Cahn, reprinted in *Consequences of Pragmatism.* The critical debate is discussed below in Chapter 3.

5. Ralph Sleeper makes an excellent point here: "If we are to see how Dewey's work hangs together, we must recognize that Dewey is not attempting to work out a theory of knowledge on the Kantian paradigm of the

279

metaphysics of experience. It would be better to say that Dewey's metaphysics is not a metaphysics of experience at all than to risk assuming that it is just another species of the kind of metaphysics embodied in Kant's *Critique of Pure Reason*" (*The Necessity of Pragmatism*, pp. 6-7).

6. William James, *Essays in Radical Empiricism*, edited by Frederick Burkhardt and Fredson Bowers (Cambridge, Massachusetts: Harvard University Press, 1976), p. 86, fn. 8.

CHAPTER I

1. Monroe Beardsley, *Aesthetics from Classical Greece to the Present* (New York: Macmillan, 1966), p. 332.

2. Stephen Pepper, "Some Questions on Dewey's Esthetics," in *The Philosophy of John Dewey*, ed. Paul Arthur Schilpp (Chicago: Northwestern University Press, 1939), p. 389.

3. See Benedetto Croce, "On the Aesthetics of Dewey," *JAAC* VI (1948) and "Dewey's Aesthetics and Theory of Knowledge," *JAAC* XI (1952); Patrick Romanell, "A Comment on Dewey's and Croce's Aesthetics," *JAAC* IX (1950); Charles Edward Gauss, "Some Reflections on Dewey's Aesthetics," *JAAC* XIX (1960), and George H. Douglas, "A Reconsideration of the Dewey-Croce Exchange," *JAAC* XXVIII (1970).

4. See *Experience and Nature*, pp. xvi, 392-93, (*LW* 1: 8, 293-94), and Chapter IX, and *Art as Experience*, pp. 25, 274, 297, 326 and 336 (*LW* 10: 31, 278, 301, 329, 339). Dewey's essay "Philosophy and Civilization" in the book of the same title should also be consulted.

5. Pepper, op cit., p. 371.

6. Ibid. p. 372.

7. Croce, "On the Aesthetics of Dewey," p. 203.

8. Ibid.

9. Croce, "Dewey's Aesthetics and Theory of Knowledge," p. 2.

10. Croce, "On the Aesthetics of Dewey," p. 204.

11. See Stephen Pepper, "The Concept of Fusion in Dewey's Aesthetic Theory," *JAAC* XII (1953). As I discuss in Chapter 5, Pepper confused the phase of "seizure," which initiates "an experience," with the fusion of funded meanings which creates consummatory closure. See *Art as Experience*, p. 145 (*LW* 10: 150), for Dewey's remark that it is undesirable to prolong the phase of seizure.

12. See Pepper, "The Concept of Fusion in Dewey's Aesthetic Theory," pp. 171-72, and Croce, "On the Aesthetics of Dewey," p. 205. For an account of the eighteenth century view, especially Baumgarten's, see Ernst Cassirer's

The Philosophy of the Enlightenment, Chapter VI; ss. vii and Croce's *Aesthetic,* Book II: Chapter iv.

13. *AE,* 130; *LW* 10:135, cited in Pepper, "Some Questions on Dewey's Esthetics," p. 371.

14. Ibid. pp. 382-83.

15. Ibid., p. 386. Perhaps Pepper's confusion arose from the fact he regarded "coherence" and "organic unity" as *cognitive* terms (as they were for the idealists), whereas for Dewey they were "felt" or "had."

16. John Dewey, "Experience, Knowledge, and Value: A Rejoinder," in *The Philosophy of John Dewey,* p. 546.

17. Croce, "On the Aesthetics of Dewey," pp. 203-04.

18. Ibid. p. 206.

19. Ibid.

20. John Dewey, "A Comment on the Foregoing Criticisms," *JAAC* VI (1948), pp. 207-08.

21. Ibid., p. 209.

22. See Pepper's "Autobiography of an Aesthetics," *JAAC* XXVIII (1970), p. 277 and footnote 3. Pepper's approach is not quite as stiff and schematic as I have represented it, perhaps. The philosophy of "root metaphors" was, after all, the basis for a pluralistic and tolerant attitude. For a sympathetic evaluation of Pepper's ideas see Douglas N. Morgan's review of *Concept and Quality,* *JAAC* XXVIII (1969), pp. 243-46. Even so, Pepper's approach seems too limited to me. In *The Basis of Criticism in the Arts* he focuses on certain philosophers' works as "the" paradigmatic instances of the four root metaphors in aesthetics: Santayana's *The Sense of Beauty* for mechanism, Bosanquet's *Three Lectures on Aesthetic* for organicism, Ruskin for formism (though he includes everyone from Plato to Aristotle to Taine here), and Irwin Edman's *Arts and the Man,* as well as his own *Aesthetic Quality* for contextualism. However distinct and consistent these works may be, I don't believe other works should be measured in terms of them.

23. Croce to the editors of *JAAC,* Sept. 23, 1952 in *JAAC* IX (1953).

24. Croce, "Dewey's Aesthetics and Theory of Knowledge," pp. 4-5. See footnote 21 in Chapter 4 below.

25. George H. Douglas, "A Reconsideration of the Dewey-Croce Exchange," pp. 498-99. This is an odd remark, because Dewey never criticized Croce for being Hegelian, but for his idealist metaphysics in general. Likewise, it is plain in *Art as Experience* that Dewey had read Croce's *Aesthetic,* was familiar with the general nature of his theory, and consciously took it into account. While Dewey ought to have been more sensitive both to the similari-

ties between his and Croce's positions and to the seminal nature of Croce's *Aesthetic*, many of these similarities can be traced to Dewey's early period, twenty years prior to the publication of *Aesthetic*, as will be indicated in the next chapter. For Santayana's evaluation of Croce, see his essay, "What is Aesthetics?" reprinted in *Obiter Scripta*, Justus Buchler and Benjamin Schwartz ed. (New York: Charles Scribner's Sons, 1936), pp. 30-40.

26. Ibid., pp. 503-04.

27. Benedetto Croce, "What is Art?" in *Guide to Aesthetics*, Patrick Romanell tr. (Indianapolis: Bobbs-Merrill, 1965), p. 9.

28. See *Art as Experience*, Chapters IX and X, especially pp. 195-202 (*LW* 10:199-205).

29. Douglas, "A Reconsideration of the Dewey-Croce Exchange," p. 501.

30. Benedetto Croce, *Aesthetic*, Douglas Ainslie tr. (New York: The Noonday Press, 1953), revised edition, pp. 50-51.

31. Croce, "On the Aesthetics of Dewey," p. 205.

32. See Croce's *Aesthetic*, I:i.

33. See *Aesthetic*, I:iii, p. 31.

34. Ibid.

35. Croce, "On the Aesthetics of Dewey," p. 203.

36. See *Art as Experience*, Chapter XIII, especially pp. 288-90.

37. Croce, *Aesthetic*, I:i, translated by Douglas Ainslie (New York: Noonday, 1955), p. 4.

CHAPTER 2

1. The essay also appears in Bernstein's *On Experience, Nature and Freedom*, and in McDermott's *The Philosophy of John Dewey*.

2. See also Dewey's biography in *The Philosophy of John Dewey*, written by Dewey's daughters in collaboration with their father, Neil Coughlan's highly entertaining, *Young John Dewey* (Chicago: University of Chicago Press, 1970), the less successful but more complete biography by George Dykhuizen, *The Life and Mind of John Dewey* (Carbondale: Southern Illinois University Press: 1973), and Morton White's *The Origin of Dewey's Instrumentalism* (New York: Columbia University Press, 1943; reprinted by Octagon Books, 1977). For Dewey's relation to George Sylvester Morris, see his early tribute, "The Late Professor Morris" (*EW* 3:3-13), and his later introduction to R. M. Wenley's *The Life and Work of George Sylvester Morris* (1917), "George Sylvester Morris: An Estimate" (*MW* 10: 109-15). See also his review of this book (*MW* 9: 336-37). The influence of Morris's *personality* rather than his ideas cannot be underestimated in Dewey's case.

3. Recorded in *Dialogue on John Dewey*, ed. Corliss Lamont (New York: Horizon Press, Inc., 1959), pp. 15-16. Like Dilthey, Dewey always maintained an interest in romanticism, however critical he may have been of its general ideas. The poets Dewey quotes most are Keats and Wordsworth. Of note also should be Dewey's remark, already quoted, that Plato was his favorite philosophical reading even in his seventies. Too often is pragmatism understood as fostering a spirit inimical to that sponsored by the Romantics. Clearly in Dewey's case we see a stern attempt to *transform* many of the ideals of romanticism into practicable and realizable goals. The romantic dimension of Dewey's thought cannot be safely ignored.

4. See "Absolutism to Experimentalism," but especially Coughlan's discussion of Morris in *Young John Dewey* and Boisvert's *Dewey's Metaphysics*, Part I, sec. 2.2.

5. Dewey here is clearly in sympathy with Aristotle, rather than Hegel, in maintaining that logic or science cannot deduce the individual from the universal. Unlike Aristotle, and like Hegel, however, Dewey is claiming that the *individual* (in this case, the Absolute Individual) is the object of knowledge. See note 49 below for a discussion of the problem of Hegel's transition from the Logic to the Philosophy of Nature.

6. See especially Dewey's remarks in Chapter X of *Experience and Nature* where philosophy is defined as the "criticism of criticisms" and his essay "Philosophy and Civilization."

7. This remark anticipates James' discussion of "The Psychologist's Fallacy" in *The Principles of Psychology*, Vol. 1, pp. 196-97, though Dewey may have encountered this criticism in James' 1884 article, "Some Omissions of Introspective Psychology." The claim that distinctions which arise from analysis should not be read *back* into the prior state as constituting its pre-existing "elements" recurs in Dewey's writings constantly. He does not address, unfortunately, the paradox that, on this theory, *nothing* can ever be said to be constituted out of elements. This is not to say that such a statement is impossible in Dewey's philosophy. With his reintroduction of the idea of potentiality, one may, as Aristotle did, speak of elements existing prior and posterior to their participation in an organized whole *potentially*. A molecule existing in an organic system is not the same as existing outside it, though, for scientific purposes, it may be identified with a molecule isolated under laboratory procedures.

8. See the "Checklist of References" in the edition of the *Psychology* constituting Volume 2 of *The Early Works of John Dewey*. Hegel's name is sedulously kept out of the text.

9. See James' remarks to Croom Robertson (recorded in Perry's *The Thought and Character of William James*, Vol. II, p. 156), "It's no use trying to mediate between the bare miraculous self and the concrete particulars of individual mental lives; and all that Dewey effects by doing so is to take all the

edge and definiteness away from the particulars when it falls to their turn to be treated." Ironically, Dewey was later to criticize James' theory for not going far enough in abolishing the idea of the self. (See "The Vanishing Subject in the Psychology of William James" reprinted in *Problems of Men*.) Hall was even less impressed than James. "That the absolute idealism of Hegel could be so cleverly adapted to be 'read onto' such a range of facts, old and new," he sputtered, "is indeed a surprise as great as when geology and zoology are ingeniously subjected to the rubrics of the six days creation" (in Dykhuizen, *Life and Mind*, p. 55). Hall, like Pavlov, rigidly separated science and religion and passionately practiced both. Dewey would later observe that reductionism as well as many dualisms arise from a misguided "quest for certainty."

10. Compare Dewey's essay of 1890, "The Logic of Verification" (*EW* 3:83 ff.) with statements made in *Essays in Experimental Logic* (especially "The Control of Ideas by Facts" and "What Pragmatism Means by Practical"), the essay "Philosophy and Civilization," already referred to, and *Logic: The Theory of Inquiry* (Chapter VIII).

11. See *Art as Experience* pp. 87-89, 264-66 (*LW* 10:93-94, 269-71).

12. See *Psychology*; *EW* 2:19 and 299.

13. See Dewey's *The Theory of Valuation* and James Gouinlock's *John Dewey's Theory of Value* (New York: Humanities Press, Inc., 1972).

14. For Dewey, the "part-whole" relation is the key to understanding the meaning of something, though this is combined with the thing's function or working. See Hubert G. Alexander's discussion of how basic abstractions of qualities, relations and functions guide thinking in his *The Language and Logic of Philosophy* (Albuquerque: University of New Mexico Press, 1972), especially pp. 156-57 on "part-whole" relations.

15. See, e.g., *Art as Experience*, pp. 192-93 (*LW* 10:196-97) and Dewey's essay, "Qualitative Thought."

16. The first four essays reprinted in EEL were Dewey's contributions to *Studies in Logical Theory*.

17. Influenced by James, Bradley came to assign a predominate role to feeling rather than thought, especially in his late work, *Essays on Truth and Reality*. See John Herman Randall's discussion, "F.H. Bradley and the Working-out of Absolute Idealism," in his *Philosophy after Darwin*, ed. Beth J. Singer (New York: Columbia University Press, 1977).

18. See James' *Principles* I, pp. 243 ff., and Dewey's remark in "Qualitative Thought" (*PC*, 99; *LW* 5:247-48).

19. Since the primary relation in idealism is knower-known, or, as in the case of Berkeley, perceiver-perceived, the tacit implication is that all other relations are degraded forms of this primary one. One finds a remarkable

anticipation of Leibniz' *"petites perceptions"* in Poltinus' *Enneads* III:viii:30, where nature's activity is described as "silent *theorein.*"

20. It seems a fundamental doctrine in idealism (and other philosophies) that one "proves" the existence of a spiritual cause by affirming that a "lower" reality (e.g. matter) cannot produce a "higher" reality (e.g. mind). See Descartes' use of this to prove the existence of God in the Third Meditation. This also is a Neo-Platonic doctrine, expressly formulated by Proclus. See *The Elements of Theology,* Proposition LXXII.

21. See *Psychology,* (EW 2:171-72). In the revised edition of 1891, Dewey describes a concept as "the power, capacity, or function of the image to stand for some mode of mental action and it is *the mode of action which is general"* (p. 179). Principles become not mere universals but "laws of construction." In the essay "How Do Concepts Arise from Percepts," published also in 1891 (*EW* 3:142 ff.), Dewey states that concepts arise from percepts by realizing the implicit meaning of the latter, but the concept *"can be grasped only in and through the activity which constitutes it,"* (144). These statements not only show the influence of James' *Principles,* which Dewey was teaching already at this time, but anticipate his discussion of concepts and universals in *Logic: The Theory of Inquiry* as general ways of acting (see Chapter XIV).

22. See *Art as Experience,* p. 266 and p. 294 (*LW* 10:270-71, 298-99). See also *Experience and Nature* p. 195 and p. 300 (*LW* 1:152, 227) and "Qualitative Thought." Dewey is critical of the Crocean and Bergsonian interpretations of intuition because it remains forever mysterious and isolated from action.

23. See Dewey's discussion of religion vs. the religious in the first chapter of *A Common Faith.*

24. For a discussion of Hegel's doctrine of "mediated immediacy," see Walter Kaufmann, *Hegel: A Reinterpretation* (New York: Anchor Books, 1966), pp. 190-91 and Hegel's discussion "With What Must the Science Begin?" at the beginning of Book I, Vol. I of the *Science of Logic.*

25. "Actual knowledge is concerned with the ideal elements. The epic of Homer, the tragedy of Sophocles, that statue of Phidias, the symphony of Beethoven are *creations.* Although having a correspondence with actual existences, they do not reproduce them. They are virtual additions to the world's riches; they are ideal. Such creations are not confined to art, nor are they remote from our daily existence" (*EW*2:77).

26. Again, see the essays "Qualitative Thought" and "Affective Thought," (*PC*, 93-125; *LW* 5:243-62; *LW* 2:104-10).

27. See especially *Art as Experience,* Chapters I and II, and pp. 147 ff. (*LW* 10:152ff.), where Dewey makes the less extreme statement that rhythm in nature is a condition of rhythm in experience, and rhythm in experience is a precondition of there being art, like poetry, which celebrates rhythm. The statement that poetry is prior to prose, which Dewey makes occasionally in

Art as Experience, should not be taken literally. It is true that we experience rhythms in life and even experience *language* rhythmically before we experience it as having specific meaning. The lullaby or Mother Goose rhymes attune us to rhythmic moods, not ideas. Later we come to discriminate specific terms.

28. See Dewey's remarks on "lived time" in *Art as Experience,* pp. 206 ff (*LW* 10:210 ff.).

29. See *Art as Experience,* p. 195, pp. 185-86 (*LW* 10:198-99, 190). What is meant here is that art creates a general mode of aesthetic perception which enhances our experience beyond the work of art and which makes our experience of the work fit into the general meaning of our lives.

30. "Imagination has no external end, but its end is the free play of the various activities of the self so as to satisfy its interests" (*EW* 2:173). See Schiller's *On the Aesthetic Education of Man,* Letter 15, and Kant's *Critique of Judgment,* Introduction, ss. ix.

31. Compare with *Art as Experience,* p. 16 (*LW* 10:21) and *Experience and Nature,* p. 96 and p. 258 ff. (*LW* 1:82, 198).

32. But see *Art as Experience,* Ch. X, pp. 229 ff. (*LW* 10: 233 ff.) where Dewey does seem to go against his own advice on ranking the arts, with literature as the highest because it communicates best. If Dewey does lapse in the book back to idealist tendencies, it is in such moments as these—surely among the book's weakest spots.

33. See Morton White's *The Origin of Dewey's Instrumentalism* and Boisvert's *Dewey's Metaphysics* for more detailed discussions of this period of Dewey's thought. White does not break Dewey's thought during his idealist period into three phases as I have done. Certainly the major influence before 1890 is that of Green through Morris and after is that of James' *Principles.* The influence of Dewey's colleagues, Mead, Angel, Tufts, and of the "Chicago School" and its experimental approach should not be underestimated, however. White's study stresses Dewey's philosophy of experience and method while ignoring, on the whole, the central issue of ethics. Boisvert divides the idealist period into two phases, the brief Kantian phase prior to Morris' influence and the subsequent Hegelian phase.

34. Thomas Hill Green, *Prolegomena to Ethics* (Oxford: 1883), p. 2. Compare with Dewey's paraphrase in "Poetry and Philosophy" (*EW* 3:123) where he says, "We must bridge this gap of poetry from science. We must heal this unnatural wound."

35. Dewey's two essays are: "Green's Theory of the Moral Motive" (*EW* 3:155 ff.) and "Self-Realization as the Moral Ideal" (*EW* 4:42 ff.). See also Dewey's review of Caird's book on Kant (*EW* 3:181 ff.). It was the influence of Caird as much as James which seemed to push Dewey closer to Hegel at this

time. These articles should be compared with Dewey's eulogistic essay, "The Philosophy of Thomas Hill Green" (EW 3:14 ff.).

36. Dewey uses this term in his book, *The Study of Ethics: A Syllabus* (EW 4:264). The passage reads: "The theory of experimental idealism (as we term the position here taken), because of its recognition of activity as the primary reality is enabled to give both thought and feeling their due." This proves that Dewey is still attempting to solve the problem stated by "The Psychological Standpoint." Dewey even briefly uses this expression as late as 1929 in *The Quest for Certainty*.

37. These crucial articles will be discussed in the chapter dealing with Dewey's theory of meaning and mind.

38. Charles Sanders Peirce, *Collected Papers*, VIII, pp. 145-47. This review also refers to Husserl, whose *Logical Investigations* had appeared three years earlier (1900-1901).

39. Dewey credits this insight to the eccentric syndicalist Franklin Ford, then a student of his. See Coughlan, *Young John Dewey*, Ch. 6. See also Dewey's letter to James (In Perry's *Thought and Character*, Vol. II pp. 517-19). Dewey says elsewhere ("Introduction to Philosophy: Syllabus of Course 5," (EW 3:234), "The aim of art is to discover the method of expression which shall secure the best organization of action; the fullest or freest movement. It aims at seeing to it that the ideal side gets a complete embodiment in the fact side; or, what is the same thing, that facts become completely permeated with their idea so as to move harmoniously and freely." Anything is aesthetic, says Dewey, in which the whole moves freely through the part.

40. See *Art as Experience*, pp. 26-27, 116-17, 176-77, 231, 260-62 (LW 10:31-33, 122-23, 181-82, 234-35, 265-67).

41. See Brand Blanshard's attack on Dewey in *The Nature of Thought*, especially pages 349-86.

42. Compare the final chapters of *The Quest for Certainty* and *Experience and Nature*.

43. Friedrich Nietzsche, *The Will to Power*, translated by Walter Kaufman and R.J. Hollingdale (New York: Vintage Books, 1967), p. 9.

44. The final name, cultural naturalism, is given in *Logic: The Theory of Inquiry*, p. 20; (LW 12:28) and indicates Dewey's growing dissatisfaction with misinterpretations of his use of "experience."

45. This is the moral consequence of Locke's *Essay*, which is, all in all, a far more radical document in terms of its social implications than the *Treatises*, which fall back on the Stoic-Medieval doctrine of "natural law" apprehended by reason innately.

46. See Dewey's operationalist discussion of mathematics in *Logic: The Theory of Inquiry* as well as such studies by Piaget as *The Child's Conception of Number*. For example, compare Dewey's comment with Piaget's: "Knowing does not really imply making a copy of reality but, rather, reacting to it and transforming it . . . in such a way as to include it functionally in the transformation systems with which these acts are linked. . . . Mathematics consists not only of all actual transformations but of all possible transformations. To speak of transformations is to speak of actions or operations . . . and to speak of the possible is to speak . . . of the assimilation of immediate reality into certain real or virtual actions. . . . To say that all knowledge presupposes some assimilation and that it consists in conferring meaning amounts, in the final analysis, to the affirmation that to know an object implies incorporating it into action schemata, and this is true from elementary sensorimotor behavior right up to the higher logico-mathematical operations," *Biology and Knowledge*, translated by Beatrix Walsh (Chicago: The University of Chicago Press, 1971), pp. 6-8.

47. The story is mentioned in Gilbert Highet's *The Art of Teaching* (New York: Vintage Books, 1950), pp. 213-17.

48. Dewey refers here to Santayana's *Life of Reason* for "the consistency and vigor with which is upheld the doctrine that significant idealism means idealization." See, for example, the first line of Chapter 9 of *Reason in Common Sense*: "Reason's function is to embody the good, but the test of excellence is itself ideal. . . ." Dewey was undoubtedly impressed and stimulated by this book, as his reviews of it indicate, which are among the most enthusiastic he ever wrote. Of the first two volumes he said that they are "the most significant contribution, made in this generation, to philosophic revision," and he dubs the position represented "naturalistic idealism," which Santayana no doubt did not appreciate (*MW* 3:319-22). Dewey's progressive puzzlement and eventual opposition to Santayana begins with the review of the last three volumes the next year (1907). Dewey admits to being most stirred by Santayana's "evaluation of the facts and motifs of human life," and selects for special comment Santayana's analysis of reason in art: not only is art rooted in "the spontaneous overflow of instinct and impulse," but it has an "instrumental function" which goes far in solving the problem of "the union of the industrial and the fine arts." Dewey finds a problem, though, in the dilemma whether art or science is a "more concrete and final expression of living reason": Dewey would propose art, where Santayana seems to propose science. Reality, Dewey indicates, from the side of "the noble, artistic, and moral 'pragmatism'" may be more than what is revealed in our cognitive endeavors (*MW* 4:229-41). By 1923, with *Scepticism and Animal Faith*, Santayana has taken just the opposite path than that suggested by Dewey. The work takes as its theme "the separation of existence and essence," which is to say of the real and the ideal. Dewey finds an affinity now with Hinduism in Santayana, a sense of resignation and a devaluation of the world of existence. Dewey holds off from a wholesale condemnation, waiting for the promised sequel (i.e., *The Realms*

of Being), but says "It is a delicate enterprise to discount practical intent and the busy life of man in behalf of aesthetic essences and their contemplation" (*MW* 15:219-22). Finally, with the appearance of *The Realm of Essence* in 1927, Dewey writes: "In the *Life of Reason* . . . he spoke primarily as a moralist and as an historian . . . of the emergence of the rational life out of the flux of blind sensation and desire. In that work, he taught or seemed to teach that the realm of ideas and ideals is rooted in nature and forms its apex: a flower of nature destined, indeed, never to bear seeds which may themselves take root in nature, but altogether lovely, the end of human experience and of human life, in the only intelligible sense of end. It now appears, however, that those who interpreted Santayana in this sense of naturalistic idealism were in error." Now we see, says Dewey, his "thorough-going dualism" which utterly separates Essence from Nature. Unlike Dewey's ideals, Santayana's realm of essence "is indifferent and inert; it has no potency nor desire to find a home in existence." Santayana has carried dualism, Dewey asserts, to its reductio ad absurdem. "But one may also take a more genial path and, setting out from the kinship of enjoyed possession of essence with appreciation of works of art, be led to interpret the doctrine in the sense of cancellation of the alleged separation of objects of thought from nature. The conclusion is that thought and its characteristic objects are, like bare action or practice, but a means for a transformation of raw nature into products of art—into forms of existence which are directly significant and enjoyed. For in the end, it is only the wisdom which is embodied in natural existence which counts. . . . The affinity of mind to pure essence is disciplinary and preparatory; that intermediate and instrumental affinity once having been developed, mind turns spontaneously to its proper object, meaning realized by art in natural existence" (*LW* 3:287-93). The meaning of this last sentence embodies the fundamental thesis of this book.

49. See the Introduction to the *Science of Logic:* "The System of Logic is the realm of shades, a world of simple essentialities freed from all concretion of sense. To study this Science, to dwell and labour in this shadow-realm, is a perfect training and discipline of consciousness," translated by W.H. Johnston and L.G. Struthers (New York: Humanities Press, Inc., 1928), pp. 69-70. See also his remarks at the end ("The Absolute Idea") where the transition from logic to nature is presented as showing "that the Idea freely releases itself in absolute self-certainty and self repose" (Vol. II, p. 486). The Idea freely gives itself over to contingency—the Idea demands to be filled in by the wealth and plurality of nature, but it doesn't demand or determine its content in detail. *How* one gets from the pure concept to the existence of nature is a problem. Findlay's comment, "In spite, therefore, of much quasi-theological mystification, there is nothing but the utmost intellectual sobriety in Hegel's transition from the Idea to Nature," must provoke a smile even among Hegel enthusiasts (*Hegel*, New York: Collier Books, 1952, p. 271). In Charles Taylor's *Hegel* we read, "Thus what emerges from the *Logic* is Hegel's vision in which the whole structure of things (including what is contingent) flows necessarily from the one starting point, that Reason (or spirit, or the Concept) must be"

(Cambridge: Cambridge University Press, 1975), p. 345. Taylor does not believe that Hegel has succeeded in showing that this follows. The problem occurs in Hegel's proof of the contradictory nature of the finite, for "it is this which allows him to derive the category of Infinity as a self-subsistent whole whose deployment is governed by necessity" (p. 346). Being and its contradiction, Nothing, leads to *Dasein*; Being must be determinate, yet this creates its opposite, which produces the synthesis of infinity, "the immortal, self-subsistent system of mortal dependent finite beings." Here Taylor comments, "But with Infinity we reach a term which does not suffer (although it contains) contradiction; rather it is a formula whose implications only need to be fully drawn out to bring us to the final reconciling synthesis" (p. 347). There are, in short, no new genuine contradictions. This, Taylor argues, leaves Hegel's philosophy an *interpretation*, not a demonstration, and without being able to come to rational certainty about the Absolute, "then Hegel's synthesis breaks asunder" (p. 349). Dewey also rejects Hegel's emphasis on necessity for a greater recognition of indeterminacy and chance: "necessity implies the precarious and contingent. A world that was all necessity would not be a world of necessity; it would just be. For in its being, nothing would be necessary for anything else. . . . A world of 'ifs' is alone a world of 'musts'—the 'ifs' express real differences; the 'musts' real connections" (*EN*, 64-65; *LW* 1:59).

50. See the second chapter of Heidegger's *An Introduction to Metaphysics*, "On the Grammar and Etymology of the Word 'Being' (*Sein*)." If one wants to find a genuine ground for comparing Dewey and Heidegger, it is not to be found in their "deconstructive" accounts of "the Tradition," as Rorty thinks, but in their ultimate, primary commitment to understanding the meaning of Being (or Existence) in terms of our temporality.

51. For the relationship between Barnes and Dewey, see Dykhuizen's *The Life and Mind of John Dewey* (Carbondale: Southern Illinois University Press, 1973), p. 221 ff. and William Shack's not unbiased *Art and Argyrol* (New York: Thomas Yoseloff, 1960).

CHAPTER 3

1. See Raymond Boisvert, *Dewey's Metaphysics*, Chapter I, sec. 1, and Richard Bernstein's introduction to *Experience, Nature, and Freedom* for an analysis of the phases of Dewey's philosophy.

2. See *Democracy and Education*, Chapters 18-19, *Human Nature and Conduct*, Chapter 20, and *Reconstruction in Philosophy*, Chapter 8.

3. See *Dewey's Metaphysics*, Chapter II, sec. 2.

4. See Philip M. Zeltner, *John Dewey's Aesthetic Philosophy* and Victor Kestenbaum, *The Phenomenological Sense of John Dewey* for discussions which simply concern themselves with Dewey's aesthetics alone.

5. "Instrumentalism" is the proper term for Dewey's version of pragmatism, though the terms are used interchangeably here. See Dewey's fine

article, "The Development of American Pragmatism," in *Philosophy and Civilization* (*LW* 2:3-21). It is important to recall that instrumentalism refers to only a part of Dewey's philosophy, his theory of knowing and meaning.

6. For the critical response to this article see: Charles Bakewell, "An Open Letter to Mr. Dewey Concerning Immediate Empiricism," *JP* II (1905), pp. 520-22; reply by Dewey, pp. 597-99; F.J.E. Woodbridge, "Of What Sort is Cognitive Experience?" pp. 573-76; reply by Dewey, pp. 652-57; Boyd H. Bode, "Cognitive Experience and Its Object," pp. 658-63; reply by Dewey, pp. 707-11. These articles are reprinted in the appendix to volume 3 of the *Middle Works*. See also Raymond Boisvert, "Dewey, Subjective Idealism, and Metaphysics," *TPS* XVIII, No. 3 (1982), as well as Boisvert's discussion in *Dewey's Metaphysics*, Ch. II, sec. 3. Whereas Boisvert convincingly shows that Dewey is free from the charge of being a Kantian idealist at heart, the question of Dewey's Hegelianism is left open.

7. See George Santayana, "Dewey's Naturalistic Metaphysics," reprinted in *Obiter Scripta* (New York: Charles Scribner's Sons, 1936), pp. 218-40 and in Schilpp, *The Philosophy of John Dewey*, pp. 234-62. The original article appeared in *JP* (1925). Note should be taken of Santayana's assumptions in his contrast between "epistemological" and "physical" categories. His is a paradigmatic misreading of Dewey.

8. See Morris R. Cohen, "Some Difficulties in Dewey's Anthropocentric Naturalism," *PR*, XLIX (1940), pp. 196-220, and H.S. Thayer's *The Logic of Pragmatism* (New York: Humanities Press, 1952), p. 80.

9. William Ernest Hocking, "Dewey's Concept of Nature and Experience," *PR* XLIX (1940), pp. 228-44. See also Dewey's responses to Cohen and Hocking, "Nature in Experience," *PR* XLIX (1940), pp. 244-58, reprinted in Bernstein *ENF*, pp. 244-60.

10. Sholom Kahn, "Experience and Existence in Dewey's Naturalistic Metaphysics," *PPR* IX (1948), pp. 316-21 and reply by Dewey pp. 709-12.

11. Paul Welsh, "Some Metaphysical Assumptions in Dewey's Philosophy," *JP* LI (1954), pp. 861-67.

12. Richard Bernstein, "John Dewey's Metaphysics of Experience," *JP* LVIII (1961), pp. 5-8.

13. Ibid., p. 9.

14. Ibid., p. 10.

15. Richard Bernstein, *John Dewey* (New York: Washington Square Press, 1966), p. 180.

16. Bernstein, "John Dewey's Metaphysics of Experience," p. 13.

17. Ibid., p. 14. Bernstein's criticism is itself plagued by the notorious ambiguities of the terms, "idealism" and "realism." The whole purpose of

Dewey's approach is to get *beyond* thinking about problems by means of static, opposed categories.

18. Roland Garrett, "Dewey's Struggle with the Ineffable," *TPS* IX (1973), pp. 95-109. Also see his "Changing Events in Dewey's *Experience and Nature,*" *JHP* X (1974), pp. 439-55.

19. Ibid., p. 108.

20. Ibid., p. 95.

21. See Richard Rorty's "Overcoming the Tradition: Heidegger and Dewey," *RM* XXX (1976), pp. 280-305, reprinted in *Consequences of Pragmatism* (Minneapolis: University of Minnesota Press, 1982), pp. 37-59, and *Philosophy and the Mirror of Nature,* Introduction and Chapter VIII.

22. Richard Rorty, "Dewey's Metaphysics," in *New Studies in the Philosophy of John Dewey,* Stephen M. Cahn, ed. (Hanover, New Hampshire: University Press of New England, 1977), p. 48. This is also reprinted in *Consequences of Pragmatism,* pp. 72-89.

23. See Thomas M. Alexander, "Richard Rorty and Dewey's Metaphysics of Experience," *Southwest Philosophical Studies* V (1980), pp.24-35, Garry Brodsky, "Rorty's Interpretation of Pragmatism," *TPS* XVIII (1982), pp. 311-38, Boisvert's criticisms in *Dewey's Metaphysics,* Ch. III, sec. 4.1, Ch. V, sec. 3.3, and Ch. VIII, and the recent exchange between Rorty and Ralph Sleeper and Abraham Edel in *TPS* XXI (1985). See also Ralph Sleeper's *The Necessity of Pragmatism,* Vol. XXI, no. 1 (1985).

24. Rorty, "Dewey's Metaphysics," in Cahn, p. 67. One advantage of Rorty's approach is that he traces problematic ideas back to Dewey's idealist period, though, in this case, only to be led astray, in my opinion. I have tried to show in Chapter 2 above that just because a continuity can be established between Dewey's earlier and later philosophy, this is no reason to jump to the conclusion that his commitments were crypto-idealist or confused.

25. See Dewey's *"de Anima,"* the immensely important Chapters VII and VIII of *Experience and Nature.* This bears comparison with Merleau-Ponty's conception of the role of the body in *The Phenomenology of Perception,* especially Part One, Chapter 6, and Part Two. Compare Rorty's remark with Croce's acerbic comment, "Dewey cannot overcome the dualism of mind and nature. He is led to delude himself that he has overcome it by means of a continuous process of nature-mind, in which the hyphen connecting two words would provide the victory which speculative logic . . . resolving . . . nature into mind, is alone capable of accomplishing," ("Dewey's Aesthetics and Theory of Knowledge," *JAAC* XI, 1952, p. 5). Note Croce's use of the term "continuous" here and how he rejects continuity for the *identity* of nature with mind. This is typical of those who fail to comprehend Dewey's "principle of continuity," as discussed below.

26. Robert Dewey, *The Philosophy of John Dewey* (The Hague: Martinus Nijhoff, 1977).

27. Ibid., p. 117.

28. Ibid., p. 167.

29. Boisvert argues for a limited, contextual theory of form in Dewey's metaphysics. Form is the organization of a complexity into an ordered whole which only comes about through interaction. Rather than being a changeless essence, Boisvert reads form as the enduring stability of a process. Thus, "forms are elicited from the events, they are not given prior to them." (*Dewey's Metaphysics*, Ch. V, sec. 3.1).

30. John Dewey, "Experience and Existence: A Comment," *PPR* IX (1949), pp. 712-13; reply to Sholom Kahn's article cited above.

31. Gouinlock, *John Dewey's Philosophy of Value*, p. 57.

32. For an interesting discussion of what Dewey means by "spiritual" see *Experience and Nature*, p. 294 (*LW* 1:223-24) and, of course, *A Common Faith*.

33. See William James, *Principles of Psychology*, I, Ch. IX, passim, and the *Essays in Radical Empiricism*, "A World of Pure Experience." Compare with Dewey's observation in his own *Psychology* on "feelings of relation" (*EW*: 2:259 ff.).

34. See Dewey's, "The Vanishing Subject in the Psychology of James," in *PM*, pp. 396-409.

35. See James, *Principles of Psychology*, I, pp. 196-97, for "The Psychologist's Fallacy."

36. For Dewey's discussion of the fallacy of selective emphasis, see *Experience and Nature*, pp. 29-30 (*LW* 1:33-34). See also the original first chapter to the book, reprinted in the appendix to *LW*: 1.

37. See especially Hegel's discussion in the first part of the *Encyclopedia*, Ch. V, "Third Attitude of Thought to Objectivity: Immediate or Intuitive Knowledge" and Ch. VIII, "Second Subdivision of Logic: The Doctrine of Essence," (translated by William Wallace as *Hegel's Logic*). Compare with Dewey's Chapter VIII, "Immediate Knowledge: Understanding and Inference," in *Logic: The Theory of Inquiry*.

38. See Woodbridge's "Of What Sort Is Cognitive Experience?" in *MW* 3:393-97. Woodbridge raises many good points, but begs the question in assuming that a "real" which is not true must therefore be false and then asks what value there is in an inquiry into false reality. Cognitive experience for Woodbridge reveals how things actually are; Dewey questions the whole presupposition that the world "actually" is what the world "really" is. That is, he raises the question of the reality of potentiality and process to an equal

status as well as questioning whether cognition simply actualizes the pre-existent structure of reality. In other words, Dewey is a far more radical Aristotelian than Woodbridge.

39. The reference is to James' essay, "Does Consciousness Exist?" in *Essays in Radical Empiricism*.

40. To summarize the criticisms of the other two articles mentioned above: Bakewell emphasized the dichotomy of immediate vs. mediate and Bode argued that precognitive experience presupposed an object of cognition. Dewey responded by saying the *continuity* overcame the difference of the immediate-mediate polarity, that the "real" was revealed in non-cognitive experience just as much as in cognitive, and that prereflective experience should not be regarded as "unfulfilled" cognition, specifically appealing to moral and aesthetic experience as examples where cognition was not an issue.

41. For an account of Woodbridge's philosophy see the discussion in C.F. Delany's *Mind and Nature* (Notre Dame: University Press of Notre Dame, 1969). Chapter V of Boisvert's *Dewey's Metaphysics* should also be noted as a careful analysis of how far Dewey can be read in light of an Aristotelian naturalism. Woodbridge's naturalism was heavily influenced by Spinozism, which accounts for the emphasis on formalism. Dewey was much more attracted to the dynamic side of Aristotle, especially the discussion of potentiality, which directly challenges the view that nature is completely structured in all respects.

42. "Biography of John Dewey," edited by Jane M. Dewey, in *The Philosophy of John Dewey*, P.A. Schilpp, ed., pp. 35-36.

43. See Georges Dicker, *Dewey's Theory of Knowing* (Philadelphia: Philadelphia Monograph Series, 1976).

44. F.J.E. Woodbridge, "Metaphysics" (1908), in *Nature and Mind* (New York: Columbia University Press, 1937), p. 96.

45. Ibid., pp. 107-08. See Aristotle's *Metaphysics*, 1003a, 21-23. I think the translation of *on* as "existence" is unfortunate. The latter comes from a late Latin coinage, "*ex + sistere*," meaning "to stand out from" rather than "to be." "Exist," strictly speaking, signifies what appears at the moment and abides through it, i.e., those individuals which "stand forth" and "show themselves" in their endurance. "Existence" fails to acknowledge all those other "modes of Being" in Aristotle's account: potential Being, possible Being and actualized, fulfilled or "energized" Being, i.e., Being that represents the fulfillment of a process. "Existence" and "Being" are not equivalent terms. "Being" for Aristotle has a temporal dimension and a richness of modality which "existence" does not possess.

46. See Ibid., pp. 108-10.

47. Gouinlock, *John Dewey's Philosophy of Value*, p. 6. This makes Dewey's position far broader and more sophisticated than those "naturalisms" which

equate reality with the objects of direct perception or of scientific inquiry (usually understood as best illustrated by the "hard" sciences of physics and chemistry). Inquiry, for Dewey, was always more than science, and nature was always more than physics.

48. See *Experience and Nature*, pp. 76-77 (*LW* 1:68) and Chapter X. Wisdom for Dewey means "opening and enlarging the ways of nature in man" to secure, expand and obtain the goods of experience, a paradigm among which, of course, are consummatory experiences. The end of philosophy, in other words, should be the enhancement of those values and meanings which render human life most significant and which are conducive to the further growth and appreciation of meanings.

49. See Charles Sanders Peirce, "Questions Concerning Certain Faculties Claimed for Man" and "Some Consequences of Four Incapacities" (*Collected Papers*, V: 213-317).

50. For places where Dewey gives examples of the "generic traits," see "Time and Individuality," "Nature in Experience," and "The Inclusive Philosophic Idea" as well as *Experience and Nature*. The chapters themselves of *Experience and Nature* indicate the general scope of the categories. In all fairness, Aristotle himself was not consistent in what the list of categories was. In Dewey's case, a generic trait or category should be regarded as a tentative tool, like a lens, which helps us see some common feature of situations in experience and thereby helps establish continuity between them and which acts as a prophylactic against erecting differences into dualisms. It becomes thus a condition of human conduct.

51. See "The Inclusive Philosophic Idea" in *Philosophy and Civilization*. The social, for Dewey, is continuity at its fullest. The social is constituted of shared meanings in which individuals participate. The social is inclusive because all other meanings come to be and are realized within it; it is the arena in which nature reaches its fullest and most complex realization. The social also establishes continuities within nature in active ways (e.g., in the creation of new substances or organisms). In short, the social stands as the domain of shared meaning and value which constitutes the context of human existence.

52. Gouinlock states, "The aim, then, of the method of experience is to see situations in their entirety; and this means to detect all of the traits of the situation in their historical continuities. . . . The method of experience implies the thorough use of criticism. It is clear that this method is the means of seeing experience in its integrity . . ., of analyzing nature in all its richness and continuities, with the end in view of clarifying and guiding life experience" (*John Dewey's Philosophy of Value*, p. 54).

53. A comparison may be drawn here to Peirce's functional realism which conceives of universals as general ways of acting or behaving. The universal has no separate being from the individuals which display behavior, yet it is a real and determining factor in the way things behave. For example, the habit

of stopping at a red light will affect the general way the individual acts, presumably toward his safety, and allows a number of various experiences to be linked significantly together. On this basis, a "generic trait" would be some aspect of a situation which allows continuities to be established between it and other situations thereby illuminating the general *ways* experience is in nature.

54. Gouinlock, *John Dewey's Philosophy of Value*, p. 12.

55. The whole point of *Art as Experience* is, of course, how "*an* experience" develops from ordinary experience, and is itself developmental. The origin of many dualisms or monisms is that they tacitly or explicitly rely on the ancient "like knows like" hypothesis, eg., how can a mental substance "know" anything which is not itself mental? For Dewey, knowing is functional, a question of coordinating activity toward valued ends by intelligence. As action becomes informed and integrated it becomes "universal" and significant (see note 53 above). Those metaphysics which place the issue of knowing upon an abstract principle of identity or which must account for difference by a principle of sufficient reason have an essentially static rather than dynamic understanding of cognition.

56. This reflects the position of a number of thinkers in America during the early part of this century which was known as "Objective Relativism" or "Perspectival Realism." See Arthur E. Murphey's articles "Objective Relativism in Dewey and Whitehead," "What Happened to Objective Relativism?" and "McGilvery's Perspective Realism" in *Reason and the Common Good* (Englewood Cliffs, N.J.: Prentice Hall, 1963). See also Boisvert's discussion, *Dewey's Metaphysics*, Ch. V.

57. John Wild, "Foreword," to Maurice Merleau-Ponty, *The Structure of Behavior*, translated by Alden Fisher (Boston: Beacon Press, 1963), p. xiii. See also Piaget's *Structuralism*, translated by Chaninah Maschler (New York: Harper & Row, 1968).

58. See Ivor Leclerc, *The Nature of Physical Existence* (New York: Humanities Press, 1972). With the rejection of Aristotelian dynamism in the 16th and 17th centuries, nature came to be conceived as an actual infinite composed of (Leibniz) or containing (Newton) individuals in pure act, i.e., individual substances having "external relations" with others but ultimately being internally self-determinate and complete. Nature is at each and every instant complete and totally determined (though Leibniz attempts to reintroduce the notion of potentiality, it is a predetermined "unfolding" of causation which has more in common with the Stoics' *logoi spermatikoi* and Augustine's *rationes seminales*). Laplace's assertion that an infinite mind could predict the future and deduce the past of the universe, given the current place and velocity of each atom, embodies this belief. Under this view, nature is pure *factum*; it is

made or *done*, and hence *finished* and *determined*. Such a universe is inherently mechanical, static and atemporal. See Peirce's brilliant criticism of this view, "The Doctrine of Necessity Examined" in *Collected Papers: VI*, Ch. 2. See also *Collected Papers: VI*, sec. 185.

59. At *Physics* 227a, 15-17, Aristotle says, "it is clear that continuity belongs to those things out of whose mutual contact a unity naturally arises. And the whole is a unity in the same way in which the continuous is a unity, whether by having been nailed or glued or mixed or having grown together" (Hope translation). Special attention should be given to the fact Aristotle says that it is a unity which "arises" or "come to be," i.e., emerges.

60. Charles Sanders Peirce, *Collected Papers: I*, ss. 175. Compare with Whitehead's use of "concrescence" in *Process and Reality* II:x, 11.

61. The idea of "power" that Dewey associates with Aristotle below is, in fact, closer to the view of the Stoics, Augustine and Leibniz (see footnote 58 above). Aristotle speaks of this sort of "active power" as potentiality in a secondary and derivative sense (see *De Anima* 417a, 21 ff.).

62. See Peirce's statement to the effect that "synechism" (Peirce's term for "continuity") is methodologically sounder than positing ultimates in one sense or another (*Collected Papers:VI*, ss. 173-74). See also Dewey's agreement with Whitehead's view of the continuity of the activity of the organism with the environment in his article, "The Philosophy of Whitehead" in P. A. Schilpp, *The Philosophy of Alfred North Whitehead* (New York: Tudor Publishing Co., 1951), p. 644.

63. Dewey to Bentley in *John Dewey and Arthur Bentley: A Philosophical Correspondence, 1932-1951*, ed. Sidney Ratner et. al. (New Brunswick, N.J.: Rutgers University Press, 1964), p. 141.

64. John Dewey, "Experience, Knowledge and Evaluation: A Rejoinder," in Schillp, *The Philosophy of John Dewey*, p. 546.

65. Ibid., p. 549.

66. Gouinlock, *John Dewey's Philosophy of Value*, p. 8.

67. Dewey to Bentley, *John Dewey and Arthur Bentley*, pp. 69-70.

68. Compare with *Experience and Nature*, 65-66 (LW 1:59-60).

69. Of course, the very means whereby atoms were defined, mass, force, gravity, etc., were *relational* concepts. It was not for over a hundred years, though, that physicists saw the implicit field-theory of Newton's ideas.

70. See Dewey's references to James in *Experience and Nature*, p. 312 (LW 1:236) and "Qualitative Thought" (PC, 93-116; LW 5:243-62).

71. See *A Common Faith*, Ch. I and *Art as Experience*, p. 195, (LW 10:199).

CHAPTER 4

1. See Everett W. Hall,,"Some Meanings of Meaning in Dewey's *Experience and Nature*," *JP* XXV, No. 7 (1928), pp. 169-18, with a response by Dewey in the same issue (pp. 345-53); Max Black, "Dewey's Philosophy of Language," *JP* LIX, No. 19 (1962), pp. 505-23; Victor Kestenbaum, *The Phenomenological Sense of John Dewey*, Ch. VII. The article by Hall and Dewey's rejoinder are particularly illuminating. Black's analysis of Dewey's theory is good, but misleading in many respects and is based on a rather narrow acquaintance with Dewey's philosophy. While Dewey's theory lacks the logical clarity Black would like, the whole point of Dewey's account is to avoid reducing meaning to questions of logic, at least as logic is understood by Black. Kestenbaum approaches Dewey from the standpoint of phenomenology and makes an illuminating comparison between Dewey and Merleau-Ponty, emphasizing the role of habit in both. He neglects, however, the overall cultural dimension of meaning nor does he treat meaning in terms of the social act of communicating, a crucial point in my view. H.S. Thayer's excellent account of Dewey's instrumentalism in his monumental *Meaning and Action* also neglects the qualitative and cultural dimension of Dewey's theory.

2. *The Phenomenology of Mind*, tr. J. B. Baille (New York: Harper and Row, 1967), p. 340. See also Daniel J. Cook, *Language in the Philosophy of Hegel* (Paris: Mouton, 1973).

3. See Charles S. Peirce, *Collected Works V:* 464 and 467, where he says that pragmatism "is merely a method of ascertaining the meanings of hard words and of abstract concepts" and is "a method of ascertaining the meanings, not of all ideas, but only of what I call 'intellectual concepts,' that is to say, of those upon the structure of which, arguments concerning objective fact may hinge." The qualifications in these statements should be emphasized.

4. The central discussion of Mead's theory of meaning can be found in his *Mind, Self, and Society*, though the topic recurs repeatedly throughout his work. For an excellent presentation of Mead's position, see David Miller's *George Herbert Mead: Self, Language, and the World* (Austin: University of Texas Press, 1973). The work of Charles Morris is also to be noted here, though his interpretation of the Dewey-Mead theory is much closer to positivism and radical behaviorism than is warranted. Once again, the cultural dimension of meaning is largely ignored in the emphasis on individual behavior.

5. On the relationship of Mead and Dewey see Neil Coughlan, *Young John Dewey*, and George Dykhuizen, *The Life and Mind of John Dewey*, Chs. 5, 6, & 7. See also Dewey's article, "The Development of American Pragmatism," in *Philosophy and Civilization* (LW 2:3-21) and his tribute to Mead in Mead's *Philosophy of the Present*.

6. For a discussion of adaptation and implementation which closely agrees with Dewey, see Jean Piaget, *Biology and Knowledge; Behavior and Evolu-*

tion, and Dobzhansky's *Genetics of the Evolutionary Process.* Dewey's own discussion occurs in Ch. II of *Experience and Nature.*

7. See again Dewey's article, "Experience and Objective Idealism," Peirce's "The Doctrine of Necessity Examined," in *Collected Papers VI,* and James' "The Dilemma of Determinism," in *The Will to Believe,* and the latter part of Ch. III in *Pragmatism.*

8. See also *Experience and Nature* pp. 71 ff. (*LW* 1:64 ff.).

9. See the discussion of this by Richard Rorty in *Philosophy and the Mirror of Nature.* Logical atomism, such as that in the early Wittgenstein or in Russell, is a good example of what is meant. The doctrine traces itself back through Descartes to Plato.

10. For Cratylus, see Aristotle's *Metaphysics* IV, 1010a 12. For the Zen Buddhist views of language, see Alan Watts, *The Way of Zen,* Part II, Ch. 3. Bergson's view can be found in his *Essay on the Immediate Data of Consciousness* (translated and "Time as Free Will" by F.L. Pogson). Bergson, like Dewey, saw experience as a whole process which is often forgotten for our schematized, analytical pictures of it. Bergson, however, does not see the flow of primary experience and analytical thinking in the interactional, functional way Dewey does. See Dewey's essay on Bergson, "Perception and Organic Action," in *Philosophy and Civilization.*

11. See Theodosius Dobzhansky's *Mankind Evolving* which takes a modified view of the radical Darwinians. "Survival" must be understood in terms of man's social and cultural self as well as his biological one. See also S. E. Luria, *Life: The Unfinished Experiment.*

12. See Maurice Merleau-Ponty, *The Structure of Behavior;* Jean Piaget, *Biology and Knowledge,* and Susanne Langer, *Mind: An Essay on Human Feeling,* vol. I.

13. Note here the use of the phrase, "an experience." To be sure, at this point Dewey has not assigned to it a technical use, but the germ of the idea is clearly present. Note also the use of the word "interpreting." In his *Study of Ethics,* Dewey says, "It is not simply that these results *do* follow, but that the child becomes *conscious* that they follow; that is, the results are referred back to the original impulse and enter into its structure in consciousness. It is evident that these mediations, or conscious back-references, constitute the *meaning* of the impulse—they are its *significance,* its *import.* The impulse is *idealized*" (*EW* 4:237). Were the last phrase modified, the passage might be from *Human Nature and Conduct.*

14. Similar views are advanced by Piaget and Merleau-Ponty. The former says, "What we should say . . . is what a colleague said in one of our seminars: 'In the beginning was the response!' " *Biology and Knowledge,* trans. Beatrix Walsh (Chicago: the University of Chicago Press, 1971), p. 8. Merleau-

Ponty states, "an excitation is determined by its relation to the whole organic state . . . and . . . the relations between the organism and milieu are not relations of linear but of circular causality" *The Structure of Behavior*, trans. Alden L. Fisher (Boston: Beacon Press, 1963), p. 15.

15. Perhaps the most detailed account of this idea is found in George Herbert Mead's *Philosophy of the Act*. Four phases are described by Mead: impulse, perception, manipulation and consummation. Mead devoted most attention to the second and third phases.

16. Selectivity on the conscious level, or choice, is continuous with individuating behavior throughout nature. Dewey says in *Experience and Nature*, "Plants and non-human animals act *as if* they were concerned that their activity, their characteristic receptivity and response, should maintain itself. Even atoms and molecules show a selective bias in their indifferences, affinities and repulsions when exposed to other events. . . . In a genuine although not a psychic sense, natural beings exhibit preference and centeredness" (218; *LW* 1:162). See also Dewey's essay "Time and Individuality" (in *Experience, Nature and Freedom*). A general comparison may be made with Whitehead's doctrine that actual entities "atomize the continuum," i.e., that every natural being, to the extent it is an actual subject, realizes ("selects" or "prehends") certain features at the expense of others, which make it just *that* individual and not another (see *Process and Reality*, Part II:ii, "The Extensive Continuum"). This idea is implicit in the Anaximander fragment and plays a major role in the philosophies of Aristotle and Leibniz.

17. George Herbert Mead, *Mind, Self and Society*, ed. Charles Morris (Chicago: University of Chicago Press, 1934), p. 129.

18. See *EN*, 232-33 (*LW* 1:179-80).

19. A comparison might be made here with phenomenological existentialists, like Sartre and Merleau-Ponty who make the same essential point. See Sartre's *Sketch for a Theory of the Emotions* (1939) and Merleau-Ponty's *Phenomenology of Perception*. Dewey himself states the "intentionality" of emotion in his essay "The Theory of Emotions": "But the full emotional experience also always has its 'object' or intellectual content. The emotion is always 'about' or 'toward' something . . ." ("The Theory of Emotion" in *EW* 4:173).

20. Victor Kestenbaum, *The Phenomenological Sense of John Dewey*, p. 35. Kestenbaum tends to ascribe emotion entirely to habit. This is an overstatement, in my opinion. Habits and opinions are phases of the situation, functionally related, but emotion tends to refer to the "tensive focus" while habit refers to active ways of mediating and structuring the situation.

21. See Dewey's remark that the impulses of an infant are "tentacles sent out to gather the nutrition from customs which will in time render the infant

capable of independent action" (*HNC*, II:i, 94; *MW* 14:68) and compare with *AE*, 67-68; *LW* 10:73.

22. William James, *Principles of Psychology*, Vol. II, p. 452.

23. See *Being and Time*, pp. 69-74 (original pagination). See also Michael Sukale's article "Heidegger and Dewey," ss. v, in his *Comparative Studies in Phenomenology* (The Hague: Martinus Nihjoff, 1976) and Dewey's *Reconstruction in Philosophy*, 87-90 (*MW* 12:129-32).

24. James, *Principles of Psychology*, Vol. I, p. 131.

25. Charles Peirce, *Collected Works*, Vol. V, 398, and 400. See also his remark, "The essence of belief is the establishment of a habit; and different beliefs are distinguished by the different modes of action to which they give rise" (V:398).

26. Kestenbaum, *Phenomenological Sense*, p. 3.

27. Merleau-Ponty, *The Phenomenology of Perception*, tr. Colin Smith (New Jersey: Humanities Press, 1962), p. 87. See also pp. 142 ff. See Kestenbaum, p. 70 and Gouinlock, *John Dewey's Theory of Value*, pp. 239 ff.

28. Ibid., p. 327.

29. Elizabeth Marshall Thomas, *The Harmless People* (New York: Vintage Books, 1965), pp. 6-7. One might point here to such famous studies as David Hall's *The Silent Language* which explores tacit communication through gesture.

30. Merleau-Ponty, *Phenomenology of Perception*, p. 142.

31. Thomas S. Kuhn, *The Structure of Scientific Revolutions* (Chicago: The University of Chicago Press, 1970), p. 116. See Marshall H. Segull, et. al, *The Influence of Culture on Visual Perception* (Indianapolis: Bobbs-Merrill Co., Inc. 1966) and Edmund Carpenter, "If Wittgenstein Had Been an Eskimo," in *Natural History*, Feb. 1980, pp. 72-77.

32. In the introduction to the *Essays in Experimental Logic*, Dewey says, "reflection appears as the dominant trait of a situation when there is something seriously the matter, some trouble, due to active discordance, dissentiency, conflict among the factors of a prior non-intellectual experience; when, in the phraseology of the essays, a situation becomes tensional" (*EEL*, 11; *MW* 10:326). It is a pity Dewey did not retain the use of the term "tensive" instead of relying on "problematical," since the latter inevitably makes one focus on simple practical "problem-solving," like fixing a tire, as Dewey's account of all speculative thought and consciousness itself. Situations are always tensional because there is always a certain amount of disequilibration. See *Experience and Nature*, where Dewey in fact defines consciousness as "The immediately precarious, the point of greatest immediate need . . . the point of *re*-direction or *re*-adaptation, of *re*-organization," (*EN*, 312; *LW* 1:236).

33. See *Human Nature and Conduct*, II:iv, 199 (*MW* 14:139). A forceful analysis of the self as a field of dramatic roles is found in Erving Goffman's classic, *The Presentation of the Self in Everyday Life*. See note 37 below.

34. On Dewey's various uses of this term along with "end," see Gouinlock, *John Dewey's Theory of Value*, pp. 130-31, 255-56, 245-46 and 151.

35. Dewey's discussion of the importance of the imagination for ethics can be found in part IV of *Human Nature and Conduct* and Chapter 10 of *The Quest for Certainty*.

36. Bronislaw Malinowski has an interesting discussion of the tribal response to death as the expression and treatment of a *social* crisis, reflected in the paradoxical double attitude toward the dead person which evokes both care and revulsion. "The death of a man or woman in a primitive group, consisting of a limited number of individuals, is an event of no mean importance. . . . A small community bereft of a member . . . is severely mutilated. The whole event breaks the normal course of life and shakes the moral foundations of society." The sense of revulsion elicits a variety of impulses (such as the desire to destroy the belongings of the dead) which threaten to break the cohesive bonds of the society. To counter these impulses, Malinowski argues that the ceremonial of death is a reintegration of the community's "shaken solidarity and . . . the re-establishment of its morale. In short, religion here assures the victory of tradition and culture over the mere negative response of thwarted instinct," *Magic, Science and Religion and Other Essays* (New York: Anchor Books, 1954), pp. 52-53.

37. Erving Goffman, *The Presentation of the Self in Everyday Life* (New York: Anchor Books, 1959). Goffman is primarily interested in the problems arising between trying to assume or project a role or character in a situation and the tacit, unintentional "impression" that one may give off. "When an individual appears before others," says Goffman, "he knowingly and unwittingly projects a definition of the situation, of which a conception of himself is an important part" (p. 242). Although Goffman does not focus on how we learn about the available "roles" we can play, his quotation from Robert Ezra Park is apropos, "In the end, our conception of our role becomes second nature and an integral part of our personality. We come into the world as individuals, achieve character, and become persons" (pp. 19-20). Mead offers a supplementary insight here, "We are more or less unconsciously seeing ourselves as others see us. We are unconsciously addressing ourselves as others address us. . . . We are calling out in the other person something we are calling out in ourselves, so that unconsciously we take over these attitudes. We are unconsciously putting ourselves in the place of others and acting as others act," *Mind, Self, and Society*, pp. 68-69.

38. Mead has analyzed this in great detail in *Mind, Self, and Society*. For example, Mead says, "Where the response of the other person is called out and becomes a stimulus to control his action, then he has the meaning of the

other person's act in his own experience. That is the general mechanism of what we term 'thought,'. . . . One participates in the same process the other person is carrying out and controls his action with reference to that participation. It is that which constitutes the meaning of an object, namely, the common response in one's self as well as the other person, which becomes, in turn, a stimulus to one's self," *Mind, Self, and Society,* pp. 73-74.

39. See *Experience and Nature,* 272-73, LW 1:208-09.

40. See Plato's *Theaetetus* 182 and commentary by F. M. Cornford, *Plato's Theory of Knowledge* (Indianapolis: Bobbs-Merrill Co. Inc., 1957), p. 97, and Aristotle's *Categories* IV lb 27, *Metaphysics* V:15, 1020 b 12 and discussion by Gottfried Martin in his *General Metaphysics,* tr. Donald O'Connor (London: George Allen and Unwin Ltd., 1968), p. 82. See also, Hubert G. Alexander, *The Language and Logic of Philosophy* (Albuquerque: The University of New Mexico Press, 1972).

41. See "Context and Thought," where Dewey says, "surrounding, bathing, saturating, the things of which we are explicitly aware is some inclusive situation which does not enter into the direct material of reflection. It does not come into question; it is taken for granted with respect to the particular question that is occupying the field of thinking. Since it does not come into question it is stable, settled" (*ENF,* 99; *LW* 6:11).

42. A significant discussion of this may be found in George Lakoff and Mark Johnson, *Metaphors We Live By* (Chicago: University of Chicago Press, 1980) and in Mark Johnson's forthcoming *The Body in the Mind: The Bodily Basis of Meaning and Imagination.* See also, however, Merleau-Ponty's *Phenomenology of Perception* and such anthropological discussions as Mary Douglas' *Natural Symbols* and Edward T. Hall's *The Silent Language* and *Beyond Culture.*

CHAPTER 5

1. In *Feeling and Form* she says, "The chief assumption that determines the entire procedure of pragmatic philosophy is that all human interests are direct or oblique manifestations of 'drives' motivated by animal needs. This premise limits the class of admitted human interests to such as can by one device or another, be interpreted in terms of animal psychology" (p. 35). Among other works, she explicitly refers to Dewey's *Art as Experience* and *Experience and Nature.* Ironically, in her later work, *Mind: An Essay on Human Feeling,* Langer goes a long way toward a naturalistic analysis of aesthetic experience, without, however, seeing any connection between the theory of experience she is groping toward and the philosophies of Dewey, James, and Mead.

2. As examples of critics illustrating these problems, see D.W. Gotshalk, "On Dewey's Aesthetics," *JAAC* XXIII (1965), E.A. Shearer, "Dewey's Aesthetic Theory," *JP* 32 (1935), Eliseo Vivas, "A Note on Emotion in Mr. Dewey's

Theory of Art," *PR* XLVII, No. 5 (1938), and George Boas, "Communication in Dewey's Aesthetics," *JAAC* XII (1958). On the other side, there have been several noteworthy articles dealing with Dewey's aesthetics from a positive approach. See in particular Dinesh Chandra Mathur, "A Note on the Concept of 'Consummatory Experience' in Dewey's Aesthetics," *JP* 63 (1966), P.G. Whitehouse, "The Meaning of 'Emotion' in Dewey's *Art as Experience*," *JAAC* XXXVII (1978), and Sidney Zink, "The Concept of Continuity in Dewey's Theory of Esthetics," *PR* 52 (1943).

3. For the institutional theory of art see George Dickie's *Aesthetics: An Introduction.* A humorous look at the social dynamics involved in the art world can be found in Tom Wolfe's wickedly insightful book, *The Painted Word.* I am not denying that Dickie's situational approach to aesthetic objects has a Deweyan (as well as Wittgensteinian) flavor to it; it simply does not go far enough. An interesting (but non-Deweyan) analysis of how something gets to be a "candidate for aesthetic appreciation" can be found in Arthur Danto's *The Transfiguration of the Commonplace.* See especially Chapter 4, which discusses Dickie.

4. See Heidegger's monumental essay, "The Origin of the Work of Art" in *Poetry, Language, Thought*, edited and translated by Albert Hofstadter (New York: Harper and Row, 1971).

5. André Malraux, *The Voices of Silence*, translated by Stuart Gilbert (Garden City, New York: Doubleday and Co. Inc., 1953), p. 13.

6. Ibid., pp. 44-46.

7. Ibid., p. 127.

8. Ibid., p. 639.

9. See Ibid., p. 624.

10. Edward Said, *The World, the Text, and the Critic* (Cambridge, Massachusetts: Harvard University Press, 1983), pp. 3-4.

11. See also his essay "Opponents, Audiences, Constituencies, and Community" in *Critical Inquiry* 9 (Fall 1982).

12. Thomas Merton quotes the following from D. T. Suzuki: "Tasting, seeing, experiencing, living—all these demonstrate that there is something common to enlightenment experience and our sense-experience; the one takes place in our innermost being, the other on the periphery of consciousness. . . . In this sense Buddhism is radical empiricism or experientialism . . . ." *Zen and the Birds of Appetite* (New Directions, 1968), p. 37. The anti-intellectualism of most Zen is, of course, unDeweyan—intelligence is part of the world that is there too.

13. In Lucien Stryk and Takashi Ikemoto, translators and editors, *Zen Poetry* (Penguin Books, 1977), p. 120.

14. See for example the articles by Shearer and Gotshalk referred to in footnote 2 above.

15. A surprising instance of this is Leon Edel's little monograph, *Henry D. Thoreau* (Minneapolis: University of Minnesota Press, 1970). Thoreau is one of those authors who invite this sort of misunderstanding because the source of their art happens to be intensely drawn from their personal lives. But Thoreau went to Walden Pond to get material for a book about human life which embodied Emerson's *Nature* and "Self Reliance." The reason why the "I" of the book leaves is just as important as why he arrives at Walden Pond. The "experiment" in recovering one's own life has been performed *amidst* his neighbors in one of the areas which has been colonized the longest.

16. See the introduction to *Essays in Experimental Logic*.

17. See Martin Heidegger's *What Is Called Thinking?*, translated by J. Glenn Gray (New York: Harper and Row, 1968).

18. *Symposium* 202 e.

19. The head caused Picasso a great deal of trouble. After Gertrude Stein had endured more than eighty sittings he painted it out and spent the summer of 1906 in Spain. In the autumn he returned and repainted the head—in the style which anticipates *Les Demoiselles d'Avignon*. It may be that the problem he confronted with the Stein portrait was how he could portray one of the founders of modernist writing in a style which was still essentially conventional. See the discussion of this event in Roland Penrose's *Picasso: His Life and Work* (New York: Harper and Row, 1973). André Malraux recalls Picasso saying of the African masks, "They were magic things. . . . The Negro pieces were *intercesseurs*, mediators. . . . They were against everything—against unknown threatening spirits. . . . I understood; I too am against everything, I too believe that everything is unknown, that everything is an enemy! Everything! Not the details—women, children, babies, tobacco, playing—but the whole of it! I understood what the Negroes used their sculpture for. . . . They were weapons. To help people avoid coming under the influence of spirits again, to help them become independent. They're tools. If we give spirits a form, we become independent. Spirits, the unconscious . . . , emotion—they're all the same thing. I understood why I was a painter. All alone in that awful museum, with masks, dolls made by the redskins, dusty manikins. *Les Demoiselles d'Avignon* must have come to me that very day, but not at all because of the forms; because it was my first exorcism-painting—yes absolutely!" *Picasso's Mask*, translated by June Guicharnaud with Jacques Guicharnaud (New York: Holt, Rienhart and Winston, 1976), pp. 10-11. Perhaps Stein was a "threatening spirit" in need of exorcism!

20. Maurice Merleau-Ponty, "Eye and Mind" translated by Carleton Dallery in *The Primacy of Perception*, edited by James Edie (Northwestern University Press, 1964), p. 162.

21. Susanne Langer, *Mind: An Essay on Human Feeling,* Vol. I (The Johns Hopkins University Press, 1967), p. 199.

22. Ibid., p. 202. She adds, "any unit of activity is an act. Taken in this way, the term has an instrumental value for building up a coherent and adequate concept of mind, and on that basis I use it in the broad sense here." Here her use of both the ideas of the act and instrumentalism are close to Dewey's.

23. Quoted in Ibid., p. 211.

24. Ibid., p. 210.

25. Ibid., p. 266.

26. Once again, this is a development of the main point of Dewey's "Reflex Arc Concept in Psychology" article.

27. For a discussion of the objectivists (like Hirsch and Betti) and the relativists (like Gadamer) see Joseph Bleicher's *Contemporary Hermeneutics* (London: Routledge and Keegan Paul, Ltd., 1980).

28. Nathan Knobler, *The Visual Dialogue,* third edition (New York: Holt, Reinhart and Winston, 1980), p. 300. This transactional model can also apply to the aesthetic appreciation of natural objects and events.

29. Malcom Cowley, "Editor's Introduction," in Walt Whitman, *Leaves of Grass* (New York: Viking Press, 1959), p. xvi.

30. For Dewey's relation to Santayana, see Chapter II, note 48, and Chapter III, section I.

31. In the *Symposium* we see an *agon* or contest between various types of *poiesis* represented by the different speakers: myth, rhetoric, natural philosophy, comedy, tragedy, dialectic, *noesis* (Diotima) and the praxis of *arete* (Alcibiades' praise of Socrates). Similar *agons* occur in the *Republic, Gorgias,* and *Phaedrus.* In Book X of the *Republic* for example we see Plato offering his new *poiesis* to replace the old mythic *poiesis* which has become discredited.

32. See Aristotle's *Poetics* 1451 b and Plotinus' *Ennead* V. 8.

33. See M.H. Abrams' *Natural Supernaturalism* and the annotated edition of Coleridge's *Biographia Literaria,* edited by James Engell and W. Jackson Bate (Princeton University Press, 1983), which draws out the influences of Neo-Platonism fairly well.

34. Immanuel Kant, *Critique of Pure Reason,* translated by Norman Kemp Smith (New York: St. Martin's Press, 1965), B 130. The fundamental question to be faced in the modern period is why reason or consciousness is interpreted as an *activity* and what exactly "activity" itself is understood as.

35. William Wordsworth, *Preface to the Lyrical Ballads in Lyrical Ballads,* edited by W.J.B. Owen (Oxford University Press, 1969), p. 157.

36. The mariner's voyage speaks of man's progressive alienation from God and Nature which isolates him from his fellow men as well. To kill the albatross, the inspirational power of imagination, brings the ship to a standstill and reveals the degree of mariner's commitment to a world which is fundamentally mechanical and dead.

37. *Preface*, pp. 173-74.

38. Quoted in M.H. Abrams, *The Mirror and the Lamp* (Oxford University Press, 1953), p. 22.

39. Ibid., p. 23.

40. O.K. Bouwsma, "The Expression Theory of Art," in *Aesthetics Today*, revised edition, edited by Morris Philipson and Paul J. Gudel (New York: New American Library, 1980), p. 262. The article can also be found in Bouwsma's *Aesthetics and Language*. See also John Hospers' discussion in his *Meaning and Truth in the Arts* (Chapel Hill: University of North Carolina Press, 1974), Chapter III.

41. Ibid., 264.

42. Ibid., p. 265.

43. Ibid. On the "physiognomy" of expression, see *Philosophical Investigations II:* xi and Beardsley's discussion of "human regional qualities" in his *Aesthetics*, (Indianapolis: Hackett Publishing Co., 1981), p. 328 ff.

44. Compare with Hospers' comment in *Meaning and Truth in the Arts*, "There are esthetic experiences without expressiveness, as when I am moved by a group of forms or colors without any life-associations whatsoever. . . . And there are experiences of expressiveness which are not esthetic" (p. 70). Dewey of course would disagree with this—one cannot have "life experiences" without "life associations" and the degree to which experience is genuinely expressive it becomes aesthetic. Hospers is using "expressive" in a rather narrow sense. See Rudolph Arnheim's discussion of expression in visual art in his *Art and Visual Perception*, Chapter X. The limits of Bouwsma's attitude were well expressed by Morris Philipson in the first edition of *Aesthetics Today*, "Bouwsma's essay reads as if it were written in a void where depth psychology had never been heard of. . . . Bouwsma makes frequent reference to the word 'emotion,' but it would be difficult to see from his essay whether he is referring to any theory of emotion more subtle than that of René Descartes. Perhaps, more than any other single element, it is this disregard of contemporary psychology by the philosophers of language-analysis that gives to their writings the quality of 'quaintness,' " *Aesthetics Today* (New York: Meridian Publishing Co., 1961), p. 142.

45. See Leonard Meyer's discussion, "Expectation and Learning," the second chapter of his *Emotion and Meaning in Music* (Chicago: University of Chicago Press, 1956).

46. For example see Beardsley's discussion in his *Aesthetics*, p. 325 ff.

47. Merleau-Ponty, "Cézanne's Doubt" in *Sense and Non-Sense*, translated by Hubert L. Dreyfus and Patricia Allen Dreyfus (Northwestern University Press, 1964), p. 16.

48. Ernest Hemingway, *In Our Time* (New York: Charles Scribner's Sons, 1970). The place of this story at the end of the selections in this book deserves special consideration.

49. Compare with Collingwood's discussion in *The Principles of Art* (Oxford University Press, 1958)., p. 109 ff. Collingwood puts the case more extremely than Dewey, "Until a man has expressed his emotion, he does not yet know what emotion it is. The act of expressing it is therefore an exploration of his own emotions. He is trying to find out what these emotions are" (p. 111). Collingwood, like Dewey, distinguishes expressing emotion from either arousing it in someone else or "betraying an emotion"—i.e., emoting. "A person expressing emotion, on the contrary is treating himself and his audience in the same kind of way; he is making his emotions clear to his audience, and that is what he is doing to himself" (pp. 110-111). Dewey would agree with all this as far as it goes, but would argue that emotion does not arise from a completely indeterminate situation nor is it articulated without the directing skills and habits which can enculture it and thereby make it "clear" to oneself and to one's audience. This is done by the artist seeking out organized modes of response. The cultural horizon, in other words, functions to structure the "generalized other."

50. The act of expression, however individual it may be, *must* constitute the appropriation *of* a public world *for* a public world, or it becomes insane. For example, André Malraux remarks of the art of the insane, "But the real madman, since he is not playing a game, has a sphere of action shared with the artist; he, too, has broken with the outside world. . . . But the madman is fettered by the predicament to which he owes his seeming freedom; his break with the world is not a conquest, a victory over other works of art, but forced on him, and it is aimless. . . . The artist's break with the world sponsors a flash of genius; the madman's is his prison," *The Voices of Silence*, p. 532. Put in more Deweyan language, the artist seeks to communicate by creatively showing the sharable or meaningful possibilities and continuity of a tradition, a network of meaning which is capable of growth and participation. Schizophrenic art is obsessively private, unconsummated by any answering gesture, seeking to stamp a final and absolute order onto the fragmentation of experience.

51. "Some Remarks on Value and Greatness in Music," reprinted in Philipson's and Gudel's *Aesthetics Today*, revised edition. The article originally appeared in *JAAC* XVII (1959). See also his *Emotion and Meaning in Music*.

52. Ibid., p. 270.

53. Ibid.

54. Ibid.

55. Ibid. It should be mentioned that Meyer is consciously using Dewey's theory of emotion and expression. See *Emotion and Meaning in Music*, p. 14 ff.

56. Ibid., p. 271.

57. Ibid., p. 272.

58. Ibid.

59. See Gregory Bateson's article, "Form, Substance, and Difference" in *Steps to and Ecology of Mind* and his *Mind and Nature*.

60. Clive Bell, *Art* (New York: Capricorn Books, 1958), pp. 17-18.

61. Ibid., p. 27.

62. Ibid., p. 34. Langer's development of Bell's concept of significant form is discussed in Chapter 3 of her *Feeling and Form,* especially pp. 32-41. Langer essentially Kantianizes Bell's Platonism. In spite of the organicism which develops in her interpretation of art in this book, the Kantian emphasis on formalism and intuitionism wins out strongly in the end: we know the import of an art symbol by a "basic intellectual act of intuition" (p. 375).

63. See footnote 50 above.

64. What Gadamer would call a fusion of horizons arising from an authentic questioning of and dialogue with the work. See *Truth and Method,* translated by Sheed and Ward, Ltd. (New York: Continuum, 1975), p. 272 ff. and p. 337 ff.

65. Once again, this seems to undercut completely the sort of criticism of Dewey one finds in the articles mentioned in footnote 1 above, especially that of Edna Shearer.

66. In *The Basis of Criticism in the Arts* (Oxford University Press, 1945), Pepper says, "It is symptomatic that Dewey frequently chooses the word 'seizure' to designate the highest aesthetic experience. It is an experience in which the total situation is absorbed in a vivid fused satisfying quality" (p. 65). The confusion of Dewey's "seizure" with "fusion" can also be found in his *Aesthetic Quality* (New York: Charles Scribner's Sons, 1937), pp. 27-28.

67. James Joyce, *Portrait of the Artist as a Young Man* (New York: The Viking Press, 1964), p. 171.

68. Ibid., pp. 42-43.

69. Ibid., p. 14, p. 22, p. 173.

70. Ibid., pp. 252-53. The irony of Stephen's identifying with Icarus should not be missed.

71. See Rudolph Arnheim's discussion of this work in *Art and Visual Perception,* Chapter X. The image of the woman has also been interpreted as

the Virgin Mary and as "Holy Wisdom." Given the whole historical orienta-tion of the ceiling of the Sistine Chapel, which progresses from the creation to the drunkenness of Noah, I believe the interpretation of the woman as Eve to make more sense, especially since the creation of Eve is the immediately subsequent panel.

72. See Joseph H. Kupfer, *Experience as Art* (Albany: State University of New York Press, 1983). I should also mention here the philosophical essays of John J. McDermott (to which Kupfer is also indebted), *The Culture of Experience* (New York: New York University Press, 1976) and *The Streams of Experience* (Amherst: The University of Massachusetts Press, 1986).

73. To see the underlying continuity of this theme in Dewey's mature period, one simply needs to compare this passage with the Introduction to the *Essays in Experimental Logic*, especially pp. 5-8 (*MW* 10:320-24).

74. See *Experience and Education*, p. 35, where Dewey again uses this passage to illustrate the principle of continuity.

75. For Dewey's discussion of the importance of embodied mind, see *Experience and Nature*, Ch. VI, especially pp. 218-33 (*LW* 1:169-80).

76. See *Experience and Nature*, pp. 245-46 (*LW* 1:188-89).

77. Dewey's defense of using the term "God" is that "aggressive atheism" is like supernaturalism in considering man in isolation from nature and vice versa. "Militant atheism is also affected by lack of natural piety," says Dewey, "The ties binding man to nature that poets have always celebrated are passed over lightly. The attitude taken is often that of man living in an indifferent and hostile world and issuing blasts of defiance. A religious attitude, however, needs the sense of a connection of man, in the way of both dependence and support, with the enveloping world that the imagination feels is a universe. Use of the words 'God' of 'divine' to convey the union of actual with ideal may protect man from a sense of isolation and from consequent despair or defi-ance" (*CF*, 53; *LW* 9:36).

78. See Rorty's description of a "Post-Philosophical" culture in the fifth section of his introduction to *Consequences of Pragmatism*. Rorty and Dewey are in agreement insofar as both seek to remove the quest for certainty and question the paradigm of philosophy as fundamentally concerned with "the" truth. But Rorty's ideal of the intellectual who "passes rapidly from Heming-way to Proust to Hitler to Marx to Foucault to Mary Douglas to the present situation in Southeast Asia to Ghandi to Sophocles" is closer to the effete image of the salon philosophe than it is to the Deweyan reformer. Dewey would agree with Marx that the purpose of philosophy is not to chat about the world or be a name-dropper; it is to change it by liberating the constructive possibilities of experience. Rorty's vision of philosophy is only radical in a very limited, academic setting.

CONCLUSION

1. See *Reconstruction in Philosophy,* 211 (*MW* 12:201) and *Art as Experience,* 275 (*LW* 10:279). The line is from Wordsworth's poem, "Elegaic Stanzas Suggested by a Picture of Peele Castle, in a Storm,"

Ah! *then,* if mine had been the Painter's hand,
To express what then I saw; and add the gleam,
The light that never was, on sea or land,
The consecration, and the Poet's dream. . . .

2. Edward Said, *The World, the Text, and the Critic* (Cambridge, Massachusetts: Harvard University Press, 1983), p. 26.

Bibliography

Two valuable guides to writings by and about Dewey are: Jo Ann Boydston and Kathleen Poulos, *A Checklist of the Writings about John Dewey,* 2nd. edition (Carbondale: Southern Illinois University Press, 1977), and Milton Halsey Thomas, *John Dewey: A Centennial Bibliography* (Chicago: University of Chicago Press, 1962).

I. Works by Dewey

A. Books

Dewey, John. *A Common Faith.* 1934. New Haven: Yale University Press, 1960.

————. *Art as Experience.* 1934. Capricorn Books, New York: G.P. Putnam's Sons, 1958.

————. *Democracy and Education.* 1916. New York: The Free Press, 1966.

————. *Essays in Experimental Logic.* 1916. New York: Dover Publications, Inc., n.d.

————. *Experience and Education.* 1938. New York: Collier Books, 1963.

————. *Experience and Nature.* 1925. Revised edition, 1929. New York: Dover Publishing Publications, Inc., 1958.

————. *On Experience, Nature, and Freedom.* Edited by Richard Bernstein. Indianapolis: The Bobbs-Merrill Company, Inc., 1960.

————. *Freedom and Culture.* 1939. Capricorn Books, New York: G.P. Putnam's Sons, 1963.

————. *Human Nature and Conduct.* 1922. New York: The Modern Library, 1930.

————. *Individualism, Old and New.* 1930. Capricorn Books. New York: G.P. Putnam's Sons, 1962.

_____. *The Influence of Darwin on Philosophy.* 1910. New York: Peter Smith, 1951.

_____. and Arthur Bentley. *John Dewey and Arthur Bentley: A Philosophical Correspondence.* Edited by Sidney Ratner et al. New Brunswick, N.J.: Rutgers University Press, 1964.

_____. and Arthur Bentley. *Knowing and the Known.* Boston: Beacon Press, 1949.

_____. *Liberalism and Social Action.* 1935. Capricorn Books. New York: G.P. Putnam's Sons, 1963.

_____. *Logic: The Theory of Inquiry.* New York: Henry Holt and Company, 1938.

_____. *The Moral Writings of John Dewey.* Edited by James Gouinlock. New York: Hafner Press, 1976.

_____. *Philosophy and Civilization.* 1931. New York: Peter Smith, 1968.

_____. *Problems of Men.* New York: Philosophical Library, 1946.

_____. *The Public and Its Problems.* 1927. Revised edition, 1946. Chicago: The Swallow Press Inc., n.d.

_____. *The Quest for Certainty.* 1929. Capricorn Books. New York: G.P. Putnam's Sons, 1960.

_____. *Reconstruction in Philosophy.* 1920. Revised edition, 1948. Boston: Beacon Press, 1957.

_____. *Theory of Valuation.* Chicago: University of Chicago Press, 1939.

B. Dewey: Articles on Aesthetics

Dewey, John. "Aesthetic Experience as a Primary Phase and as an Artistic Development." *The Journal of Aesthetics and Art Criticism,* IX (1950), 56-58.

_____. "Affective Thought." *Later Works 2:* 104-10.

_____. "A Comment on the Foregoing Criticisms." *The Journal of Aesthetics and Art Criticism,* VI (1948), 207-09.

_____. "Art in Education—and Education in Art." *Later Works 2:* 111-23.

_____. "Experience and Existence: A Comment." *Philosophy and Phenomenological Research,* IX (1949), 709-13.

_____. "Qualitative Thought." *Later Works 5:* 243-62.

_____. "Subject Matter in Art." *The New Republic,* XC (1937), 335.

_____. "Time and Individuality." *On Experience, Nature, and Freedom.* Edited by Richard Bernstein. Indianapolis: The Bobbs-Merrill Company, Inc., 1960., 224-43.

II. Works on Dewey

A. Books

Bernstein, Richard. *John Dewey.* New York: Washington Square Press, 1966.

Boisvert, Raymond. *Dewey's Metaphysics.* Fordham (forthcoming).

Boyston, Jo Ann, ed. *Guide to the Works of John Dewey.* Carbondale: Southern Illinois University Press, 1970.

Cahn, Stephen, ed. *New Studies in the Philosophy of John Dewey.* Hanover, New Hampshire: The University Press of New England, 1977.

Coughlan, Neil. *Young John Dewey.* Chicago: The University of Chicago Press, 1975.

Damico, Alfonso J. *Individuality and Community.* Gainesville: University Presses of Florida, 1978.

Dicker, Georges. *Dewey's Theory of Knowing.* Philadelphia: Philadelphia Monograph Series, 1976.

Dykhuizen, George. *The Life and Mind of John Dewey.* Carbondale: Southern Illinois University Press, 1973.

Geiger, George. *John Dewey in Perspective.* New York: Oxford University Press, 1958.

Gouinlock, James. *John Dewey's Philosophy of Value.* New York: Humanities Press, 1972.

Hook, Sidney. *John Dewey, An Intellectual Portrait.* New York: The John Day Co., 1939.

Kestenbaum, Victor. *The Phenomenological Sense of John Dewey: Habit and Meaning.* Atlantic Highlands, New Jersey: Humanities Press, 1977.

Lamont, Corliss, ed. *Dialogue on John Dewey.* New York: Horizon Press, Inc., 1959.

Rosenstock, Gershon George. *F.A. Trendelenburg—Forerunner to John Dewey.* Carbondale: Southern Illinois University Press, 1964.

Rosenthal, Sandra, and Bourgeois. *Pragmatism and Phenomenology.* Amsterdam: B.R. Gruner Publishing Co., 1980.

Schillp, Paul Arthur, ed. *The Philosophy of John Dewey.* Volume I of *The Library of Living Philosophers.* Edited by Paul Arthur Schillp. La Salle, Illinois: Open Court Publishing Co., 1970.

Schneider, Herbert. *A History of American Philosophy.* 2nd edition. New York: Columbia University Press, 1963.

Sleeper, R.W. *The Necessity of Pragmatism.* New Haven: Yale University Press, 1986.

Smith, John E. *Purpose and Thought*. New Haven: Yale University Press, 1978.

Thayer, H.S. *Meaning and Action*. 2nd edition. Indianapolis: Hackett Publishing Co., 1981.

White, Morton. *The Origins of Dewey's Instrumentalism*. New York: Columbia University Press, 1962.

Zeltner, Philip M. *John Dewey's Aesthetic Philosophy*. Amsterdam: B.R. Gruner Publishing Co., 1975.

B. Articles

Alexander, Thomas M. "Richard Rorty and Dewey's Metaphysics of Experience." *Southwest Philosophical Studies*, V (1980), 24-35.

Ames, Van Meter. "John Dewey as Aesthetician." *The Journal of Aesthetics and Art Criticism*, XII (1953), 145-68.

Bakewell, Charles. "An Open Letter to Professor Dewey Concerning Immediate Empiricism." *The Journal of Philosophy*, II (1905), 520-22. Reprinted in John Dewey, *The Middle Works*, vol. 3, pp. 390-92.

Bernstein, Richard. "Dewey's Naturalism." *The Review of Metaphysics*, XIII (1959), 340-53.

————. "John Dewey's Metaphysics of Experience." *The Journal of Philosophy*, LVIII (1961), 5-14.

Black, Max. "Dewey's Philosophy of Language." *The Journal of Philosophy*, LIX (1962), 505-23.

Boas, George. "Communication in Dewey's Aesthetics." *The Journal of Aesthetics and Art Criticism*, XII (1953), 177-83.

Bode, B.H. "Cognitive Experience and Its Object." *The Journal of Philosophy*, II (1905), 653-63. Reprinted in John Dewey, *The Middle Works*, vol. 3, pp. 398-404.

Boisvert, Raymond, D. "Dewey, Subjective Idealism, and Metaphysics." *Transactions of the Charles S. Peirce Society*, XVIII (1982), 232-43.

Brodsky, Gary. "Absolute Idealism and Dewey's Instrumentalism." *Transactions of the Charles S. Peirce Society*, V (1969), 44-62.

————. "Dewey on Experience and Nature." *The Monist*, XLVIII (1964), 366-81.

Cohen, Morris Raphael. "Some Difficulties in Dewey's Anthropocentric Naturalism.". *The Philosophical Review*, XLIV (1940), 196-228.

Croce, Benedetto. "Dewey's Aesthetics and Theory of Knowledge." Translated by Frederic Simoni. *The Journal of Aesthetics and Art Criticism*, XI (1952), 1-6.

————. "On the Aesthetics of Dewey." Translated by Katherine Gilbert. *The Journal of Aesthetics and Art Criticism*, VI (1948), 203-07.

Douglas, George H. "A Reconsideration of the Dewey-Croce Exchange." *The Journal of Aesthetics and Art Criticism*, XXVIII (1970), 497-504.

Eames, Elizabeth. "Quality and Relation as Metaphysical Assumptions in the Philosophy of John Dewey." *The Journal of Philosophy*, LV (1961), 179-95.

Eames, Morris S. "The Cognitive and the Non-Cognitive in Dewey's Theory of Valuation." *The Journal of Philosophy*, LVIII (1961), 179-95.

Edman, Irwin. "Dewey and Art." *John Dewey: Philosopher of Science and Freedom*. Edited by Sidney Hook. New York: The Dial Press, 1950.

Garrett, Roland W. "Changing Events in Dewey's *Experience and Nature*." *Journal of the History of Philosophy*, X (1972), 439-55.

————. "Dewey's Struggle with Ineffable." *Transactions of the Charles S. Peirce Society*, IX (1973), 95-109.

Gauss, Charles Edward. "Some Reflections on Dewey's Aesthetics." *The Journal of Aesthetics and Art Criticism*, XIX (1960), 127-32.

Gotshalk, D.W. "On Dewey's Esthetics." *The Journal of Aesthetics and Art Criticism*, XXIII (1964), 131-38.

Graña, Cesar. "John Dewey's Social Art and the Sociology of Art." *The Journal of Aesthetics and Art Criticism*, XX (1962), 405-12.

Hall, Everett W. "Some Meanings of Meaning in Dewey's *Experience and Nature*." *The Journal of Philosophy*, XXV (1928), 169-81.

Hocking, William Ernest. "Dewey's Concepts of Experience and Nature." *The Philosophical Review*, XLIV (1940), 228-44.

Honeywell, J.A. "Dewey's Transcendentals." *New Scholasticism*, XLV (1971), 517-46.

Kahn, Sholom J. "Experience and Existence in Dewey's Naturalistic Metaphysics." *Philosophy and Phenomenological Research*, IX (1948), 316-21.

Kaminsky, Jack. "Dewey's Conception of *An* Experience." *Philosophy and Phenomenological Research*, XVII (1957), 316-30.

Mathur, Dinesh Chandra. "A Note on the Concept of 'Consummatory Experience' in Dewey's Aesthetics." *The Journal of Philosophy*, LXIII (1966), 225-31.

Pepper, Stephen Coburn. "The Concept of Fusion in Dewey's Aesthetic Theory." *The Journal of Aesthetics and Art Criticism*, XII (1953), 169-76.

————. "Some Questions on Dewey's Esthetics." *The Philosophy of John Dewey*. Edited by Paul Arthur Schillip. La Salle, Illinois: The Open Court Publishing Co., 1970.

Romanell, Patrick. "A Comment on Dewey's and Croce's Aesthetics." *The Journal of Aesthetics and Art Criticism*, VIII (1949), 125-28.

Rorty, Richard. "Dewey's Metaphysics." *New Studies in the Philosophy of John Dewey*. Edited by Stephen Cahn. Hanover, New Hampshire: The University Press of New England, 1977, pp. 45-74. Reprinted in Richard Rorty, *Consequences of Pragmatism* (Minnesota: University of Minnesota Press, 1982).

Rosenthal, Sandra B. "John Dewey: From Phenomenology of Knowledge to Knowledge as Experimental." *Philosophy Today*, XXII (1978), 43-49.

Santayana, George. "Dewey's Naturalistic Metaphysics. *The Journal of Philosophy*, XXII (1925), 673-88. Reprinted in George Santayana, *Obiter Scripta*, edited by Justus Buchler and Benjamin Schwartz (New York: Charles Scribners's Sons, 1936).

Shearer, Edna Aston. "Dewey's Esthetic Theory." *The Journal of Philosophy*, XXXII (1935), 617-27; 650-64.

Stuhr, John J. "Dewey's Notion of Qualitative Experience." *Transactions of the Charles S. Peirce Society*, XV (1979), 68-82.

Sukale, Michael. "Heidegger and Dewey." Chapter VII of his *Comparative Studies in Phenomenology*. The Hague, Netherlands: Martinus Nijhoff, 1976.

Vivas, Eliseo. "A Note on Emotion in Mr. Dewey's Theory of Art." *Philosophical Review*, XLVII (1938), 527-31.

Welsh, Paul. "Some Metaphysical Assumptions in Dewey's Philosophy." *The Journal of Philosophy*, LI (1954), 861-67.

Zink, Sidney, "The Concept of Continuity in Dewey's Theory of Esthetics." *Philosophical Review*, LII (1943), 392-400.

Index

Absolute: xv, 5, 22, 25, 27, 42ff., 58, 75f., 83. See Hegel, idealism, Spirit.
act, the: 124ff., 135, 139f., 155. See reflex arc.
action: 8ff., 26f., 33, 41f., 73, 76, 96, 101f., 114, 127, 149, 153, 155, 161, 171, 196, 203, 208, 220, 256. See situation, transaction.
aesthetic-artistic experience: xiv, xixf., 60, 117, 206f., 211f., 233. See an experience, art, continuity experience, intelligence.
aesthetic theories: Croce's, 2ff., 7ff.; idealist, 3f., 35ff.; institutional (Dickie's), 187; Kant's 38f., 187f.; Pepper's, 3ff. See criticism, formalism, mimesis, psychic distance theory, romanticism.
aesthetics: xiiif., xix, 1, 5, 10f., 60, 63, 68f., 104, 189ff.
an experience: xiii, xix, 10f., 102, 115, 127, 135, 175, 185f., 198ff.
appreciation: 206f., 230ff.
Aristotle: xvii, 5, 15, 18, 40, 49, 86, 89, 94, 99ff., 114, 125f., 135, 171, 214, 234, 283 n.5, n.7, 294 n.45, 296 n.58. See potentiality.
art: xiiif., xixf., 36ff., 42ff., 53ff., 60, 102, 105, 183ff., Chapter 5 pas-

sim.; importance for philosophy: xii, xix, 1ff., 10ff.
Art as Experience: xvff., 1ff., 60, 183ff., Chapter 5 passim.
art for art's sake: 190, 234. See formalism.
artist: 36, 207f., 214ff., 274.
art product (vs. artwork): 187, 209, 236.
artwork: xx, 187, 213; working of the work of art, 209, 229, 235, 246. See an experience.

Barnes, Albert C.: 55.
Beardsley, Monroe: 1, 221.
Bell, Clive: 233f., 239, 246, 249f. See formalism.
Bentley, Arthur: 105, 108f.
Bergson, Henri: 126, 133f., 181.
Bernstein, Richard: 65f., 90, 291 n. 17.
Black, Max: 119f, 298 n. 1.
body: xix, 141ff., 151f., 182, 231.
Boisvert, Raymond: xii, 58f., 68, 279 n. 2, 291 n. 6, 293 n. 29, 294 n. 41.
Bouwsma, O.K.: 213, 216ff., 221.

care: 207, 220.
Castaneda: Carlos, 178.

319